THE LAND OF TOO MUCH

THE LAND OF TOO MUCH

AMERICAN ABUNDANCE AND
THE PARADOX OF POVERTY

Monica Prasad

HARVARD UNIVERSITY PRESS

Cambridge, Massachusetts

London, England

2012

Library of Congress Cataloging-in-Publication Data

Prasad, Monica.
  The land of too much : American abundance and the paradox of poverty / Monica Prasad.
    p.   cm.
  Includes bibliographical references and index.
  ISBN 978-0-674-06652-6 (alk. paper)
  1. United States—Economic policy.   2. United States—Social policy.
3. Fiscal policy—United States.   I. Title.
HC103.P843 2012
338.5'2120973—dc23   2012010526

For Stefan

CONTENTS

Figures

Tables

One of the central questions of comparative political economy is why there is so much more poverty in the United States than in any other developed country. In any way that we can measure poverty, the United States fares worse than other countries, even if we control for factors such as the different racial composition and immigration history of the American population. For almost a century scholars in sociology, political science, and economics have studied this question, and they invariably come to the same conclusion: the United States, they tell us, has more poverty because the American government does not do anything about it. Market inequality is similar in the United States and other countries, and only after the intervention of the state through taxes and transfers do we see a marked divergence in poverty rates. In other words, we know how to solve poverty, or at least to reduce it to European levels, but we decide against doing so. The centuries-long tradition of comparative political economy has produced a range of theories that attempt to explain this situation by pointing to the racial fragmentation of American society, the culture committed to the free market, the weakness of labor, or the political strength of business. These theories disagree on particulars, but they all agree that American political economy is characterized by minimal state intervention or by state intervention that reinforces market differences, that the United States is a "liberal" or laissez-faire country that distrusts the state and favors the free market.

At the same time, research in the past two decades in history and the historically oriented social sciences has thoroughly dismantled any possibility of believing that the United States is a minimally interventionist state. The interdisciplinary research program termed "American political development," for example, has taken apart what William Novak refers to as "the tired myth of the 'weak' American state" (2008, 754). But if comparative political economy ignores this historically oriented scholarship, it is also true that the historical literature cannot explain why there is more poverty in the United States and why capitalism looks so different in different countries. If the United States is and always has been interventionist, the relevant differences between the countries become harder to explain.

This book is an attempt to make a fresh start in comparative political economy by acknowledging what the historical scholarship has to teach us but using this knowledge to answer the question posed by the comparative literature—why are there such differences between the United States and Europe? Why does the American state intervene so heavily in some ways that help workers, consumers, and the poor—such as consumer regulation and taxation—but not in other ways—such as a welfare state?

In this book I argue that the United States has greater poverty because a set of progressive interventions backfired. The American state is not less interventionist in general, but rather, American intervention took a different form, one that has been less successful in the fight against poverty. To explain why American intervention took this peculiar form and exactly how it backfired, this book develops a "demand-side" theory of comparative political economy that focuses on how states structure mass consumption. The argument begins with the observation that the key difference between Europe and the United States from the mid-nineteenth to the mid-twentieth centuries was the explosive economic growth of the United States compared to the economic difficulties of Europe. When American productivity and the size of the American market caused price declines throughout the world, particularly in agricultural products, most European countries responded by closing their borders from the American invasion through protectionism; while Americans also turned to protection, tariff barriers were not enough, because the problem was the productivity of American farmers themselves. Consequently, the United States saw a powerful agrarian movement aimed at reordering the political economy. The nineteenth century populists set down important precedents for this reordering, but the crucial moment in this new economic order was the Great Depression, which at the time many diagnosed as a result of "overproduction." "The land of too much" was a phrase Huey Long coined in the 1920s to name the riddle of how *wealth,* in the form of an unusually successful harvest, could become *catastrophe* in the form of plunging prices that left farmers unable to repay their debts. Long, like many others, drew a straight line from those plunging prices to farm foreclosures, from there to bank instability, and from there to the Great Depression. The Depression was not a problem of having too little but of having too much. "People are starving," Long said, "and yet we have more wheat, corn, meat, milk, cheese, honey and truck in this land than the whole human race in America can consume if everyone were turned loose to eat what it wanted. . . . There is something wrong when people starve for food and shiver for clothes and can not get them because there is too much in the land" (Long 1930). Like many others, he settled on the argument that the problem was concentration of wealth into a few hands, which prevented those who were starving and shivering from translating their needs into market demand for the glut of products rotting on American farms. He argued for a fundamental transformation of capitalism, because "if we spread our great wealth enough that all are served in the land of too much—then there would be a transfusion into business, a lift to the forgotten, a hope for our nation" (Long 1933d).

Since the 1980s, many observers, including most social scientists, have argued that "spread[ing] our great wealth" is a distinctly un-American thing to do. But for a century before that, that is precisely what America did, for the reasons that Long gives. The American state was shaped by attempts to respond to problems of abundance while a politically divided Europe struggled to generate economic growth. It turns out that "spread[ing] our great wealth" is a deep-rooted American tradition.

Spurred on by agrarian politicians who held key swing votes, the United States settled on a pattern of progressive taxation and a form of agrarian regulation that ended in the democratization of credit and strict regulations on business. The pattern of state intervention in areas important to the agrarian agenda, such as in the regulation of business, is what historians writing about the remarkably interventionist American state have noticed. However, progressive taxation and reliance on consumer credit undermined political support for the welfare state—in a complex process traced in this book—and this is the main feature that scholars of comparative political economy have examined.

Acknowledging the power of agrarian statism helps us to understand contemporary developments in the United States. As the stable growth rates of the early postwar period gave way to the oil price shocks of the 1970s, progressive taxation unleashed a taxpayer revolt in the United States, while strict regulations led to calls from across the political spectrum for deregulation. Under deregulation, easy credit created financial volatility that spread to the rest of the world. Surprisingly, none of our sophisticated theories of comparative political economy has had much to say about the financial crisis that has recently roiled our economy. This book traces how agrarian intervention led to a form of "mortgage Keynesianism" that fueled American growth for several decades, and identifies a trade-off across the industrial countries between reliance on the welfare state and reliance on credit-based consumption. I suggest that developing the public welfare state would benefit economic growth in the United States by loosening the grip of mortgage Keynesianism, thereby lowering the demand for finance and reorienting political efforts and resources away from the financial sector and towards more stable sources of growth.

In tracing the developing power of the American state since Reconstruction, the use of that power for interventionist and redistributive purposes, the consequences of that power for the development of the public welfare state, and the backlash to this mode of governance in the 1980s, this book demonstrates that the major sociological, political science, and economic theories about the comparative dimensions of capitalism are based on the false premise that the United States is a liberal or laissez-faire state. These theories are therefore unable to explain some central facets of capitalism, such as the greatest financial crisis since the Great Depression. Attention to how capitalist societies shape consumption—a "demand side" theory—makes better sense of many otherwise inexplicable features of capitalism and of the American state.

THE LAND OF TOO MUCH

PART ONE

EXPLAINING AMERICAN STATE INTERVENTION

1

Doctors began to notice the first cases of the strange disease in 1959. Thousands of babies with stunted limbs and other severe birth defects were being born all over Germany, Britain, Sweden, Australia, dozens of countries. Many died from their deformities at birth. Others would experience difficulties as they grew, including heart disease and spina bifida. Through 1960 and into 1961, all around the world, the number of cases mounted. (Daemmrich 2002; Sherman and Strauss 1986; Kelsey 1965; Taussig 1962; Carpenter 2010)

In 1961 two doctors traced the problems to a sedative called Contergan that had been developed in Germany and marketed worldwide under other names. Contergan was prescribed for insomnia and for nausea. It did not seem to have side effects and was not toxic in overdose, and it became so popular that it was called "West Germany's baby sitter" (Daemmrich 2002, 139). But as the incidents rose, pediatricians began to suspect and then to document an extremely strong association between the birth defects and Contergan taken in the first trimester of pregnancy. It was withdrawn from the market in 1961, and eventually conclusive evidence emerged of how the drug caused the malformations (Daemmrich 2002). By then it had already affected over 10,000 children in "one of the greatest medical disasters of modern times" (Akhurst 2010, 370).

Amid the calamity, a stunning and justly celebrated act of resistance came to light: under the name Thalidomide, the drug had been kept off the American market by Frances Kelsey, a researcher at the Food and Drug Administration (FDA) with a hunch and a streak of self-confidence that led her to delay approval again and again, until the truth was finally known. Kelsey was well prepared for the task. She had done her graduate work in pharmacology at the University of Chicago (she was admitted on the assumption that "Frances" was a male name) in the lab that had identified the toxicity of an over-the-counter drug that had killed 107 people in 1937. The lab's work led to the Food, Drug, and Cosmetic Act of 1938. During the war, Kelsey's work on pregnant rabbits had shown her that drugs can cross the placental barrier and that pregnancy can change the body's response to a drug. (Bren 2001)

The Thalidomide application was Kelsey's first case at the FDA. Kelsey realized that the manufacturer's and distributor's studies documenting no adverse effects in animals were irrelevant because the drug also did not cause sleepiness in those experimental animals as it did in humans; it simply worked differently in humans. She called it "a peculiar drug" (Mintz 1962, A8). Because the drug was aimed at relieving minor symptoms, she chose to wait for better evidence of its safety.

While there was no rush for Kelsey, there was a rush for the American distributor, Richardson-Merrell, which wanted approval in time for Christmas—Christmas apparently being the high season for sedatives—and sent representatives to make repeated visits and phone calls to Kelsey. As the months dragged on, nineteen months in all, the company complained to her superiors that Kelsey was being unreasonable. But she held her ground. Again and again the company resubmitted the application, arguing that any effects were so rare as to be negligible, and again and again Kelsey returned it for insufficient evidence of safety (Bren 2001). Soon the European doctors had pieced together their conclusions, and Thalidomide stayed off the American market.[1] Twenty cases of birth defects from suspected administrations of Thalidomide in the first trimester were documented in the United States, from travelers bringing the drug from Europe with them and from an early trial distribution of the drug.[2] But the widespread tragedy that would have occurred had Kelsey been less persistent had been averted.

Historians of the episode have emphasized the role of Kelsey, and it is true that Kelsey's ability to resist industry pressures requires the kind of explanation that cannot be reduced to social context and can really only be plumbed by close attention to the mysteries of human character. But there is one element in the story that does point to social context, and it does not reduce Frances Kelsey's heroism to note the circumstances that allowed her resistance to be so powerful: the U.S. government has a long history of disapproving drugs available in other countries, a "drug lag" that has been the source of complaints from doctors as well as industry. This history of stronger drug regulation placed Kelsey in a position to disapprove Thalidomide. In Britain at the time, "any drug manufacturer could market any product, however inadequately tested, however dangerous, without having to satisfy any independent body as to its efficacy or safety" (British Member of Parliament Kenneth Robinson, quoted in Ceccoli 2002, 139). Germany had a tradition of self-regulation by pharmacists and physicians. All that the government could do was recommend that a drug be removed from the market after the fact (Daemmrich 2002, 140–141). In these countries there were no Frances Kelseys because there were no FDAs.

The divergent responses to the Thalidomide tragedy also demonstrate the tradition of stronger American drug regulation. Although Europe was more heavily hit, it was the United States that responded with tougher drug laws, so much so that by the 1970s, a widely reported study by physician William Wardell (1973) found that Great Britain had introduced four times as many drugs onto the market as the United States throughout the 1960s. A follow-up study by Wardell and Louis Lasagna (1975), head of Johns Hopkins's Division of Clinical Pharmacology, found the United States lagging France, Great Britain, and Germany by one to two years in drug approvals. One particular drug for hypertension was introduced in Europe ten years before it was approved in the United States, and Wardell wondered how many deaths had been caused by that delay. In 1985, one study found that it took thirty months to approve a drug in the United States compared to six months in France and Britain; and other research showed that in Britain, 12% of drugs were found unsafe after having been introduced onto the market compared to only 3% in the United States, indicating a stricter preapproval process in the United States (see Wiktorowicz 2003, 625; Ceccoli 2004).

Although the drug-lag debate fed into a building deregulatory fervor, the issue of drug regulation did not allow for easy solutions. For example, one drug that Wardell had held up as an example of an important drug unnecessarily kept off the American market—Practolol—was later shown to have serious side effects and was eventually withdrawn from the market in Europe (Wright 1975; Daemmrich and Krücken 2000). Although the case did not receive much publicity, the FDA had once again been right where other countries had been wrong. While analysts tried to estimate and weigh the suffering caused in Europe by rushed approval, as in this case, against the suffering caused in the United States by delayed approval in other cases, the uncertainties ensured that the FDA would continue on its cautious path throughout the 1970s.[3]

The story of Thalidomide has been interpreted from many different angles—as a tale about the predations of the drug industry, as a warning about the risks of unfettered scientific advance, as a parable of the difficulties of assessing risk in our complicated societies, as a way into the study of the social location of science. But the most surprising fact about it is that in this case it was the laissez-faire United States—the country that supposedly hates state intervention, the country allegedly most favorable to the market—that was the most successful at using the state to protect consumers from a pharmaceutical company wanting to market a dangerous drug, while the drug was welcomed all over statist Europe (Carpenter 2010).

This is a surprise as all our theories of comparative political economy, in the disciplines of sociology, political science, and economics, insist that the United States is a liberal state with a strong tradition of minimal state intervention (using "liberal" here in the classical sense of an ideal of limited government). Within sociology, some analysts argue that national differences in political economy follow different cultural patterns, that the United States has a political culture that is "oriented to the reinforcement of market mechanisms to ensure economic liberties and effect growth, and the prevention of other forms of government meddling with economic life" (Dobbin 1994, 24) and that the United States "proclaims more than any other [economy] its conformity to the laissez-faire ideals that anchor the dominant streams of modern economic theory" (Fourcade 2009, 254). Others argue that because of its weak labor movement and absence of a labor-backed political party, the United States has not been able to pass the policies that "modify conditions for and outcomes of market distribution" (Korpi 2006, 173; Korpi 1983). Within political science the dominant tradition of comparative political economy, the "varieties of capitalism" approach, sees the United States as a "liberal" regime in which "deregulation is often the most effective way to improve coordination" (Hall and Soskice 2001, 9), coordination problems are resolved through market-based rather than state-based solutions, and state intervention is used only to reinforce—not to undermine—market outcomes. The equally strong tradition of historical institutionalism argues that the American state has been unable to develop because of the multiple checks and balances in the political structure (Steinmo, Thelen, Longstreth 1992). Within economics, two prominent scholars have recently given the national culture argument a familiar twist, arguing that greater racial heterogeneity in the United States has led to persistent preferences for minimal state intervention because citizens believe that intervention will benefit those from other racial groups (Alesina and Glaser 2006).

If the United States is so market oriented, so beholden to the weakness of labor, so liberal, and so suspicious of state intervention, where did

6

that pattern of stricter drug regulation come from? Hundreds or thousands of Americans are walking around today with intact limbs and bodies because of the successful intervention of the American state against the market.

If drug regulation were the only policy to show this pattern, we would be justified in considering this story an absorbing trifle or in brushing it away with teleological arguments that consumer regulation preserves the market. (For the actual history of the development of the FDA, which involves the temperance movement, the rise of chemistry, muckrakers, and the Grange, see Swann 2004; Hamowy 2007; Carpenter 2010.)

But in recent years, historically oriented scholars have shown that this example is not an exception—indeed, it seems to be the rule. William Novak summarizes this new generation of scholarship: "[T]he American state is and always has been more powerful, capacious, tenacious, interventionist, and redistributive than was recognized in earlier accounts of U.S. history" (2008, 758). So far, none of this nearly two decades' worth of work has made it across the disciplinary divide to reorient comparative political economy. All of our theories of comparative political economy— with their implications for our understanding of economic growth and poverty reduction—have been built on a picture of American history that is turning out to be incorrect.

It is not hard to see why the belief in a weak American state persists, as the United States is different from other industrialized countries in many ways (Table 1.1): Americans today are considerably richer than the citizens of other industrialized countries. They work more and use more energy than the citizens of other countries. Americans are less likely to be in unions and much more likely to be in jail, somewhat less likely to be unemployed, and likely to die a few years earlier despite much higher levels of expenditure on health. Wage inequality is higher in the United States than in other countries at the top and bottom of the income distribution. Americans pay lower taxes overall than citizens of other countries and have only recently legislated universal health care, fifty to a hundred years after other countries. There is less public ownership of business. Because of the smaller welfare state, there is more poverty in the United States. American labor regulations are harsher than those of other countries, repression of labor has been more violent in the United States, and there has never been a truly working-class party in the United States at the national level. Surveys find Americans more likely to believe in God, to pray, and to attend religious services than the citizens of most European

Table 1.1. The United States compared to other industrialized countries

	United States	Other industrialized countries
Wage inequality: ratio of 90th percentile wage to 10th percentile wage, 1990s	4.6	2.8
Collective bargaining coverage: percentage of workers covered by a collective bargaining agreement, 2000	14	67.7
Rates of incarceration: prisoners per 100,000 population, 2003–4	726	101
Life expectancy for total population in years, 2003	77.2	79
Health expenditure as % of GDP, 2003	15.0	8.8
Per capita GDP, 2004 (in 2004 dollars)	$39,732	$29,562
Unemployment rate, 2005	5.1	6.5
Annual hours per worker, 2004	1,817	1,582
Hourly labor productivity, 2000 (U.S.=100)	100	95
Per capita energy use: kg of oil equivalent, 2003	7,843	4,766

Source: Baker 2007, 6–27. Includes the following countries: for wage inequality, Australia, Austria, Belgium, Denmark, Finland, France, Germany, Italy, Japan, Netherlands, New Zealand, Sweden, U.K. (6); for collective bargaining coverage: wage inequality countries+Canada and Norway (9); for incarceration: collective bargaining coverage countries+Spain, Portugal and Ireland (12); for life expectancy, wage inequality countries+Canada, Greece, Ireland, Norway, Portugal, Spain (14); for health expenditure: life expectancy countries+Luxembourg (15); for per capita GDP, life expectancy countries+Switzerland (20); for unemployment rate, incarceration countries (22); for hours per worker, incarceration countries (25; for labor productivity, incarceration countries+Switzerland (21); for energy use, health expenditure countries+Switzerland (27).

countries (Norris and Inglehart 2006, 226–227). American foreign policy often goes its own way, often despite strenuous European opposition (Robert Kagan 2003).

Things are not as clear as they seem, however. As recent scholarship is showing—and as we will consider in greater detail below—the United States has lower tax revenue because all of the other countries collect a large amount of revenue from national sales taxes, which the Democratic base has successfully rejected on multiple occasions for their regressivity. Although other countries have more public ownership of business, that public ownership is often used in the interests of capital rather than in the interests of workers—as in France, where nationalized industries were the leading edge of capitalism (Prasad 2005). Labor parties have been vibrant at the state level, and many of them "seize[d] the Democratic party label" (Shafer 1999, 453; on the strength and political orientation of labor at the state and local level see, e.g., Fink 1973; Kazin 1987). Moreover, many of the trends that make the United States seem so different are of recent vintage: only in the 1980s did the United States begin to surpass France and the United Kingdom in inequality, for example (Piketty and Saez 2003, 36), and the foreign policy of Ronald Reagan was very different from that of Richard Nixon. Across history, working hours were higher in some countries and some sectors and some time periods, and lower in other countries and other sectors and other time periods, than in the United States (see, e.g., Huberman 2004). These are not timeless characteristics of the American state, and much that we see as timelessly American stems only from the 1980s.

But this mixed picture was somehow spun into a story about state weakness that has taken over the social sciences. The full story of the rise of what Novak calls "the myth of the 'weak' American state" remains to be written, but Daniel Rodgers has recently given an interesting clue to one moment in the development of this myth. In the early twentieth century, middle-class Progressive reformers took sociological tours of Europe in order to compare and contrast welfare and economic policies. "Would you like to take tea with the London Commissioner of Prisons . . . ?" asks an advertisement headlined "Sociological Trip to Europe" from a 1931 magazine (reproduced in Rodgers 1998, 209). "Would you enjoy going as special guest to world-famous settlements and meeting their leaders, to a large industrial plant, and to government departments to learn about Old Age Pensions and Unemployment Insurance? How about a visit to a Welsh coal mine, a housing scheme, a cooperative organization?"

From the 1890s into the first three decades of the twentieth century, the respondents to ads such as these went, sipped, explored, and compared. Rodgers identifies a busy transcontinental circulation of ideas of reform and tracks the American Progressives as they compare the American state's failings in health care and social legislation to the health care policies of Catholic and pronatalist France, the social legislation of anti-socialist Germany, the bargains of corporatist Sweden, and the great rumblings of the rising Labour party in England. The idea of the laggard United States was born, and was nurtured over time by the middle-class students of the middle-class Progressives into a coherent narrative. This work would eventually feed the streams that raged into the river of Gabriel Kolko and the other historians of the "corporate liberal" school who accused the United States of being in the grip of business, and whose writings laid the foundation for our theories of comparative political economy.

It was middle-class reformers who could afford to go on these tours and make these comparisons. They created a newly international social science education and fused an urban and labor bias into our understandings of comparative political economy. But Progressivism was not just a middle class phenomenon. Many of the great achievements of the Progressive era, certainly most of the policies that shaped American political economy, were initiated by the Populist strain of Progressivism— those cantankerous old farmers of the 1890s who bequeathed their hopes and opposition to the new century. As many historians and social scientists have argued and as Elizabeth Sanders has recently reminded us, farmers gave the original push to the development of American intervention in the crucial period of the late nineteenth and early twentieth centuries. Farmers and their political representatives were central at the beginnings of the fights that resulted in "the redefinition of trade policy; the creation of an income tax; a new, publicly controlled banking and currency system; antitrust policy; the regulation of agricultural marketing networks; a nationally financed road system; federal control of railroads, ocean shipping, and early telecommunications; and agricultural and vocational education" (Sanders 1999, 7–8)—indeed, all of the main features of American intervention (for other scholars who have examined the importance of farmers to the development of American political economy see, e.g., Lipset 1950; Esping-Andersen 1990; Clemens 1997; Schneiberg and Bartley 2001; Verdier 2002; Postel 2007; Schneiberg, King, and Smith 2008; Carney 2010, among many others).

But farmers were not the ones taking the tours of Europe, comparing what they saw with what they hoped to see, and returning to write research monographs and train generations of students. Farmers were not part of the "Atlantic connection" that Rodgers identifies as central to the international movements of social reform around the issues of poverty, prisons, women's rights, and urban planning. What would those farmers have seen if they could have taken those tours, and what would our vision of Progressivism look like if it had been shaped by comparisons among the things that interested farmers, rather than comparisons among the things that interested urban middle class reformers? Because these questions have been neglected in the comparative scholarship, it is not possible to give a systematic answer to this question. In most cases, the comparative studies of these policy domains simply do not exist, and in all of them the literature is nowhere near as sophisticated as the literature on the welfare state. Luckily, some studies do exist, particularly on the four issues of greatest concern to farmers—monopoly power; monetary reform; taxation; and regulation of business—and we can take a "tour" through that literature, a nonsystematic exploration that will nevertheless teach us some important things.

Monopoly Power

The farmers' first concern would no doubt have revolved around the question of the trusts, the "moneyed trusts" of the northeast that were the target of so much resentment and rage at the turn of the century. Well versed in the weaknesses and flaws of the Sherman Antitrust Act and the attempt by American courts to subvert it, tourist farmers would have stood ready to examine antitrust policy in other countries with a microscope. They might have hoped to take tea with antitrust lawyers in the several countries and dutifully headed off to hunt down a monocled Queen's Counsel or a professor of *Jura* specializing in antitrust—only to discover that there were no such things because no European country had anything like American antitrust law. The farmers would have realized that "[e]xcept in North America, laws designed to curb cartels and monopolies were rare until after the Second World War .... associations to protect business interests were authorized by French law [in 1884] and thereafter the prohibition of price-fixing was attenuated, first by judicial interpretation and later, in 1926, by amendment of the penal code"; Sweden, starting in the 1920s, "provided for investigation of monopolies but for no subsequent corrective action" (Edwards 1967, 3). Although German workers and the public had expressed enough dissatisfaction with cartels to force a review of cartel policy in 1902, no action was taken until 1923, when the Weimar Republic passed a law *legalizing* cartels but regulating their practices. Cartels in Germany grew from a few hundred at the turn of the century to a peak of over three thousand in 1926 (Edwards 1967; Feldenkirchen 1992).

Britain's case is not far from the continental norm. In 1888, the Mogul Steamship Company sued a cartel for having set its prices so low that Mogul was forced out of business. But ten of the eleven judges in the House of Lords could see nothing wrong with this. It was not the court's business,

11

they intoned, to "prescribe to the business world how honest and peace-able trade was to be carried on" (Freyer 1992, 125)—a quotation that shows the interpretation prevalent at the time that antitrust represents state intervention into the market. They were unclear on the question of whether cartel agreements could actually be enforced in the courts, how-ever, and this remained the great question of British anti-cartel policy for the next two decades, with the courts attempting to affix a "rule of reason-ableness" that would determine when such contracts could be enforced. Eventually in 1914 the Lords decided that the businesses themselves are the "best judges of what is reasonable as between themselves" (131), that is, that cartels were not only legal, but could actually be enforced in the courts. That the United States also had something called a "rule of reason-ableness" has led to some confusion in the scholarship. But "reason" was being used in the American case not to determine whether cartel agree-ments could be enforced, but rather, whether cartels were legal at all, a principle that had already been settled in Britain in the Mogul decision.

Our farmers would have been stunned. They might have begun to develop a theory of "laggard Europe." They were well aware that Ameri-can reforms had not succeeded in taming business, that despite antitrust prosecutions "the structure of corporate oligarchy shook, but never col-lapsed" (McGerr 2003, 159), that "the most powerful element in the market—that is, big business—remained supreme in society" (Dawley 1991, 170). They would have known that antitrust provisions attempt-ing to harness big business ironically ended up contributing to a wave of mergers that reinforced the corporate oligarchy (Lamoreaux 1985). But in Europe it seemed that the state was not even attempting to "shake" the structure of corporate oligarchy, much less trying to make it collapse. How could it be that big business "remained supreme" and no one seemed bothered by it? Obviously, the farmers would have thought, Europe was in the grip of business power.

From our perspective we know that this approach to monopoly would not change until the late twentieth century when the European Union (E.U.) brought American-style competition policies to Europe. In France, the strategy of creating "national champions"—firms that would be large enough to compete against the flood of American goods and thereby en-able the country to kick its way towards industrialization—was a corner-stone of the *trentes glorieuses*. Sweden's ineffective 1925 antitrust law was strengthened only after the Second World War. This was the context in which, during the middle of the century, Crawford Greenwalt, chairman of Dupont, complained: "Why is it that I and my American colleagues are being constantly taken to court—made to stand trial—for activities that our counterparts in Britain and other parts of Europe are knighted, given peerages or comparable honors?" (quoted in Verdier 1994, xv).

Of course, the unusual American approach to antitrust has been visible to theorists of comparative political economy, but they interpret this massive state intervention against concentrated economic power as a victory for the free market. As discussed more fully in Chapter 2, the history does not support this interpretation, and the farmers agitating against trusts would certainly have considered absence of antitrust a problem. If the collapse of "the structure of corporate oligarchy" and attacks on "the most powerful element in the market . . . big business" are our measure of Progressivism—as two of our most prominent scholars of Progressivism suggest—then the United States was clearly more progressive than its European counterparts.

Monetary Reform

After the role of trusts, American farmers touring Europe in the Progressive era would have been most interested in European attitudes on monetary issues given that one of the main demands of the Populists was abandonment of the gold standard. Milton Friedman and Anna Schwartz (1963) famously vindicated the Populist farmers, arguing that an easier money supply would have kept price levels more stable in the rapidly growing economy. Barry Eichengreen sums up their explanation: "Had free silver coinage been maintained in the United States and Europe, more money would have chased the same quantity of goods, and this [late nineteenth century] deflation could have been avoided" (2008, 18). Some credit the Populists with pioneering the understanding of this role of money in the real economy (Niemi and Plante 2008, 442). Certainly the farmers revitalized interest in closer analysis of the role of money, including drawing economist Irving Fisher to pay attention to this question and ultimately to lay the foundations for monetarism (Allen 1993, 71–72; see also Carruthers and Babb 1996; Ritter 1997; note that, quite the opposite of the picture of "practical men" being "slaves to some defunct economist" (Keynes [1935] 1964, 383), the economists were following the lead of the practical men who had worked out their own understanding of their situation, as they would do again during the Great Depression).

Rather than touring world-famous settlements and interviewing their leaders, our touring Progressive farmers would have wanted to visit banks and interrogate European financiers to see how they were handling issues of deflation and the money supply. On the narrow issue of the gold standard, they would have found that the United States was neither particularly progressive nor particularly conservative. England, France, and Germany, like the United States, had adopted a pure gold standard by the 1870s only to see it collapse because of wartime financial exigencies. All of the countries adopted it again in the 1920s (the United States ahead by a few years) and abandoned it again in the 1930s (Germany in the lead with France the last of the major countries to do so). The international scope of the gold standard meant that the actions of one country affected the decisions of others, and there was little divergence among the advanced industrial countries. What divergence there was goes in an unusual direction, for France turned out to have been the champion of the gold standard at mid-century. Led by neoliberal economist Jacques Rueff, France adhered to the gold standard longer than the other major powers and was the most vocal supporter of the gold standard even after its demise (Chivvis 2010).

The gold standard, however, was only the mechanism through which the farmers were expressing their main interest, which was in a rapidly expanding money supply and easy availability of credit (Ritter 1997). As Niemi and Plante summarize the farmers' understanding: Gold produced deflation. "Deflation was a force for default. Default produced sharecropping" (2008, 437). What the farmers opposed was deflation—particularly, deflation caused by the inability of the money supply to keep pace with growth in output—and opposition to the gold standard and support for free coinage of silver were means to that end.

The touring farmers would have asked whether other countries managed to keep the money supply growing with growth in output. They would have found little concern for this issue. For example, although the Bank of England dates to 1694, only centuries later did the bank begin to understand itself as having responsibilities regarding the money supply. At its origins the bank saw itself as a profit-making enterprise and secondarily as a source of credit to government (Wood 2005). But it is also worth noting that in no other country was this question as pressing, because in no other country was productivity—including agricultural productivity—as high as in the United States. As Robert Gordon (2004, 2) notes, "Starting from the same level of productivity and per-capita income as the United

States in the mid-nineteenth century, Europe fell behind steadily to a level of barely half in 1950." This was not purely the result of the two world wars. Breaking the trend down into epochs, Gordon writes: "Europe fell steadily behind the United States through 1913, then suffered downward dislocations associated with both world wars, followed by a sharp reversal and catch-up during the golden years 1950–1973 and then an evident failure to close the remaining gap after 1973" (5). For many reasons, which we will explore below, the United States was witnessing a world historical rise in productivity in the nineteenth century and was grappling with the consequences of that productivity. European countries did not face this issue, and therefore European countries that had central banks were not unduly concerned about the issue of expanding the money supply to fight deflation.

Our farmers would have turned next to the other great monetary issue of concern to them: the handling of debt. If expansion of the money supply was one avenue to easing the situation of farmers, the other was expansion of credit. In all of these countries, farmers in the late nineteenth century were keenly interested in questions of credit, and all of the countries saw attempts to make credit more easily available. But on the question of what happened to those who could not pay their debts, the United States—because of the political power of agrarians—diverged sharply from other countries. As David Skeel writes, "Bankruptcy law in the United States is unique in the world" (2001, 1). Although the United States originally borrowed its bankruptcy law from England, over the years the two diverged drastically. Today, in England, "when an individual debtor files for bankruptcy in England, she faces close scrutiny from an official receiver, generally without the benefit of counsel. The official receiver rather than the debtor is the one who determines the debtor's treatment, and debtors rarely are given an immediate discharge. Far more often, the court, at the recommendation of the official receiver, temporarily delays the discharge or requires the debtor to make additional payments to her creditors" (2). By contrast, in the United States, "the debtor is the one who gets to choose" whether to "turn her assets over to the court and have her obligations immediately discharged (that is, voided), or to keep her assets and make payments to her creditors under a three-to-five-year rehabilitation plan" (7).

The situation in other countries is similar to Britain: "Before the [nineteen-] nineties, the European consumer bankruptcy law was next to nonexistent. . . . Often the costs of bankruptcy and the inconvenience caused by it are so huge that non-business citizens are, in practice, excluded. More important is that the bankruptcy did not and does not offer relief of debt (discharge) at all, and is therefore useless from the point of view of the small-asset debtor" (Niemi-Kiesiläinen 1997, 133–134). Only in the late twentieth century would other countries begin to consider and adopt the American approach to bankruptcy. Even after the American bankruptcy reform of 2005, the complete discharge of debts that is available to American debtors is rare elsewhere (Tabb 2005).

Their tour of the issue of the money supply and their observation of how bankruptcy laws worked to the benefit of creditors rather than debtors in other countries would have led our farmers to come away with an appreciation both for the unique situation of the United States and a sense that European countries were more beholden to the needs and wishes of capital.

Taxation

Instead of visiting a government department of pensions, the farmers' next concern might have been to visit a government revenue department to investigate the progress of tax legislation, as a graduated income tax was the next big fight of the era. The touring farmers would again have come away with an impression of a Europe not particularly concerned about the rise of the free market and the concentration of capital. In France, the farmers would have found suspicion of the state and its agents to be so widespread that the state was unable to meet its revenue needs through direct taxation, resorting to hidden means of taxing its citizens. Instead of the American wish to "soak the rich," in the late nineteenth and early twentieth centuries the French were terrified by the prospect of "fiscal inquisition" from the state (Morgan and Prasad 2009). Rather than a concern over capitalism and trusts, the concern was over the growing powers of the state. This concern was so strong that it channeled tax policy down lines that the French state would follow for the next century, such that scholars were still finding more progressive taxes in the United States than in France until the rise of neoliberalism in the late twentieth century (Piketty and Saez 2007). Far from being the best protector of private property, the United States also had more progressive inheritance taxation than France or Germany (Beckert 2008).

Germany and Sweden both introduced progressive income taxes in the early decades of the twentieth century as part of the attempt by elites to head off socialist sentiment (Steinmo 1994), but our farmers would

16

have been appalled at these systems' evolution in the coming decades, as taxes on labor and consumers rose while taxes on capital and corporations were kept low (see Chapter 6). For example, the Swedish value added tax did not even exempt basic necessities like food and clothing (Steinmo 1993), and in Sweden in the 1980s, "the effective net tax rate on personal capital income was actually negative for the top 60 percent of the income ranks" (Lindert 2004, 240).

Only in Britain, the birthplace of the general income tax, would the farmers have been satisfied: a rising Labour party had forced the Liberals to turn to the left and introduce progressive taxation at the turn of the century. The "People's Budget" of 1909 had proposed several heavy taxes on the wealthy. Lloyd George eventually succeeded in implementing graduated income taxation with the revenues to be used for pensions and social insurance proposals. More important than the specific measure were the principles it introduced into Britain, which would guide British politics until the advent of Margaret Thatcher seven decades later and even beyond: redistribution, class politics, and the end of any real power held by the House of Lords (Daunton 2001).

Our farmers, discussing these observations in their newspapers and journals, might have tossed around a theory of the Anglo-American mode of market regulation, which privileges an interventionist state, counterposed to the continental version, which seems to fear the state and leave business to itself in all of these domains that interested the farmers. In these domains European countries saw businesses as the "best judges of what is reasonable as between themselves," privileged creditor concerns over debtor concerns, and worried about the "fiscal inquisition" of the state. The farmers would note that these developments tracked the rising political power of the working classes in the United States and Britain and the underdevelopment of suffrage on the continent. An intellectually inclined farmer might have drafted a treatise on "laggard France" and its irrational hatred of the state. Such a farmer would have wondered where this exceptional French resistance to the state comes from—the Revolution, perhaps, which had inculcated in French national character a resistance to any form of centralized authority? Or even further back, to the medieval jacqueries, which had created boundaries between citizen and state that were reproduced with every street protest? Or were myths of resistance to Roman rule passed down in the old Gallic tribes along with recipes for black pudding and tripe? Studies would have proliferated showing that the nationalizations of the postwar period were merely symbolic and actually functioned in the interests of capital, and that the French welfare state was biased towards the middle classes and the wealthy, reinforcing rather than undermining market outcomes (on nationalization working in the interests of capital see Prasad 2005; on the middle-class bias of the French welfare state see Cameron 1991). Scholars would have insisted that state expenditure on health care was actually a *market-reinforcing* intervention, because it produced healthy laborers ready for capitalist production and relieved firms from the burden of paying for health insurance. French child-care institutions, like Swedish ones, would have been seen as freeing up female labor for the market (Swenson 2002, 7). There was just something about the French character, the farmers would have mused, that insists on freedom and the market and cannot tolerate state intervention or collectivism.

Regulation

Turning finally to the last stop on the tour, the tourist farmers would have examined the regulation of business including those food and drug regulations that several decades later would enable Frances Kelsey in her stance against the pharmaceutical manufacturers. Again they would have been satisfied to see a lively public debate in Britain over the sale of fraudulent foods, with legislative results that included a required listing of the contents of foods, investigations into practices of food adulteration, and implementation of a Food and Drugs Act in 1899. The farmers would have been astonished, however, to see the debate center on whether margarine can be passed off as butter. Where were the issues of hygiene and worker safety that so exercised the readers of Upton Sinclair? The British obsession seemed to be with guaranteeing that products sold on the market were what they claimed to be—not on whether these products were actually effective or safe (Phillips and French 1998). The framework that guided regulation from 1875 to 1938 assumed "that the processes and ingredients of food manufacturing were essentially safe and that regulation's real target should be the retailers who tampered with manufactured goods before selling them" (Phillips and French 1998, 356).

In Germany, the farmers would have been astounded to see that industry patrolled itself. The government cared not at all for a drug's safety, although it did investigate the question of whether the drug had been diluted. The main German response to the rise of the era of pharmaceuticals was to pass a law in 1872 that outlawed their sale except by apothecaries. While apologists for the German pattern might point to informal

18

social controls on apothecaries or other means of informal regulation, the Thalidomide example demonstrates the failure of such controls. In Germany there was no oversight of manufacturing or of drug testing nor were there restrictions on labeling or on advertisements. Worries about the expanding scope of pharmaceuticals led to proposals for government oversight, but business interests repeatedly squelched these—five times between 1928 and 1941 (Daemmrich 2004).

By now, heading to France, our farmers would no longer have been surprised to learn that the 1905 Food Adulteration Act was a law against falsification and fraud, and was not designed to enhance safety or effectiveness (Dessaux 2006). Clearly, American food and drug regulation was more stringent than any of the European countries. By Frances Kelsey's time, the United States seemed to be more stringent in every domain of regulation, not just food and drugs. For example, until the neoliberal deregulations of the 1980s, scholars found that in this period the United States was more adversarial on vehicle emission standards than Sweden (Lundqvist 1980), was more adversarial in regulating possible carcinogens than several European countries (Brickman, Jasanoff, Ilgen 1985), and was more adversarial in both food and environmental regulation than Europe (Jasanoff 1991). American occupational safety regulations (Kelman 1981), procedures for vinyl chloride regulation (Badaracco 1985), and health and safety regulations were more strict and adversarial to industry (Wilson 1985). The United States was more punitive in the regulation of mines (Braithwaite 1985). When the ozone layer was threatened, the United States quickly passed a ban on CFCs, but only Norway and Sweden did so in Europe while the E.U. only acted under U.S. pressure (Benedick 1998). The regulation of water pollution was more stringent in the United States than in Germany (although not more effective, Verweij 2000). As will be discussed in more detail in Chapters 7 and 8, the United States emerged from the Great Depression with tighter controls on financial firms than any other country, including prohibitions against branch banking and universal banking. These patterns help to explain why it was France—not the United States—that created the neoliberal global financial architecture of the 1990s (Abdelal 2007).

Frances Kelsey was a hero. But her heroism was made possible by an American context of stringent regulation that lasted from the late nineteenth century to the late twentieth century.

This tour through the recent historical and historically oriented social science literature shows that if we compare the United States to other industrialized countries according to the metric of what farmers were interested in at the turn of the twentieth century—rather than according to the metric of what middle-class urban Progressives were interested in—the American state looks much less liberal. The American state attacked big business and taxed the wealthy more than European states did, the American state aided debtors at the expense of creditors, and the American state regulated corporations more extensively.

While the emphasis here has been on the issues that would have seemed most relevant to farmers conducting this comparative assessment, it is worth noting the many other ways in which recent historical work dismantles the idea of an individualistic, market-oriented, or business-driven United States counterposed to statist, corporatist, or more social democratic European countries. For example, a study of comparative trade policy at the turn of the century shows that while the United States paid attention to popular considerations, other countries were beholden to business forces (Verdier 1994). On the question of corporatism that ruled political science for a generation, recent historically attuned work is showing that the American state resembles European states more than we have appreciated (see, e.g., Gordon 1994; Block 2008; Berk 2009). Balogh (2009) has documented that the nineteenth century United States featured a stronger national government than scholars have generally assumed. Amenta (2000) and Skocpol (1995) have shown that at times in history the American welfare state has been a leader, not a laggard. Even the American process of industrialization as uniquely driven by mass production has been called into question, and scholars have shown the existence of alternative regional production processes in the late nineteenth century that might have won out (Scranton 1997; Berk 1997), while comparativists have noted the existence of subcultural logics of production in other countries (Piore and Sabel 1984; Herrigel 2000; for a reinterpretation of regulation in America see Novak 1994). This historical work calls our theories of comparative political economy into question, and these theories will need to be reformulated to take account of the actual history. This work also suggests that scholars in the last half century, working with an urban and labor bias, have exaggerated the differences between the United States and other countries.

To be clear, the point here is not that history demonstrates uniformly greater state intervention in the United States than in other countries. In order to show exactly how much our theories obscure, I have emphasized here the areas in which the United States is more interventionist. But of course there are many examples where there is more state intervention in other countries than in the United States, such as in the regulation of genetically modified organisms, or in rates of environmental taxation, or in labor regulations throughout American history; and American regulation has weakened since the rise of neoliberalism in the 1980s (Echols 1998; Hines 2007; but see Orren 1991 on the English inspiration for American labor laws). Rather, the point is that all advanced capitalist countries intervene in the market, and in every country some of these interventions promote the market while others undermine it. Because of this, we need better ways to conceptualize the differences between the states than any of our theories of comparative political economy have been able to provide.

But there is a problem with the revisionist historical scholarship as well. Simply pointing to the existence of heavy state intervention in the United States or alternative logics in each of the countries is not enough, because this literature cannot answer three questions. First, if the United States had and continues to have state intervention in many domains, why is there more poverty in the United States than in other countries? This is the great question that underlies all theories of comparative political economy. Attempts to measure state intervention are imprecise and subject to many judgment calls. But there is one finding that remains stable no matter how we measure it: the United States has more poverty than the countries of Europe. Rainwater and Smeeding (2004) show in their examination of childhood poverty that this remains the case even if we examine absolute poverty and even if we examine only whites and the native born. In a well-known paper, Buhmann, Rainwater, Schmaus, and Smeeding calculated poverty in different countries in several ways and found that, overall, the calculation of poverty was highly sensitive to the assumptions of the model used to calculate it—with the exception that "[f]or all scales and lines the United States has the highest poverty rate" (1988, 32). The Organisation for Economic Cooperation and Development (OECD), using a different data source, finds the United States having the highest relative poverty of the advanced industrial countries of the west for almost all combinations of household form and labor market participation; the United States also achieved the second-lowest reduction in absolute poverty from the mid-1990s to the mid-2000s (OECD 2008). Even when we use absolute rather than relative measures of poverty, the United States remains near the top of the list of advanced countries with the highest poverty; for example, Smeeding (2005, 960–961) uses purchasing power parity to estimate absolute poverty in eight nations, and finds the standard of living for the poor second lowest in the United States, a picture that worsens when we consider that in the United States the poor need to buy things that are provided for free as part of the welfare state in other nations (on absolute poverty see also Smeeding 2006).

Moreover, this discrepancy does not seem to be the consequence of a market that produces more poverty, as poverty levels are similar in the developed countries before taxes and transfers. Rather, poverty levels vary because of state actions. As David Brady argues, "[T]he fundamental cause of poverty is politics" (2009, 9; see also Rainwater and Smeeding 2004; Kenworthy 2004). The historical literature on state intervention in the United States has to be able to explain these features—if the United States had a strong state, why was that state not addressing poverty? If there are alternative traditions and important subcultural logics within each country, then what explains the persistence of this overarching discrepancy?

Second, the historical literature does not do a good job of explaining the attack on state intervention that arose in the United States in the 1970s and 1980s. Even if the United States has not always been more unequal than other countries, it is now. Table 1.1 shows considerable differences today that a full theory must be able to explain. If the United States had a strong state in the early part of the twentieth century, what happened to it starting in the 1970s and 1980s? What explains the rise of neoliberalism in recent decades?

Finally, neither the historical scholarship nor the comparative politics literature has been able to shed light on the most consequential economic event of recent years: the financial crisis of 2007–2008. Indeed, the crisis has revealed how little we really understand about capitalism, with the most central members of the economic establishment publicly confessing the limits of their understanding.

This book aims to knit together the historical scholarship showing heavy state intervention in the United States with the scholarship in comparative political economy to answer these questions. I will attempt to show that calling attention to the American style of state intervention gives us a better understanding of the development of the American state, *including* the question of why there is more poverty in the United States than in other advanced industrial countries—the very question that has exercised urban and middle-class Progressive reformers for over a century. Paying attention to these issues gives a more convincing explanation of the underdeveloped public welfare state in the United States. Second, examining the history of the rise of these elements of the American state can help explain the rise of neoliberalism in the 1970s and 1980s. And a proper understanding of comparative political economy, one that is attuned to history, is crucial for an understanding of how the financial crisis unfolded.

Unless we can provide a better theoretical explanation for patterns of greater intervention in the United States, these instances of state intervention will always be treated as exceptions, no matter how many of them we find. Skocpol and Finegold note the successes of the Department of Agriculture during the New Deal, but call it "an island of state strength in an ocean of weakness" (1982, 271). Daniel Carpenter thoroughly catalogues the Food and Drug Administration's regulatory power, but believes it is only "a partial contrast to the comparative portraits of the state in which the United States appears laggard, weak, or exceptional in its reliance on private mechanisms" (2010, 22). Fred Block traces the emergence of a developmental state in the United States but sees this as "swimming against the current" of predominant policy (2008, 169). David Vogel summarizes his findings on regulation as, "The United States remains exceptional, but . . . this exceptionalism is precisely the opposite of what much of the literature on American politics would have led one to expect" but cautiously adds "at least with respect to this dimension" (Vogel 1986, 28). Even scholars who are aware of the wide range of interventions in the American economy have tried to reconcile this with the belief in an economy that favors the market. Novak (2008), whose important essay calls attention to many aspects of state strength, ultimately concludes that the interventions he catalogues are used to favor capital, and even briefly implies that they are used to exercise violence over the governed (771–772; see also Block 2007 on this point). All capitalist states do pass policies to help capital, but they also pass policies to control capital. The United States resembles other states in the former, and Novak's formulation cannot help us explain the latter. Another recent attempt to square the evidence of state intervention with the belief in laissez-faire is the argument that the American state has remained invisible or submerged (Balogh 2009, Sheingate 2009, Quinn 2010, n.d., Mettler 2011). While helpful at elucidating some aspects of American power, these arguments are less helpful at explaining the extremely visible movements for government intervention at the turn of the century and during the Depression and New Deal, or the historical moments during which America has been a leader in the visible patterns of redistribution that

today characterize European countries, or highly visible government regulations, or that one of the most striking and consequential features of
American taxation is its *greater* visibility, as discussed in Chapter 6.

The United States currently anchors the liberal pole of all comparative historical frameworks, as we will see in Chapter 2. The varieties of
capitalism theory, for example, argues that several different models of capitalism, including the liberal American one, can function well. Neoclassical
economists point to the higher per capita Gross Domestic Product (GDP)
of the United States and attempt to argue that minimal state intervention
leads to higher growth (e.g., Tanzi and Schuknecht 2000). But if the
United States is as interventionist as other countries then it may be that
no capitalist state has survived, or can survive, without extensive state
intervention. Such a demonstration would be extremely important for our
understanding of how economies grow, of relevance to those advising
developing countries today, as well as to those struggling to understand
crises of capitalism.

Conservatives today like to argue that the United States is and always
has been a country that favors the free market and fears state intervention,
seeking to limit the scope of political action to fit the contours of that
belief. But if there has been a strong strand of state intervention in the
United States, then the scope for politics is wider than this. For very different reasons, activists on the Left also seek to adhere to this argument, in
the hopes of shaming the United States into following European models.
But a politics that takes account of, rather than ignores, the strong state
intervention of the United States may yet manage to achieve an American
model of poverty reduction. While I explore the political implications of
these arguments in the conclusion, my primary aim in this work is not to
propose policy solutions but to produce a more accurate historical por-
trait. Certainly all political actors, no matter their ideological predilec-
tions, have an interest in clearing away misconceptions about the past.

2

COMPARING CAPITALISMS

Many countries achieved sustained economic growth over the course of the twentieth century. Almost as interesting as the phenomenon of economic growth itself is the story of how scholars have sought to understand it. From the beginning, it was clear that the countries were not all following the same line. Every country that attained rapid or sustained economic growth seemed to have its own recipe for how it did so, and every few decades the fortunes and relative standing of the different models shifted. In the early twentieth century, attention turned first to Sweden, which in the interwar period seemed to be pioneering a model midway between capitalism and socialism, causing analysts to draw lessons from the strength of the Swedish Social Democrats. After the Second World War, the rapid recovery of France made it the poster child for planned capitalism, so analysts gave careful scrutiny to the role of the state in economic growth. The economic crisis of the 1970s shifted the focus to the Japanese model, which seemed to have survived intact, leading to fascination with cultural differences between Japan and other countries. Today, attention focuses on Germany, which despite the shock of reunification seems to have maintained for many decades stable economic growth and widespread participation in the benefits of economic growth.

Two urgent questions have driven this scholarship. First is whether capitalism can benefit everyone in a society. The original question of scholars imbued with Marxist suspicions was whether capitalism could benefit the working classes; but as the decades passed and it became clear that some models of capitalism were benefiting not only the working classes but also the poor, scholars began to wonder why some countries were more successful at dealing with poverty and inequality than others. The second question, which becomes particularly pointed in times of economic crisis, is which model of capitalism can best produce sustained economic growth. A central question in this tradition is whether the programs that reduce poverty and inequality in some countries have hindered economic growth, as neoclassical models of the economy would predict. Because the welfare states of Europe are more successful at reducing poverty and inequality but do not seem to have suffered greatly for it, there is great interest in examining their record. While the demise of the European welfare state has been regularly prophesied in the American press for twenty years, a combination of minor reforms appears to have preserved the core features of these systems (see, e.g., Vail 2010 on France and Germany). It is difficult to predict the consequences of the current crisis in Europe, but Europe has posted a record of over fifty years of economic growth with low poverty, a unique achievement in the history of capitalism that merits continued attention.

The case of the United States was always an important contrast, explicit or implicit, in all of these theories: the absence of a national labor-based party made it a stark contrast to the Swedish model; the resistance to planning and industrial policy made it a contrast to French statism; the supposed individualism of the United States was drawn in contrast to supposedly collectivist Japanese culture; and today, its uncoordinated market is used as a foil to the German coordinated model of capitalism.

An early version of the question of why the United States was so different arose from the Marxist tradition. In the early twentieth century, the Marxist scholar Werner Sombart ([1906] 1976) wondered why there was no "socialism" in the United States. This absence contradicted, in Sombart's eyes, Marx's prognosis that socialism would be most advanced where capitalism was the most advanced. As Eric Foner (1984) has pointed out, the question was never very crisply defined. There was no socialism in any of the western capitalist countries, after all; and there *was* a labor-based party in the United States at the time the question was being asked, its demise during the First World War a result not of its weakness but of its commitment to the international principles of socialism. But the investigation took on a life of its own, and scholars would wrestle for another century with many of the same hypotheses that Sombart first pinned down: that a uniquely pro capitalist or antistatist culture existed in the United States; that early suffrage had undermined class-based politics; that the two-party political system siphoned off more extreme agitation; that greater material benefits led workers to acquiesce in the system; that westward expansion provided an escape valve from social conflict. Over the years, scholars added other variants to these answers, most importantly that racial and ethnic diversity had undermined the cohesiveness of the working class and that fragmented political institutions had made redistributive policies difficult.

Class-Based Arguments

Perhaps the most sustained and fascinating debate in comparative political economy today is between those who find the sources of different political economic traditions in labor and those who see employers and employer organization as the main difference. The best examples of scholars in the former tradition include John Stephens (1979), Walter Korpi (1983), Alexander Hicks (1999), and Evelyne Huber and John Stephens (2001). The basic argument is that redistribution in capitalist states is a function of the power of unions and labor-based parties, either alone or as an essential partner in political coalitions. Korpi argues for taking "class and the distribution of power resources" (1983, 14) as the starting point for any analysis of politics. Scholars in this tradition argue that labor markets distribute risks and the resources to cope with risks differently, such that those facing the most risks have the least resources to cope with them: "Such features generate a potential for class-related collective action. Political parties based in socioeconomic categories relatively disadvantaged in terms of economic resources and relying largely on labor power are expected to be protagonists in welfare state development aimed at modifying conditions and outcomes related to market distributive processes" (Korpi 2006, 168). This natural asymmetry ensures that class will remain a prominent social division within any capitalist society.

According to this view the distribution of power resources is historically structured, with capital always having the upper hand but labor able to organize and fight back under certain historical conditions—for example, where industrial unions join together in confederation, where a socialist party is popular, or where capital is centralized and concentrated (Korpi 2006, 172; Stephens 1979). In Sweden, labor had been able to ally with the state and win policies that improved the lives of workers. In short, "The distribution of power resources between the main collectivities or classes in a country affects the form and direction of public intervention in the distributive processes and thereby the extent of inequality in a country" (Korpi 1983, 195). Class matters, and politics matters as well.

This theory, which was perhaps the dominant vision of comparative capitalism during the 1980s, has been criticized for overgeneralizing from the unusual Swedish experience (see, e.g., Esping-Andersen 1990, 17; Iversen and Soskice 2009, 439). As Peter Baldwin argued in an exhaustive examination of one hundred years of welfare policy in five European countries, "None of the supposed benchmarks of social democratic social insurance . . . were initially or in any essential way determined by the Left or its core constituency. Bourgeois and rural interests were the origin of what Social Democrats have later successfully claimed as their own" (Baldwin 1992, 156). Such arguments suggest that the correlation between labor power and social spending is spurious (as we will discuss further in Chapter 3). The power resources theory is also difficult to apply to American history because as several scholars have shown, the dominant feature of the American welfare state is a precocious development in the early part of the twentieth century followed by an underdevelopment, particularly in the area of national health insurance, after the Second World War (Skocpol 1995; Amenta 2000; Swenson 2002). This unusual trajectory does not fit well onto patterns of labor or union power in the United States, as the highest unionization rates are found after the Second World War. Moreover, the class-based argument ignores or cannot make sense of the strength of labor at the state level discussed in Chapter 1 or the fact—explored more fully below—that in the United States labor did not want some of the main elements of the welfare state at mid-century. Such arguments end up assuming that labor and the Left will be champions of the welfare state, an assumption that does not always hold. Even in Europe labor has often identified its interests with a broadly growing economy, and has pushed for welfare policies as part of over-arching agreements for economic growth (see, e.g., Eichengreen 1996 and the discussion in Chapter 3). Class-based arguments also have difficulty explaining why policy usually does not return to the prior pattern when a different class constellation acquires power. And such a theory does not generalize well beyond the case of the welfare state, because as we have seen, some of the strongest protections of workers and consumers are in the United States, which analysts in this tradition see as having a relatively weaker labor movement.[1]

Another version of the argument for the importance of class to American exceptionalism is found in Gøsta Esping-Andersen's discussion of welfare state regimes. Drawing on the work of Karl Polanyi ([1944] 2001), who warned of capitalism turning human beings into commodities, Esping-Andersen proposes that we analyze states by the degree to which they make it possible for people to live without turning themselves into commodities: "[t]he outstanding criterion for social rights must be the degree to which they permit people to make their living standards independent of pure market forces" (1990, 3). Using this framework Esping-Andersen suggests a tripartite classification of welfare states in advanced industrial countries: the liberal welfare states, such as the United States, Canada, and Australia, "in which means-tested assistance, modest universal transfers, or modest social-insurance plans predominate" (26), the conservative or corporatist welfare states such as Austria, France, Germany, and Italy, in which decommodification goes hand in hand with status differentiation, and the social-democratic welfare states such as Sweden, with their more universal welfare principles and their commitment to full employment.

Esping-Andersen argues that it is not labor but agrarian classes who are the main determinant of welfare state development: "One of history's paradoxes is that the rural classes were decisive for the future of socialism. . . . Political dominance was, until after World War II, largely a question of rural class politics. The construction of welfare states in this period was, therefore, dictated by whichever force captured the farmers" (1990, 30–31). He argues that continental Europe was hostile to farmer-labor coalitions, while the Scandinavian countries and the United States were both hospitable to such coalitions "but with the important difference that the labor-intensive South blocked a truly universalistic social security system and opposed further welfare-state developments" (30) while in Norway and Sweden farmers supported the welfare state in return for agricultural subsidies.

In this explanation, the underdevelopment of the American welfare state ultimately turns on the question of a certain kind of production in the South. Although Esping-Andersen does not cite any specific authors, in his argument for the southern veto he seems to be drawing on the work of Jill Quadagno (1984) who has elaborated on this perspective at greater length in her study of the 1935 Social Security Act. This vision of American agrarians as having vetoed the welfare state is dominant in historical studies of social policy. But the main provision of the Social Security Act of 1935, old-age pensions, eventually developed into the one welfare area in which the United States is not a laggard (Finegold 1988; Hacker 2002; Scruggs and Allan 2006). Although the pension legislation in the Social Security Act was distinctly shaped by the interests of southern capitalists and blocked from becoming more universal at its origins, it nevertheless grew into a more universal old-age program whose effects are similar to those of public pensions in other countries. Certainly the ability of southern Congressmen to block New Deal welfare proposals is an important part of the history of the American welfare state, but their veto is not the end of the story.

I will argue below that while Esping-Andersen is right to focus on the political preferences of agrarians, the story is more complicated than a veto from the labor-repressive South. American agrarians, even southern agrarians, were not always resistant to the development of the state, but their statist interventions had consequences that they could not have foreseen.

More generally, it is empirically inaccurate to argue that the goal of reformers has been to become "independent of pure market forces," even in the most developed welfare states. In most cases, the goal has been an improved market position and better working conditions in an expanding economy, not decommodification at all (Eichengreen 1996; see Thane 1984 for a review of why the working class might not have preferred welfare measures). Indeed, even the Swedish experience does not always support the decommodification thesis, as one of Sweden's traditional successes was precisely in getting the unemployed back into work rather than in allowing them to remain outside the labor market.

Varieties of Capitalism

Given the difficulties of the class-based arguments, about a decade later scholars began to develop a new argument to explain both the different outcomes regarding poverty and inequality and the possibility of sustaining economic growth with more than minimal state intervention. Formulated most thoroughly in Hall and Soskice's *Varieties of Capitalism* (2001), this theory drew on the attention of a prior generation of political scientists to corporatist bargains between labor, employers, and the state. But where the earlier generation of scholars like Korpi had been impressed by labor's ability to strike bargains in this corporatist triangle, Hall and Soskice, along with scholars such as Peter Swenson (2002) and John Zysman (1983), shifted the focus to employers. Firms, Hall and Soskice argue, face specific problems in carrying out production: the need to secure the cooperation of a skilled workforce and the need to acquire reliable finance, supplies, and channels of distribution. Capitalism can be analyzed as the history of how firms solve these problems. In a set of economies that Hall and Soskice call "liberal market economies," these problems are solved through competitive arm's-length market exchanges between the firm and each of its partners, whereas in "coordinated market economies" the firm interacts with its partners to solve these problems. For example, in liberal market economies firms are not involved in training their workers, and the school-to-work transition is a chaotic and haphazard process compared to the structured apprenticeships found in coordinated market economies (Thelen 2004). Hall and Soskice also suggest that different elements of the political economy will work in concert, evidencing "institutional complementarities": "nations with a particular type of coordination in one sphere of the economy should tend to develop complementary practices in other spheres as well" (18).

These two modes of capitalism fill different and complementary niches in the global market. Coordinated market economies are best at producing high quality products, particularly capital goods, that retain enormous loyalty from customers and require highly specialized workers, while liberal market economies specialize in generating completely new products or radical changes in production process that require only generally skilled workers. Thus, *both* the liberal market economies and the coordinated market economies are capable of generating economic growth. But Hall and Soskice argue that liberal market economies produce more inequality and longer working hours, while the welfare state is actually complementary to the institutions of a coordinated market economy; this is because secure jobs, welfare benefits, and good working conditions are necessary to convince workers to specialize in the highly specialized tasks that firms in coordinated market economies need (50–51). According to this logic, firms in coordinated market economies will have an interest in supporting high levels of benefits, whereas in liberal market economies, firms have less interest in doing so. (For a fuller discussion of the development of the welfare state according to the varieties of capitalism perspective, see Mares 2003.)

The sophistication of the varieties of capitalism framework has had a magnetic effect on the field of comparative political economy. Most scholars are now positioned either within this framework or in opposition to it, and the literature extending or critiquing the framework has become vast. The most instructive insights for our purposes come from the debate between the supporters of class-based explanations and the supporters of varieties of capitalism. Walter Korpi (2006) along with other scholars points out that firms in coordinated market economies have not, by and large, welcomed the welfare state. Korpi argues that varieties of capitalism scholars "have mistaken employers' consent to expansion as evidence for their first-order preferences for such reform" (171). Korpi argues that there is plenty of employer opposition to the welfare state in coordinated market economies; and the differences that do exist in employer *acquiescence* to the welfare state reveal not just employer preferences but also employer bargaining power. (On these points see also Prasad 2006, 203–224.)

In recent years, in the face of clear historical evidence, varieties of capitalism scholars have backed away from the claim that employers actively prefer or choose welfare policies in the coordinated market economies. In a detailed response to Korpi's criticisms, Iversen and Soskice (2009) argue that employers have *come to accept* the welfare state, and that class-based or power-resources arguments are unable to explain why large welfare states do not seem to diminish economic growth (439).

Iversen and Soskice then outline an approach that traces the divergent economic fates of nations in the twentieth century to the organization of guilds and cooperatives. In the nineteenth century and earlier, some countries, for exogenous reasons, developed cooperative institutions, and in the first decades of the twentieth century these were formalized into systems of proportional representation. These systems then promoted labor strength and unification and also—separately—promoted redistribution. In other words, Iversen and Soskice argue that the correlation between labor strength and redistribution does not show that labor strength causes redistribution—rather, the truth is the other way around. Institutions that promote redistribution strengthen the hand of labor.

Iversen and Soskice's work is a strong attempt to deepen and refine the varieties of capitalism perspective. It represents the frontier of theories of comparative political economy. But it falls short of an explanation of comparative political economy on several counts. First, the feature that distinguishes the United States from other states is not the size of its welfare state but the public versus private nature of the welfare state (Jacoby 1998; Hacker 2002; Klein 2003). Private welfare—such as firm-level health and pension plans—should be found in the *coordinated* economies, where worker loyalty to specific firms matters because such measures may help attract or keep workers. In the liberal United States, with its economic system based on generalized skills, workers are not indispensable and consequently we should not see private systems of health and pensions. Of course, it is precisely in the United States that we do see such systems. Second, Iversen and Soskice argue that their main dependent variable, inequality, is a result of wage compression. If that were true, we would see greater equality in the coordinated market economies *before* taxes and transfers; while parts of the pre-tax distribution are more unequal in the United States, overall liberal and coordinated economies are similar in levels of inequality before taxes and transfers, and what differences emerge do not go in the directions predicted by varieties of capitalism (Figure 2.1). This suggests that taxes and transfers rather than collective bargaining are predominantly responsible for the patterns Iversen and Soskice see.

Moreover, an unrealistic assumption is required for the authors' argument about proportional representation and redistribution to work:

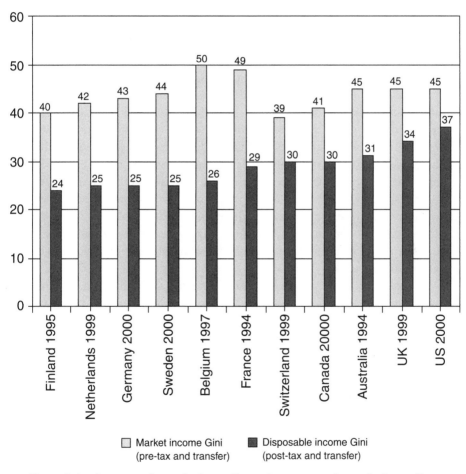

Figure 2.1. Pre-tax and transfer inequality and post-tax and transfer inequality. (*Source:* Smeeding 2005, 972.)

that governments can never pass policies that help the rich at the expense of the poor. Iversen and Soskice argue that voting in democracies can be modeled as a system with three voters (the lower class, the middle class, and the wealthy). In proportional representation systems with three parties representing the lower, middle, and upper classes, the lower classes and the middle classes will unite in order to tax the wealthy (452). In majoritarian systems, on the other hand, with only two center-left and center-right parties, there will be a center-right bias. Using the acronyms L, M, and H for lower, middle, and upper class respectively, Iversen and Soskice write that in majoritarian systems "M has less to fear from an MH government moving right than from an LM government moving left. The former leads to lower benefits going to M but also to lower taxes on M, while the latter implies higher taxes on M with the proceeds redistributed to L" (453). This explains the asymmetry that biases proportional representation systems towards center-left policies and majoritarian systems to center-right policies. But Iversen and Soskice's arguments stand only if taxation is the sole policy that determines voters' choices. This asymmetry does not exist in a world in which the government can take actions that voters believe help the wealthy at the expense of the middle classes and the poor—such as agricultural subsidies for large landowners only, financial sector policies that benefit the very top of the income distribution but threaten economic stability for the middle classes, draconian criminal sanctions for minor crimes, or exemptions to pollution laws for well connected donors. In such a world M has an incentive to align with L against such policies even in majoritarian democracies, because an MH government moving right represents a threat to M.

Moreover, the scholarship is quite clear that the redistribution of the large welfare states does not work by taking from the rich and giving to the poor. Several scholars have noted that the large welfare states seem to be based on forms of taxation that hit the lower classes more heavily, such as payroll taxes and sales taxes, and at least until the neoliberal tax reforms of the 1980s, the welfare states of Europe taxed capital much more lightly than the United States did (Carey and Rabesona 2004; Mendoza, Razin, and Tesar 1994; Volkerink and de Haan 2001; Sørensen 2004; and see Chapter 6.) On the spending side, it is well known that welfare states have a bias toward the middle and upper classes. Because middle and upper classes are in a better position to take advantage of state-subsidized higher education and costly end-of-life health care and because many welfare states target benefits to earnings, the large welfare states follow what Korpi and Palme call "the biblical *Matthew Principle* of giving more, in absolute terms, to the rich than to the poor and also, in relative terms, having limited low-income targeting," which serves to solidify support for the welfare state across classes (Korpi and Palme 1998, 672; on this point see also the magisterial work of Peter Baldwin 1992). Welfare states do reduce poverty and inequality, but the Robin Hood picture that Iversen and Soskice rely on—a picture of taking from the rich and giving to the poor—has been dismantled by careful cross-national studies. Redistribution seems primarily to occur within classes, from young to old, healthy to unhealthy, and uneducated to educated, in Arthur Stinchcombe's (1985) terms, rather than across classes from rich to poor.

And of course, the varieties of capitalism perspective would predict less heavy regulation in the United States because the United States is said to be a liberal market economy in which "deregulation is often the most effective way to improve coordination" (Hall and Soskice 2001, 49)—an odd sentence, as it implies prior regulation that the theory has no way of explaining. The varieties of capitalism perspective is an extraordinary intellectual achievement, but in recent years its limits have become clear.

National Culture

Another set of scholars explain greater American poverty as an outcome of a greater American cultural predilection for free markets. One of the most famous of this strand of explanations is by Lipset and Marks (2000), who advance a thesis that socialism failed in the United States because American culture is largely bourgeois, which meant socialists were always "trying to swim against the tide of American culture" (266; for the classic statement see Hartz 1955).

These explanations are difficult to square with the evidence, however. For example, when faced with clear evidence of a quite radical Marxism in the American socialist movement around the First World War and moments of labor militancy from the early nineteenth century to the Great Depression, instead of using this evidence to qualify their thesis, Lipset and Marks argue that this proves their thesis: American socialists failed because of their "dogmatism," their ideological commitment to uncompromising Marxism (2000, 195–202; 272–273). But this dogmatism rooted in American sociological and ideological worlds would seem to show that American culture—out of which the socialist movement arose—has strains that are quite hostile to capital, whatever their tactical results. On the other hand, when socialists *did* compromise during the Second World War, instead of revising their thesis about the dogmatism of American socialism the authors argue that it was this compromising that doomed them to failure, because it sowed confusion in the socialist ranks (214). When faced with opinion polls showing general support for nationalization and other socialist measures in the 1930s, Lipset and Marks do not use this evidence to qualify their thesis of "antistatism and individualism" (266) in American culture, even at exceptional moments, but respond only that "by that time the Socialist party was in no condition to take advantage of this" (267).

Like the class-based theories, the cultural arguments also have trouble explaining the specific historical trajectory of welfare legislation in the United States, particularly the early twentieth century through the New Deal when the United States was a leader in welfare state legislation, followed by the later decades of welfare state underdevelopment (Skocpol 1995; Amenta 2000; Swenson 2002). These cultural theories tend to see an unchanging national culture or a switch from a culturally-determined market pattern to a pragmatically-driven state intervention during the Great Depression (e.g., Dobbin 1993, on industrial policy), but this does not match the history that scholars have found of a precocious welfare state that began to lag after the Depression and the Second World War.

Although cultural arguments receive a mixed hearing in the social sciences, one argument that comes from this camp has become accepted wisdom: that American antitrust regulations should be interpreted not as state intervention but rather as attempts to preserve the market. Frank Dobbin argues that antitrust regulations are "designed to guard economic liberties by preventing restraints of trade and enforcing price competition" (1994, 3). This interpretation of antitrust regulation as favoring market efficiency is widely accepted. Dobbin uses it to support his argument that there are "distinct ideas about order and rationality in different nations" (1994, 2) that drove the regulation of railroads in different countries in the nineteenth century (for a very different interpretation of national railroad regulation in the nineteenth century see Dunlavy 1992, 1994).

But in later work Dobbin himself has emphasized that in the nineteenth century the original "Proponents of antitrust policy raised the specter of baronial power; they *did not argue that antitrust would improve industrial efficiency.* Only later were [the Interstate Commerce Act and the Sherman Antitrust Act] framed as means to support competition" (Dobbin and Dowd 2000, 635, emphasis added).

Recent research on the origins of antitrust supports the later Dobbin: antitrust legislation was implemented not because it was seen to improve market efficiency but as an attempt to tame monopoly power. Only later, in the early twentieth century, did it come to be interpreted as favoring competition (Berk 2009). There is still much debate on the origins of antitrust, but the debate revolves around the question of whether antitrust legislation resulted from the demands of consumers or small businesses— no analyst seriously argues that it was an attempt to increase efficiency. For example, the debate on the origins of the Sherman Antitrust Act is divided into three camps, those who see farmers and consumers as key, those who see small business as reacting *against* the greater market efficiency of the trusts, and those who see a combination of the two (see Troesken 2002, 275; Letwin 1956; Stigler 1985). None of these camps claim monopoly power was attacked for producing efficiency but rather only because monopolies were hurting small business or agrarians. The self-interested demands of small business or the agrarian sector for legislation that would protect them is a thin reed on which to base the claim that antitrust legislation was implemented by a "political culture" that values the "natural selection" of the free market.

Indeed, the best recent evidence is that antitrust was a blow *against* the free market and its efficiencies. DiLorenzo (1985) argues that monopoly power in fact led to lower prices. This also seems to have been the view at the time. Historian Sanford Gordon examined scholarly literature and found that most economists of the time believed that "high fixed costs made large scale enterprise economical" (1963, 166). As George Stigler wrote, "A careful student of the history of economics would have searched long and hard, on July 2 of 1890, the day the Sherman Act was signed . . . for any economist who had ever recommended the policy of actively combatting collusion or monopolization in the economy at large" (Stigler 1982, 3, quoted in Hazlett 1992, 274).

Small businesses were well aware of the economies of scale that large businesses enjoyed. Libecap (1992) argues that antitrust was a way for small businesses to preserve inefficient practices and insulate themselves against the free market. Small business wanted antitrust not only because the large trusts were engaging in anticompetitive practices but also because in some cases the large trusts were able to employ economies of scale that smaller businesses could not (Troesken 2002, 276). Sherman himself "intended to protect small and inefficient firms from their larger competitors, regardless of the effect on consumer welfare" (276–277).

Troesken uses documentary sources to conclude that Sherman's "actions are inconsistent with the idea that he wanted to promote competition and lower prices" (291–292). Rather, Sherman wanted to protect small businesses against the efficiencies that large firms were able to achieve. This is a particularistic argument on behalf of small business rather than an argument that competition should be protected because "natural selection mechanisms in free markets is the mainspring of growth" (Dobbin 1994, 3)—instead, the attempt here is to *preserve inefficient modes of production against more efficient modes of production* and precisely to *prevent* the natural selection of the free market.

Boudreaux and DiLorenzo (1993) likewise conclude that the particularistic interests of small business drove antitrust. They direct attention to the roots of the state-level antitrust acts that preceded the national act and conclude, "The political impetus for some kind of antitrust law came from the farm lobbies of mostly midwestern, agricultural states, such as Missouri. Rural cattlemen and butchers were especially eager to have statutes enacted that would thwart competition from the newly centralized meat processing facilities in Chicago. The evidence on price and output in these industries, moreover, does not support the conjecture that these industries suffered from a monopoly in the late nineteenth century. . . . These industries were fiercely competitive because of relatively free entry and rapid technological advances such as refrigeration . . . antitrust was a protectionist institution from the very beginning" (1993, 93). They see American policymakers acting as British policymakers are supposed to in Dobbin's framework, protecting entrepreneurs from the market.

Thus, rather than demonstrating preferences for the "natural selection" of the free market, there is evidence that antitrust was the opposite: a demand for state intervention against the natural selection of the free market. While interpretations of antitrust as preserving the efficiency of the market did develop in the early twentieth century (see Gerald Berk 2009), Dobbin himself has shown elsewhere that the cultural interpretation of antitrust changed radically as a *result* of the passage of the policy: "The architects of antitrust policy sought to prevent the rise of aristocratic power in American industry—they did not have a new model of the modern economy in mind. . . . [But after it passed, antitrust policy] was soon described not as a form of state intervention to prevent concentrated power but as a pro-growth policy . . . as the foundation of a true market economy" (Dobbin and Dowd 2000, 653).

Just as European capitalists discovered that there were benefits to the welfare state, American capitalists learned to live with antitrust and even discovered its benefits. Elements of the prior understanding of antitrust as a tool of state intervention against the free market remain, however, and understanding this helps to resolve some otherwise inexplicable phenomena, such as the lack of enthusiasm among neoliberal Republicans (those most in favor of the free market) for enforcement of antitrust policy in the 1980s (Davis and Stout 1992). If there is a political culture in the United States that sees antitrust enforcement as defending the free market, those who originally implemented antitrust were not part of this culture, and those who currently favor the free market are not part of this culture.

A more general criticism of the cultural arguments is that other cultures also possess pro-market and individualistic strains. Consider French reactions to the British Poor Law in the Third Republic, which Timothy Smith describes in ways that sound like what the cultural scholars would call American: "To liberals, the Poor Law was expensive, a threat to individualism and, they feared, it would lead straight to communism" (Smith 1997, 999–1000). He notes: "the image of the Poor Law was so very negative that it explains in part the oft-noted lag in French social policy development. . . . The message was simple, and it was driven home ad nauseam: no nationally mandated public relief system, no culture of poverty" (Smith 1997, 999). Smith argues that this resistance broke only when military experiences heightened popular concern over the need to create plentiful healthy French soldiers. As Peter Baldwin (1992) has shown most thoroughly, even in France and Germany, two of the most well-developed welfare states, social provision was underdeveloped for decades precisely because of middle class unwillingness to support the poor; these welfare states only began to grow to their current levels when the middle classes realized that welfare programs would benefit *them* (30). The United States is not unusual in its cultural attitudes of resistance to policies that redistribute towards the poor; it is unusual for not having developed welfare policies that benefit the middle classes, for reasons that we will examine in Chapters 6 and 9.

Racial Fragmentation

National culture arguments—arguments explicitly attributing causation to national cultural traditions—have waned in sociology in the face of criticisms that they cannot explain sub-cultural differences and that they ignore the malleability of cultural discourses and meanings, change over time, different policy principles in different domains, and the diffusion of cultures across national boundaries. But as sociologists move away from these arguments, economists have rediscovered them. Recently two prominent economists made a modified national culture argument the center of their explanation for the divergent shapes of welfare states, arguing that the racial fragmentation of the United States undermines the welfare state by leading to less support for redistribution (Alesina and Glaeser 2006; they also point to other factors, such as the importance of socialist parties and the fragmentation of political institutions that we have discussed above and below. See Pontusson [2006] for a refutation of nearly the whole of Alesina and Glaeser's argument). This is a reprise of earlier arguments from scholars such as Jill Quadagno (1984, 1994), Thomas Sugrue ([1996] 2005), and many others.)

Alesina and Glaeser's evidence for this argument consists of contemporary surveys that find a correlation between racial attitudes and support for redistribution within the United States and cross-sectional studies that find a correlation between racial homogeneity and generosity of welfare benefits across countries as well as across states in the United States. The problem with the first of these is that it ascribes social spending to popular preferences for social spending. But we know that citizens increase their support for redistributive programs after they are passed. As many scholars have argued, welfare programs are difficult to scale back because once they are implemented, they become popular with the public (Therborn 1984; Therborn and Roebroek 1986; Le Grand and Winter 1986; Pierson 1995; but see Mishra 1990, 32–42). This happens because interest groups (such as the AARP in the United States) arise devoted to generating support from them, because familiarity and the absence of disaster lessens opposition to them, and because they structure flows of information in particular ways (for example, because their benefits are often highly visible while their costs remain diffuse and obscure). But if support for redistributive programs rises after they are passed, then correlating existing levels of support for social spending with existing levels of racial fragmentation will lead to spurious results. We cannot read current opinion back into history and conclude that public support was a reason for the welfare state's origins; as discussed above, before the rise of the welfare state there was in fact resistance among European middle classes to policies that would redistribute to the poor.

Similarly, there is reason to think that the correlation between racial fragmentation and smaller government across countries is not causal. As Pontusson (2009) notes, this correlation does not hold within the advanced industrial countries. It holds only if several developing countries are included. As will be suggested by the argument developed in Chapter 3, both racial fragmentation and low social spending may be the consequence of different patterns of settlement, such that the racially heterogeneous countries are the ones that were settled more recently, and countries that were settled more recently are more likely to have smaller governments because of their role in export markets and the particular politics that this leads to.

The correlation between racial fragmentation and social spending among states and countries, also brings up another issue: why should racial fragmentation lead to low levels of overall social spending rather than high levels of *within-race* social spending? Recently, Evan Lieberman (2003) has argued that racial fragmentation can lead to preference for within-race redistribution. Lieberman asks why racially fragmented and segregated South Africa was able to establish a progressive tax collection regime while racially democratic and integrated Brazil was not. He argues that upper-income white South Africans felt collective racial solidarity and a sense of responsibility for lower-income whites and were therefore more willing to pay income and property taxes that they believed would benefit those of their own race. Absence of this kind of racial solidarity in Brazil prevented the development of progressive taxation. But if this is the case, it is unclear why there should be within-race solidarity on the question of taxation but not on the question of social spending. It is possible to envisage the development of an extensive welfare state that would have been restricted to whites—a more developed version of the initiatives that Ira Katznelson (2005) points to. For example, we have noted above the ways in which the pension provision of the Social Security Act was originally written to exclude African-American laborers (Quadagno 1984) but nevertheless developed into a generous and universal welfare provision system over time (Hacker 2002). This leads to the question of why this could not have happened for the welfare state as a whole.

One can imagine an alternative political history in which the United States developed a public welfare state along European lines but restricted it to whites, developing cross-class solidarity on the basis of racial solidarity, and one can imagine this welfare state gradually being extended to incorporate all races in the latter part of the twentieth century, just as the 1935 pension provisions of the Social Security Act gradually developed in both the percent of the old-age population they covered and the generosity of the benefits they delivered. This suggests that simple correlations are unconvincing in the absence of the demonstration of historical mechanisms producing those correlations. The missing mechanism, as will be argued below, is that racially fragmented states are settler states with extensive agrarian production, and agrarian states did not develop the kinds of problems for which social spending by the state is the solution; they developed an alternative set of problems that led to alternative forms of state intervention.

Race is such a crucial structuring principle in American life that it would be impossible to expect no effects at all from the country's long history of slavery and segregation. But racial fragmentation leading to preferences for less state intervention cannot have been the key mechanism at work, because public preferences were not the main reason for the development of European welfare states, racial fragmentation has been shown to work in favor of progressive policies such as progressive taxation, and racial fragmentation can allow the development of racially-based welfare programs that slowly become universalized. Moreover, racial fragmentation cannot help us explain the moments when the United States has been a welfare state leader nor can it help us explain the instances of greater intervention catalogued in Chapter 1.

Much of the argument in this book turns on the fragmented nature of the political system, and this fragmented structure is, of course, partly a legacy of slavery and the different modes of production that characterized the North and the South during the colonial period and of the political attempt to piece together a government out of such disparate parts. But this is race as economic interests concretized into political institutions, not race as people's preferences for helping or harming others of different ethnicities. If we understand race as concretized in political institutions, then race does have much to tell us about the unique path of American political economy, an issue to which we now turn.

State Structures and Historical Institutionalism

The theory that receives the most support from the history examined in this book is that the fragmented nature of the American state shapes the policies the state can pursue. This theory, or set of theories, is associated with several different movements within the social sciences, most prominently the movement to "bring the state back in" of Theda Skocpol and her collaborators (Orloff and Skocpol 1984; Skocpol 1985; Evans, Rueschemeyer, and Skocpol 1985; Skocpol 1995; Steinmo 1993; Steinmo, Thelen, and Longstreth 1992). These scholars examine how state actors and state agencies may for specifiable historical reasons become partially autonomous from the societal structures that brought them into being and how the structure of the state and the nature of preexisting policies influence the shape of legislation. The piece of this complex of arguments that is most relevant to the story here is that fragmented states—states in which policy-making power is divided both vertically across levels of government and horizontally across several competing and equally powerful decision-making centers—have distinctly different patterns of policy-making than centralized states.

Ellen Immergut (1990) has offered the most useful specification of this argument: in fragmented states, "[p]olitical decisions require agreement at several points along a chain of decisions made in different arenas. The fate of legislative proposals . . . depends upon the number and location of opportunities for veto along this chain" (1990, 396). This theory of "veto points" has been enormously influential across the social sciences, and it has been particularly helpful in explaining how the checks and balances of the American system—the division of government into different levels as well as the fragmentation of power within each level—have prevented many policy proposals from proceeding to the stage of implementation in the United States. This explanation, for example, fills in Quadagno's explanation above and details *why* the South was able to exercise disproportionate influence in the 1935 Social Security Act (Weir, Orloff, and Skocpol 1988, 24).

Nevertheless, what this theory of veto points predicts—as given by its very name—is inaction in the presence of multiple veto points. It is thus useful for an explanation of why the United States did not act in ways that other countries did, for the United States has many more points at which action can be vetoed than most other countries. However, as we have seen in Chapter 1, in many cases the United States acted *even more extensively* than the countries of Europe. It is hard to explain these areas of state intervention with the theory of veto points alone.

As we will see below, the real story is that a fragmented power structure changes the shape of the legislation in subtler but no less consequential ways. For one thing, a fragmented structure can make small minorities disproportionately powerful, giving them the swing vote on key pieces of legislation. But the content of their preferences explains how they will use that swing vote and whether they will use it to resist action or impose different kinds of action. Moreover, although the fragmented state structure was the reason for agrarian power in the United States, agrarians were powerful in other states as well, for different historical-institutionalist reasons. Understanding what American agrarians did with their power and why it took a specific shape requires combining this perspective with other theoretical perspectives (as theorists in this camp would no doubt agree: no scholar making these arguments argues for a single-factor theory of history).

The theories described above are unable to explain the tradition of greater American state intervention that we saw in Chapter 1 and, in several cases, are unconvincing on their own terms; but comparing their strengths and their weaknesses gives us a guide for what a fuller theory of comparative political economy should do.

First, a good theory should explain the heavier state intervention in some domains in the United States *as well as* the less developed public welfare state in the United States that results in greater poverty and inequality. Second, a good theory should explain why European states were able to combine economic growth with redistribution for several decades. And a good theory of comparative political economy should be able to explain the origins of the divergences in the American and European trajectories. We also have some warning about what not to do. First, we should not presume that state intervention always undermines the market. Europeans have come to believe that the welfare state is an integral part of market capitalism, just as Americans have come to see antitrust as so important to the market that they have almost forgotten that it was originally a demonstration of state power against the power of capital. And we should not ignore the actual history. Some of the dead ends that the other theories have reached (for example, the argument about wage bargaining as the primary mechanism for reducing inequality from the varieties of capitalism theory, or the inability to see the further development of the 1935 Social Security Act) seem to result from an absence of sustained dialogue with the historical record—a record being explored today not only in the discipline of history, but across the social sciences.

Although none of these theories alone can adequately explain the events, the argument below draws on particular elements from each the-

44

ory. The cultural theories received an important elaboration in Frederick Jackson Turner's famous essay of 1893, "The Significance of the Frontier in American History" (incorporated in Turner [1920] 1996). While Turner took his thesis of the importance of the frontier's role in an unconvincing cultural and cognitive direction, he was absolutely right to focus on the role of the frontier, as we will see in Chapter 3. From class-based theories, we take the focus on the importance of interest groups. It was clearly the case that groups were able to define collective interests, act in those interests, and occasionally, when the opportunity was right, to influence the course of policy. However, as Esping-Andersen does, we will shift our focus from labor to agrarians, for reasons explained in Chapter 3. From institutional theory, we learn when the opportunity is right—at several points in the story below we will see the central importance of the fragmentation of American power and how it amplified the political voices of some groups. And finally, from varieties of capitalism we take a particular understanding of time and of history, of the importance of corporatist bargains between capital and labor, and of the importance of the nineteenth century as the key moment when the institutions of our economic world were first forged.

For what each of these theories misses is a major fact about this nineteenth century moment: the United States was experiencing and responding to very different problems than any of the European countries. This has been obscured by the attempt to treat the countries as comparable units that can be indexed by variables such as the degree of labor or employer power they possess. While these types of comparisons are certainly useful for arriving at partial answers in some domains (and will be deployed in this work where relevant), they must always be combined with an overarching awareness of the very different roles the countries played in world history. As an agricultural exporter, the United States witnessed a strikingly different pattern of agrarian politics than did the importing countries of Europe. At the moment of what O'Rourke and Williamson (1999) call the "first" era of globalization in the late nineteenth century, these divergent trade patterns spelled out divergent politics that would bear fruit during the Great Depression and would go on to undermine the public welfare state and construct a society of credit-financed consumption in America.

45

3

A DEMAND-SIDE THEORY OF

COMPARATIVE POLITICAL ECONOMY

Describing his youthful conversion to communism, Arthur Koestler wrote:

The event that aroused my indignation to a fever pitch never reached before was the American policy of destroying food stocks to keep agricultural prices up during the depression years at a time when millions of unemployed lived in misery and near starvation. . . . its effect on Europeans was that of a crude and indeed terrifying shock which destroyed what little faith they still had in the existing social order. By 1932 there were seven million unemployed in Germany which means that one in every three wage earners lived on the dole. In Austria, Hungary and the surrounding countries the situation was similar or worse. Meat, coffee, fruit had become unobtainable luxuries for large sections of the population, even the bread on the table was measured out in thin slices; yet the newspapers spoke laconically of millions of tons of coffee being dumped into the sea, of wheat being burned, pigs being cremated, oranges doused with kerosene to ease conditions on the market. . . . Woe to the shepherds who feed themselves but feed not their flocks! Indignation glowed inside me like a furnace. At times I thought that I was choking in its fumes; at other times I felt like hitting out, and shooting from a barricade or throwing sticks of dynamite. . . . Echoes of the hundred days of the Hungarian Commune; echoes of the indignant wrath of the Hebrew prophets, and of the forthcoming Apocalypse according to St. Marx; the memory of my father's bankruptcy, the sound of the hunger-marchers' broken-down boots on the pavement and the smell of fresh wheat being burned in the fields all these ingredients fused into one emotional experience. (Koestler 1961, 273)[1]

In September 1933, under the Roosevelt administration's price support programs, six million pigs were killed and a quarter of the cotton crop for the year plowed under. Europeans were not alone in being appalled, as unemployment and hunger were widespread in the United States as well. The slaughter of the pigs seems to have hit a particular nerve among the American public, as the policy specifically targeted piglets and pregnant sows. The tiny pigs that were rounded up from the farms routinely escaped through the cracks of slaughterhouse fences designed for much larger animals and were found roaming city streets. While much of the pork that resulted from the livestock destruction was given to relief agencies, some of the pigs were so small that their meat could not be effectively harvested by the machines or even used as fertilizer, and they were summarily dumped—sometimes to the consternation of the suburbs that ended up as the dumping destination. At one point the processing facilities became so overtaxed that $330,000 worth of pigs were simply chucked into the Mississippi River (Blakey 1967; *Chicago Daily Tribune* 1933a; *Wall Street Journal* 1933).

The White House was flooded with letters and editorials angrily denouncing the policy. "Why, oh why destroy what is so good to eat?" asked Mr. and Mrs. George Biddle, when their family had "not had a pork chop or any part of a hog in . . . years?"; "When men, women, and children are hungry, I say that no defense can be made either in law, morals or religion for throwing wholesome meat into a fertilizer vat," one newspaper writer thundered, "I tell you there are some things that are just too much" (both quoted in Poppendieck 1995, 15–16). Arthur Dixon wrote: "I've lived in the U.S. seventy years. . . . in all the seventy years I've never seen so much foolishness in legislation as is going on right now. The killing of a million piggy sows and four million little pigs, and the destruction of cotton, wheat, etc., is the most damnable, ridiculous, and vicious legislation I have ever heard of" (Dixon 1933). An Indiana newspaper felt the same aversion as Arthur Koestler to "the enormity of the latest offense against every law of God and man" (quoted in Blakey 1967, 53). The program seemed to contradict every principle the American farmer had been taught, every program of increasing productivity that the scientific agriculture movements of the turn of the century had yielded: "What, one asks, is the value of the 4-H pig clubs and the big litter contests, if it only results in the production of pigs which are to be wasted?" (Jones 1933; on the history of early agricultural efficiency efforts, see Danbom 1979; Fitzgerald 2003; Olmstead and Rhode 2008).

Secretary of Agriculture Henry Wallace complained of the critics: "They contended that every little pig has the right to attain before slaughter the full pigginess of his pigness" (quoted in Blakey 1967, 49). Even three years later, a defensive Democratic senator made the issue part of his keynote speech at the Democratic Convention: "They have shed these tears over the premature deaths of pigs as if they had been born, educated and destined for the ministry or for politics" (quoted in Blakey 1967, 56).

It was a sensitive issue for the Democrats, who had been driven to this radical measure of destroying crops and livestock by the desperation of American farmers. The policy solution of destroying pigs was on the face of it a completely logical reaction to the situation. Prices for pigs had plummeted in the 1920s and early 1930s to levels that had not been seen since the nineteenth century. From a peak of $17.85 per hundred-weight in 1919, the average price of slaughter hogs had fallen to $3.83 per hundred-weight in 1932 (Olmstead and Rhode 2006). Similar price declines hit farmers all over the country, so that by the mid-1930s only 16% of farm households were earning the national median income (Kennedy 1999, 192).

Hit with prices that did not allow them to recoup their investments and repay their debts, farmers reacted with violence. In January 1933 the head of the Farm Bureau had warned: "Unless something is done for the American farmer we will have revolution in the countryside within less than twelve months" (quoted in Schlesinger [1958] 2003, 27). Events seemed to be bearing him out. Over the spring and summer farmers tried to bodily prevent foreclosures and to disrupt the transportation of food with pickets, road blockades, attacks on bridges and railway lines, and even bombing of warehouses. In April a mob of farmers in Iowa nearly lynched a judge for refusing to waive foreclosures. In May picketers attempting to blockade the delivery of milk clashed with guardsmen just outside Milwaukee and again in northern Wisconsin, leading to dozens of injuries and two hundred jailed. (*Chicago Daily Tribune* 1933b; Schlesinger [1958] 2003; Shover 1965).

Moreover, as farmers defaulted on their loans, small banks in an environment without deposit insurance began to fail (Chandler 1970, 78–84). Falling prices were leading to agitation in the financial system as well. This was the context for the Department of Agriculture's price support programs: something had to be done to keep prices up, or there would be chaos in the countryside and disruptions to the nation's food supply as well as continued turbulence in the financial system. Because it was too late to prevent the breeding of pigs for that year, the program had to be to cull the results of that breeding, so supply would go down and prices would go up.

The "ridiculous and vicious" legislation had a relentless logic to it. Still, it led to a much larger and more disturbing question. When all of the United States's energies had for decades been bent on increasing agricultural productivity, how could it be that the problem was now one of too much? How could having too much be a problem at all? It was not just pigs, either, but cotton, wheat, corn, sugar, tobacco, indeed all of the crops that formed the backbone of American agriculture whose prices had to be supported with government programs. It was not just the paradox of poverty in the midst of plenty but the further paradox that plenty seemed to *create* poverty. Increased supply led to plunging prices, which drove farmers to ruin and pulled the wider economy into recession.

In this context it is not hard to see why an impressionable young European would flee into the arms of the Communists. Something seemed seriously awry with capitalism, and if others did not respond as fiercely as Koestler did, nevertheless the worry was widespread. One observer documented it as "the general feeling of worldwide unrest, the vague discontent evoked by the thought: 'Why does the fact that we produce more than ever at less effort than heretofore mean that we must have less to enjoy?'" (Deutsch 1935). Analysts such as A. Philip Randolph quickly identified the problem not as one of literal overproduction because "[t]he workers want to buy. They can consume the goods produced. But they cannot buy the goods produced because their wages are inadequate" (Randolph 1933). As one observer said, "We still pray to be given each day our daily bread. Yet there is too much bread, too much wheat and corn, meat and oil and almost every other commodity required by man for his subsistence and material happiness. [The problem is that W]e are not able to purchase the abundance that modern methods of agriculture, mining and manufacturing make available in such bountiful quantities" (quoted in McElvaine 1984, 50). A British member of Parliament explained the Communist temptation: "It is only the modern workman who can find himself condemned to extinction through the ability to produce sheer abundance of all that is necessary to live a proper and ample life. The unemployed workman is the most grotesque irony of the ages. . . . Can there not be some planned relationship between production and consumption to avoid this economic contradiction and idiocy of the misery and squalor of the masses amidst abundance?" (Ben Pillet, quoted in Randolph

1933). Marxist theorists saw in the unfolding events a resounding vindication of Rosa Luxemburg's arguments about capitalist overproduction crises ([1913] 2003).[2]

President Roosevelt agreed on the diagnosis, proclaiming in a campaign speech, "Our task now is not discovery, or exploitation of natural resources, or necessarily producing more goods. It is the soberer, less dramatic business of administering resources and plants already in hand, of seeking to reestablish foreign markets for our surplus production, of meeting the problem of underconsumption, of adjusting production to consumption, of distributing wealth and products more equitably" (quoted in Kennedy 1999, 373). Driven by Adolf Berle, Rexford Tugwell, and other members of the Brain Trust, the administration hurriedly passed several policies in 1933 to address the problem, including the Agricultural Adjustment Act (AAA) with its destruction of pigs and cotton, the Commodity Credit Corporation (CCC), which intended to support farm prices, and the National Industrial Recovery Act (NIRA), which sought to establish precisely such a "planned relationship between production and consumption," but one that would remain this side of communism by encouraging industries to set codes of competition, edging the United States closer to European-style corporatist negotiations between government, industry, and labor. The goal of all of these acts was, Roosevelt said, "the prevention of foolish over-production" (quoted in Schlesinger [1958] 2003, 97) through the control of overzealous competition. The NIRA and AAA would be found unconstitutional a few years later, but the AAA returned in a slightly altered form in 1938, and the price support and farm subsidy programs that the AAA and the CCC introduced have become so deeply entrenched that even the Reagan administration, the most ideologically antistate administration in recent times, actually increased farm subsidies (Lake 1989; on the NIRA and AAA more generally, see Hawley 1966; Finegold and Skocpol 1995; Sheingate 2001; Schlesinger [1958] 2003).

This analysis of the Depression as caused by overproduction resonated across the political world, from Roosevelt's advisers to southern agrarians to Marxist theorists. Paul Baran and Paul Sweezy would prepare the most cogent statement of this perspective a few decades later, arguing that the overproduction crisis was an inevitable result of the productivity of monopoly capitalism, which outstrips demand and can only be accommodated by military expenditures and other large-scale public works projects (Baran and Sweezy 1966).

But most American economists dismiss the diagnosis of overproduction as "arrant nonsense" (Rothbard [1963] 2008, 56)—though they are usually more diplomatic in saying so. Rothbard argues, "There is no reason why prices cannot fall low enough, in a free market, to clear the market and sell all the goods available. If businessmen [here, the farmers] choose to keep prices up, they are simply speculating on an imminent rise in market prices. . . . If they wish to sell their 'surplus' stocks, they need only cut their prices low enough to sell all of their product" ([1963] 2008, 56). To the argument that farmers could not sell their output below cost because they had borrowed in order to produce and were dependent on receiving a certain price in order to repay their debt, Rothbard retorts: "now the discussion has shifted to a different plane. We find no overproduction, we find now that the *selling prices* of products are *below* their cost of production. But since costs are determined by expected future selling prices, this means that costs were previously *bid too high*" (57, emphases in original). That is, farmers paid much more and borrowed much more than they should have, given that prices were going to fall: they simply forecast prices incorrectly, and they invested too heavily in unproductive ventures.[3] This view, associated with the Austrian school, sees the Depression as caused by the collapse of the unsustainable credit expansion in the 1920s that had led those farmers to their overeager expansions. This credit expansion in turn was caused by the introduction of a central bank in 1913. Instead of instituting a central bank to smooth fluctuations in credit and their macroeconomic consequences, as it had done after the Bankers' Panic of 1907, Rothbard and the Austrian School argue that the government should have simply stepped back and let such crises play themselves out.[4] In Rothbard's view, the ultimate cause of the Depression was the decision to establish the Federal Reserve System and the Fed's subsequent loose monetary policy in the 1920s; but these decisions themselves are outside of the explanatory framework, a policy mistake and a historical contingency. That the establishment of the Federal Reserve was a direct response to an economic disequilibrium is not part of Rothbard's story, and the Austrian view ultimately requires sanguinity in the face of economic crisis that may not be possible in democracies. Rothbard also neglects the fact that debts were denominated in nominal terms, as we will discuss further. Also unsatisfying is the inability to explain why prices plunged when there was a need for the products all over the country and the world. In the Austrian view this indicates some sort of sectoral imbalance, with agriculture growing much more quickly than other sectors, perhaps because of easy credit to agriculture in the 1920s that was again the consequence of an inexplicable policy mistake. But in some ways this seems simply to restate rather than answer the question: what the Austrians call a credit boom or a policy mistake, observers of the time called overproduction. How could policymakers have made such a momentous mistake?

While Rothbard represents an unorthodox branch of economics, many mainstream economists share his dismissal of the overproduction argument, pointing to the unmet demand all over the country as a reason to be skeptical that the country was literally producing more than was being demanded. Even at the time, Irving Fisher was appalled by the idea of constraining production: "We can scarcely feed the hungry more bread by destroying material of which the bread is to be made nor clothe the naked by destroying the material of which the clothes are to be made" (quoted in Pavanelli 2004, 298). He concluded: "The reason, or a reason, for the common notion of over-production is mistaking too little money for too much goods" (Fisher 1933, 340). Several decades of elaboration and data collection have strengthened the argument that the anomalous situation that puzzled Koestler was caused by a restricted money supply. Although there are still many open questions, such as why interest rates did not rise if a constricted money supply was the main causal agent (Temin 1976), economists of all stripes—monetarist/neoclassical as well as Keynesian—generally agree with this view most famously defended by Milton Friedman and Anna Schwartz (1963). Friedman and Schwartz argued that the Federal Reserve contracted the money supply at an inopportune moment, turning what would have been a normal recession into a depression (see also Romer 1992 on the role of monetary factors in ending the Depression, and Irwin 2010 on the effects of French monetary policy; see Gordon and Krenn 2010 for a defense of the role of fiscal policy; on contemporary scholarly views of the Great Depression see Parker 2007, and Bordo, Goldin, and White 1998).

Overproduction of the kind envisaged by Roosevelt plays no role in this conception. Rather, according to this explanation the origins of the Depression are again to be found in a policy mistake by the Fed, but in this telling the mistake is the opposite of the Austrian explanation: too little money in the 1930s rather than too much money in the 1920s. Friedman and Schwartz ask, "Why Was Monetary Policy So Inept?" when the necessary knowledge was available to the Board of Governors: "pursuit of the policies outlined by the System itself in the 1920's, or for that matter by Bagehot in 1873, would have prevented the catastrophe" (407). Friedman and Schwartz trace the problem to the untimely death of one man, New York Federal Reserve Governor Benjamin Strong, and to the consequent power vacuum in the absence of Strong's domination: "A committee of twelve men, each regarding himself as an equal of all the others and each the chief administrator of an institution established to strengthen regional independence, could much more easily agree on a policy of drift and inaction than on a coordinated policy involving the public assumption of responsibility for decisive and large-scale action" (415). Friedman and Schwartz are apologetic about this explanation, acknowledging that it seems "farfetched" (419), and it does smack of post hoc rationalization. One could point out that a great deal of research suggests groups are *more* likely to take risky action than individuals (Isenberg 1986). It is an oddly weak foundation stone for their majestic explanation of the Depression. More recently Allan Meltzer (2003) has shown, based on internal Fed documents, that there was more continuity between Strong and the subsequent committee than Friedman and Schwartz appreciated and that the Fed in general seems to have believed "that the proper function of the System was well expressed in the phrase . . . 'The Federal Reserve supplies needed additions to credit and takes up the slack [i.e., withdraws credit] in times of business recession' . . . We have been putting out credit in a period of depression, when it is not wanted and cannot be used, and we will have to withdraw credit when it is wanted and can be used" (318). The Fed thought that credit was needed in times of boom and needed to be taken out of the economy in times of recession—that is, recessions have nothing to do with Fed policies, are not caused by lack of money and credit, and "correction must come about through reduced production, reduced inventories, . . . and the accumula- tion of savings through the exercise of thrift" (318), essentially the Roth- bardian position and one version of Herbert Hoover's position. But why they believed this remains puzzling. And for the monetarists as for the Austrians, the decision to establish the Fed itself remains exogenous to the explanation.

Although explanations of overproduction were rolled in with Keynes- ian explanations at the time, Keynes himself had no such theory of over- production. He made the much less radical argument that at moments of economic uncertainty rational consumers will decide to hold greater cash reserves, which will lead to a decline in consumption that damages busi- ness ([1935] 1964). Recent versions of Keynesian explanations for the

Depression are more accurately described as a hybrid of Keynesian and monetarist explanations: while they may see nonmonetary factors such as autonomous drops in consumption as important in *initiating* the recession, they also see a strong role for monetary factors in turning what might have been a normal recession into a depression, as well as in the eventual recovery. Peter Temin (1989) is perhaps the central exponent of a contemporary Keynesian view of the Great Depression. Temin elaborates an argument (revising his earlier views) that the disturbances of World War I, propagated by an unnecessary adherence to a gold standard regime— even before the gold standard itself was officially resumed—caused a deflationary bias that was the ultimate source of the instability. Temin argues that this gold standard regime required monetary contraction in countries facing downward pressure on their currencies but did not require monetary expansion in countries facing upward pressure; this asymmetry produced a deflationary bias throughout the system. Because of this, countries that abandoned the gold standard earliest suffered least and recovered most quickly (see also Eichengreen 1992; Mishkin 1978; Bernanke and James 1991). This explanation for the propagation of the Depression is also widely accepted, but Temin does not explore the reasons for the choice of the gold standard and the possible alternatives to it. Policymakers adhered to the gold standard because they thought that without it capital flows necessary for reconstruction would wither if exchange rates became volatile; why did this argument, which seems rational on the face of it, ultimately prove so destructive (James 1990)? Most importantly, although the gold standard did not require expansion, Meltzer (2003, 275–277) argues that it did not compel contraction; the contraction of the Federal Reserve remains to be explained. For Keynesians as for monetarists, the central issue is money supply contraction by the Fed, which remains outside of the theoretical framework.

It may be that the Fed's tight money policy is simply inexplicable. It may be one of those contingent events that some scholars claim ultimately determine the course of history and that the best we can do is tell nuanced stories rather than grasp the underlying forces at work. But it is also possible that we need broader ways of thinking about the Great Depression. For the elephant—or perhaps the giant pig—in the middle of the room is a factor that is not even mentioned by any of these explanations; the most consequential event of the late nineteenth and early twentieth centuries in the Western world was the unprecedented economic growth of the United States. It was growth of a kind that no one had seen before and that no one really knew how to handle—not the farmers making their forecasts nor the bankers tuning their monetary indices nor the European countries that struggled with its consequences. But to explain why this is the main issue, we will have to step back in time and move from twentieth century depression to the age of colonialism.

In 1719 and 1720 a clever Scotsman named John Law established and promoted a scheme for French investment in the New World that has become known as one of the biggest speculative bubbles of all time. Law had convinced the French government to give his company, the Mississippi Company, exclusive rights to trade in the new colony of Louisiana as well as in the Indies, and he sold shares to the French public. The scheme was abetted by the introduction of paper money, which Law presciently realized could solve the problem of underutilized resources, but the foundation of the scheme was the promise of fabulous wealth based on the minerals and natural resources that abounded in the New World and in the Indies. Law distributed literature emphasizing "the richness of the soil, the abundant resources . . . the presence of treasure such as Spain had found in Mexico and South America" (Webb [1952] 1980, 224). The frenzy that resulted has been lovingly catalogued by historians, with tales of the crowds that swelled the Rue Quincampoix where Law traded, the noble families who pawned their jewels to purchase shares in the company, the strategies that Frenchmen and -women cooked up to be allowed to see Law and purchase shares. One enterprising woman, unable to fight through the crowds to see him in his chambers, rode around for days until she caught sight of Law on the street and then faked an accident so he would rush to her aid. Violence on the street was common, and there was even a murder when a young aristocrat and two aides ganged up on a successful speculator. Many poor workers found themselves suddenly wealthy—and then just as suddenly poor again, for the whole enterprise crashed within a few years. The bubble led to the founding and rapid settlement of New Orleans by thousands of prisoners from France and landless farmers from Germany, but the hoped for riches did not emerge. Law fled to Venice while the French burned effigies of him. The Mississippi Scheme is one of the case studies of delusion in Mackay's *Extraordinary Popular Delusions and the Madness of Crowds,* and it has gone down in history as a classic example of misguided speculation (Mackay [1841] 2003; Kindleberger 1978; Garber 1990; Ferguson 2008).

But it turns out that in the end John Law was right. If the parts of the Company that traded in the East never lived up to the promise, the New World did abound in fabulous wealth to a degree that justified the speculation. Law's miscalculation was that his timing was off by over one hundred years, which is the amount of time it took to turn those resources into material abundance.

James Belich (2009) has recently drawn attention to the process that he calls the "Settler Revolution." From the fifteenth through the eighteenth centuries, European countries not only sought to colonize and bring under control the dominions of Asia and Africa but also to form new colonies on the lands of the Americas and of the South Pacific by killing or displacing their prior residents. "Settler colonialism," a term common in Australian social science, is the unique formation that resulted, in which the colonizers remain permanently in the new land. Belich argues that the histories of the United States, Australia, Canada, and New Zealand should all be read as part of this larger process (see also Janoski 2010; Elkins and Pedersen 2005; Denoon 1983; Veracini 2010; Go 2008; Steinmetz 2005; for an early exploration of the theme see Webb [1952] 1980; and for a brilliant analysis of the effect of New World resources on Europe as compared to China, see Pomeranz 2000). As Kevin O'Rourke notes, the settler revolution dictates "[m]any of the great themes of the next four centuries—slavery, the extension of the frontier, voluntary mass migration" (1997, 775–776) and the genocide of Native Americans, the themes that we describe as American history itself.

For our purposes, the most important aspect of settler colonialism is the dramatic economic growth it caused, particularly in the Unites States. Long-term comparative statistics on economic growth are not well developed. Absence of reliable records, the tedious and time-consuming nature of the task, and lack of rewards in the academy for this kind of labor all mean that we have very few sustained attempts to examine the economic development of different nations comparatively over the course of centuries. Fortunately, we do have some. The most recent serious effort at gathering good cross-national data was made by Angus Maddison of the University of Groningen, whose long-term series provide the foundation for most arguments about long-run growth. To ensure that his data are comparable both across countries and over time, Maddison uses a form of purchasing power parity called "International Geary-Khamis dollars," which takes into account price volatility over time as well as exchange rates and purchasing power across countries.

On the question of comparative economic growth in the advanced world over the nineteenth and early twentieth centuries, Maddison's (2006 and online updates) figures show that this period was the age of the settler countries. As Table 3.1 shows, in 1820 the settler countries (Australia, Canada, New Zealand, and the United States) were not as rich as the United Kingdom or the Netherlands. By 1870, Australia had surpassed the United Kingdom, and New Zealand was catching up; by 1950, the race was over, with all of the settler countries richer than all of the countries of old Europe. After 1950 Germany raced ahead and the gap between the European countries and the United States narrowed but has never entirely closed. According to Maddison's figures, in 2008 per capita GDP in the United States stood at 31,178 International Geary-Khamis dollars, compared to 20,801 in Germany, 22,223 in France, 23,742 in the United Kingdom, 24,409 in Sweden, and slightly over 25,000 in Canada and Australia; the closest to the United States was Norway, at 28,500.

Some of Maddison's data are controversial, as he has made liberal assumptions where data are scarce.[5] For the period after 1820, however, and for the countries that Maddison identifies as "advanced capitalist countries" Maddison's work is more careful (see Maddison 1995, 96–97). There are still some questions about the rapid rise of Australia in the early nineteenth century, and it may be safest to restrict our attention to

Table 3.1. GDP per capita, in international Geary-Khamis dollars

	1820	1870	1913	1950
Belgium	1,319	2,692	4,220	5,462
Denmark	1,274	2,003	3,912	6,943
France	1,135	1,876	3,485	5,186
Germany	1,077	1,839	3,648	3,881
Italy	1,117	1,499	2,564	3,502
Netherlands	1,838	2,757	4,049	5,996
Norway	801	1,360	2,447	5,430
Sweden	819	1,359	3,073	6,769
U.K.	1,706	3,190	4,921	6,939
Australia	518	3,273	5,157	7,412
New Zealand	400	3,100	5,152	8,456
Canada	904	1,695	4,447	7,291
U.S.	1,257	2,445	5,301	9,561

Source: Maddison 2006 and online updates http://www.ggdc.net/MADDISON/oriindex .htm.

the period after 1870, for which the numbers are most reliable. Even restricting our attention to this period, it is clear that the settler countries grew more quickly than the European countries and the United States in particular—previously hampered by its dual economic structure and then by Civil War—rapidly took the lead.[6]

This conclusion is supported by other sources. The bitterest feud in the world of comparative economic statistics is between authors such as David Landes, who uses Maddison's figures to argue that Europe was already wealthier than the rest of the world in 1800, and Paul Bairoch and his followers, who argue that it was not. But on the question of relative wealth within the advanced industrial countries over the late nineteenth and early twentieth centuries, Bairoch's figures support the Maddison picture. For example, Bairoch's figures on per capita industrialization from 1860 to 1953 show that West European countries grew but not as fast as the settler countries. Over this period industrialization in France grew by a factor of 4.5, in Germany by a factor of 9.2, and in the United Kingdom by a factor of 3.3. Swedish industry was more productive, growing by a factor of 10.9 but was outpaced by Canada and the United States; Canada grew by a factor of 26.4 and the United States by a factor of 16.9 (Bairoch 1982, 281).

The other main source of long-term comparative economic statistics is Brian Mitchell's *International Historical Statistics* (1993, 1998), and this also gives a similar picture. Although Mitchell's coverage is not as extensive as Maddison's, for the United States, Britain, France, Germany, and Sweden from 1870 to 1913, Mitchell finds the United States industrializing at a much faster pace than Germany or Sweden, and all three of these countries industrializing much faster than Britain or France (Figure 3.1; for links to the data for all of the graphs, see endnote 1, page 273). Germany's industrialization figures look much better than its per capita GDP figures do, but the United States is considerably ahead in both. Recent research suggests that comparisons of industrialization such as this one overstate the poor economic performance of France (e.g., Berg 1994), but no scholarship has yet revised the picture of startling economic growth in the United States.

American economic growth was particularly impressive in agriculture (Figure 3.2). Between 1869 and 1911 agricultural output doubled in several countries but increased by a factor of 2.5 in the United States. In manufacturing output the United States is also highly productive, but the Scandinavian countries are equally productive (Figure 3.3); and by some measures the Scandinavian countries outgrew the rest of the world in the late nineteenth century on a per capita basis (O'Rourke and Williamson 1999).

Per capita measures and indices of growth do not give the full picture however, because the size of the United States dwarfed these and all other countries in terms of absolute amounts being produced (Figure 3.4).

The absolute amount of production is the central issue because by the beginning of the twentieth century the Americans were able to flood the world market as no other country could. The productivity of the American economy became a problem for the whole world. Although elements of the American experience were also occurring in each of the other settler countries, the scale of habitable land in the United States made it qualitatively different from any other country. More than simply the *rate* of growth or of productivity, it was the *scale* of economic activity in the United States that was the issue for the global economy, particularly as new developments in transportation brought that material abundance to

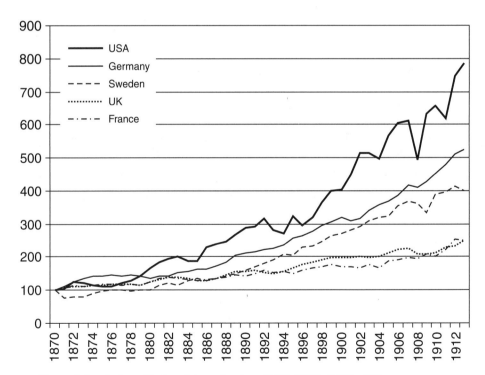

Figure 3.1.   Index of industrial production, 1870–1912. 1870 = 100.
(*Source:* Brian Mitchell, International Historical Statistics 1993, 1998.)

all corners of the world. This scale of activity was unlike anything that had been seen in previous centuries. Although the Italian city-states, the Netherlands, and England had all seen dramatic economic growth in earlier eras, the resources of the American landmass produced growth of a quantitatively and qualitatively different order. For example, Maddison's figures show that at its peak in 1900, the United Kingdom produced just under 10% of world product (Italian and Dutch shares of world product are even lower at their peaks, but it is not clear how reliable the data are for these earlier years). At its peak in 1951, the United States produced over 25% of world product.

According to Maddison's figures, in 1950 the United States was wealthier in the aggregate than Australia, Canada, France, Germany, Italy, Sweden, Switzerland, and the United Kingdom *combined*. No wonder John Law foresaw fabulous wealth in the New World. The Mississippi Com-

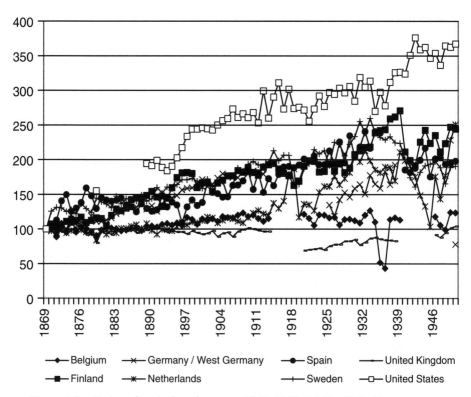

Figure 3.2. Index of agricultural output, 1869–1950 (1869 = 100). (*Source:* Maddison 2006.)

pany stock prices were ten times higher at the peak of the bubble than at their original issue (Garber 1990, 42–46). But U.S. GDP was more than a hundred times higher in 1950 than at the end of the eighteenth century. If John Law's investors could have held on until 1950, they would have attained and surpassed the fortunes of their dreams.

Western Europe watched these developments, astonished, as its prior colonial domains outgrew the home countries. Britain, France, and Germany then began a frantic effort to catch up that can be clearly documented in qualitative sources. For example, the rising astonishment can be traced in (and was partially created by) the series of international expositions or

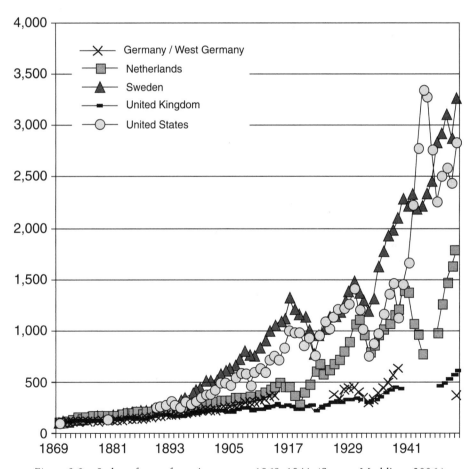

Figure 3.3. Index of manufacturing output, 1869–1941. (*Source:* Maddison 2006.)

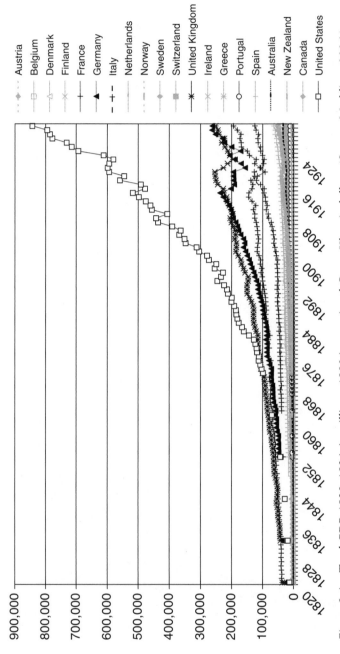

Figure 3.4. Total GDP, 1820–1924, in millions, 1990 international Geary-Khamis dollars. (*Source:* Maddison 2006.)

"world's fairs" that proliferated in the late nineteenth century, such as the World's Columbian Exposition in Chicago in 1893 and the Great World's Fair in Paris in 1900. These fairs offered exhibitions of slices of life in many different countries, from recent technological innovations to art, culture, education, and even social organization. Merle Curti (1950) examined official European reports on American participation at these fairs and finds increasing appreciation for American progress capped by the triumphant Chicago Columbian Exposition of 1893, at which startled observers witnessed the arrival of a new world power. Soon after, books began to appear in Europe with titles like *The American Invaders, The Americanization of the World,* and *The American Invasion*—the first but not the last time that the world would panic about the rise of American power (Wright 1990, 652).

The causes of the more rapid economic growth of the United States at the turn of the century are not fully understood, but scholars have identified several possible sources. Nathan Rosenberg (1994) argues that the conditions of American life led to a particular kind of manufacturing which was resource-intensive, mechanized, and standardized, and this kind of manufacturing had more productive possibilities than the kinds of labor-intensive manufacturing more appropriate in Europe at the time. Gavin Wright (1990) argues that this mechanization led to an intensification of natural resource extraction in particular and Nelson and Wright (1992) argue that natural resource extraction has been a continuing complement to American industrialization. David and Wright (1997) give an overview of the institutions that ensured that the mineral wealth of the land was put to productive use in the nineteenth century—unlike the mineral wealth of Russia, or the British Empire. Bensel (2000) argues that in the Republican Party the United States possessed a political organization firmly devoted to the goal of development. Another important influence was the role of the states in financing geological mapping; a European invention, the geological survey turned out to be a form of industrial policy central to the rise of American wealth (Hendrickson 1961). Alfred Chandler (1990) argues that American organizational capacities were more sophisticated at an earlier date than in Great Britain or Germany. Others have suggested that the American financial system was unusually conducive to growth (Rousseau and Sylla 2005); as a unified market, the United States had opportunities that Europe would only achieve after its political conflicts subsided in the twentieth century (Gordon 2004); and because of its size the United States could benefit from the new technologies of transportation and communication of the nineteenth century along with the advantages to scale they brought (Gordon 2004). During and after the First World War the American lead was only furthered when the United States quickly electrified. The United States also exploited new (German) developments in the design of the internal combustion engine to develop a fleet of personal automobiles and business trucks "while Europe was distracted by wars and interwar economic chaos" (Gordon 2004, 1).

These dynamics are clarified by comparison to the other countries settled by European colonizers. Lange, Mahoney, and Hau (2006) argue that natural resources do not matter as much as the institutions that allow societies to take advantage of them; the countries settled by Spain were unable to take advantage of their mineral wealth as those settled by Britain did. The institutions of Spain were less conducive to economic growth than those of Britain, so that where there was the *most* Spanish colonization there was the *least* growth in Latin America. All the countries colonized and settled by Britain, on the other hand, shared institutions that were friendly to economic growth, which led to the most development where there was the most intensive colonization. This work helps to explain why the United States and other settler countries grew faster than the parts of Africa and Asia that were colonized less intensively by the British.

To sum up, we know that the lands where British settlers from the seventeenth through the nineteenth centuries overwhelmed the native populations turned out to be extraordinarily productive and grew much more rapidly than any of the European countries, countries settled by other colonial powers, or countries settled less intensely by Britain. The United States in particular, with its vast tracts of land (in habitable climates, unlike Canada and Australia, whose populations remained small) and favorable institutions, witnessed levels of material production unmatched by the other countries, levels unseen in world history. Several different quantitative sources indicate this while qualitative sources confirm it. The availability of the New World's resources, together with a particular set of institutions that led to the intensive use of those resources, and new transportation technologies that brought increasing returns to scale and brought American productivity to all corners of the world, created an explosion of abundance that rippled throughout the world and produced a new epoch in history.

For our purposes, the causes of this growth are not as important as its consequences. For the irony of this great wealth is that while Americans were richer than they had ever been in the late nineteenth century, accounts of the time are filled with tales not of mobility and luxury but of struggle and woe. The stunning rise in the GDP numbers does not match the lived experience. A Tennessee farm woman asked in 1890, when the United States was twice as wealthy as it had been twenty years ago, "Why is it, that in the great middle class to which we belong as compared with twenty years ago we find ourselves so much lower down in the scale of real possessions?" (quoted in Lester 2006, 19). The Omaha Platform of 1892 began, "[W]e meet in the midst of a nation brought to the verge of moral, political, and material ruin" (quoted in McMath 1992, 161). Efforts at organization were difficult because members were too poor to organize, as the leader of a sub-alliance in the Farmers' Alliance wrote the state head in 1890: "I wish to know whot to do with my alianc. The members is all so pore that the[y] cant pay thare duse" (quoted in McMath 1975, 119). What E. P. Thompson had said of Britain in the mid-nineteenth century was equally true of Americans in the late nineteenth century: "[M]ost people were 'better off' than their forerunners, but they suffered and continued to suffer this slight improvement as a catastrophic experience" (1963, 212).

Many of the difficulties of the late nineteenth century can be laid at the feet of the gold standard, which artificially constrained the money supply at a time of unbounded productivity. Increasing economic integration had led the nations of the western world to fix the value of their currencies to gold. By doing so, they hoped to smooth the exchange rate fluctuations that could be so devastating to international trade. In theory, if one country was more productive than another then prices for its products would fall until demand in other countries for those products rose enough to reestablish equilibrium. But in practice, American farmers were so productive and prices fell so far that farmers were ruined not only in America but also in Europe. In the abstemious language of modern economics, "the deflation in the late nineteenth century gold standard era . . . reflected both positive aggregate supply and negative money supply shocks" (Bordo, Lane, and Redish 2004, 15). In the nineteenth century the effects of the gold standard were compounded by the American wish to return to the standard at prewar parity, which required prices to fall, by the ending of the flow of gold from the 1840s gold rush, and by the removal of Civil War greenbacks and other government currency from the money supply (Rockoff 1984, Bordo and Rockoff 1996, Friedman and Schwartz 1963). Even in later periods, when there was not literally a lack of gold, monetary authorities often "sterilized" the inflows of gold, not allowing incoming gold stocks to raise the money supply (Eichengreen 1992, Irwin 2010). It is the workings of the official gold standard itself along with the contractionary tendencies of monetary authorities, even when countries had abandoned the official gold standard, that Temin (1989) calls the gold standard "regime," which he sees as lasting well into the 1930s. In theory a tight money supply can be mitigated by a rising velocity of money, but the late nineteenth century as well as the early Depression years were both periods of declining money velocity (Friedman and Schwartz 1963, 640–641; Bordo and Jonung 1981), presumably because consumers would not have wanted to part easily with money that was rapidly gaining in value.

Falling prices were thus the gold standard regime's main weakness. As the quantity of goods rose but the quantity and velocity of money did not, prices fell. Karl Polanyi, the great student of price volatility, writes, "While, in the long run, changes in selling prices need not affect profits, since costs will move up and down correspondingly, this is not true in the short run, since there must be a time lag before contractually fixed prices change. . . . Hence, if the price level was falling for monetary reasons over a considerable time, business would be in danger of liquidation accompanied by the dissolution of productive organization and massive destruction of capital. Not low prices, but falling prices were the trouble" ([1944] 2001, 201).

In recent years scholars have expanded on the reasons why money is not a neutral signal of underlying phenomena but a causal element in its own right. If debts are denominated in nominal terms, price deflation can lead to inability to repay debts. Critics often object that this occurrence simply moves money from one group (creditors) to others (debtors) and does not reflect aggregate decline in income. But these nominal movements can have real effects if creditors thereby become unable to lend, drawing to a halt projects that might have increased aggregate wealth or productivity (Bernanke 1983). Through this causal chain, increased productivity can lead to economic decline—Koestler's paradox.

There were two main episodes of severe deflation that can be chronicled in the price series (Figure 3.5), and both are the consequence of wartime price rises inducing greater productivity. The wholesale price index is a measure of costs to business rather than costs to end consumers and measures the wholesale price of a basket of representative commodities; consumer price indices show the same pattern. Prices jumped during the Civil War and again during World War I. In both cases, disturbances in supply chains had led to skyrocketing prices during the war, which led producers to invest in increasing supply, ultimately causing deflation when the war ended. The first major episode, in the 1880s, is sometimes called the "great deflation." The difficulties of agriculture during the Civil War, when labor was desperately short, caused a price spike in the 1860s. This catalyzed changes in the American agrarian workforce, partly through the increasing development of midwestern agriculture to replace disrupted Southern supplies, partly through mechanization and partly through increasing use of women and children as commercial agricultural laborers (Craig and Weiss 1993; Rasmussen 1965). But once in place, these changes did not fade away after the war. They led to rapid growth in postwar agricultural output, magnified in coming decades with the development of the railroad network and shipping and refrigeration technologies. From 1870 to 1913, exploitation of the American frontier and developments in transportation meant that New World grain flooded European markets until, on the eve of the First World War, the United States was feeding Europe (O'Rourke 1997). European farmers suddenly found themselves competing with the endless supplies of cheap grain, causing farm prices all over the west to plunge.

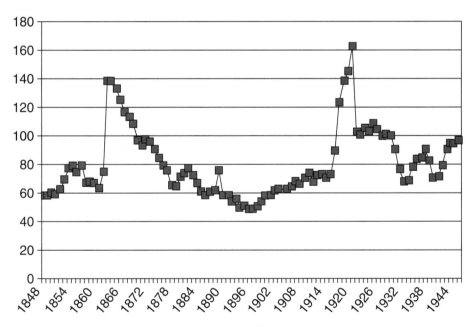

Figure 3.5. Wholesale commodity price index, 1848–1943. 1929 = 100. (*Source:* Mitchell, International Historical Statistics, 1993, 1998.)

A similar sequence was repeated during World War I. Henry Wallace of pig slaughter fame summed up the reasons for the deflation that followed that war: "First, there was the wartime expansion of cultivated crops when farmers patriotically plowed up 40 million extra acres of land to help win the war. Second, there was the abrupt change of the United States after the war from a debtor to a creditor nation, making it more difficult for foreign nations to buy our surplus farm crops. Third, there was the displacement of the horse by the automobile, truck and tractor and the releasing of 35 million acres that had formerly been used for the production of feed. Fourth, there was the movement of European nations to produce all their own food so as not to be starved out in another war. Fifth, there was the new farm competition in other exporting countries such as Argentina and Australia. . . ."[7] Once again war had led to a sequence in which farmers "patriotically plowed up" extra land (or perhaps just responded to the much higher prices their crops could command because of European markets being disturbed by the war) and raised productivity, only to find themselves facing a glut of crops as the war ended and foreign markets recovered. Although the deflation of the late nineteenth century lasted much longer, the deflation of the 1920s and 1930s had more severe short-term effects; the price drop in 1921 alone remains the worst single-year deflation in American history, with consumer prices falling by 10% and wholesale prices and farm products falling by 40% (Lindert and Sutch 2006; Hanes 2006).

Polanyi argued that human societies will never accept the devastation that rapidly rising or falling prices can cause ([1944] 2001). He suggests as an anthropological law that there will always be intervention that impedes the free play of prices. His remarks were aimed at Friedrich Hayek's arguments (1944, 1948) that prices reveal important information about complex systems that cannot be gathered in other ways, and price fluctuations should therefore not be circumvented through legislation. If prices were falling, this was a signal to farmers to plant other crops or to move to other industries altogether. But this was easier said than done. Prices for all crops seemed to fall together, and investing in new equipment to diversify did not make sense when there was no guarantee of stable or rising prices in any crop; moreover, in many areas, farmers simply did not have good crop alternatives (Cochrane 2003, 14). Although some farmers did abandon agriculture, the uncertainties of urban life suggested the wisdom of holding on to a farm, as this would at least guarantee subsistence (Woofter, 1935–1936). Compounding the difficulty of making a rational decision between staying on the farm or moving to the city was the problem that no one really knew how much farmers made, not even the farmers themselves (Danbom 1979, 7). Faced with this profile of options, many farmers decided that the most rational course was to stay where they were and take the Polanyian route of trying to force more systematic change through collective action. Economic difficulties because of the occasional drought were easy to understand, but bad weather cannot explain the long-term decline in the prices, and it was maddening to watch prices fall when farmers were doing everything right and the weather was cooperating. Thus, both episodes of deflation seen in the price series were followed by political action rather than by natural processes of market adjustment.

But while the response to the deflation was everywhere a turn to politics, this political response took different shape in different countries.

In the first episode of price deflation in the late nineteenth century, European countries responded to the invasion of American grain with protectionist tariffs. France, like the rest of Europe, had been flirting with free trade in the 1860s. But after defeat in the Franco-Prussian war, French nationalists and manufacturers found a strong ally in the agricultural sector, which resented the natural advantages that New World agriculture enjoyed. Tariffs rose dramatically in the late 1880s and 1890s, with the Méline tariff of 1892 attaching stiff duties to most agricultural imports (aside from raw materials) and signaling the new era of protectionism. In Germany, too, a period of experimentation with trade integration ended as a coalition of industrialists and Junkers, the alliance of iron and rye, succeeded in raising tariffs at the turn of the century. Many see in these developments the watershed in which Europe abandoned nineteenth century integration and turned towards protectionism. Italy followed these general trends as did Portugal, Sweden, and Norway; Belgium and Switzerland also adopted tariffs, although at lower levels. Only Britain, with its dwindling agricultural labor force, and Denmark and the Netherlands, where livestock agriculture benefited from cheap grain, largely held to free trade against the protectionist tide. Several scholars have interpreted this sequence of events in terms of the discovery of the New World and its abundance of land providing a resource shock to the whole world once this land was integrated into the global economy. The sudden availability of so much more land disturbed the economic position of landowners, and the position of landowners in different polities was key to the political response. (Gourevitch 1986; Hobson 1997; Tracy [1964] 1989;

Kindleberger 1951; Koning 1994; O'Rourke 1997; O'Rourke and Williamson 1999; Rogowski 1989; Swinnen 2009). As two scholars sum up this episode, "Transport cost declines led to distributional changes, which in turn prompted an attempt by the losers to insulate themselves from the international economy . . . [I]t seems that globalization undermined itself" (Findlay and O'Rourke 2003, 39).

An important point to keep in mind is that the problem was more severe in agriculture than in manufacturing. Although both sectors took advantage of the new transportation and refrigeration technologies, it was land that was in particular abundance in the New World, and this land came to Europe in the form of cheap primary products (food and raw materials). The New World exported primary products and imported manufactures. However, the imbalance was much greater in primary products than in manufactures. For example, in the period 1896–1900 the United States and Canada exported over a billion American dollars worth of primary products but imported only $550 million; and the United States and Canada exported 240 million American dollars worth of manufactures and imported $325 million. There was an imbalance in manufactures, but it was much less severe than the imbalance going in the other direction in primary products. Meanwhile, over this same period, the United Kingdom and Ireland exported 212 million American dollars worth of primary products and imported over $1.6 billion; and the United Kingdom and Ireland exported over one billion American dollars worth of manufactures and imported only $350 million. The countries of northwestern Europe (Finland, Sweden, Norway, Denmark, Germany, Belgium, Netherlands, France, Switzerland, and Austria) in 1896–1900 exported 1.5 billion American dollars worth of primary products but imported $2.9 billion; and the countries of northwestern Europe exported nearly 1.5 billion American dollars worth of manufactures and imported only $685 million (Yates 1959, 227–230).

These patterns are stable from the 1870s to the 1920s. Throughout this period the European countries were receiving primary products and sending out industrial manufactures, while the United States was receiving industrial manufactures and sending out primary products. But throughout this period the trade imbalance remained greater in primary products than in manufacturing. This whole period can be characterized as one in which New World primary products overwhelmed European markets. While imports from other agricultural countries, particularly Russia, Argentina, and Australia, also contributed to the "European grain invasion" (O'Rourke 1997), imports from the United States were dominant. For example, in 1913 imports from the United States accounted for a larger share of imports than imports from any other non-European country in the United Kingdom, Germany, Italy, Spain, and Portugal (as well as in the smaller European countries combined); only in Belgium/Luxembourg and France, with their overseas colonies, was this not the case and even there American imports ranked second or tied for first respectively (Svennilson 1954, 177).

On the other side of that great invasion, the invaders themselves, the American farmers, were suffering from the same collapse in prices. The United States was also highly protectionist—indeed, it had initiated the late nineteenth century round of protectionism—but as American farmers were the exporters and their own productivity was the problem, protectionism was not enough of an answer for American agriculture. Instead, the low prices led to a widespread period of collective soul-searching and political agitation that we call populism.

Price deflation, particularly of staple commodities, was the central complaint of the American populists. For many years scholars took the populists at their word, and economic determinist explanations of populism were orthodox (e.g., Hicks [1931] 2009). Starting in the 1940s, historians began to question whether the populists' situation was as bad as they claimed. Douglass North (1966) argued that price deflation alone could not have been the culprit, because as the prices farmers received for their commodity crops fell, so did all other prices, including prices for their supplies and consumption needs, and in fact over the period of the populist revolt, other prices were falling faster than the prices of the main commodities grown in the United States. Subsequently, historians reinterpreted populism as not an economic phenomenon so much as a cultural one. Anne Mayhew (1972) famously argued that farmers were protesting not falling prices but rather the sudden importance of prices in their lives from commercialization. Other scholars argued for the importance of the cooperative movement, or cultural traditions and community ties, to the spread of populism (Goodwyn 1978; McMath 1975).

More recent work has supplied some missing links, however, that make the populists' own complaints, and therefore an economic interpretation of populism, more compelling (see, e.g., McGuire 1981, and see Postel 2007 for a thorough refutation of the idea that populism was a protest against modernity or progress). First, as David Lake notes, we know that when the economic troubles disappeared in the early decades of the twentieth century, agrarian radicalism subsided. New discoveries of gold at the turn of the century increased the money supply, leading to rising agricultural prices, which "transformed the nature of agrarian politics. Farmers substantially reduced their political agitation and once again began to work within the existing party system . . . with favorable economic conditions, agrarian conflict was defused, and public debate focused on essentially technical and relatively depoliticized issues" (Lake 1989, 93–94). When the economic problems were tamed the farmers were not so troubled by the cultural changes; but we know that this was not simply a matter of having become accustomed to the cultural changes, because when the agrarian economy fell into trouble again in the 1920s agrarian radicalism heated up again. The most intense phase of the activism is during the price declines.

Second, recent research has shown the importance of credit to the settler economies. As Sarah Quinn (2010) notes, even if the land that the settlers received was itself free, they nevertheless needed to borrow to finance the tools and material necessary for turning the land into profitable farms. We know that price deflations made borrowing problematic, because farmers borrowed at nominal prices and repaid the loan with money that was worth much more because of deflation. Eichengreen (1984) argues that mortgage interest rates were not higher than would have been expected given the risky nature of farming in unsettled territories and given variation in interest rate legislation; he also argues that price deflations could not have been so consequential, given that mortgages were very short in duration (just a few years) at the time. But this understates the effect of price deflation. Figure 3.6 uses Eichengreen's data to calculate a real interest rate for the years 1869 through 1885. This value quantifies how much extra a farmer paid in real terms for a mortgage of $100 taken out in that year compared to how much the farmer would have paid if prices had been stable. Mortgages at this time would have been "balloon mortgages," in which the borrower paid only the interest each year and then paid the balance of the sum at the end of the loan period (or more likely, simply took out a new loan for the new balance). Thus, the real interest rate captures how much more the amount of the loan is worth in real terms at the end of the loan period. The usual loan period was very short, with many loans due in just two or three years, so the real interest rate has been calculated for 2-, 3-, 4-, and 5-year loan periods.

Using this method, we can see that the farmers were often paying real interest rates twice as high as the nominal interest rate. Perhaps even more striking is the volatility of the real interest rate: a continuous price decline throughout the period might have convinced mortgage lenders that interest rates could be safely lowered (as Eichengreen suggests) but in the early 1880s prices suddenly rose for several years, such that a farmer who had taken a five-year loan in 1878 paid almost half as much real interest as nominal interest. This unpredictability explains why mortgage lenders would have been wary of lowering interest rates. Consequently those who took out loans in the mid-1870s or in the early 1880s found themselves stuck with huge real interest rates. These price deflations must have pushed some farms that would have been viable at stable prices into

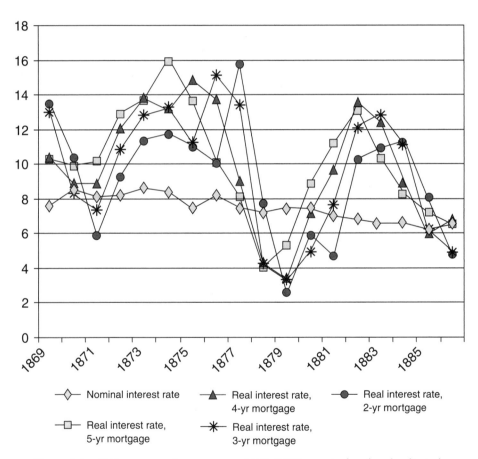

Figure 3.6. U.S. mortgage interest rates, 1869–1885, nominal and real, adjusted for deflation. (From data in Eichengreen 1984.)

default. Whether they actually led to foreclosures or to refinancing, they certainly led to political outrage. Clearly in some years and some circumstances farmers would have done well (such as borrowing on a five-year loan in 1878), but the overall trend of price deflation put them on the losing end of the bargain in most years. This explains why farmers might have been protesting price deflation even if prices for the goods they bought were also falling.

Jeffry Frieden (1997) argues that indebtedness itself could not have been the problem, as heavily indebted homeowners in the East were not clamoring for silver. Rather, farmers fought for a looser monetary policy because it would make American crops cheaper for the export market. He shows that if we control for region, debt by itself does not correlate with support for soft money in Congress. Frieden portrays this finding as inconsistent with traditional understandings of populism, but he has ignored the role of divergent interest rates in different regions. For example, in the South and West mortgage interest rates were often twice as high as in the East (Quinn 2010, 62), partly because of interest rate ceilings in the East and partly because of the greater risks of settling the land further west. It is no wonder that Frieden finds greater support for soft money in the South and West, even controlling for levels of indebtedness, as debt at 5.5% interest is quite different from the same amount of debt at 10% interest. Frieden has also ignored the kind of debt at issue, with the crop-lien system particularly difficult to manage in the South, where the land had been devalued after the Civil War. Nevertheless, even if Frieden underestimates the importance of indebtedness, he is correct that farmers were also concerned about the export market. These are both economic concerns, supporting an economic interpretation of populism.

The revisionist scholarship aims to show that no one was exploiting the farmers: the interest rates are reasonable given the amount of actual risk involved in settling southern and western land. In that case, what the populists were complaining about was the *actual risk* of life in an unsettled land. Whether or not they were being exploited, settling the land required borrowing money, but borrowing money under a gold standard in a booming economy was a clear economic risk; populism was the response to that risk, an attempt to solve economic difficulties through the political process.

The economic productivity and the resulting price collapse had consequences throughout American politics because farmers were in a pivotal political position: in the fragmented and geographically structured

American government, votes from agricultural constituencies played a major role in determining the structure of political economy. The price declines led to a serious rethinking of what "money" is and how it functions, what role credit should play in the economy, and what the distribution of wealth might have to do with the functioning of the economic system.

In the late nineteenth century it also led to a focus on the issue of monopoly power because the rapid growth was incarnated in American firms that were much larger and wealthier than firms in other countries, which a wave of mergers at the turn of the century had made even larger (Lamoreaux 1985). Recent research has revealed some surprises in the comparative analysis of firm size, but all accounts agree that the largest firms were larger in the United States than anywhere else. Even the revisionist scholarship of Kinghorn and Nye, for example, which calls the orthodox picture of smaller firms in France into question, agrees there was considerably greater industrial concentration in the United States and, in terms of assets or capital, American firms were considerably larger than French and German (Kinghorn and Nye 1996—U.S. Steel and Standard Oil were so large that they had to be dropped from their graph. See their figure 1, 102).

The wealth of these corporations and the men who owned them provided a jarring contrast to the increasingly visible poverty of the urban concentrations that housed the workers of the corporations. The wealth of the country also supported the development of a public sphere that could highlight and dramatize these juxtapositions, a public sphere that painted the large corporations as heartless to labor, neglectful of safety standards, and ruthless against small business. And the wealth of the country supported a class of social reformers who could devote their lives to thoughtful campaigns against corporations and in uplift of the poor. (Goodwyn 1978; Cooper 1990; McGerr 2003; Postel 2007)

The antimonopoly politics that resulted was a break from what had gone before. Of course, there has been a subculture of suspicion of big business in the United States ever since Thomas Jefferson, but similar subcultures are seen in all countries. Agrarian and anti-big-business ideologies formed part of the nineteenth century debate over industrialization in Germany, for example, and featured prominently in Nazi rhetoric (Barkin 1970; Turner 1985). Even France, which after the Second World War explicitly adopted a policy of promoting large firms, has always had a strong subculture of suspicion of big business and Jefferson-like championing of agrarians and *petits commerçants,* from the Comité Mascuraud and Pierre

Poujade to José Bové (see, e.g., Nord [1986] 2009; Moss 1977). The real divergence here comes not at the level of culture but at the level of action.

While the size of the firms was one factor in the emergence of monopoly politics, Morton Keller (1980) has argued that what was further unique about the United States is that the large firms developed before political institutions had been formed to control them. But perhaps the most important difference between the United States and Europe is that, because of the different position of agrarians in export markets, European agrarians could be appeased with protectionism whereas American agrarians could not; American agrarians consequently became central in the fight against concentration of wealth, an attack on the industrial economy that directly threatened their interests.

These nineteenth century precedents, established during the first period of deflation, flowered into a new political economy during the second episode of deflation in the 1920s and early 1930s. This second period of deflation has not traditionally been seen as a continuation of the populist period. Most historical accounts consider populism to have ended by the turn of the century. But this book aims to demonstrate that these are two acts in the same larger story, which is a story of the disequilibrium caused in the world economy as a result of American abundance. These two deflationary episodes were interrupted at the turn of the century by a period of years in which the discovery of new gold stocks temporarily resolved the deflationary problem. But this was an interlude and not a resolution. The problem of deflation caused by extreme productivity under a gold standard regime remained, and when the new gold stocks were no longer sufficient to cover the new productivity catalyzed by World War I, prices fell again and another round of agrarian protest resulted.

In the 1920s and early 1930s, in a direct repeat of the events of the 1890s, tariffs were the "first line of defence" (Tracy [1964] 1989, 120–123) against the invasion of American grain for most European countries, including France, Germany, Italy, Switzerland, Austria, Sweden, and Finland and at somewhat lower levels in Belgium. In 1931 even Britain, that relentless supporter of free trade, adopted weak tariffs on some agricultural products. Some of these European movements came in retaliation for the Smoot Hawley Tariff Act of 1930. Beyond tariffs, countries also experimented with various other protectionist policies, from requiring the purchase and usage of domestic raw materials to setting import quotas. Only after these steps had been exhausted did European countries begin to experiment with other kinds of intervention into agricultural markets such as price controls (Tracy [1964] 1989). Eventually, European countries did adopt price support programs, stockpiling, and production controls (Libecap 1998), but the focus on protection and on the role of foreign surpluses kept much of the political attention fixed on tariffs. Farmers in other countries also had an outlet that farmers in the United States did not: if conditions deteriorated, they could emigrate to America. In Sweden, for example, which had a powerful agrarian movement, the agrarian crisis of the 1880s led to massive emigration to the United States as well as to tariffs on agricultural products (Micheletti 1990, 35).

In this second episode of deflation, however, a new response began to be seen: policymakers in several European countries began a top-down effort to regenerate capitalism and catch up to the United States. It was at this time that several elements of a unique growth model were laid down that many European countries would follow for the rest of the century—indeed, that they still follow today. This European growth model was "wage moderation and export growth" (Eichengreen 1996, 41). This growth model focused on keeping wages relatively low so that profits could be reinvested in firms, allowing them to generate a stunning rise in exports, which grew at a rate of over 8 percent per year in the postwar period (41). While the corporatist bargains that yielded this growth model have been examined thoroughly, the scholarship on corporatism tends to focus on the form of the agreement—the tripartite bargain between business, labor, and the state—and its consequences for the welfare state rather than emphasizing the point that the content of these agreements was a *restraint of consumption* and a privileging of "supply-side policies for the reconstruction of . . . industry" as Christopher Allen writes for Germany (1989, 263). Wage moderation required deferral of present consumption in the interest of using resources to build up productive capacities

This strategy had its origins in efforts to repair the damage to productivity and industrial capacity from each war. Between 1913 and 1919, per capita GDP grew modestly in the United States but fell in Belgium, Germany, Denmark, France, and Sweden. The effects of the Second World War were even more dramatic. Between 1939 and 1945, per capita GDP grew modestly in the United Kingdom, Canada, Australia, and New Zealand, while it declined in *every* continental European and Scandinavian country. Meanwhile American per capita GDP grew from $6,561 in 1939 to an astonishing $11,709 in 1945, an annual growth rate of over 10% (Maddison, 2006 and online updates).

After the First World War, European countries had attempted to reconstruct on the basis of a revived gold standard, a strategy that failed spectacularly. After the Second World War several countries turned to an export-led strategy of reconstruction based on the foundation of wage moderation and specifically avoided encouraging consumption. Although this model was not universal across Europe, it was particularly strong in the two key economies of Germany and France, where it only became stronger in the postwar period. For example, as historian Jan Logemann writes for Germany in the 1950s, "time and again concerns for price-stability and inflation worries would undercut overtly demand-side oriented growth strategies. Not the promotion of domestic consumption but rather shoring up capital for rebuilding industry and fostering exports were at the forefront of economic policy" (Logemann 2007, 82). There is debate among historians as to whether Germany's response to the Depression can be called Keynesian (as we will discuss further in Chapter 8), but German demand-stimulus policies did not include encouragement of *private* consumption. Rather, as several scholars have pointed out, Keynesianism took different forms across countries, and European countries including Germany adopted a variant of "social Keynesianism" in which the demand stimulus came from public spending (Weir and Skocpol 1985; on this point see also Piore and Sabel 1984, 91; Logemann 2007; Crouch 2009; Watson 2010). Meanwhile, in France after the Second World War, "[t]he economic situation was in fact one of shortage . . . the main economic choices of the period were thus totally foreign to the Keynesian problematic" (Rosanvallon 1989, 189; see also Milward 1984). The wars had revealed France's relatively low productivity level compared to Germany, and Jean Monnet and the planners around him concluded that "[c]apital investment was the key" to recovery (Kuisel 1981, 222). Although attracted by the American consumer economy, the planners decided that the problem for France was increasing productivity and therefore "[t]he planners wanted to lower the output of consumer goods as much as possible without arousing opposition to the [plan]. . . . The planners chose investment over consumption, modernization over reconstruction, or the future over the present" (Kuisel 1981, 225). The question was how to finance this investment. In looking for funds for industry even "essential" consumer goods were accorded lowest priority because "[f]inancial resources would be available, it was held, if consumption were controlled through such means as rationing. Then personal savings would accumulate and furnish the necessary investments" (Kuisel 1981,

233–234). Because of this, Keynesianism in France was "a polite way of being a socialist" (Simon Nora, quoted in Rosanvallon 1989, 190) and a means of legitimating technocratic economic management rather than a specific policy of encouraging consumption. Perhaps France's greatest contribution to the European growth model was its steady (if imperfect) drive to lower trade barriers through the piecemeal development of the institutions of the European Union. (Kuisel 1981; Milward 1984; Adams 1989)

In other countries this strategy of wage moderation and export growth is seen to varying extents. In Finland the "policy model has displayed a rather one-sided emphasis on supply, cost, and competitiveness factors . . . emphasis has been placed on the need to enhance the competitiveness of industry by curtailing its costs through fiscal measures" (Pekkarinen 1989, 322, 324). In Sweden the economists of the Stockholm school had developed policies of promoting consumption even before Keynes, but they adopted a "social Keynesian" strategy focusing on public works rather than on the explicit encouragement of private consumption (Weir and Skocpol 1985). Early 1930s policies were ultimately viewed as inadequate, perhaps because of the small size of Sweden's domestic market (Gourevitch 1986, 131–135). As a consequence "Keynesian policy prescriptions were broadened early on to tackle problems of industrial structure and inflation as well as those of aggregate demand" (Pekkarinen, 1989, 319). Italy has always been a partial exception to the supply-side orientation of European economies and has suffered for it (Eichengreen 2007, 113). Norway and Denmark have been mixed, with some receptivity to consumption-oriented policies as well as strong emphasis on supply-side factors (Pekkarinen, 1989).

Britain is the most prominent exception to this European growth model. The response to the Depression in Britain was weaker than in the United States, Germany, and Sweden, and there was no immediate policy of stimulating demand. Gourevitch argues that this is because high finance managed to impose deflationary policies onto domestic markets and the small and diminishing agrarian workforce "deprived labor and dissident business elements of . . . allies with whom to challenge that orthodoxy" (1986, 136). But after the war Britain did turn to Keynesian policies, and it was never very successful at wage restraint. It was also less successful than the continental European countries in focusing on an export-oriented strategy because of its separation from the Common Market, for which the Commonwealth was not a perfect substitute, and because its declining export-oriented industries were replaced by new industries oriented to domestic production (Owen 1999; Musson 1978, 281). However, it was also the case that the wartime damage to Britain's industrial capacity rendered some of its problems "foreign to the Keynesian problematic." For example, we will discuss in more detail in Chapter 8 the policies of subsidizing demand in housing that were so central to the American response to the Depression. In Britain after the Second World War, the problem in housing was *supply* of materials, as steel, softwood, and labor were being carefully allocated among competing uses (Jones 2000, 110). These different problems ensured that even in Britain the political economic model that emerged would focus to some extent on the tasks of reconstruction and engineering growth. As Britain slipped into a half-century-long obsession with the question of why it was falling behind the United States and Germany in productivity, its postwar policy responses tacked between attempts to increase productivity and attempts to increase wages. (Although we are focusing on the contrast between the United States and Europe here, see Garon 2012 and Park 2011 on restraint of consumption and channeling of savings to reconstruction in Japan.)

European welfare states grew partly as byproducts of this model of investment-oriented economic growth, either as part of explicit bargains of wage restraint in return for welfare or as piecemeal efforts to address the instabilities that the economic growth model was causing. These bargains have of course been examined intensively in the literature on European welfare states, but understanding the focus of European economies on finding resources for productive investment sheds new light on the question of why employers were willing to extend welfare provisions. Such provisions were not attempts to retain worker loyalty, as the varieties of capitalism perspective argues, but rather, an explicit quid pro quo for wage moderation and consequent restraint of private consumption. As Eichengreen summarizes:

> In Belgium, the first postwar government adopted a social security scheme in return for labor's adherence to a 1944 social pact limiting wage increases. In return for the unions' promise of wage restraint, the Norwegian government offered legislation mandating paid vacations and limiting the length of the workweek. The Dutch government introduced unemployment insurance and old-age pensions, while extending social security coverage, as a quid pro quo for wage moderation. Starting in 1955, the Swedish government offered com-

pulsory health insurance, an expanded system of disability insurance, and an array of retraining programs in return for labor's acquiescence to policies of wage restraint and solidarity. The Danish government offered an expanded system of sick pay in 1956, when the agreement to link wage increases to productivity negotiated during the reconstruction phase showed signs of breaking down. The Austrian government extended tax and social insurance concessions to labor in return for wage moderation. (2007, 33–34)

Even when there was not such an explicit quid pro quo of welfare policies for wage restraint, the pressures of the growth model drove policymakers to expand welfare spending as a way of reconciling citizens to the policies of investment-oriented growth, even in advance of citizen pressure for such policies (Vail 2010, Allen 1989).

This book does not present a full accounting of approaches to consumption in European countries, nor does it identify the reasons for adherence to or divergence from this model over time and how this affected the welfare state. Rather, the aim here is merely to demonstrate that this has been a strong strain in several European countries for much of the twentieth century, in order to set American developments in comparative perspective. For the United States followed a path that is the mirror-opposite of this. During the second deflation of the 1920s, and then in the Great Depression, the United States pioneered a politics of increasing consumption that it has also adhered to until today. As one writer observed in the 1960s: "President de Gaulle not long ago 'declared that France's economic future depended on more savings, more investment, and less consumption.' By contrast, the United States Treasury, at almost the same time, emphasized that its recent tax moves—the Revenue Act of 1964 and the Excise Tax Reduction Act of 1964—'provided a substantial stimulus to consumer demand.' What the United States seeks to achieve is exactly what France seeks to avoid" (Norr 1966, 390). As the European countries were restraining consumption and orienting themselves towards export production, the United States was laying the foundations for a growth model based on consumption. Alexander Gerschenkron had suggested in 1962 that this was a general law of capitalism, writing, "The more backward a country's economy, the greater was the stress upon producers' goods as against consumers' goods. . . . The more backward a country's economy, the heavier was the pressure upon the levels of consumption of the population. . . . The more backward a country's economy, the greater was the part played by special institutional factors designed to increase supply of capital to the nascent industries" (Gerschenkron 1962, 354). But understanding how exactly this worked out historically, and how a consumer economy emerged in the United States, requires closer examination of the era in which this growth model first arose—the Great Depression.

We saw above that the most prominent explanations of the Great Depression ultimately trace it to contingent events, particularly the inexplicably tight monetary policy of the 1930s. The structural issue that underlies this contingency is that American growth rates made it difficult to discern the appropriate monetary policy. Take the question of the stock market boom. Between 1927 and 1929 the value of U.S. stocks doubled (Calomiris 2010). Were those rising stock prices the result of changes in underlying fundamentals, for example, the yield of communication and transportation technologies finally recovering from the war, or were they bid up by speculators and easy credit? The Fed thought the latter and restricted the money supply in an attempt to gently deflate the bubble. But some contemporary observers thought the high stock valuations were justified. Irving Fisher, in a spectacularly mistimed quote, said in October 1929 that stock prices had reached "what looks like a permanently high plateau" (*The New York Times*, October 16, 1929). Fisher has been ridiculed mercilessly ever since, but in fact scholars have recently argued that the high stock prices were justified given the many fundamental changes in the 1920s. McGrattan and Prescott show that the high stock prices of 1929 actually matched the fundamental value of corporations as measured by tangible and intangible assets: "with regard to the value of the 1929 stock market, Irving Fisher was right" (2004, 1003). Examining patent citations to measure the significance of technological and managerial innovations in the 1920s, Nicholas (2008) finds their value consistent with the run-up of the market in the 1920s and inconsistent with the much lower value of the market after the crash, suggesting that it was the post-crash low prices, presumably caused by the tight money supply, that were unjustified. Other scholars using different measures argue that the stock market was in fact overvalued (e.g., De Long and Shleifer 1991). But if we are nearly a century later still discovering evidence on both sides of the debate, observers at the time can be forgiven for not understanding the events they were living through—whether it was artificial growth generated in the 1920s through artificially easy credit, or whether it was sound economic growth based on the fundamentals of a historically unprecedented rise in productivity. What American abundance had introduced was a context of uncertainty. In this context the Fed's decision to try to deflate the stock market with tight money to avoid a worse collapse down the road does not seem as inexplicable as Friedman and Schwartz suggest. Federal Reserve bankers placed emphasis on "checking the speculative wave," because they thought it was "a fake prosperity destined to end in a crash" (quoted in Meltzer 2003, 279). Nor does farmers' inability to forecast price declines seem as inexplicable as Rothband suggests.

Charles Calomiris notes why it would be historically inaccurate to have expected actors of the time to know what we (think we) know today. Calomiris writes: "The period 1914–1947 was an unusually unstable three decades in U.S. history. The sequence of large and unique shocks, along with the changing economic structure of the economy, was not conducive to learning about monetary policy" (Calomiris 2010, 17). As evidence of these shocks and changes in the structure of the economy that made prediction difficult, Calomiris lists a range of measures demonstrating unusual progress, e.g., "the 'fastest rate of multifactor productivity growth over the last century and a half, and probably two centuries' . . . In 1919 there were roughly 7 million automobiles in the United States; by 1929, there were more than 23 million. Electricity became widespread in the 1920s, even in rural areas. Annual radio sales grew from $60 million in 1922 to $843 million in 1929. . . . Cities saw the spread of skyscrapers of ever-expanding ambition. The first real estate boom and bust in Florida, amid an awakening appreciation of the unique opportunities for development there, occurred from roughly 1920–1926" (18–20). Even more confusingly, under the general troubles of the 1930s, many sectors and industries were operating profitably (Bernstein 1987), just as the general prosperity of the 1920s had hidden a period of agricultural distress and bank foreclosures, "the worst rural mortgage foreclosure outcomes and the highest rural bank failure rates up to that point since the 1830s" (Calomiris 2010, 18).

Taking a closer look at one instance of this uncertainty can help to explain the confusion. While some have argued that agricultural growth during the 1920s was excessive and financed by an unjustified credit boom, a look at Figure 3.7, which shows the progress of agricultural output up to just before the Great Depression, explains why observers of the time might have found it to be perfectly rational: what we see here is certainly rapid growth, but the growth seems to be in keeping with a generally rising trend since the turn of the century, particularly after the volatility of the war years had been overcome. It would be hard for someone looking at this figure to predict the 15% drop in agricultural output that occurred in the early 1930s. As one observer of land prices in the 1920s wrote, "In retrospect it may seem remarkable that [agricultural] land buyers in 1919 and 1920 had such extremely optimistic expectations. Nevertheless at the time, their optimism seemed quite reasonable. Unusually rapid gains in farm incomes and farmland values during the late wartime and early postwar periods marked the climax of a long period when incomes and land values had been steadily rising. Indeed, farm incomes and farmland values had risen consistently in most parts of the country since the late 1890's" (Johnson 1974, 180). Some scholars even today contend that despite occasional volatility, agriculture showed slow and steady growth all the way to the Great Depression (Federico 2005). No one knew anymore what was rational or what to expect.

The orthodox understanding is that these agrarian sector difficulties caused or worsened the Depression. As Christina Romer sums up, "the great expansion of agricultural lending during World War I left the American farm sector unusually heavily in debt. When deflation started in 1930, farmers were the first to default, and this sent undiversified rural banks into failure. . . . The unique conjunction of undiversified banking and a particularly large increase in agricultural indebtedness in the 1920s

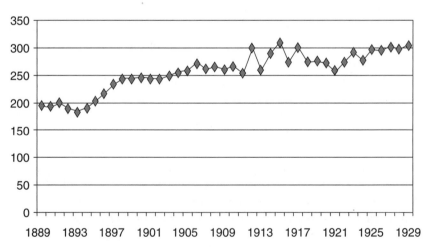

Figure 3.7.   Index of agricultural output, 1889–1929. 1869 = 100.
(*Source:* Maddison 2006.)

made the financial panics in the United States both more severe and more persistent than in other countries" (1993, 34).

In short, overproduction *was* a problem, although not exactly in the way many contemporaries envisaged it. It was not literally the case that the economy was producing more than could be absorbed, as Roosevelt argued at the time or as scholars such as Baran and Sweezy argued later. Rather, the sustained economic growth of the United States had created a disequilibrium in the world economy starting in the late nineteenth century, as seen in the price volatility caused by inability to market that growth. This disequilibrium introduced a deflationary bias into the system because policymakers could not quite believe the growth rates and did not allow the money supply to keep pace with the growth rates even before the gold standard had been officially resumed. The unprecedented growth made accurate forecasting impossible. The growth of the American economy does not explain everything about the events, but it is a major background factor. Unusual growth in agricultural supply, caused by technological advances as well as by settling of new land, kicked off the volatility that confused policymakers, and triggered agrarian statism. It was the background for the popularity of the consumption-oriented policies of the time.

It is not the aim of this work to present a new explanation of the Great Depression. The main outlines of the Depression are by now well understood, although, as we have seen, several important riddles remain unsolved even at this date (including how, or even if, the failure of rural banks contributed to the overall crisis, Federico 2005). Rather, this discussion has aimed to illustrate the context of crisis and uncertainty that formed the background for the policies that we will trace in the next chapters and that laid the foundation for divergent political economies. The concern of this book is not with the policies that in fact caused or resolved the Great Depression but the many policies implemented as an attempt to address the Depression that went on to have other consequences—the side effects of the Great Depression.

We saw above that a dominant response of the European countries was protectionism and then after the Second World War, adoption of a policy of wage restraint and export orientation in return for extensions of welfare protections. While the United States was as protectionist as any other country—indeed, passage of Smoot Hawley was a central episode in this cycle of protectionism—as an agricultural exporter it was hurt by European tariffs. Thus, a key difference is that in the United States the agrarian concern with price volatility became translated into a concern first with overproduction and then with the concentration of wealth. In the United States, just as they had done in the original populist moment, plunging commodity prices in the 1920s meant ruin for agrarians in the sequence that led eventually to the killing of the pigs and the cotton ploughed up that so vexed Arthur Koestler. The theme of overproduction drove much of the policy response, and proposals for solutions abounded. Policymakers experimented throughout the 1920s and 1930s with higher tariffs, then lower tariffs, renewal of wartime credits to Europe, the Dawes and Young plans to help revive European demand for American exports by reviving the European economy, voluntary agricultural cooperatives, acreage reductions, and marketing agreements, and they tried to subsidize below-market-price sales of surplus crops directly in the McNary-Haugen proposals (vetoed by Coolidge), all in the attempt to shore up prices. Efforts intensified after the Depression widened to the broader economy and the White House changed hands (Finegold 1982), but the theme of overproduction and the attempt to support prices continued. Policymakers passed the Guffey-Snyder and Guffey-Vinson Acts to support coal prices, the Connally Act to counteract falling prices in the oil industry, the Robinson-Patman Act, which criminalized certain types of price discounts, and the Miller-Tydings Act which aimed to protect small retailers from price-cutting competition, and President Roosevelt created the Commodity Credit Corporation, which provided loans to farmers at market prices with crops as collateral (Finegold 1982; Lake 1989; Benedict 1966; Libecap 1998). It was in this context that the crop and livestock destructions of the early 1930s took place, and the Agricultural Adjustment Act included many other price support proposals, such as domestic allotments and the "ever normal granary," Henry Wallace's idea to guarantee prices by having the government purchase and store surplus produce (Nourse 1940, 923; Sheingate 2001). The public sphere was rife throughout this time with creative ideas for getting rid of surplus crops (see, e.g., Figure 3.8). The diagnosis of poverty in the midst of plenty had led to a period of ideological ferment—examined more fully in Chapter 5—during which radical methods for economic restructuring of many different kinds were proposed. Through this experimentation "New Deal agricultural policies carved out an unprecedented role for the state in controlling farm prices and the level of farm output" (Hooks 1990, 32). While the early 1930s were the high point for these policies, the Second

New Deal was also marked by concern for price stabilization and over-production (Kennedy 1999, 241–248; Schlesinger [1960] 2003).

The main solution that ultimately arose from these experiments, and a solution we continue to follow today, posited that the money supply needs to keep pace with economic growth. This was an understanding of

Figure 3.8. A suggestion for what to do with excess wheat: "Send some of our good cooks abroad to start the pancake habit." (Source: *New Orleans Morning Tribune,* August 14, 1931, 8. Courtesy of the Collections of the Louisiana State Museum.)

money pioneered by agrarians, and it continues to rule American politics. But other solutions proposed at the time were equally important to the development of political economy: in particular, a key diagnosis that resonated with many was that the plenty the farmers were producing could not get into the hands of those who needed it because the wealthy were hoarding all the money. This was also a theme of the agrarian Populists of the 1890s that was picked up by the agrarians of the 1920s and early 1930s. Several groups and movements converged on the argument that the depression was a problem of *purchasing power,* because wealth was concentrated in so few hands that for the majority of people, needs could not be translated into effective market demand. Even before Keynes had published his defense of consumption-oriented economic policies, the United States developed a model of economic growth that Meg Jacobs (2005) calls the "purchasing power paradigm" and that Lizabeth Cohen (2003) has called the "purchaser consumer paradigm."

These terms refer to the growing belief during the Depression and the New Deal that "[t]he prosperity of the nation is built upon spending, not saving" (quoted in Cohen 2003, 55). Such thinking was widespread, found among economists such as Robert Nathan, who argued that the nation now "must increase consumption and reduce savings" (quoted in Garon 2012, 327), as well as representatives of labor who used it to argue for higher wages for male workers: "Unless a worker's earnings can support his family, we [will] find our whole capitalistic set-up deprived of the market for the great production of which it is capable" (quoted in Cohen 2003, 154). It was found within the government, where Harold Ickes's National Resources Committee noted that the country's "rich abundance of natural resources and an undreamt-of capacity to convert this natural wealth into useful goods and services" required that "the consumers of the Nation are able to buy the output of goods and services which industry can produce" (quoted in Garon 2012, 327). As we have seen, it reached Roosevelt himself. Although during the Second World War the government would attempt to restrain consumption and credit in the hope of fighting inflation (with important consequences examined in Chapter 6), episodes such as this were the exception rather than the rule at mid-century, and stimulating consumption, directly as well as by fighting concentration of wealth, became a predominant concern of American political economy.

Jacobs and Cohen both argue that the importance of consumption that emerged in twentieth century America was not a natural product of capitalism, and it does not reflect the absence of politics. To substantiate their case they each show us, in the place of the depoliticized, apathetic consumer of Frankfurt School theory, example after example of highly politicized consumers taking to the streets to protest price rises, writing letters to policymakers complaining of the unavailability of meat, and hunting for bargains with price lists in hand. Jacobs interprets the National Recovery Administration (NRA), the National Labor Relations Board (NLRB), and the Office of Price Administration (OPA) as policies that were ultimately driven by belief in the "purchasing power paradigm," which saw purchasing power in the hands of workers as the key mechanism to regenerate capitalism. If socialism foundered on the shoals of roast beef and apple pie, Jacobs argues that getting those apples and that cow from New England and Chicago onto the kitchen table at a price that most families could afford required as much focused political effort as anything seen in any other country.

At the level of policy, however, Jacobs's work is less convincing. The NRA was not particularly long lasting, and cannot be said to have been a key influence on the development of the consumer economy. The OPA's failure may have been important for closing off one path of development, but this does not explain the direction the country did take. Jacobs convincingly argues that the Wagner Act was propelled by believers in the purchasing power paradigm, but she does not trace the role of the Wagner Act in developing the consumer economy. Labor unions were as strong or stronger in other countries but did not always fight for higher wages and did not create consumer societies; indeed, as we have seen, in Europe labor unions were essential in enforcing wage restraint on the working classes. Simply pointing to policies that strengthen labor does not get us to a consumer society. (On the role of collective bargaining in the purchasing power paradigm in the United States see also Piore and Sabel 1984, 80–82.)

Lizabeth Cohen is more convincing on this score, directing our attention, as other scholars have also done, to the vast change in the American landscape that propelled the focus on consumption (see also Jackson 1985; Massey and Denton 2003). She notes the importance of the Federal Housing Administration (FHA) in particular, which underwrote a mortgage-based consumer economy and helped to catalyze an infrastructure of credit. While Cohen masterfully tracks the social consequence of this policy, however, she is less interested in tracing its causes.

One element that both of these scholars have missed is the role that *agrarian concern for the concentration of wealth* played in forming the American consumer economy. As we will see in the following chapters, congressmen from agrarian states were key to two policies that would prove consequential: the fight for progressive taxation, which constrained the fiscal base of the state and kept taxes on consumption low in comparative perspective, and the resistance to branch banking, which brought the financial sector into crisis and required the creation of a new infrastructure of credit.

Agrarians were not the only ones involved in developing the purchasing power paradigm, and agrarians were not successful in all of their goals; indeed, from the turn of the century to the First World War agrarians were much less active, largely satisfied with the increasing money supply, while urban reformers carried the burden of policy change. But agrarians were particularly influential in these two polices. Drawing on the antimonopoly politics that the first wave of price volatility had bequeathed, farmers developed a specific focus on breaking up concentrations of wealth. It was farmers who carried this into politics because the sectional division of the American state put them in positions of power. But this politics was not simply about breaking up concentrations of capital to allow the free play of market forces: it was state intervention of a different kind. As the growing nation developed its tax structure, politically powerful agrarians ensured that taxes would be collected in a progressive manner, repeatedly defeating the national sales tax for its regressivity. Propelled by their diagnosis of the overproduction problem and empowered by their pivotal role in the political structure, agrarian voices argued that the tax system was a necessary lubricant of the capitalist wheel. They saw progressive taxation as necessary to get money back into the hands of those who needed the results of that American productivity—like Fisher, they thought the problem was not too many goods but too little money in the hands of those who needed the goods and decided to address this problem directly. Second, a series of regulations designed to break up monopolies in the financial sector worsened the financial crisis of the 1930s and prompted the development of an infrastructure of home mortgage financing that was largely intended as a means of propping up demand in the financial sector.

Both of these policies came out of the political actions not of the consumers whom Jacobs and Cohen focus on but rather of agrarians. These policies arose not because of inflation, as Jacobs suggests, but out of episodes of deflation that had catalyzed farmers into political action. And rather than following a script written by their main proponents, both these policies had consequences that were often in direct opposition to what their supporters had intended.

90

One of those unforeseen and unintended consequences is that these two policies helped to undermine the welfare state and helped to develop a credit-financed consumer economy, as traced in Chapters 6 and 9. The American welfare state also did not benefit from the kinds of pacts of wage moderation in return for welfare seen in Europe because those pacts were in service to an overarching goal of economic growth, whereas the overarching concern in the United States was "not . . . producing more goods [but rather] adjusting production to consumption . . . distributing wealth and products more equitably" in Roosevelt's words quoted above (quoted in Kennedy 1999, 373). Instead, high wages became the focus of labor concern as a means of redistributing all that excess wealth. The answer to why the United States has more poverty than the countries of Europe is that the United States for most of the twentieth century adopted a consumption-oriented growth model while other countries emerged with an economic approach that commentators today might call "supply-side" because of its focus on exports and restraint of consumption. American social democracy took the form of a focus on consumption while the European welfare state was a political consequence of that restraint on consumption. These divergent growth models had very different effects on the welfare state and on poverty.

There is nothing uniquely American about the problem of price volatility or the problem of business cycles that result in surplus and declining prices. Indeed, the inspiration for one of Henry Wallace's price support programs, the ever-normal granary, was a Chinese invention, the *chang ping tsang*, dating from the fourth or fifth century B.C., and other such policies have been found independently in other times and places (Bodde 1946). Business cycles and agrarian surplus are normal episodes in history, as is government intervention to support prices. Abbott (2012) has even argued that problems of abundance are so common that the concept of abundance should be the normal lens through which to examine social life rather than the concept of scarcity. Contra Koestler's assumptions, European countries also experimented with crop destruction programs at this time, as for example, wine in France (Sheingate 2001).

There are two important ways, however, in which the European response at this time was different from the American response. First, at this particular moment, for Europe the agrarian surplus was largely coming from abroad. The European countries were struggling to generate productivity, and for them the problem was how to manage American abundance. The policies that the countries adopted were therefore largely oriented toward addressing this foreign threat, and this was the key focus of agrarian politics. In France and Germany the two world wars seemed to have destroyed capitalism. No European country was doing as well in productivity or wealth as the United States. In France, for example, at the end of the First World War "many fields were in ruin, and more than 10 percent of the active agricultural population was dead" (Sheingate 2001, 91). At the end of the Second World War "there were no more trains. Canals, river ways, and ports were unusable. Electric lines were cut. Three thousand ports had been blown up. Of every ten motor vehicles, nine could no longer run and the tenth was out of fuel" (quoted in Eichengreen 1995, 18). The wars had exacerbated the economic troubles of Europe compared to the United States. The second difference is that when European farmers were pressed to the wall, they could emigrate to the United States. Agrarian sectors in other countries had an escape valve that was lacking in the United States after the end of the major movement of westward expansion. These differences channeled agrarian politics in European countries down different lines, ultimately allowing the emergence of very different growth models in the different countries.

We can conceptualize these differences between the countries as different orientations towards consumption. One of the intellectual legacies of neoliberalism has been heightened attention to the social structures necessary for the provision of goods and services, such as the sources of innovation, the conditions conducive to entrepreneurship, and the forging of mass production. We see this in the flowering of the varieties of capitalism literature, which asks: what does it take for firms and producer groups to be able to create and maintain supply, and what historical traditions have led to public policies that enable firms and producer groups to do so? But another important question that has been relatively neglected recently concerns the "demand side" of the economy—the question of how public policies and historical traditions have generated and structured widespread consumption. One consequence of industrialization was the inability of individuals and households to survive outside of the market. As the citizens of developing countries were increasingly brought into dependence on the market, the question arose of what to do about those who did not have the ability to provide for their own consumption.

It is important to be clear here that I am not asking whether it is necessary for the government to stimulate or manage demand. This endlessly debated question has obscured the equally important point that, whether or not it is necessary for governments to manage demand, they have historically done so. Governments manage demand by collecting taxes, providing subsidies, setting interest rates, and passing legislation to ease or restrict the availability of credit—monetary and fiscal policies—and these policy tools have macroeconomic consequences.

Consumption has, of course, been extensively studied across the social sciences, but by and large studies of consumers and consumption examine one society at a time and implicitly or explicitly treat consumption and the structuring of consumption as a feature of the transition to modernity that is common across countries (e.g., Aglietta 2000, 23; Appadurai 1996; Cohen 2003; Slater 1997). Even studies that take a comparative approach (e.g., Kuisel 1993; De Grazia 2005) have missed the growing importance of institutional innovations that fostered consumption in the United States in the postwar period compared to institutions that restrained consumption in European countries. Only very recently, spurred by the financial crisis, have comparative historians begun to explore the differences in consumption and particularly in credit-financed consumption across countries (e.g., Logemann 2007, 2008, 2012; Trumbull 2010a, 2010b, 2012; Garon 2012; and see the contributors to the "Cultures of Credit" conference, Logemann 2010). The picture emerging from this research is of a history of restrained consumption and restrained consumer credit in Europe over the postwar period, counterposed to a history of increasing consumption and increasing credit-financed consumption in the United States.

A theory of comparative political economy that begins from these observations—a demand-side theory of comparative political economy—makes better sense of empirical differences between the United States and Europe. As we will explore in more detail in the next chapters, because of the United States's much higher growth rates, demand management became an issue in the United States more so than in Europe. While European countries focused on top-down efforts at reconstructing their economies by focusing on production and restraining consumption, the United States pioneered a form of "mortgage Keynesianism" in which mortgage finance was a primary mechanism for sustaining economic growth. These developments in turn yielded a political economy that undermined the public welfare state and established dependence on the development of credit-financed private consumption for economic growth, in contrast to the production-oriented economies of Europe.

To summarize, I argue in this book that comparative differences in political economy are best explained as the development of different approaches to demand management that arose during the interwar period and the Great Depression. In the continental European states, the problem was to regenerate capitalism where it seemed to have been destroyed. In the United States, however, the problem was taming a capitalism that was so successful that it seemed to produce poverty as a consequence of too much wealth. These different problems emerged from the different role that these countries played in the imperial project as settled colonies or as colonizers. Responding to these different problems, the countries established different traditions of monetary and fiscal policy that have been stable over decades and have influenced the development of other areas of political economy, including the welfare state. The United States attempted to foster demand by regulating the market and expanding the availability of credit, while European countries focused on encouraging supply and restraining consumption. Building on Elizabeth Sanders's (1999) demonstration of the importance of agrarian statism in the United States, I show that the unusual productivity and disproportionate political power of American farmers during this period had crucial effects on political economy that resound to this day.

This argument implies that although every single one of the theories of comparative political economy discussed in Chapter 2 places the United States at the "minimal state" end of the continuum, in fact no successful capitalist country has had a minimal state, and even the United States boasts a remarkable degree of state intervention against the market (on this point, see Chang 2007; Reinert 2007). Of course, we cannot draw any conclusions from this about whether or not state intervention is economically necessary—these countries might have grown even more, or grown faster, if there had been less state intervention. But it remains true that, at least to date, capitalism has everywhere been accompanied by massive state intervention. The mystery of the absence of correlation between state intervention and economic growth that Iversen and Soskice point to is no mystery at all. There is no correlation because there is no variation on the independent variable. The states the varieties of capitalism scholars call "liberal" are heavily interventionist in other ways. As Karl Polanyi ([1944] 2001) suspected on the eve of the postwar capitalist miracle, the social dislocations caused by capitalism led everywhere to state action to encourage growth and overcome resistance to growth. Even if state intervention is not economically necessary or is even economically harmful, it does seem to be ubiquitous.

The remainder of this book investigates the two policies that resulted from this process that are particularly relevant for political economy today.

Chapters 4 to 6 explore American taxation and its consequences for the welfare state. Chapters 7 to 9 examine the peculiar American credit-based economy and its consequences. The main narrative in each set of chapters is that American farmers and their representatives in Congress implemented in the interwar period a form of state intervention that was unique in the western world; and this intervention had unexpected consequences in the postwar era that undermined the American welfare state, preventing the elaboration of European-style political economy and setting the United States on a path of mortgage Keynesianism. However, the function of the two sets of chapters for the development of the argument in this book is slightly different. Chapters 4 to 6 conduct an in-depth historical examination based on archival sources to pin down how American actors linked the issue of overproduction to the solution of a particular kind of progressive intervention. In Chapters 7 through 9 the focus is broader and more explicitly comparative, aiming to show how and why the United States departed from other countries in developing its peculiar regulatory apparatus and its focus on credit-driven consumption. This is not a systematic comparative historical analysis, as I do not examine other cases in detail; rather, this work aims only to place the American experience in comparative perspective, drawing on the histories of other countries only where they are useful for shedding light on American developments. Chapter 10 draws policy lessons from this history.

PART TWO

THE AGRARIAN
REGULATION OF TAXATION

Perhaps the most surprising of the areas of greater state intervention toured in Chapter 1 is the issue of tax progressivity. Sven Steinmo (1989, 1993) first brought to widespread attention the possibility that American taxation may be more progressive than taxation in other advanced countries. In the last decades several additional studies have confirmed that welfare states seem to be smallest where the tax structure is the most progressive, even controlling for the effects of inequality on tax progressivity (Mendoza, Razin, and Tesar 1994; Cusack and Beramendi 2006; Lindert 2004; Prasad and Deng 2009) Moreover, the United States seems to be a particular outlier in having a progressive tax system. Tax progressivity is difficult to calculate, and conclusions about comparative progressivity must remain tentative. Nevertheless, there are three reasons for believing that the American tax structure is unusually progressive. First, the United States is the only advanced industrial country without a national sales tax. While the American states do impose sales taxes, partly because of competition between the states these are levied at much lower levels than national sales taxes in Europe, so that the total American sales tax burden, including state and local sales taxes, adds up to less than one half of the sales tax burden in most other countries (Mendoza, Razin, and Tesar 1994; Carey and Rabesona 2004; Kato 2003; Hines 2007). Sales taxes are generally thought to be regressive, because lower-income households spend much more of their income on consumption, and sales taxes do not take the taxpayer's economic situation into account. Some scholars argue that if seen on a lifetime basis sales taxes are not regressive, but Graetz (2005, 248–250) argues that a lifetime perspective is inappropriate given fluctuations in tax rates, and the politics of sales taxation does seem to proceed on the assumption of regressivity, as we will see below. Some argue that exemptions for necessities and higher rates on luxuries lessen the regressivity of the sales tax, but Beramendi and Rueda draw on OECD figures to argue that "the vast majority of the taxation on goods and services in industrialized democracies is concentrated on products that are consumed by the general population. Hence, taxes on consumption can be taken to be essentially regressive across OECD countries" (2007, 621–622). The second reason for thinking that the American tax structure is unusually progressive is that before the neoliberal policies of the 1980s the American income tax seems to have been more progressive than income tax in other countries, although whether and how this has changed in recent years is less clear (Piketty and Saez 2007; Prasad and Deng 2009). As Thomas Piketty notes, "very high taxes on the very rich—that was invented in the United States" (quoted in Lowrey 2012). Third, at least until the 1980s and maybe even after that date, taxes on capital were heavier in the United States, while taxes on labor were heavier in the countries of Europe (Carey and Rabesona 2004; Lindert 2004; Sørensen 2004; Cusack and Beramendi 2006).

Chapters 4, 5, and 6 explore these three different facets of the American tax state. This chapter asks: why is there no national sales tax in the United States? I argue that at the moment when national sales tax was most likely, first farmers, and then the Democratic base more generally, rejected it for its regressivity.

Why No National Sales Tax?

A general sales tax or consumption tax is a tax levied at the point of purchase on all items of sale. A value added tax (VAT) is a specific kind of sales tax, imposed only on the value that has been added to the product at each stage of production; in practice, each buyer in the supply chain gains back taxes paid when she sells on the product, making the final consumer bear the whole tax. France was the first country to adopt a partial value added tax in 1954, which was expanded in 1968. Between 1964 and 1973 the countries of the EU adopted VAT as a condition of membership. Between 1986 and 1991 several other countries adopted it, some of them in an effort to make the tax structure less progressive (part of a general neoliberal attempt to increase the ease of capital accumulation). Switzerland adopted it in 1995, and Austria adopted it in 2000, making the United States the only advanced industrial country without a national VAT (Kato 2003; Lindert 2004).

The theories discussed in Chapter 2 give unsatisfactory answers to the question of why the United States resists a national sales tax. For example, the class-based approach would predict a class divide in support for national sales tax, and indeed, as we will see below, labor opposed sales taxes for their regressivity, while employers tended to support them. But this would lead to a prediction of an unusually strong labor movement in the United States, which has been able to successfully impose its preferences on national sales tax. This would seem to be at odds with the class-based argument that the United States has an underdeveloped welfare state because of the *weakness* of labor. The varieties of capitalism approach would suggest that to explain the absence of the national sales tax we should examine the role and preferences of employers. But employers were consistently in favor of national sales taxation in the United States—as will be shown below—and were consistently defeated.

Cultural explanations are equally unsatisfying as they predict the opposite of what we find in this case. For example, Marion Fourcade considers the United States "an economist's economy," one where "the language of economics carries greatest social authority both in the wider public sphere and in specific institutional settings such as corporations, courts, public policy" (2009, 254). But in fact economists favor sales taxes, because sales taxes penalize work and income less than income and capital taxes do and therefore create less distortion in a free-market economy (see, e.g., Hines 2007; Lindert 2004, 235–245; Summers 1981; Lucas 1990; and the discussion in Chapter 6). In this case, it is the European countries that are closer to the teachings of economics while the United States flouts those teachings. More generally, explanations that point to national culture are unconvincing because while sales taxes have failed at the national level, they have been prevalent at the state and local level in the United States.

Could those state and local sales taxes have undermined the push for a national sales tax? Perhaps state governments, jealous of the revenue raising capacity of sales taxes, wanted them reserved to the states. But state and local sales taxes largely came *after* the failure of national sales tax proposals. The major defeats of the national sales tax occurred in 1921 and 1932, and it was not until 1932 that the first state sales tax was implemented in Mississippi (Portney 1980, 89—although Michigan had experimented with a short-lived value added tax earlier). Only after it became clear that the national government would not adopt a sales tax did more states begin to adopt them (Haig and Shoup 1934; Hansen 1983). In 1921 the federal government was indeed wary of treading on state revenue sources, such as estate taxation (*Chicago Daily Tribune* 1921j), but sales taxes had not yet been established as the prerogative of the states. In later years some (including Franklin Roosevelt on the eve of his Presidency) argued sales taxes should be reserved for the states, and this theme was strongest in 1932; but as we will see, others thought the preliminary experience with sales tax in the states showed it could be adopted at a national level. The existence of state sales taxes cannot, by itself, explain why the first option was chosen rather than the second.

Historical institutionalist explanations bring more insight but are incomplete on their own. Sven Steinmo's path-breaking comparative study of taxation (1989, 1993) argued that the veto points of the American political system allowed opposition to sales tax to carry the day. But if the fragmented polity is a central factor when explaining the absence of a national sales tax, how do we explain the presence of the unusually progressive taxes on income and capital that Steinmo also identifies as characteristic of the American tax system? It seems the defenders of capital should have been able to veto these taxes. The veto-points explanation needs to be combined with attention to other factors, as Steinmo himself notes in the last chapter of his work.

Junko Kato (2003) argues that regressive taxes are more efficient at raising revenue than progressive taxes and that new taxes generate more opposition than raising rates on old taxes; consequently, after the economic crisis of the 1970s, states that had not yet adopted efficient, regressive mechanisms of revenue generation were unable to introduce such options and thus were unable to maintain welfare state spending. Kato focuses on the value added tax, and her analysis (discussed further in Chapter 6) is helpful in explaining the different politics of the value added tax before and after the economic crisis. But the VAT in most countries simply served to rationalize the administration of a tax structure already marked by other kinds of national sales taxes. By 1954, when the VAT was first introduced in France, a national sales tax had already been in place in Germany (since 1918), Canada (1920), France itself (1920), Belgium (1921), Luxembourg (1922), Austria (1922/1923), Italy (1923), Australia (1930), the Netherlands (1933), Norway (1933), Finland (1941), and Switzerland (1941). Other countries had experimented with a national sales tax, and the United Kingdom had instituted a "purchase tax" that, while only applied to select goods, constituted a substantial amount of revenue (Due 1955a, b; Williamson 1921; Buehler 1932; Hindman 2010). Because VAT is a rationalization of taxes that were already in place, in focusing on value added tax Kato's analysis is less helpful for clarifying the historical dynamics that led to a national sales tax in some places but prevented it in others.

Steffen Ganghof, in a critique of Kato's work, argues that regressive taxation is chosen precisely because policymakers anticipate that it will allow the state to grow: "The basic differences between taxes [in terms of their revenue-raising capacities] have long been known and taken into account" (2006, 365). Indeed, European policymakers seem to have suspected these differences for centuries.[1] But it is implausible to ascribe these motives in the case examined here because, as we will see below, manufacturers and their political defenders were the most strident supporters of sales tax throughout the twentieth century. If Ganghof's critique of Kato were correct in this instance, we would have to believe that capitalists and Republicans wanted the state to expand and supported sales taxes for that reason. It is not clear exactly what American policymakers believed about the revenue raising capacities of sales taxes at this time, as this was not a main feature of the debate, which turned instead on the issue of progressivity and regressivity.

Beramendi and Rueda (2007) have argued that indirect taxation is a function of corporatism; having offered redistribution to labor and low taxes on capital to capital, governments in corporatist settings have no choice but to turn to indirect taxes, whereas in noncorporatist settings Beramendi and Rueda predict that indirect taxation is an outcome of partisanship. But using their own definitions of the relevant variables and their own data source, the United States is the country with the least left-wing partisanship (see their table 1), so their argument is unable to explain U.S. resistance to a national sales tax. Moreover, their thesis predicts that tax decisions will be made after, or concurrently with, decisions on welfare state spending. While this is the case for payroll taxes, it is not the case for sales taxes: American resistance to sales taxation—and European embrace of sales taxation—precedes the major development of the welfare state.

Eccleston (2007) argues that VAT fails because expert opinion, which unanimously agrees on VAT, carries less weight in the American political context than in other countries. This is true, but not all policies on which experts agree fail. For example, the United States adheres to low tariff barriers and other free trade policies that generate expert agreement and populist opposition. If some policies on which experts agree succeed and some policies on which experts agree fail, there is some factor other than expert agreement at work.

In short, there is still something left to explain.

Three Failed Attempts

Although it has not been implemented in the United States, the national sales tax has never been far from political discussion, from the First World

War through the latest presidential campaign.[2] A national sales tax has come up for vote on the floor of Congress three times, in 1921, 1932, and 1985. In 1921, the United States, like many other countries, considered a national sales tax in order to help retire its war debt. Defeated in Congress by a coalition of Democrats and Progressive midwestern Republicans, the issue lay dormant for a decade. The inability to deal adequately with war debt brought it up again in 1932, the second time the issue reached the floor of Congress. It was defeated again, partly because of the same sectional split and partly because, in the interim, state governments had started to claim sales taxes as their rightful revenue source. The national sales tax did not come up for vote on the floor of Congress for the next half century, but there were two occasions in those intervening years when the issue was broached by politicians. The first was during the Second World War, when Congress and the Roosevelt administration tried various ways of making the sales tax work but were ultimately defeated. The reasons for the defeat were the unfamiliarity of the tax and the continued resistance of farmers and labor to the tax's alleged regressivity. The wartime failure meant that the United States would emerge from the war with a tax state based on income taxation (including an efficient mechanism for withholding tax from paychecks that, in one of the ironies of history, was devised by a group that included Milton Friedman; Friedman and Friedman 1998, 122–123). The rapidly rising incomes of the postwar period meant the income tax was capable of generating large amounts of revenue, giving policymakers no reason to look for new revenue sources. Thus, the national sales tax was occasionally discussed but not with any seriousness until 1979. In that year the head of the House Ways and Means Committee, Al Ullman, proposed a value added tax. His defeat in 1980 gave birth to a Beltway legend that his support for a VAT had caused his downfall. The national sales tax came up for vote on the floor of Congress for the last time in 1985 but only as a mechanism for financing the Superfund environmental cleanup. It was defeated because a tax targeted on polluters was seen as less regressive and more distributionally just. Ever since then VAT has remained a perennial talking point but has never moved beyond the stage of discussion.

1921: Reed Smoot v. the Farmer-Labor Bloc

The closest the national sales tax has come to enactment in the United States was in the summer and fall of 1921, when Senator Reed Smoot of Utah backed the measure with his weight as a ranking member of the

Senate Finance Committee. Smoot, a Republican whose name has gone down in conjunction with the Smoot-Hawley tariff, was known for supporting manufacturing interests. The discussions that eventually resulted in the Revenue Act of 1921 were primarily concerned with the need to raise revenue to retire the debt from World War I. At the beginning of the episode, public opinion was thought to favor the sales tax (*The New York Times*, 1921b). President Harding supported it, and business organizations had always favored a national sales tax. But farmers' publications complained, "At present, the income tax and the excess profits tax are not bothering farmers to any extent, but with a sales tax they would all have to pay" (*Indiana Farmer's Guide* 1921), and the American Federation of Labor opposed the tax because it would "shift the burden of taxation from capital to labor" (*The New York Times* 1921e) and because "[t]he cost of government should rest more heavily upon those who receive the greatest benefits, upon accumulated wealth, upon accumulated earnings. . . . The sales tax is in contradiction to this theory because in operation it would collect from the poor and the unfortunate" (*The New York Times* 1931a; but see also *The New York Times* 1921k).

In general, manufacturers' groups and business groups (including chambers of commerce) testified in favor while labor and farmers' groups, as well as some public utilities, testified against. The groups that testified in favor were the Tax League of America, Music Industries Chamber of Commerce, Boston Chamber of Commerce, Philadelphia Trades Council, Manufacturers' Club of Philadelphia, National Association of Real Estate Boards, National Association of Manufacturers, National Retail Dry Goods Association, National Association of Retail Clothiers, National Retail Shoe Dealers' Association, National Garment Retailers' Association, National Automobile Chamber of Commerce, New York Board of Trade, National Automobile Dealers' Association, and the fur industry. Groups that testified in opposition were the American Farm Bureau Federation, National Association of Credit Men, National Electric Light Association, American Gas Association, American Electric Railway Association, National Industrial Conference Board, National Grange, Farmers' National Council, People's Reconstruction League, Farmer-Labor Party, National Association of Retail Grocers, American Federation of Labor, American Mining Congress, National Lumber Manufacturers' Association, and representatives of public utilities. (*Chicago Daily Tribune* 1921a; *Chicago Daily Tribune* 1921b; *Chicago Daily Tribune* 1921c; *Chicago Daily Tribune* 1921d; *Chicago Daily Tribune* 1921e;

Chicago Daily Tribune 1921h; *Los Angeles Times* 1921a; *Los Angeles Times* 1921b; *Los Angeles Times* 1921c; *The New York Times* 1921d; *The New York Times* 1921f.; *Wall Street Journal* 1921).

Several experts, including E. R. Seligman and T. S. Adams, the leading tax experts of the time, testified strongly against the tax, arguing that countries that had adopted it had done so out of desperation rather than "sound principles" and that in fact, sales taxes were passed on to the consumer more than the excess profits tax. Their arguments in favor of retaining the excess profits tax rather than implementing a sales tax was said to have "deeply impressed" the senators, and the hearings closed without generating "as much sentiment for a sales tax among members of the committee as expected" (*Chicago Daily Tribune* 1921f; *Chicago Daily Tribune* 1921g, *The New York Times* 1921c; *The New York Times* 1921g). The bill that eventually emerged from the House did not include sales tax.

Unsatisfied with this outcome, in late August Smoot offered a completely new bill with a 3% manufacturers' sales tax as the single largest source of revenue (*The New York Times* 1921i). This proposal took a dizzying number of turns between August and November. First the number shrank to 1%, then the proposal seemed to die when at a late night conference on October 5, a group of Progressive Republicans came out against any movement toward a sales tax: "Last night, just before midnight, the agricultural bloc of Senators took action at the home of Senator Capper which practically insures the passage of the pending tax bill and the defeat of the substitute sales tax bill proposed by Senator Smoot. The conference was attended by most of the Senators from the Middle and Far West, and by Senator Lodge, Republican leader of the Senate. . . . Senator McNary of Oregon explained that the proposed sales tax would work a great hardship on the agricultural producers, and all support for this measure then was withdrawn by the Senators attending the conference" (*Los Angeles Times* 1921d).

But Smoot and other proponents managed to bring the sales tax to a vote in early November, three times, only to see it defeated on all three occasions despite some speculation that it might be coupled with a soldiers' bonus (*Chicago Daily Tribune* 1921i; *Chicago Daily Tribune* 1921k; *Chicago Daily Tribune* 1921l; *Los Angeles Times* 1921e). The first vote, on November 3, was for a 1% tax. The second, on November 4, was for a 1/2% tax, and when this failed a last ditch effort was made to reinstate the 3% manufacturers' tax. The third vote is not recorded, but the patterns of votes on November 3 (for a 1% tax) and November 4 (for a 1/2% tax) were similar: all the Democrats voted against the sales tax in both cases, and most of the Republicans from the Northeast voted in favor in both cases. But the midwestern Republicans were split, with enough of them voting against the sales tax to kill the measure. (*The New York Times* 1921l; *The New York Times* 1921m; *The New York Times* 1921n).

Closer analysis of the Republican votes shows that midwestern Republicans in particular were driving the Republican results (Table 4.1). The table shows only Republicans because all Democrats voted against the sales tax. While northeastern, southern, and western Republicans voted in favor of sales tax, the majority of midwestern Republicans voted against. If 9 of the 12 midwestern Republicans who voted against sales tax on November 3—or 11 of the 13 voting against on November 4— had, instead, voted with their party, the result of the vote would have been reversed. The table shows a statistically significant association between region and voting behavior.

A few months later an effort was made, supported by President Harding, to pass a sales tax to pay for a bonus for veterans of the First World War, but this never made it out of a Ways and Means subcommittee, whose members "had become convinced that the farm-labor bloc had sufficient votes in combination with the Democrats to prevent" such a bill (*The New York Times* 1922). This ended the 1921 episode.

Why were these midwestern farmer-labor politicians so firmly against sales tax? Why, for that matter, were the Democrats united against it? We will explore reasons for support of progressive taxation in more detail in

Table 4.1. Regional voting on sales tax in Congress, November 3 and 4, 1921, Republicans only

	November 3, 1921				November 4, 1921			
	Northeast	South	Midwest	West	Northeast	South	Midwest	West
Yes	6	3	5	11	7	3	5	10
No	1	1	12	3	3	1	13	4
Fisher's exact		.012*				.036*		

Source: Votes from *Congressional Record* 1921, 7254–7255, 7298.
Notes: Definition of regions in all tables from U.S. Census Bureau.
Fisher's exact test of independence between region and voting.
* $p < .05$, ** $p < .01$, *** $p < .001$

Chapter 5, but one suggestion in the scholarship is that sectional cleavages of this nature reflect the different economic interests of the respective states (Bensel 1984; Sanders 1999). Although there were large industrial corporations in some midwestern cities and states, the midwestern states were still disproportionately agricultural at this time. Indeed, the congressmen from these states sometimes called themselves, and were called by others, the "Farm Bloc" (e.g., O'Brien 1973). In the sales tax episode, complaints abounded of "the terrorism of the 'Ken-Cap-Clan' of the agricultural bloc, led by Senators KENYON [of Iowa] and CAPPER [of Kansas] under the banner with the legend 'Soak the Rich'" (*The New York Times* 1921j). The agrarian/industrial cleavage between the states mapped onto the geographically fragmented structure of the American government, as the labor/capital cleavage did not.

Agrarian states would have been particularly vulnerable to the plunge in grain prices in 1921 shown in Chapter 3, a 10% decline in average prices that remains the worst price deflation in American history (Vernon 1991). As discussed in that chapter, farming as an industry was heavily reliant on credit in the 1920s, with land, labor, and supplies borrowed against the eventual sale of the crop. When the price deflation hit this credit-heavy structure, it wiped out many farmers, spawning a wave of farm foreclosures that was the highest the nation had yet seen (although it would be dwarfed by the number of foreclosures in the next decade [Alston 1983]).

This period of agricultural distress had many consequences. As Hoffman and Libecap (1991) explain, the farmers and their representatives in government first attempted to establish agricultural cooperatives that would keep products off the market in order to raise prices (405). When that did not work, they turned to politics. The early 1920s are characterized by the rise of the Farm Bloc, an aggressive and successful coalition in Congress (Hansen 1991, 31–37). As Arthur Link notes: "By maintaining a common front from 1921 to 1924 [the Bloc] succeeded in enacting the most advanced agricultural legislation to that date, legislation that completed the program begun under Wilsonian auspices. It included measures for high tariffs on agricultural products, thoroughgoing federal regulation of stockyards, packing houses, and grain exchanges, the exemption of agricultural cooperatives from the application of the antitrust laws, stimulation of the export of agricultural commodities, and the establishment of an entirely new federal system of intermediate rural credit" (1959, 845).

Link and other historians have not noticed that resistance to the national sales tax also belongs on this list. Farmers were particularly united against sales tax because the geographic division of the economy meant that farmers were largely exempt from paying income tax, which fell mostly on the wealthy northeast, whereas sales tax would have raised the cost of farm implements and supplies and lowered the quantity of products farmers could sell (Murnane 2004). Moreover, the greater revenue potential of sales taxes that we will consider in Chapter 6 was not a predominant theme and may not even have been understood. The choice as farmers saw it was *not* between a large amount of taxes raised regressively (and perhaps spent progressively) versus a smaller amount of taxes raised progressively. Rather, the question as they saw it was who should bear the burden of taxes, the rich or the poor. The farmers and their representatives were quite clear about their answer to this question.

Although economic factors may have been paramount, the fact that it was midwestern *Republicans* who were the key constituency should warn us away from a strictly economic determinist interpretation, for the development of party structures is also a crucial factor in how the events played out. Democrats everywhere were opposed to the sales tax; but the ability of the Republican Party in the Midwest to send agrarian Republicans to Congress played into the sales tax issue by weakening Republican Party cohesion at a crucial moment. As the *New York Times* noted, explaining why midwestern Republicans would be willing to break party lines, "With many of the Congressmen from the agricultural sections of the West . . . the political rule of 'safety first' applies. They conceive that the sales tax will be made unpopular among their constituents by the Democratic contention that it is a consumption tax which will be burdensome on those whom Mr. Bryan called the common people. They also conceive that the electorate in their sections may be led to believe that the repeal of the excess profits tax [which passage of the sales tax would have allowed] will be in the interest of great corporations in the principal industrial States, none of which is West of the Mississippi" (1921h).

1932: John Nance Garner and the Rise of the States

The sales tax came to the floor of Congress for a second time in 1932. By 1931 the United States like many other countries was still managing the debt caused by the costs of the First World War and the Depression. Blakey and Blakey (1932) suggest that the tax cuts of the 1920s had worsened the situation, particularly given the new demands on revenue from new spending commitments at local and state as well as at federal levels. The situation was so grave that the deficit increased substantially over the months that Congress discussed what to do about it. Mellon and the Treasury preferred to meet the budget shortfall with a series of excise taxes on particular goods, but the automobile industry, which would have been particularly hard hit, convinced the House that sales taxes on specific products were not the best way to raise revenue (Blakey and Blakey 1932). Instead, the House debated a manufacturers' excise tax of 2.25% influenced by a similar Canadian tax (Schwarz 1964, 166). When debate began, opposition to this tax was intense, if scattered. Blakey and Blakey write, "The opposition was led by the representatives of labor and agriculture who contended that sales taxes are passed on to consumers generally instead of falling principally upon those most able to pay taxes" (630). As the days passed, the opposition coalesced and organized, with Fiorello LaGuardia of New York leading the Republican rebels and Robert Doughton of North Carolina leading a band of fifty rebel Democrats (Schwarz, 167). On March 24, the rebels won a preliminary skirmish (Schwarz, 167), and on April 1 the House again rejected a proposal for a 2.25% sales tax, 236 to 160 (170). Schwarz writes of the sales tax proposal: "Every national political leader, from the President to the leaders of the parties in both houses of Congress, had pleaded for its adoption. Most of the prominent journals of the nation considered it necessary for the nation's welfare. Yet when La Guardia and Doughton sought popular approval of their opposition, they found it in abundance" (171–172).

The rejection of this tax—which had been the central element of the leaders' plan to meet the deficit—ended the House's role in the revenue act. In the Senate, Democrat David I. Walsh of Massachusetts and Republican David A. Reed of Pennsylvania were the strongest supporters of the national sales tax. Reed proposed in the Senate Finance Committee to reinstate the sales tax, but the committee voted against it, 12 to 8 (Schwarz, 178). On May 30, a group of 35 Democratic Senators presented a petition with this statement: "In order to expedite the passage of a revenue bill to balance the budget and to prevent unnecessary prolongation of debate thereon, the undersigned now declare that they will at this time vote against every form of general sales tax on the pending bill" (cited in Blakey and Blakey 1932, 635) while the Republicans presented a statement from 20 Senators (19 Republicans and one Farmer-Labor) to the same effect. Meanwhile, Franklin Roosevelt signaled his opposition—in part because he preferred reserving the sales tax for the states—and even when President Hoover himself came to the Senate during the lame duck session later in the year to speak in favor of sales tax, the Senate did not budge (Schwarz 1964, 179).[3] Walsh proposed an amendment for a 1.75% sales tax, which was defeated in a 53 to 27 floor vote. The sales tax would not come to the floor of Congress for another half century.

A sectional split was again evident in this episode, but this time the strongest trend pits the northeastern votes against the rest. Table 4.2 shows the April vote in the House, the signing of the petition and the May vote in the Senate. In each of the votes there is a statistically significant association between region and voting, and in the signing of the petition there is a statistically significant association between region and signing. The Northeast emerged as the strongest supporter of sales tax, and the other three regions were, to varying degrees, ambivalent or opposed. Even northeastern Democrats began to support sales tax at this time, and midwestern Republicans in the House were more ambivalent than in the 1921 episode. But as in the 1921 episode, the opposition was concentrated outside of the manufacturing Northeast. In 1932 this opposition extended beyond the Midwest for Republicans, while southern Democrats remained in opposition, unlike the northeastern members of their Party.

Congress did not seek testimony on the specific issue of sales tax, so it is not possible to establish the support or opposition of interest groups as expressed systematically to Congress. However, a few witnesses did spontaneously express their views on sales tax during hearings on the general tax bill, and other groups expressed their views to the press or conducted campaigns on the issue. Favoring the sales tax were the Cleveland Chamber of Commerce, National Manufacturers' Association, Connecticut Manufacturers' Association, Reynolds Candy Company, and a large contingent from the automotive industry and other industries that would otherwise have been hit by excise taxes. In opposition were groups including the American Farm Bureau Federation, National Grange, Farmers' Union, American Federation of Labor, Associated Industries of America, Retail Dry Goods Association, National Association of Retail Druggists, Merchants' Association of New York City, Associated Dress Industries, United Women Wear's League, United Infants' and Children's Wear League, and Industrial Council of Cloak, Suit, and Skirt Manufacturers (*Wall Street Journal* 1932a; *Wall Street Journal* 1932b; *Washington Post* 1932; *Fleming* 1932b; *The New York Times* 1932a; *The New York Times* 1932b; *The New York Times* 1932c). A new pattern is visible in

111

Table 4.2. Regional preferences for sales tax in Congress, 1932

	Republicans				Democrats			
	Northeast	South	Midwest	West	Northeast	South	Midwest	West
April 1, 1932 vote, House								
Yes (reject tax)	15	8	46	14	10	100	40	3
No	55	3	41	11	27	15	4	4
Fishers' exact		0.000***				0.000***		
Petition, 1932								
Signed (reject tax)	0	1	10	8	0	22	5	9
Did not sign	14	3	8	4	4	6	1	1
Fisher's exact		0.000***				0.007**		
May 31, 1932 vote, Senate								
Yes (support tax)	13	2	3	2	4	2	1	0
No	0	1	11	8	0	19	5	9
Fisher's exact		0.000***				0.001**		

Source: Votes and petition signatories from Congressional Record 1932, 7324, 11563–64, 11664.

Notes: Fisher's exact test of independence between region and voting behavior. In the April 1, 1932, a "yes" vote is a vote to reject the national sales tax. In 1932, signing the petition indicates rejection of the national sales tax. In the May 31, 1932, vote a "yes" vote is a vote to support the national sales tax

* p<.05, ** p<.01, *** p<.001

that representatives of retailers have come out in opposition, but the lines of support from general business and manufacturers' groups, and opposition from farmers and labor, remains as in 1921.

However, the real fight on the issue was waged not by interest groups, but within Congress. During the debate in the House, "[a]ttacks on the bill—especially on the sales tax feature—came almost uniformly from Democrats with rural constituencies. . . . The popular cry was that the sales tax, backbone of the proposed budget-balancing program, was but a policy of 'soaking the poor'" (Fleming 1932a). As in 1921, the economic crisis that generated the need for revenue in the first place had extremely dire consequences for farmers, with foreclosure rates immortalized in Depression-era literature. Once again the crisis called a political coalition around agricultural interests into being, which, while not particularly successful on other agrarian issues (O'Brien 1973), was central to the rejection of sales tax. (LaGuardia himself was in fact the only member of the New York delegation to oppose the bill in the House [*Baltimore Sun* 1932].)

This time the crisis hit cotton and tobacco as well, and so the various leaders of the opposition were as likely to come from the farm states of North Carolina and Louisiana as from Kansas (Blakey and Blakey 1932; *The New York Times* 1931d; *Washington Post* 1931; Snyder 1984; O'Brien 1973). In the Senate, two months after being sworn into office, Louisiana's Huey Long—whom we will examine more carefully in Chapter 5—was denouncing taxes on "the people," that is, sales taxes: "There is not going to be any knocking at their doors by visitors bringing glad tidings, but when the knock is heard at the door and the humble citizen rises from the table to meet the visitor for whom he has been waiting for so many years, instead of a visitor bringing the necessary and needed help for the distressful conditions of this country he finds the tax gatherer coming to levy a tax of 2 1/4 per cent on everything he buys" (*Congressional Record* 1932b, 6542).

In this episode, the issue of reserving sales taxes for the states also began to be voiced. But only Mississippi had actually begun to implement a sales tax at this point, and the outlook for this tax was not at all clear, as it was the subject of ongoing protest within the state (*New York Times* 1932d). While Schwarz (1964) interprets the 1932 sales tax episode as a victory for the states, the concern for consumer purchasing power and regressivity voiced by agrarian congressmen helped to *determine* the states' victory in the domain of sales tax.

1942: Morgenthau's Morning Glory

The exigencies of wartime financing kept the sales tax on the agenda throughout the Second World War. In addition to wartime revenue needs, some political elites worried about inflation (a major concern at the time, given the recent experience of hyperinflation and its consequences in Weimar Germany) and thought that adopting a sales tax would remove purchasing power from the public—a concern European policymakers shared. But whereas in European countries this concern prevailed, in the United States it did not.

One episode during the war years that clarifies the dynamics behind the repeated failure of sales tax is Treasury Secretary Henry Morgenthau's proposal for a progressive national sales tax as part of the Revenue Act of 1942. As the act was making its way through Congress it became clear that the budget would be in shortfall (Blakey and Blakey 1942). The Treasury proposed a "graduated spendings tax," a tax on spending to be levied at progressive rates. The Finance Committee rejected this plan on the day it was proposed; the Committee then went on to propose a new wage tax, the "Victory Tax," which brought the total revenue projections to $9.6 billion (Barkley, 1942). Not all of these provisions survived the legislative process, but the tax remains the largest in American history to date. The main feature of the act was the lowering of exemption levels on income tax—in other words, the extension of income tax onto lower income groups. The Victory Tax also introduced collection at the source. This technique developed, the following year, into the introduction of withholding, the most momentous change in the administration of tax collection, probably responsible for allowing the American state to rely on income tax rather than on sales tax. It "entered the tax tent by the camel's nose method in the form of the 'Victory' tax" (Blakey and Blakey 1942, 1081; see also Zelenak 2010a).

Thus, the failure of Morgenthau's graduated spendings tax is a key episode in the failure of the national sales tax. Had it survived and become part of the Revenue Act of 1942, it would have been established as part of the keystone of the American tax state.

Morgenthau's proposal was a hybrid of two parts: a temporary flat-rate 10% sales tax to raise $6.2 billion to be refunded after the war, and a nonrefundable $2 billion sales tax levy, which was to be levied at progressive rates (10% to 75%) with exemptions for low incomes. It would have required taxpayers to report their spending each quarter. When it was introduced a poll of the House was said to have found an "over-whelming majority" of members in favor (*Chicago Daily Tribune* 1942b). On September 8, a majority of Finance Committee members were reported to support the sales tax; but on the very next day they unanimously re-jected it—12 to 0—and "[t]he chorus of opposition to the Treasury's spending tax plan among members of the committee was almost without a dissenting note" (Trussell, 1942). Of those who gave an opinion to the press about their reasons for rejecting the plan, seven complained that it was too complicated: "the most complicated and unworkable that has been submitted by tax experts to the Senate Finance Committee in the nine years of my membership. It has all the evils and none of the virtues of a sales tax"; "If it's as confusing to the taxpayer as to the committee I don't think it will be adopted." "The most complicated monstrosity I've seen." "The taxpayers won't understand it." The most positive comment was from Robert LaFollette, who despite opposition to the way the plan would hit lower income levels, said, "I appreciate how the Treasury, in a complex way, is trying to cushion the regressive effects of a sales tax" (MacCormac 1942). The *Chicago Daily Tribune* called it "one of the most decisive and immediate rebuffs ever suffered by the treasury on a tax proposal" (Fisher 1942).

The speed of the events was most surprising. Morgenthau's plan had been prepared carefully for weeks but was rejected in one day. Commen-tators dubbed it "Morgenthau's morning glory," because discussion on it opened and closed on the same morning (Albright 1942b). On Septem-ber 8, the head of the Finance Committee was reporting that a majority of members favored the sales tax; on September 9, it was dismissed with only one (rejected) attempt to make it more progressive. One reporter wrote that it was dismissed "after about five minutes of formal consider-ation" in the Finance Committee (Trussell 1942). It did not receive the same sustained attention sales tax received in 1921 and 1932, not even coming up for a vote of the full House or Senate.

Public opinion in the early 1940s ran in favor of the tax. In 1943 Gallup would find 53% of respondents favoring sales tax if a tax was going to be necessary, and only 34% favoring income tax (Gallup, 1943; see also Zelenak 2010a). In the spring of 1942 letters on the subject of sales tax to Senator Walter George, the Chairman of the Senate Finance Commit-tee, ran heavily in favor of the sales tax—115 in favor with only 24 op-posed. Royal J. Spettell favored it because "[p]eople wanting things would then pay according to their ability to spend," a point echoed by

Mrs. Vernie Johnson: "A federal sales tax would make the ones pay more that buy more." One writer liked sales tax because it could be collected "without drafting an army of civilian clerks, and a bunch of high salaried loafers." Others noted the tax's capacity to reduce buying power, which was presumed to curb inflation. Several correspondents mentioned that their state or city (Iowa, Mississippi, Indiana, California, Massachusetts, New York City) had a general or specific sales tax that had been working well, while others mentioned observing the general sales tax in operation in Canada and Brazil. Many favored sales tax to the alternative of heavier income taxation: "IF WILD IDEAS AND TAXATION throws the load on the GOOSE THAT LAYS THE EGGS some thing ROTTEN IS GOING TO BE HATCHED." A member of the Ladies' Garment Workers' Union claimed, "[I]n spite of what high union officials say, the rank and file of the union do not oppose a sales tax." And several made a moral argument that even the poor should be asked to contribute to the general defense: "It is *our* Government and should be supported by everybody 'From the gentleman of leisure in his mansion so grand, to the poor groveling wretch on the street.'" "It is a long run dangerous thing to have one-third of the population believing they're not taxed." "Why should not [the whole population] pay the cost of this grand organization if from the unfortunate we were to get but a crumb from the floor?" Eben Adams thanked Senator George for his "manly discussion of the new contemplated Tax Bill."[4]

While letters to Congress do not reflect a cross-section of public opinion, the heavy predominance of letters favoring sales taxes in these files suggests that Congress was aware of what the Gallup poll also revealed, namely, if taxes needed to be raised then general public sentiment was in favor of sales tax.

If public opposition cannot have been the reason for the sales tax's failure, perhaps the reason was simply the tax's complexity. Bank (2002–2003) argues that as soon as policymakers attempt to make the sales tax less regressive by moving away from a flat rate sales tax, the tax becomes too complex to be workable. But this explanation raises a further question. The 1942 tax certainly did fail because the attempt to create a hybrid made the act seem to be too complex. But where did the need to create this hybrid come from? Morgenthau proposed a compromise because a straight sales tax had been projected to fail due to its regressivity. One reason that has been suggested for this is Roosevelt's opposition to taxes that would fall on workers and producers. This is what early observers of the time saw in Roosevelt's tax policies: "Roosevelt's profound devotion to a democratic tax system—taxation according to ability to pay, taxation which will encourage initiative, enterprise and economic freedom, taxation which will discourage monopoly, speculation and tax dodging—stands out as the beacon guiding the President in hewing out tax policy" (Hellerstein 1950).

But as historians later noted, Roosevelt was not averse to all regressive taxes. Thorndike (2009) points out that Roosevelt had supported the highly regressive tax on food that was part of the Agricultural Adjustment Act of 1933. Leff (1983) notes that a major aspect of the New Deal revenue structure, the financing of the Social Security Act of 1935 through payroll taxes, was regressive. It is hard to explain these instances if the Administration was opposed to regressivity on principle. It is not clear why the administration was unwilling to bend the principle of progressivity for this case as it had for other cases. If Roosevelt was mollified by the expected progressivity of Social Security payments or the use of the funds to pay farmers in the Agricultural Adjustment Act, he could likewise have earmarked regressive sales taxes to progressive ends. If he had, Morgenthau would not have needed to complicate the plan to try to reduce the regressivity, bypassing the objections of complexity.

The most systematic study of New Deal taxation is Mark Leff's (1984) argument that taxation policies at this time can be explained by Roosevelt's strategy of passing mildly progressive symbolic policies in order to head off any real attempts at redistribution. In this argument, Roosevelt was afraid of scaring off business and did not want to generate real revenue; he adopted mostly empty symbols of progressive taxation rather than more substantial redistributive policies. But in his resistance to sales tax, Roosevelt was doing the opposite of what business wanted and was doing exactly what his constituents wanted. The defenders of capitalism— manufacturers and their political protectors—were the ones in favor of sales tax, while Roosevelt's supporters opposed the sales tax. At least in this case, Roosevelt sided against the plutocrats.

Examination of the testimony before the House in March and April of 1942 and before the Senate in July and August reveals that the groups that testified in favor of sales tax were the New York Board of Trade, New York State Chamber of Commerce, National Association of Manufacturers, National Retail Dry Goods Association, Brooklyn Chamber of Commerce, American Federation of Investors, Commerce and Industry Association of New York, American Retail Federation, and United States Chamber of Commerce. Testifying against were the United Electrical,

Radio, and Machine Workers, Railway Labor Executives Association, Congress of Industrial Organizations, American Federation of Teachers, Union for Democratic Action, American Federation of Labor, National Negro Council, United Government Employees, League of Women Shoppers, United Automobile Workers, and New York City Consumers' Union. In July and August 1942, during testimony to the Senate Finance Committee on sales tax, the groups in favor were the Atlantic Rayon Corporation, National Retail Dry Goods Association, American Retail Federation, New York State Chamber of Commerce, Chamber of Commerce of the United States, Associated State Chambers of Commerce, National Association of Manufacturers, and Illinois Federation of Retail Associations, while the Congress of Industrial Organizations and American Federation of Labor testified against (though the AFL was willing to accept a tax on luxuries). (Dorris 1942a; Dorris 1942b; *Wall Street Journal* 1942a; *Wall Street Journal* 1942b; *The New York Times* 1942a; *The New York Times* 1942b; *Washington Post* 1942; *Chicago Daily Tribune* 1942a; *Chicago Daily Tribune* 1942c; *Chicago Daily Tribune* 1942d; *Los Angeles Times* 1942; Albright 1942a; Hamilton 1942).

Of course, American labor unions are known to be more pro-capitalist than labor unions in other countries. But if opposing the sales tax is the more pro capitalist position (because sales taxes are the way to raise real tax revenue), then it seems that labor unions are actually more procapitalist than capital. A more likely explanation is that the administration opposed sales taxes because of the clear and demonstrated opposition to it among the Democratic base—whereas other regressive taxes, tied to specific benefits, had not yet engendered coalitions in opposition, the sales tax aroused a visible and vocal resistance from labor, teachers, government employees, and African American groups. The tax did not come up for a vote in either chamber, but it is clear from the testimony that the Democratic base opposed the sales tax in 1942; and that sales tax called forth a well-organized response, a response rooted in a history of resisting sales tax that was already two decades old. This opposition to the tax among Democratic constituents explains Morgenthau's attempt to make the tax less regressive, an attempt that in turn made it too complicated to generate support on the Finance Committee.

More generally, if American progressive taxation is merely symbolic, one may see it as symbolic to the same extent that European welfare states are, as welfare state policies have also substituted for more substantial reform. Certainly at the origins of these two approaches it was not clear which would be the more deep-rooted response to poverty and the inequalities of capitalism. The arguments that progressive taxation was merely symbolic are implicitly comparing the tax system to a socialist or utopian redistribution of resources; but within the range of efforts attempted by other capitalist countries, the weaknesses of progressive taxation as a strategy were not clearly visible at the time, and we should not read our current evaluation of it backwards onto historical actors.

Blakey and Blakey (1942) write, "The Revenue Act of 1942 marks a new high in American finance; in fact, it reaches a new high for any country. According to official estimates . . . in a full year of operation the new law will increase federal tax revenues by . . . about 50 per cent more than would have been received if the existing law had not been changed, and four times as much as the greatest tax measure of World War I" (1069). The final rejection of sales tax from this act ensured that the American state would enter and emerge from the war with a progressive tax structure in place at the national level. The sales tax was briefly proposed again in 1943, and roundly defeated again by the same forces, with even less difficulty (*Chicago Daily Tribune* 1943).

Note that at this point, agrarian groups are no longer a dominant voice on the issue. Having won a decisive victory with the price support programs of the New Deal, agrarian political energies would from this point forward be concentrated on protecting narrow gains and would no longer feed into the creative rethinking that upended American political economy in the first part of the century. As Lipset notes, "The New Deal program, setting a floor under agricultural prices and providing crop insurance and extensive federal government aid programs, gave farmers what they wanted and destroyed the embryonic radicalism" (1950, 17). In tax policy, while agrarian energies were crucial in the 1921 and 1932 episodes, by the Second World War the legacy they bequeathed of progressive taxation was being carried by other groups. Agrarian statism also declined as the share of farmers in the population declined. Their corporate descendants have been very effective at maintaining price supports for agriculture (and in establishing new programs such as food stamps to do so [Finegold 1988]), but they have left behind the broader politics of the early twentieth century. The farmers' legacy was to have introduced a policy around which the Democrats could coordinate a fractious coalition that included labor, consumers, and other groups, and the appeal of this policy continued even as farmers passed from the stage as a political force in history.

119

Postwar Attempts

The national sales tax did not come to the floor of Congress for the next four decades. Congress flirted with a sales tax during the Korean War, and supporters of it argued that it could help to stem inflation, but by this point Robert Doughton—one of the two architects of the rank-and-file rebellion against sales tax in 1932—had graduated to the chair of the Ways and Means Committee. He came out in such staunch opposition that the idea moved no further, and he justified his nickname of "Muley Bob" (*The New York Times* 1951; *Wall Street Journal* 1952). By this time the states were also fully in opposition, having established infrastructures of revenue collection that depended on sales tax (*The New York Times* 1953). Richard Nixon floated a trial balloon 1.5% sales tax first as part of a tax reform that would also cut personal income taxes and corporate taxes, which was immediately shot down by labor (Walker 1958), and then again in the early 1970s as a replacement for property taxes, an effort that ran aground on the states' jurisdiction over property taxes (Martin 2008, 81–82). The surprise of the 1960s and 1970s is how *little* discussion there was of sales tax, with no more than a handful of newspaper mentions from the early 1950s to the late 1970s, and no serious attempts at national sales taxes. But perhaps this should not be surprising, as historians have shown that there was no particular need for new sources of financing in this era, since the state's revenues rose automatically with increasing prosperity (Brownlee 1996).

This changed in the 1970s, when the end of the era of generally rising prosperity led to a search for new revenue sources. In 1979 the chairman of the Ways and Means Committee, Oregon Congressman Al Ullman, championed a value added tax. Despite backing from the chairman of the Senate Finance Committee, the proposal withered on the vine in DC. (Pine 1980a). But back in Oregon it pricked the ears of an ambitious opponent. Unseating Ullman, a twenty-three-year veteran of Congress at the pinnacle of his power, should have seemed unthinkable. He was respected on the Hill, instrumental in important legislation and popular at home, and "responsible for more landslides in this part of the country than Mt. St. Helens" (Neal 1980). Nevertheless his opponent zeroed in on Ullman's VAT effort: "Smith contends the VAT eventually would result in increased taxes for business and individuals—with higher spending levels to boot. . . . He also criticizes the tax as 'regressive' . . . and he echoes complaints that the VAT would be inflationary" (Pine 1980b). He also argued that having "lost touch" with the district explained Ullman's willingness to raise taxes (Pine 1980b).

Ullman rushed back home, dropping in for coffee with constituents, touring local plants, visiting the elderly, courting local reporters, and showering pork on the district (Rattner 1980). And he desperately back-pedaled on the VAT, insisting that he had only been testing the waters, or that it would be a substitute for other taxes and would not raise taxes overall (Pine 1980b). It was too late. Ullman was swept away in the anti-incumbent tide of 1980, dampening congressional willingness to experiment with a VAT in future years.

A value added tax was discussed in the mid-1980s as part of the general rethinking of taxation that the Reagan administration's first-term deficits had incited. Ironically, where Ullman and other supporters of VAT often tried to push it by arguing that it would not raise overall taxes but would merely substitute for inefficient taxes, Donald Regan's Treasury concluded that substitution was not a good enough reason for VAT: "The Treasury Department has concluded that the advantages of a national sales tax are not sufficient to justify this level of expenditure merely to reduce reliance on the income tax." The Treasury report acknowledged that business supported VAT because of its greater efficiency but complained that a new tax would require 20,000 additional tax staff and $700 million in enforcement costs while also being regressive, causing a one-time increase in prices, intruding into a revenue area relied on by local governments, and allowing greater spending (Gerth 1984; Seaberry 1984).

In 1985 a proposal for a VAT to finance hazardous waste cleanup (the "Superfund") cleared the House and Senate Finance Committees and the Senate but was voted down in the House (*Washington Post* 1985). Perhaps because it was tied to a clear spending purpose, this was the closest the VAT would come to approval since 1932. However, the availability of a tax targeted on polluters as an alternative to the VAT makes this episode incomparable to the previous cases or to other contexts in which no single group could be identified as appropriately responsible for the tax burden. Nevertheless, it is striking to note that the legend of Al Ullman was prominently paraded on the floor of Congress as a reason not to vote for this tax: "The question has to be, Are we ready to give birth to a new form of taxation, namely, VAT? Now, if we were to ask that same question to a former Member of this House, a former chairman of the Ways and Means Committee, Mr. Al Ullman, his answer would be 'no,' because if there is one thing that brought his defeat, it was his sponsor-ship of VAT. When he went home to face the electorate, they said with loud voices, 'We don't want VAT.' The question is whether or not this House or whether the American people now want VAT. I say that they do not. I think we ought to consider that before we vote on this matter" (Del Latta, see *Congressional Record* 1885, 35610).

After this episode, value added tax has been perennially discussed but never seriously attempted. Bruce Babbitt proposed a 5% VAT with ex-emptions or credits to lessen regressivity in the 1988 campaign, but he did not make it past the first primaries. The other candidates, including the eventual Democratic nominee, opposed the tax, arguing that it "would soak the middle class," "leave the wealthy laughing all the way to the bank," and was "a Republican idea" (Passell 1988). VAT next turned up during the 1992 campaign, when Democrats proposed a 10% VAT as a means to finance health care (Rich 1992). It received some support from administration officials during the economic summit Clinton held before taking office (Hilzenrath 1992), but the proposal never moved beyond the stage of preliminary discussions. In 1995, several plans to reform the tax code were proposed, including a straight sales tax and the "U.S.A. tax" (for "Unlimited Savings Allowance"), essentially a way to turn the income tax into a sales tax by exempting all savings (Passell 1995). These did no better at gaining political traction, although supporters kept the flame burning throughout the second Clinton administration and into the first administration of George W. Bush. In 2004 Bush himself said the VAT was "kind of an interesting idea that we ought to explore seriously" but later a spokesman clarified: "I don't think he meant a national sales tax per se. I think what he means is a tax reform that might disadvantage sav-ings and investment less" (Andrews 2004). The Obama administration was rumored to be considering a value added tax to finance health care in 2009, but the tax was not mentioned in either of the bills voted out of Congress (see, e.g., Rampell 2009). As of this writing, the most recent proposal for a national sales tax was made by Republican primary con-tender Herman Cain but gained no political traction and collapsed with his campaign. As Lawrence Summers once commented: "'Liberals think it's regressive and conservatives think it's a money machine.' If they re-verse their positions, the VAT may happen" (Rosen 1988; see Zelenak 2010b for some recent discussions of VAT and other national sales taxes).

The United States does not have a national sales tax because from the 1920s to the 1940s—when many other countries adopted it as a means of retiring war debt—the national sales tax was repeatedly defeated by representatives of farmers and labor as well as by other elements of the Democratic base. This coalition defeated the national sales tax because its greater revenue-raising capabilities had not been demonstrated, and the question posed by the national sales tax seemed to them to be a simple question of who would bear the tax burden. More sophisticated analyses of whether sales taxes really are regressive, for example, if viewed on a lifetime basis, were far in the future (see Graetz 2005 and Prasad and Deng 2009 for a criticism of this argument). Because the sales tax seemed to raise prices consumers and workers would pay and lower the quantities that farmers would sell—and because income tax was borne by northeastern manufacturing—midwestern, southern, and western representatives worked to keep the burden of taxes away from their constituents. Although there is a paucity of research on why labor and agrarian groups were unwilling or unable to resist national sales tax in other countries, Morgan and Prasad (2009) examine the case of France and conclude that, although sales taxes were not popular, the opposition to them was muted because the dominant concern of agrarians was protectionism; and because, given the slower pace of industrialization in France, agrarians were not as concerned about issues of progressivity as in the United States. Indeed, rather than concentrations of wealth, French farmers were concerned about the concentration of state power, and they attempted to resist this power by resisting direct methods of taxation.

The choices taken in the 1930s had significant consequences. When faced with drastic new revenue needs during the Second World War, American policymakers fell back on the tax they knew best, creating a tax state based on the template of progressive income taxation (Thorndike 2009). The unusual features of the American tax state were set. While this did not matter during the period of rising economic growth, in the 1970s the unpopularity of progressive taxation in a climate of economic austerity gave birth to a politics of general tax reduction, which made the introduction of new taxes extremely difficult. After the worldwide recession of the 1970s American politicians were unable to implement any new taxes, particularly after the dramatic defeat in 1979 of Ways and Means chair Al Ullman.

There were two reasons the United States never left the path of resistance to sales taxation. First, during the thirty years after the war, politicians did not *need* a new source of revenue. In the era of easy finance (Brownlee 1996) tax coffers were being replenished without effort, obviating the need for a new tax. The increasing prosperity after the war hid the actual increase of taxes in generally rising paychecks. Taxpayers consented to this higher level of taxation both because it was less visible (hidden in those larger paychecks through the mechanism of withholding) and because the returns of those taxes were highly visible in the form of a rapidly developing country. But once this era of prosperity ended, politicians were no longer *able* to introduce new sources of revenue because, in the absence of ever-growing prosperity, citizens began to feel the tax bite and protested. While income and property taxes elicited the most central protests, politicians interpreted these protests as a general antitax sentiment, and the possibility of implementing a "less visible" consumption tax was over. Wartime was the one moment when politicians needed to introduce a new pattern of financing that would generate much higher levels of revenue, *and* taxpayers were willing to finance this revenue. Because of this, the path the countries adopted during the war was fixed for decades afterward. (See Kato 2003 for more on these arguments.)

This chapter shows that by ignoring American Progressivism, the literature on comparative political economy has missed a key cause of the divergent shapes of capitalist states. One reason for a smaller state in the United States is that agrarians and labor undermined the state's revenue-raising capacity at a crucial historical moment. On the other hand, historians have missed one of the key consequences of American Progressivism: as Chapter 6 will argue, resistance to sales tax prevented the elaboration of a European-style welfare state.

While resistance to regressive taxation is a central element in preserving the unique features of the American state, another is the positive focus on progressive taxation, the subject of Chapter 5.

5

THE LAND OF TOO MUCH

The American focus on progressive taxation is unusual in comparative perspective. It was spearheaded by several actors from the South and the Midwest who discovered the popularity of progressive taxation. Without their efforts, the United States may well have ended up with a tax system resembling that of Europe's. To examine why these actors were so intent on progressive taxation, this chapter first briefly traces the late nineteenth century agrarian movement for progressive taxation, and then moves to a detailed exploration of one twentieth century figure, Huey Long, governor and senator from Louisiana. The aim of the chapter is to show how the issue of overproduction led to the solution of progressive taxation.

The Origins of Progressive Income Taxation in the United States

In the late nineteenth century American industrialization upset the delicate political balance that had been achieved on the issue of protective tariffs. For decades, tariffs on manufactured products had served both to raise revenue and to protect the infant industries of the Northeast (Mehrotra 2004:167; Hansen 1990; Skocpol 1992). Southern and midwestern political acquiescence was bought by selectively extending tariffs to a few key agricultural products (Sanders 1999; Seligman 1916), but this political bribe became less tenable with industrialization, as mechanization led to increasing agricultural productivity, and farmers in the South and Midwest found themselves able to compete internationally. They also found themselves hurt by the high, protected prices of manufactured goods. Thus the sectional division of modes of production led the western and southern states to argue that the burden of taxation should be shifted to wealthy manufacturers in the Northeast (Bensel 2000).

A temporary income tax had been put in place during the Civil War, but the drive for a permanent income tax first took shape within the Populist political movements of the late nineteenth century (Ratner 1942, 164). Farmers joined forces in organizations such as the Grange Party, the Greenback Party, and the Southern and Northern Alliances, and in 1892 the Populist Party officially demanded an income tax in its famous Omaha Platform (Baack and Ray 1985, 608–609). Populists were also developing a nascent theory of overproduction, that unfettered capitalism "makes the seller unable to buy back as much labor value as he sold and so leads to glutted markets" (Pollack 1962, 73), but the income tax was predominantly defended in ethical terms. In the South, these farmers were represented by Democrats. But in the midwestern states, the Republican Party machine was all-powerful, and the midwestern Republicans who represented these agrarian constituencies increasingly came to oppose the party leadership.[1] These "insurgent Republicans" from the farm belt first began to split from the main body of the party over the issue of free silver and eventually became bold enough to challenge the leadership and side with Democrats on the tariff and progressive taxation.

The Democratic Party as a whole had not previously favored income taxation and was initially hesitant to embrace the issue of tariff reduction in part because labor unions were split on the issue, with workers in protected industries favoring tariffs (Mehrotra 2004). This changed as labor leaders came to believe workers were bearing the costs of tariffs. Although labor was never entirely unified on the question, the leaders came to support tariff reform and the income tax (Mehrotra 2004). The Democratic Party also unified in opposition to the tariff in the late 1880s because of the efforts of President Cleveland (Klinghard 2005). Democrats began to favor the income tax not only as a means to replace the revenue lost from tariff reduction but also because they began to see the electoral appeal of an income tax that would be paid for by rich industrialists.

The income tax was seen as the quickest route to shifting the burden of taxation from tariffs paid by consumers to those with high incomes. An income tax was "by far the most effective weapon for use against the Plutocratic policy. . . . There is nothing which those Eastern Plutocrats dread so much as that. . . . At the present juncture I am quite sure there is nothing which could be so effectually used to put a cog in the wheels of the Plutocratic program" (C.H. Jones, quoted in Ratner 1942, 172). One legislator thought that income tax "will mark the dawn of a brighter day . . . with more of sunshine, more of the songs of birds, more of that sweetest music, the laughter of children well fed, well clothed, well housed" (quoted in Ellis 1940, 239).

Thus farmers and labor came together into a broad-based movement against tariffs, and in favor of income tax, as a means of curbing excesses of wealth generated by industrialization and redistributing the burden of taxation upward. Although agrarian Populists hurt by tariffs had been the initial impetus for the income tax movement, and the representatives of agrarian Populists provided key votes in Congress at a pivotal moment, the income tax had become a nationwide and broadly popular issue.

The income tax was particularly popular in comparison with what it was replacing. Up to that time central government revenues were largely reliant on indirect taxes, specifically, tariffs and excise taxes, while direct taxes were the province of local and state governments. Both sets of taxes were unpopular. Tariffs and excise taxes were criticized for their regressivity and for raising prices on common products (Mehrotra, 2004). As for the direct taxes collected by local and state governments, the bulk of revenue came from the "general property tax," the workhorse of the nineteenth century American tax system (Higgens-Evenson 2003; Yearley 1970). This was a tax on all property (meaning on all assets, not only real estate), and by all accounts it was universally loathed for the extreme variation in tax burdens across local and state boundaries, for the fact that industrialization was creating new forms of wealth that escaped this tax, for its regressivity, and for much else besides (Yearley 1970; Seligman 1890). These difficulties led to widespread tax evasion, to the point that a commission called the tax a "tax upon ignorance and honesty" (Seligman 1890, 30–31).

In this context, the income tax was an appealing alternative because it addressed the failings of the existing system: the centralization of the income tax would even out the variation of local tax burdens, and the focus on income would capture new forms of wealth, thus addressing the central weaknesses of the local and state (direct) tax system. Inquiry into the taxpayer's ability to pay would allow the application of progressive rates, thus addressing the central weakness of the federal (indirect) tax system. There were worries over the inquisitorial character of direct taxes, but these seem to have been allayed for many by the fact that *someone else* would be paying this tax: because the tax was progressive it would fall largely on the wealthy manufacturing Northeast, and observers in the West and South believed that the revenue raised from a national income tax (and paid by others) would reduce the often crushing local and state tax burdens that they themselves carried (Westin 1953). This meant that the income tax was not seen as an exercise of power from the center over the provinces (as it was in France, for example, [Morgan and Prasad 2009]) but rather as redistribution from the (economic) center to the rest of the country.

These forces generated a twenty-year battle over the income tax. In 1893 southern and midwestern Democrats in the House added a federal income tax measure to a bill that reduced tariffs, but the Supreme Court declared this income tax unconstitutional. There is no clear partisan split in the voting, but all except one of the known votes divides along geographic lines, with justices from the Northeast voting against the tax and justices from the South voting in favor (Weisman 2002; Ratner 1942; Corwin 1938).

McKinley's two victories (1896 and 1900) were seen by the Republican Party as vindication of their political position on tariffs. But midwestern voters continued to send anti-tariff Republicans to Congress, and support for the income tax for its redistributive effects continued to grow. Finally, in 1909, Republicans in Congress and President Taft concluded that the Democrats and insurgent Republicans had the votes to pass an income tax. Attempting to stave off more radical proposals, they proposed a constitutional amendment enabling the income tax. They expected the amendment to fail, thus bringing the income tax issue to an end, and this was an expectation that many supporters of the measure shared (Mehrotra 2004, 184; Ratner 1942, 279).

To the shock of all involved, the amendment was overwhelmingly ratified by 1913 (Solvick 1963; Weisman 2002). The agricultural states supported the amendment disproportionately (Baack and Ray 1985).[2] But between 1909 and 1913, the elections of 1910 and 1912 had brought Democrats (and reformist Republicans) into power in many state legislatures all over the country, not just in the agricultural states (Buenker 1985). At the national level, Republicans lost control of the House in 1910, and in 1912 Democrats took control of the presidency and both chambers of Congress. The division over tariffs, rising prices, and the start of African-American voters' abandonment of the Republican Party all contributed to the defeats. The surprising electoral reversal made passage possible—indeed, in some states where the amendment had been rejected before the election, it was taken up again after the election and ratified (Buenker 1985).

Once the amendment had been ratified, the way was cleared for the Democratic Congress and presidency to pass the income tax law in 1913. The first income tax was limited in its reach, with a high exemption that relieved virtually all middle class families from paying the tax. Brownlee (1996, 56–57) estimates that only 2% of households were subject to this income tax. Thus, the 1913 law created a progressive income tax that reached only a small proportion of the population—part of the reason for its tremendous popularity.

This law helped to finance American military needs in World War I, but in the 1920s Republicans in power began to scale back levels of taxation. Only with the deflation of the 1920s and 1930s would the fight for progressive taxation once again flare up. It came from the same sources that we came across in Chapter 4: midwestern and southern activists and legislators. To examine this fight in more detail, the remainder of this chapter focuses on one such activist and legislator, Huey Long of Louisiana. Long played a key role in the passage of the Revenue Act of 1935, but the goal of this chapter is not to argue for the centrality of Long to the American tradition of progressive taxation. Long was clearly influential, as will be shown below, but his influence depended on the general popularity of progressive taxation, a cause that was being promoted by many agrarian politicians at the time, including Floyd B. Olson of Minnesota, Lynn Frazier of North Dakota, Olin Johnston of South Carolina, Claude Pepper of Florida, and Cordell Hull and Al Gore Sr. of Tennessee (Mayer 1951; Gieske 1979; Vallely 1969; Newman and O'Brien 2011). Not all politicians favored progressive taxation, not even all southern Democrats did; indeed, Pat Harrison of Mississippi was an influential opponent (Swain 1978). But the support was widespread and deep across the country. Rather than making a claim for Long as a singular force in the struggle for progressive taxation, this chapter focuses on him in depth in order to uncover how actors of the time put together the problem of overproduction with the solution of progressive taxation. Long's story is one of several similar stories occurring all across the country at the time—although his story is perhaps one of the more colorful political episodes of the twentieth century.

Huey Long and Progressive Taxation

Huey Long's term as governor of Louisiana was a picaresque journey featuring fisticuffs and raids on gambling clubs, a failed impeachment and charges of murder and kidnapping, an international incident over green silk pajamas, a national debate on whether "cornpone" should be dunked or crumbled in "potlikker," and a political feud that somehow managed to embrace tragedy and farce at once—with the state of Louisiana having for one week three self-proclaimed governors, a situation that may have cost the state millions of dollars and may well have originated in a falling-out over a crime of passion (*The New York Times* 1927; *Washington Post* 1928; *Los Angeles Times* 1929; *The New York Times* 1930; *Washington Post* 1930; *Atlanta Constitution* 1931; *Los Angeles Times* 1931; *Chicago Daily Tribune* 1931; *The New York Times* 1931b; *Atlanta Constitution* 1929). Observers of the time were captivated. The "light political farce," Long's boyish features, the accusations of flirtatious New Orleans nights and the scenes of fainting in the legislature all made such riveting theater that contemporaries can hardly be blamed for not noticing that through his antics Long was slowly casting the foundations of a progressive program (Coad 1928; *Chicago Daily Tribune* 1929a; *Chicago Daily Tribune* 1929b).

The elements of the program were simple: taxation of Standard Oil and other corporations combined with the floating of bonds (taxation of future generations) to pay for highways and free textbooks, with the program to generate its own support through the patronage that highway jobs would offer plus the electoral appeal of both the material benefits and the symbolic attacks against corporations. Long's last editorial, written shortly before his assassination, summed up his legacy in Louisiana, pointing to progressive taxation and sound finances as well as to spending on education, prisons, hospitals, and textbooks, plus the beginnings of a tourism infrastructure with "the prettiest capitol in the world . . . the greatest airport . . . a bathing resort on Lake Pontchartrain that is 7 miles long" (Long 1935d). He did not live long enough to boast about the elimination of the poll tax, which came into effect just before his assassination.

Historians have not done much better than contemporaries at understanding Long's Progressivism, despite considerable attention to Long himself. The scholarship on Long has been underdeveloped due to an overarching focus on one question: was Long a dictator? (Williams 1981; Brinkley 1982; White 2006) Long managed to acquire near-total power over Louisiana through a combination of appeal to the rural masses, conversion of that appeal into patronage and control of funds, and compromises extended to enemies through the judicious use of that patronage and those funds. Given his Populist backing and the international context of his times, it is not hard to see why historians have wondered if he was the home-grown version of fascism (indeed, when Hitler first came to American attention one national newspaper described him as "a sort of Huey Long without pajamas" Folliard 1930). But the attention to this question has led to neglect of the subtler but no less world-historically important accomplishments of Long during his brief political career.

At the national level, one of the main elements of Long's Progressivism was a commitment to progressive taxation. Evidence of several kinds reveals that Long was central to the formation of the Revenue Act of 1935, which, as part of Roosevelt's Second New Deal, established a tradition of high tax rates on the wealthy. Long had recently organized a movement of Share Our Wealth clubs around the country committed to redistribution and progressive taxation. Historians have argued that Share Our Wealth was not a particularly vibrant or vital movement, as shown by its rapid dissolution after Long's assassination. But whether or not the clubs were powerful, Long had created the perception of power and used it to force change. As Amenta, Dunleavy, and Bernstein (1994) have demonstrated, we know this from four kinds of evidence. First is the timing of the introduction of Roosevelt's progressive taxation plank. While most of the Second New Deal had been in the works before the pressure from Long, and while forces within the administration itself were pressing for these other policies, there is one proposal that appeared suddenly in 1935 as a late addition to the platform: soak-the-rich taxation. This was a central element of Share Our Wealth, but it was not a central element of Roosevelt's programs before the pressure from Long's movement (cf. also Kennedy 1999, 243). The second piece of evidence for Long's influence is a secret poll that the Roosevelt administration conducted that specifically attempted to measure Long's popularity; it concluded that, while Long had no hope of winning, his presence in the presidential race would take away several states from Roosevelt and throw them to the Republican candidate (Amenta, Dunleavy, and Bernstein 1994, 691). The Democratic Committee chairman who had conducted the poll concluded that Long "might have the balance of power in the 1936 election . . . the result might spell disaster" (quoted in Kennedy 1999, 241). The existence of the poll itself in this time when polls were expensive and infrequent indicates Roosevelt's concern with Long, and the contents of the poll's findings could not have reassured him. Third, Long was most influential in states where Roosevelt spent the most on

Works Progress Administration funding (Amenta, Dunleavy, and Bernstein 1994, 691–697), and Roosevelt directly attacked Long by blocking federal funds to Louisiana and by subjecting Long to an Internal Revenue Service investigation (Kennedy 1999, 237), suggesting that Roosevelt was putting his money and his efforts where his fears were. And finally, according to an aide, Roosevelt himself admitted Long's influence by identifying Long as one of the two "most dangerous men" in America. He was said to have told aides that he was attempting to "steal Long's thunder" with his policies (Amenta, Dunleavy, and Bernstein 1994, 678; Kennedy 1999, 237).

It would be inappropriate to draw from this a "great man" conclusion about the ability of Long alone to influence history. Roosevelt would hardly have worried about Long if Long did not represent a broad movement that was unusually durable because of the depth of the economic difficulties it was attempting to address. Long is an index of a general prewar commitment to progressive taxation in America at this time. There is reason to believe that this commitment to progressive taxation shaped the possibilities of tax collection during and after the war. Although the Revenue Act of 1935 did not itself generate substantial revenue, disappointing those who had hoped for greater redistribution (Leff 1984), it did set the foundation for a system of progressive taxation prior to the Second World War, a system that endured at least until the neoliberal policies of the late twentieth century (Thorndike 2009).

What has been less carefully investigated, however, is why Long was so interested in progressive taxation. If Long's pressure on Roosevelt was one of the reasons for introducing progressive taxation, why was that pressure not exercised in other ways—for example, on the question of health care? In comparative perspective, the long-delayed introduction of national health care is a key distinguishing characteristic of American political economy, responsible for higher levels of poverty and significantly lower tax collections in the United States. Scholars have argued that in Canada—the country most resembling the United States in other ways—pressure from outside the two major parties was crucial to the passage of universal health care. "By contrast, the absence of an independent voice for the left in the United States ensured that the agenda for national health reform would be set within the limits of the Democratic party coalition" (Maioni 1997, 414). Long was certainly an independent voice, but he used his voice for progressive taxation rather than health care. In Louisiana, Long had built a network of charity hospitals, so it is not obvious why health care was not part of the Share Our Wealth program. This chapter addresses this issue by tracing several sources of influence on the development of Huey Long's thinking. Long was certainly not the only champion of progressive taxation in the United States, and the Revenue Act of 1935 was not the only legislative embodiment of the Progressive ideal. But studying this particular actor and this particular moment gives us clues into why the politics of progressive taxation was so popular in mid-century America.

Although casual observers from outside the state assimilate him to the general category of racist southern demagogue, Long was an unusual southern Populist in many ways. For one thing, he made real attempts to improve the lives of black people. Although he could have made Populist hay by limiting his programs for the poor to whites, in most cases he did not do so, in an era when other southern Populists were fixated on the political power of racist appeals. Long was not above demagoguing on occasion, but race was never his main concern. Indeed, he was much loved by blacks throughout the state, with many naming children after him (including the parents of Black Panther Huey P. Newton),[3] at a time when other southern politicians were building strong political machines on segregation and occasionally coming out in favor of lynching. As a New Orleans African American newspaper wrote on Long's death: "While certain forces inimical to the Negro and his progress may have pointed out that Long never did any specific thing for his benefit, those who admired his shrewdness have been equally as quick to show that he had never done anything specifically against him. However, this much is certain. The lamented Huey Long was for the common man, definitely throwing all his legislation in their favor, and as Negroes are certainly classed with the commoners, they benefited by Long's work. They shared the good roads, and bridges, public school free text books, debt moratorium, reduction in taxes, automobile licenses, and phone, gas, and electric rates. In his last special session of the state law-making body he caused a bill to be passed which will affect Negroes particularly, in view of the fact that money lenders wax fat on the numerous small loans made to them" (*Louisiana Weekly* 1935).

Long's motivations on the issue of race are not entirely clear. Some speculate that he expected blacks to be enfranchised eventually—or even planned to enfranchise Louisiana's black population himself—and would not have wanted to alienate a potential group of voters. To some observers he seemed to be genuinely concerned about the black poor. Perhaps his views are best summed up in an article he published in the *Louisiana Progress* in August 1931: "Now, just a word about the poor negroes. We have 700,000 negroes in Louisiana. They're here. They've got to be cared for. Don't let people hollering that a negro may be working for somebody affect you toward your neighbor just because he is giving the negro something to do. The poor negroes have got to live, too. You wouldn't want to starve them to death if you could. I've fed a many [sic] hungry negro in my life and I will do it again. That's one thing the southern white man will do. In the north they call the negro mister, but they are not so careful about feeding him as we are down here. The southern white man don't do any of that 'mister' business, but he will feed the negro when no one else will do it" (Long 1931d). Tellingly, the column lies next to an extremely racist piece of demagoguery in the newspaper, an article criticizing a political opponent for belonging to a club that had a black vice-president, a theme that was pursued across several issues of Long's newspaper. "They're here. They've got to be cared for" was the extent of Long's concern. That even this minimal appreciation—not doing "anything specifically against" blacks, and not specifically excluding them from government programs—led to widespread and enduring affection for Long among Louisiana's black population suggests what they had been accustomed to before him.

On the question of prejudice against Catholics and Jews, one acquaintance affirmed that Long didn't have any religious prejudice, "But, he didn't have much religion either."[4] Interestingly, Long was a key factor in the campaign of the first woman to win election to the U.S. Senate, Hattie Caraway of Arkansas. Long was not particularly feminist—he was campaigning for her because she supported Progressive policies, he hated one of her political opponents, and he wanted to demonstrate his own power—but it is worth noting that he was not opposed to a woman in the Senate. Indeed, one of the key members of his staff was Alice Lee Grosjean, a 24-year-old whose appointment as secretary of state caused Long no end of trouble because of the inevitable rumors, but who in fact seems to have been a highly capable executive (see, e.g., White 2006, 153). By the standards of his time, Long was remarkably progressive on questions of race, religion, and gender.

Long considered all of these issues distractions from the real issue: class. Born in an unusually progressive part of Louisiana (the only parish to have once voted a socialist candidate into the legislature, and one of the few to vote against the state's secession from the union on the grounds that slavery was a "rich man's cause" Brinkley 1982, 10), Long worked first as a traveling salesman—a glamorous occupation at the time—criss-crossing the rural South and absorbing lessons about the preoccupations of that slice of early twentieth century America.

Long then trained as a lawyer and went to work opposing the oil corporations that were beginning to transform Louisiana, eventually entering politics with well-formed ideas of the responsibilities of the wealthy to society and convinced of the electoral potential of class-based appeals. His quick ascent from the head of the Public Service Commission to the governor's office was marked by attacks on large corporations, particularly Standard Oil. As governor, Long presided over the implementation of Populist policies such as distributing free textbooks to schoolchildren. He also oversaw an extensive program of road-building, as well as an attempt to tax Standard Oil that led his opponents to try, unsuccessfully, to impeach him. After only three years he was elected to the U.S. Senate and was making a name for himself as an economic Populist when an assassin stopped him in 1935 (Williams 1981; Brinkley 1982; White 2006).

The main policy results of Long's efforts within Louisiana were an extensive roads and highways program—a stunning achievement, placing Louisiana's highway system at the head of the country—as well as expenditures on education, particularly the funding of Louisiana State University, and welfare programs such as the establishment of charity hospitals. All of this came years before the Works Progress Administration would take up similar causes nationwide. One observer notes that "within three years after Huey Long took office, state expenditures increased from $29 million to $84 million"(Jennings 1977, 228) although other scholars argue that those expenditures did not raise the state's standing in comparative rankings and that much of the money was wasted in corruption (Jeansonne 1993).

Long's most notable legacy, however, was outside Louisiana. In influencing Roosevelt to adopt progressive taxation, Long played a key role in cementing the American approach to taxation.

All that is known about the origins of Share Our Wealth is that the idea came to Long one night during his Senate career. As far back as his days as a traveling salesman, Long had been used to waking up in the middle of the night to scribble ideas on a little notebook kept by his bed. According to the story, in early 1934, "Early one morning, about three o'clock according to some versions of the incident, Huey Long summoned his secretary, Earl Christenberry, and the Reverend [Gerald] Smith to his rooms, and excitedly explained that he had just thought of a national organization, without dues of any sort, to be known as the Share-the-Wealth

Society; something to be welded into a national Huey Long political unit on the basis of a platform whose principal plank was the decentralization of fortunes" (Deutsch 1935).

The club's principles were drawn up that night. The main purpose was to limit wealth in such a way as to provide a minimum income and pensions as well as "to limit the hours of work, to balance agricultural production against what can be consumed, to care for the veterans of all wars, and to provide collegiate professional training for all young men and women who demonstrate mental capacity to profit by it" (Deutsch 1935).

Because of the paucity of sources the story of the origins of the club must remain circumstantial, and scholars have focused on the events surrounding the formation of the club (particularly, a decline in Long's political fortunes in the latter part of 1933) rather than on detailed questions such as why Long concentrated on taxation in particular. Nevertheless, it is possible to reconstruct some of the issues that Huey Long was concerned with when he formulated the Share Our Wealth clubs, the problems that he was trying to solve in developing his support for progressive taxation, and the events and conjunctures that transformed his general interests and concerns into specific programs. This close examination will give us some indication of why progressive taxation came to the fore at this moment, rather than issues such as health care.

Long's support for progressive taxation drew on two important sources in his background. First was Louisiana's unusual legal history as "the only solid, durable enclave of civil law" (Friedman 2005, 116). Louisiana's legal tradition draws on the Napoleonic legal code to a greater extent than all other states, as well as on Spanish law. In areas that affect economic competitiveness the state has revised its Code and adopted laws similar to other states over the years. But while much of the code has been changed, one idea has continued from the earliest date to today— the idea of "forced heirship." In France, unlike the United States, testators do not have complete freedom to determine who shall inherit their estates. Rather, a portion of the estate is required to be inherited by the children and the close relatives. The original idea for this in France was that it would prevent the accumulation of dynastic fortunes. Louisiana adopted this—and still abides by it, although in a much more limited form today. Huey Long learned about forced heirship during his legal education and career, and it seems to have left a strong impression on him. Note that Long was drawing on *French* influences to articulate what a superficial observation might lead us to call an *American* fear of large fortunes (Gruning 2003–2004; Friedman 2005).

Another rhetorical resource was the Jubilee—the Biblical tradition of forgiveness of debt every certain number of years. Long once advised a young man who, as Long had done, wanted to teach himself the law: "In between the civil code and corporation law on the schedule [Long] inserted a lengthy exhortation to study the Bible. Start in at Genesis and read several pages a day, he commanded. Keep reading, no matter how 'wearsome it becomes;' keep the 'begats' in mind 'just enough to trace generations.' But 'when you get to the Hebrew Law study carefully all the way: It's the basis of all law' " (Williams 1981, 76). The Hebraic code had first come up in a long conversation he had had with his professor, Charles Payne Fenner, on the Louisiana tradition of forced heirship. Either Fenner, or Long himself, recalled Biblical precepts on the redistribution of property, and Long began to give the Bible serious study. "[W]hat struck him particularly were the commandments that every seven years there should be a release of debts and that every fiftieth year, the 'Jubilee' year, there should be a return of possessions to every man. . . . [T]hrough the study of law his attention was directed as it never had been before to the question of the redistribution of wealth" (Williams 1981, 77).

Biblical rhetoric featured often in his speeches and writings. In 1931 Long writes, "God gave us the law. He gave us the rules of life. He told us what to do and what not to do. He told us if we would keep our wealth distributed among the people that we would lie down and sleep in safety and dwell in peace, but that, if we didn't we should perish as others have before us. He told us how to handle these things. Will we do it?" (Long 1931b). Just two months after being sworn in as a senator in 1932 Long was thunderously quoting Scripture (or alleged Scripture) in defense of the redistribution of wealth through the taxation of profits: "So the Lord spoke further. 'If you distribute this wealth, then,' the Scripture says, 'you will lie down at night in a land of safety and peace, and dwell in a land of comfort and plenty for all. But if you will not do it, there is no country that is going to survive with the accumulation of wealth in the hands of a few people' " (*Congressional Record* 1932a, 6544). He wondered why Christians apply Biblical precepts selectively, "[W]e follow the law that the Lord gave us against murder, against stealing, and against nearly everything else, but we have eliminated the law written in the same phrases and in the same paragraphs, written so plain that the most ignorant cannot fail to understand, written extensively from the 24th to the 27th chapters of the book of Leviticus, commanding that the race of people should not allow its wealth to be gathered into a few hands, so that there was luxury, super-luxury, abandonment, great delight and hilarity with a

few, and starvation and impoverishment with the many" (Long 1931c).
"[W]hy observe His statutes against murder, stealing, and many other
things and not observe His statutes on how humanity should handle the
profits of the land and take care of the race? . . . 'And ye shall hallow the
fiftieth year and proclaim liberty throughout all the land unto all the in-
habitants thereof; it shall be a jubilee and ye shall return every man unto
his possessions' " (Long 1931a).

However, these cultural resources might have remained decorative
filigrees around Long's politics, if not for the cotton crisis of 1931. Cotton, the source of southern economic life, was too plentiful that year,
driving prices lower than could have been imagined possible, and driving
cotton farmers into difficulties all over the region (Snyder 1984). As we
have seen, the problem was not restricted to cotton but had touched
many primary commodities; in Louisiana, however, where cotton was
still king, it was cotton that was particularly consequential. Long, like
many observers, was flabbergasted by a system that could turn an unusually successful harvest into catastrophe: "People are starving, and yet
we have more wheat, corn, meat, milk, cheese, honey and truck in this
land than the whole human race in America can consume if everyone
were turned loose to eat what it wanted," Long writes in 1930; he pin-
points the problem as "[t]he man owning these commodities has no market because no one has money to buy them," a situation that is "[m]ost
remarkable." "There is something wrong when people starve for food and
shiver for clothes and can not get them because there is too much in the
land" (Long 1930). Through the collapse of the price of cotton Long began to participate in the general struggle to understand overproduction
during the Depression.

Long played a central role in attempting to engineer a "cotton holiday," a one-year ban on planting cotton across the South that would
have driven up the current year's prices. The word *holiday* was borrowed
from the Farmers' Holiday Associations of the 1930s (Shover 1965), but
the plan was more precise than any of the production control plans that
had been mooted up to that point. Essentially, the cotton holiday was a
way to get past the prisoner's dilemma that every individual farmer
faced—where collapsing prices led individual farmers to try to make up
for it by planting more cotton, but if everyone planted more cotton then
the price declined further—by collectively binding the farmers to produce only as much cotton as was being demanded, an outcome that was
mutually beneficial for all but could only work if it was breached by

none. The plan has been said to have originated with a group of northern Louisiana farmers (Snyder 1984) or from Representative John Sandlin of Minden, Louisiana, in the northwestern part of the state (*Morning Tribune* 1931). Long cleverly avoided the problem of the possible unconstitutionality of forced acreage reduction by proposing that the reason for acreage reduction would be given as eradication of the boll weevil, which was clearly constitutional. Through Long's efforts the ban came tantalizingly close to being passed, and Long even dreamed at one point of taking it international (*Times-Picayune* 1931b). But the ban failed when Texas, the largest cotton growing state, refused to join, and Long seems to have drawn the lesson that a more stable method of widespread distribution of the fruits of technological capacity was required. But what would that more stable method be? (Snyder 1984)

What followed for Long were years of intellectual casting about. He did not immediately turn to taxation. In a 1927 speech at Alexandria, Long had mentioned taxes only to complain about government waste: "Our tax moneys have frequently been uselessly spent. . . . We should . . . make way for a reduction of taxation wherever the same may be practical or possible, in the economic administration of the State's business."[5] A Louisiana tax officer under Long's governorship could not recall Long having a systematic philosophy of taxation used to redistribute wealth, claiming only that Long wanted low taxes on everything.[6]

Long came to the issue of taxation through a series of steps that can be traced in his writings for his newspaper, the *Louisiana Progress* (later the *American Progress*). In every issue of the paper Long wrote an editorial on whatever he was involved in at the moment, from local politics to harangues against Roosevelt. While the *Progress* was published irregularly, it lasted in some form from 1930 to 1940. The issues from 1930 to Long's assassination give a glimpse into his evolving political ideas.

An early diagnosis was that the problem of overproduction was caused by the plenty of the land being bottled up by the monetary mechanism. "The farmer can raise hides but he hasn't the money to buy back shoes for his children. He can sell cotton so low that he can't buy back calico and gingham to clothe the family . . ." (Long 1931a). In August 1931, Long was proposing barter as a solution to the overproduction crisis: "Do you remember when your father or mother swapped a cup of beans for a cup of sugar; or your father traded a sack of potatoes for a sack of oats; etc.? Well, now, we've got to get right back to that to keep from starving to death in this country this fall and winter. . . . Forget these little old hard feelings and jealousies that may exist between you and some-body living close to you. . . . If you need to build a shed, see if your friend hasn't some lumber that he will trade you for some corn or potatoes; if your stock needs feed, and you are out, try to trade something to some one else for feed. Keep a good garden summer and winter. Don't forget turnips in all seasons. Remember pot-likker and cornbread alone can go a long ways." And he mentions a "little market letter that we are having Harry D. Wilson put out. In it he lists whatever you've got you want to trade and then he lists what the other man has that he wants to trade to you" (Long 1931d).

The whirlwind tour with Hattie Caraway in 1932 was an important point at which the seeds for what would eventually become the Share Our Wealth appeal were sown. It was Long's first campaign on the theme of "too much."[7] Long is said to have spoken extemporaneously, but what is said to be a stenographic report of one of the speeches survives. Long begins with backcountry humor then quickly launches into what was be-coming his new trademark: "Why is it? Why? Too much to eat and more people hungry than during the drought years; too much to wear and more people naked; too many houses and more people homeless than ever before. Why? This is a land of super-abundance and super-plenty. Then why is it also a land of starvation and nakedness and homlessness [sic]?"[8] By all accounts the whirlwind tour was an unparalleled triumph. A week before the election, "Mrs. Caraway was not conceded even an outside chance to get any ponderable proportion of the total vote of her state. . . . One week later, when the votes were counted, it was found that she had received more ballots than all six of her opponents combined. A spot map later made it plain that in the counties the whirlwind tour of Huey Long over the state with her—39 meetings in as many county seats scattered along 2,103 measured miles of motor highway—visited, she got her votes. In the counties that were not touched in that amazing itinerary she got a mere inconsiderable sprinkling of votes, not enough to wad the proverbial shotgun."[9] Deutsch writes, "The Share-the-Wealth movement had not yet been born. But the idea back of the present organization over-turned the political structure of the state of Arkansas in the space of a single week." After one of the speeches a telegram was sent to Long's rival: "A cyclone just went through here and is headed your way. Very few trees are left standing, and even these are badly scarred."[10] For Caraway, Long's speeches spelled victory in the Senate; for Long, they were a demonstration of the political power of the theme he had tapped.

In the following years the early thought experiments with barter gave way to more consequential suggestions for debt moratoria (Long 1934i) and for the expansion of the money supply. Long wrote several editorials supporting the remonetization of silver as an answer to the problem of declining purchasing power: "The currency should even be further expanded to give the people money enough for easy trade intercourse" (Long 1933b). The money, he seems to have decided, was locked up in banks: "With so many banks closing in early March, and before, we have tied up several billion dollars in deposits. They no longer circulate. Added to that, the Federal Reserve Board is acting now about like it always wanted to act, it has not put out more money; it has taken in a billion or so more the last we heard from it" (Long 1933b).

Long's struggle, his groping through the crisis, rises from the pages of the newspaper: "The total volume of money in our land is around six billion dollars. Our normal wealth is three hundred sixty billion dollars, or $60.00 in wealth to $1.00 in money. There is not enough money to make a good medium of exchange. . . . You go crazy listening to arguments and reasons for and against it. But I am convinced beyond a doubt that nothing but great good can come from remonetizing silver. . . . And even safer than that, a cure for every woe is to redistribute wealth through progressive taxation so that a dozen men do not control what is needed by 120,000,000 people" (Long 1934b).

It is this latter theme of progressive taxation that emerges over the months and years as Long's principal policy solution. Long's attention was called to taxation because of national and state-level attention to taxation. As we saw in Chapter 4, Long was involved in the 1932 attempt to reject a national sales tax. Instead of a sales tax, Senate radicals, including Long, wanted to raise money by raising rates on the wealthy. This fight cemented Long's attention to taxation, which only grew over the next few years. A tax reform in Louisiana in 1933 reinforced the idea of attempting to tax the wealthy (*Los Angeles Times* 1933). And a series of studies in the mid-1930s on tax evasion by the wealthy drew widespread attention to the issue of taxation (Thorndike 2009).

Another impetus for Long's turn to taxation was Roosevelt's National Recovery Administration, implemented as part of the National Industrial Recovery Act of 1933. The NRA was perhaps the main catalyst for Long's break from Roosevelt (Kennedy 1999, 237). Long opposed the wage and price limits the act established, arguing that these constituted "transfusion with one's own blood"—that the limits would affect small businesses more than large businesses and that redistribution from small businesses was simply pushing around peanuts. The NRA, Long said, "will do some good, but unless wealth is spread among the masses it cannot go far enough. It purports transfusion. From where? From among the rank and file—from one to the other of the common people. It purposes to raise up the men in the mire, by what? By their own boot straps? . . . If we spread our great wealth enough that all are served in the land of too much—then there would be a transfusion into business, a lift to the forgotten, a hope for our nation" (Long 1933d).

The NRA drew Long's focus onto the issue of redistribution because it aimed to redistribute, as he saw it, from the masses to the masses. The natural thing to do, he concluded, was to get more money into the hands of the masses by taking it from where there is too much of it. As Long explained, "The President wants to get more money into the hands of the masses. The masses have not the money to hand to one another. A few people have all of the wealth tied up, and we can only get wealth into the hands of the masses by taking it from the classes who have it all" (Long 1933f).

The elements of the eventual policy were coming into clearer focus: concentration of wealth was a problem not only for ethical reasons—as Long had always insisted—but also because it deprived the masses of purchasing power and brought the economy to a halt; the circulation of money might be one response to it but another was "taking [the wealth] from the classes who have it all." And once the idea of raising taxes on the wealthy was in place, the rest of the program fell into place. Long had always criticized the concentration of wealth, but in late 1933 and 1934, almost every single one of his editorials was a harangue against the concentration of wealth. Long argues that the cause of redistribution of wealth is supported by many, from "Thomas Jefferson, Daniel Webster, Andrew Jackson, Theodore Roosevelt . . . William Jennings Bryan" (Long 1933a), "Abraham Lincoln . . . Francis Bacon, Sir Thomas More, Jean Jacques Rousseau, Thomas Edison [to] the famous Mayo brothers of medical fame" (Long 1934h), to radio pioneer Guglielmo Marconi, John D. Rockefeller's pastor, and the Pope (Long 1934f, 1934g). He finds support for it in the Constitution, the Bible, and the Greek philosophers (Long 1933c, 1934h). He attempts to link the fight for redistribution of wealth with the American Revolution (Long 1934f). He insists that redistribution of wealth will eventually help the wealthiest capitalists, because it will make the system more stable (Long 1933g, 1933i). He argues that maldistribution of wealth has been the cause of the fall of empires: "Greece faded, Rome fell, Egypt, Babylon and all went their way from one course, the rich few and impoverished millions. Can national confusion obscure that fault?" (Long 1933h). He blames the Depression itself on the concentration of wealth (Long 1934a).

In late 1933, Long finally concludes "Taxation is the only source of insuring a redistribution of the wealth. The load being carried by the man at the bottom should be shifted not only to be borne by the wealthy at the top, but so that the enormous fortunes may be pulled down to a reasonable size, the government supported thereby, and the common man of the streets built steadily from the surplus resources until he has reached an average station in life. Such systems of taxation should continue to siphon from the top and to build from the bottom until there was a fair living for everyone, sufficient that he might not only enjoy the necessities and conveniences of life, but a fair share of the luxuries" (Long 1933e).

And in 1934, he spells out the famous program: "By limiting the sizes of fortunes through the employment of a progressive income tax, by forbidding the inheritance of billion-dollar fortunes through the enactment of inheritance taxes, by decreeing that no one man can earn more than $1,000,000 a year—that no one man can inherit more than $5,000,000— that no one man can own a fortune of more than $100,000,000—by making into law these provisions, then, and only then, will we achieve what the NRA has failed to do, viz., the return of prosperity to America for all time" (Long 1934h). While taxation was the center of the program, the Share Our Wealth societies also involved expenditures on education, because education not only trained the young, it also took them out of the labor force while calling back into the labor force those currently unemployed who could teach their trade: "All in all, the program is one of national organization; it means no great or burdensome outlay because there is a surplus of the goods and things needed for the care of all students, and the consuming of the same will immediately aid our problems of over-production" (Long 1935a). Also, "Coupled with this program will be the old age pensions to all people over 60 years of age; the complete care for veterans of our wars; a limit to the hours of toil; a caring for all agricultural production by having the Government take over the surpluses of such crops as may be necessary in the particular years when they are not needed. This will make it necessary that the Government do certain public works in the section where particular crops are not planted for that year" (Long 1934c).

143

America as a land of plenty, and the enigma of poverty in the midst of plenty, were the central themes in Long's writings just before, during, and just after his formulation of the Share Our Wealth clubs: "Here we have hewn a country out of a wilderness to where it is worth $400,000,000,000.00 in normal times, maybe more" (Long 1934d). "When I look around America today and see people going hungry in one section while food rots on the ground in another, when I see people living in box cars in one state and thousands of vacant homes in another, when I read of little children clad in rags in our cities while farmers plow up cotton in the South, when I see the government destroy 5,000,000 pigs in the Middle West while 5,000,000 people are hungry in the East—when I see all these things happening I wonder on what road are we traveling, where are we headed" (Long 1934h).

But where in the early 1930s Long had simply been confused by it, by 1934 he had a concrete proposal to give, the Share Our Wealth Society: "Are we going to let the money masters of America say that they propose inequality to such an extent that, in a land flowing with milk and honey, the children born into existence in America will even be denied the sustenance of life when they were all declared to be created equal? . . . Let everyone put his shoulder to the wheel. Let him see his neighbor and ask him to join a Share Our Wealth Society . . . to the end that All the People of America Will be Aroused, Active and Alert and All determined that in the land where there is food, All will eat; in the land where there are plenty of clothes, Everyone will be clothed; in the land where there are plenty of buildings, there will be homes for All" (Long 1934e).

Thus, progressive taxation became the central issue for Long because the problem that he was trying to solve was, as he saw it, the problem of overproduction and the distortions of purchasing power that it caused. The general background for Long's support of progressive taxation was an attempt to grapple with how to make capitalism work and, especially, how to make it work for the poor. Long was fond of noting the contrast between the world of his boyhood, where the independent effort of a family was sufficient to provide for all of its needs from building its own shelter to growing its own food, and the world he was living in now, with its complex web of interdependencies. Particularly troubling to him, as to many observers of the time, was the riddle of overproduction—cotton lying in the fields while children went unclothed. In his own attempt to come to terms with this world, he drew upon the resources of his legal training in Louisiana, as well as elements of the Bible, to formulate poli-

144

cies against the concentration of wealth. His attention was channeled into taxation, in particular, because of a fight in the early 1930s over how to raise revenue to retire the war debt, a fight whose resolution set the pattern upon which the American state would go on to raise revenues during the Second World War. Progressive taxation became a response to overproduction. Although Long does not explicitly discuss problems such as health care, which simply seem to drop out from his thinking, examining the development of his ideas makes it clear that such issues were secondary to the main problem that consumed all of his energies, the question of how to battle overproduction.

Scholars have been unduly uncharitable to Long in dismissing his arguments. Alan Brinkley, for example, argues that Long was drawing on decades-old studies. But as Long did not hesitate to point out (e.g., Long 1935b), recent studies supported his points about the concentration of wealth, including Harold Loeb's *The Chart of Plenty* and an investigation by *The Daily News:* "So at the end of twenty years' time which I have devoted, trying to force to the attention of the American people the necessity for the redistribution of wealth into the hands of our people, so that there will not be starvation and nakedness in the land of too much to eat and too much to wear—I say, at the end of these twenty years of turmoil and labor, the ice has begun to thaw, the clouds have begun to break; there is not only a silver lining, but a blue spot in the sky, which is growing in proportions day by day" (Long 1935c).

Of course, Long was not the originator of these ideas and debates in which he participated. They were collective debates, triggered by an anxious society-wide search for the levers of economic growth. This episode should remind us of the degree to which the Depression had begun to denaturalize the market system, leading observers and politicians of many stripes to consider the socially constructed nature of the economic world. It is a point that can be easily forgotten. Alan Brinkley, for example, implies that the devastation Long saw around him was natural, that prices had fallen "of their own accord" (1982, 40). This echoes traditional critiques of the issue as simply a natural economic phenomenon.

But many of the general ideas that Long, like many Americans, was trying to think through have in the end been vindicated. Long wondered if lack of purchasing power was a reason for the Depression, and although the specific argument about overproduction was rejected by most academic observers, concern with purchasing power dominated the postwar American economy. Long wondered if the constrained money supply was the reason for the Depression, and Friedman and Schwartz followed this line of thought to its conclusion; the explanation of the Depression as having been caused by unduly restrictive money supply is now conventional wisdom. Long was right to draw attention to those problems even if his proposed solutions were not what analysts with the advantage of decades of scholarship eventually settled on. Long was not a scholar, and his approach included contradictions, evolutions in understanding, and incorrect calculations. For example, as Brinkley and others have pointed out, Long miscalculated the amount of taxation that could be borne by the wealthy and redistributed, and he blithely ignored the difference between liquid and illiquid assets. But the American political world has remained committed to the general principle of progressive taxation. If Long was struggling to articulate policies that were not natural, we live in the nonnatural world that those policies created.

This close evaluation of Long's ideas gives us a clue to Long's popular appeal. Long's appeal is often described as something hard to understand, as some magical or mystical charisma. Charisma may play a role, but the ultimate reason for Long's success was that he was seriously attempting to think through the important economic questions of the time. His ideas resonated with a radical rethinking of economic institutions in the 1930s.

Long's approach was also more firmly grounded in an American tradition of state intervention than has been appreciated. The particular challenge for the United States in the early part of the twentieth century was managing its sudden and growing wealth; in comparative perspective, the United States was much more productive than any of the European countries. Being "the land of too much" led to problems of price volatility and instability. Many of the unique features of the American state can be traced to these issues. As the nation struggled with these problems, solutions emerged that led to a focus on using the concentrated power of the state against the concentration of capital. The ultimate goal of this tradition—as in every other western capitalist country— was to make capitalism work, and to make it work for the people. Long's attempt was part of the general attempt in the western world to make capitalism work by radically rethinking notions of private property and distribution of wealth. But unlike Europe, where wartime devastation led to attempts to use the state to regenerate capitalism through a focus on exports and restraint of consumption, in the extremely productive turn of the century American economy the attempt was to use the power of the state to break up wealth in the interests of economic growth that would benefit the people. Progressive taxation is part of that story.

The story of Huey Long and progressive taxation allows us to rethink another key element of American history. Southern politicians are usually seen as obstructing Progressivism. But Huey Long was a southern Populist who found a way to make a Populist appeal that was also progressive, a Populist appeal that did not depend on race. Long takes his rightful place among that Progressive tradition. Those who criticize American taxation for not being even more progressive have ignored its unusual progressivity in comparative perspective. While the Progressive era had laid down important foundations for progressive taxation, during the Great Depression Long and others like him drew on a less common strain of populism to reinterpret progressive taxation not just as a moral good but as an economic necessity.

Before we turn to a Progressive celebration of Long, however, it is worth noting the historical irony of the story. As discussed in Chapter 6, several scholars have argued that regressive taxes underpin every single European welfare state, while progressive taxes consign a state to a difficult path of revenue generation. If this is true, then Long's Populist appeal did as much, if not more, as the racist appeals of other southern politicians to undermine the welfare state, at least in the long run. In the short run, the income tax turned out to be a flexible and successful revenue raising instrument that underpinned a growing state, including the fledgling welfare state. But scholars have argued that as the advanced industrial countries hit the economic crisis of the 1970s, the limits of a progressive tax system became visible. If the thesis that regressive taxation facilitates the development of the welfare state is true—a question we take up in Chapter 6—then by focusing on progressive taxation and firmly rejecting regressive taxation, Huey Long and the agrarian statists undermined the long-term revenue raising capacity of the American state, thereby setting the United States on the distinct path that it still follows.

6

PROGRESSIVE TAXATION AND

THE WELFARE STATE

Chapters 4 and 5 examined the formation of two distinct features of the American progressive tax regime: the failure of sales tax and the commitment to progressive income tax. This chapter will analyze the consequences of these features for the welfare state. Although the welfare state is an extensively investigated topic in the social sciences, studies of the welfare state are often divorced from studies of taxation. This leads to one-sided interpretations of politics that assume welfare programs can be understood as reflections of prevailing opinions about the poor, as if the wish for revenue automatically resulted in revenue. Rooting our explanations of politics in the fiscal capacities of states yields a more realistic picture and shows that the manner of tax collection can have independent—and sometimes surprising—effects on welfare states.

Despite the overarching trend of ignoring the link between taxation and welfare spending, there is a small, but increasingly sophisticated body of work that does so. One of the first scholars to argue that the manner of tax collection may carry implications for the welfare state was the sociologist Harold Wilensky. Echoing classical Italian public finance theories of "fiscal illusion," Wilensky (1975) observed that the Swedish welfare state in the 1970s seemed to be increasing indirect forms of taxation such as the value added tax and other sales taxes. Over the next three decades Wilensky developed the argument that "the squeeze on real disposable income due to rising prices and government expenditures creates most tax resistance in countries foolish enough to rely too much on painfully visible taxes, especially on income taxes and property taxes on households" (2002, 379). Wilensky calculates a "backlash score" of the intensity and duration of tax protests that achieved political success between 1965 and 1975 and finds a correlation between tax backlash and the proportion of visible taxes in the revenue structure. He categorizes direct taxes such as income, property, capital gains, and inheritance and gift taxes as visible taxes, "taxes taken in one or two big bites from taxpayers who believe that they will not receive direct benefits in line with contributions" (715). Thus, the mechanism that makes taxes visible, according to Wilensky, is infrequency and size of payments, but of equal importance is the invisibility of the benefits such taxes are purchasing. Sales taxes, on the other hand, are collected in frequent small payments, which, in Wilensky's schema, the taxpayer does not feel, whereas payroll taxes (which directly fund the welfare state) are tolerated because their benefits are visible. While Wilensky does not elaborate on this, one may also note that to implement a tax that discriminates by income, the state needs fine-grained information on taxpayer income. The process of collecting this income can become a painful ritual for the taxpayer, as it puts information about tax costs directly into the hands of taxpayers, unlike forms that do not discriminate based on income such as consumption taxes.

In a direct rebuke of the politics of Huey Long that we explored in Chapter 5, Wilensky argues: "Among the myths embraced by the American Left, the most misleading is that the road to equality runs through progressive income taxes on business and property. . . . In fact, the most egalitarian and civilized democracies have slightly regressive tax systems and highly progressive spending programs" (715).

Wilensky's backlash scores have not been replicated quantitatively, and several important questions remain to be worked out, such as why it should be the proportion of visible taxation rather than the absolute levels of visible taxation that seems to be the relevant criterion: when measured as a percent of GDP, visible taxes in the developed welfare states are high, and it is only when measured as a percent of total tax revenue that the relative standings that Wilensky discusses become clear. The implication is that citizens are weighing *visible* costs against *overall* benefits derived from government, but this has not been empirically demonstrated.

Nevertheless, there is evidence in support of Wilensky's arguments at both micro and macro levels. Psychological experiments support Wilensky's claims about the importance of tax visibility to tax attitudes at the micro level. For example, Chetty, Looney, and Kroft (2009) show in a field experiment that including the sales tax in the posted price of a product so that shoppers are more aware of it reduces sales of the product, even though shoppers know that sales taxes will be added even when they are not posted. Finkelstein (2009) shows in a field experiment that charging tolls electronically so that drivers are less aware of them increases toll collections by 20–40%. And Gallagher and Muehlegger (2011) show that offering a tax rebate as a sales tax waiver has more effect than offering it as a less visible income tax credit. Surveys on attitudes towards different taxes have produced mixed results (e.g., Advisory Commission on Intergovernmental Relations 1993, 1; Hadenius 1985; Dornstein 1987). However, survey protocols first call to mind a particular tax and then ask if respondents like it, and this would not seem to be the best way to assess *whether* respondents think about a particular tax in the course of their normal lives. The experimental evidence seems more convincing.

Historical case studies also find support for Wilensky's argument at the macro level. My work on the comparative success or failure of neoliberal movements in the United States, United Kingdom, France, and West Germany (Prasad 2006) found the histories unfolding exactly as Wilensky suggests: the most unpopular taxes in the United States, the ones that triggered the neoliberal revolt and caught policymakers' attention, were property taxes and income taxes; in Britain, Thatcher's government anticipated the unpopularity of income tax increases and actually raised sales taxes instead when faced with a budget shortfall; in Germany and France, however, taxation was tied to spending in ways that made the benefits of taxation visible and made it difficult for politicians to gain much political leverage from tax cuts.

An important extension of Wilensky's work is Junko Kato's (2003) argument that having introduced a value added tax before the economic difficulties of the 1970s allowed policymakers to raise the overall revenue level when economies began to contract, whereas absence of this instrument before the 1970s left policymakers struggling to establish a new tax in a low-growth environment. Kato argues, "As a flat-rate regressive tax on a broad base, the VAT, when implemented, has a strong revenue-raising power that the income tax lacks. The broad tax base on consumption, which does not fluctuate as much as income during economic ups and downs, guarantees large amounts of revenue even with a slight increase in a flat tax rate" (27). But if a country did not introduce VAT in prosperous times, opposition to VAT after the 1970s prevented its development into a successful revenue-raising instrument. Thus, Kato adds a historical element to Wilensky's analysis, arguing that it is not simply the form of taxation that matters but also when the tax is introduced. The most successful tax regimes were those that grew based on less visible taxes during the prosperous decades after the Second World War.

Peter Lindert (2004) argues for a second type of link between tax systems and welfare states. Where Wilensky emphasizes the political consequences of progressive taxation, Lindert focuses on the economic consequences, suggesting that reliance on regressive labor and consumption taxes is a more stable strategy than reliance on progressive capital and income taxes because labor and consumption taxes are less economically distorting: "Contrary to what many have assumed about redistributive welfare states, [their style of taxation] tends to raise GDP and inequality, relative to the tax mixture in the lower-spending countries. In some high-tax high-budget social democracies, the taxation of capital accumulation is actually *lighter* than the taxation of labor earnings and of leisure-oriented addictive goods" (235). The Scandinavian countries in particular are marked by low capital income taxation alongside their large welfare states. One reason for the greater success of consumption taxes is that capital taxes can lead to capital flight: "[C]apital is internationally mobile and would take positive productivity effects with it when it is migrating" (241). In a series of publications Steffen Ganghof (2006, 2007, 2008) has argued that the main reason regressive taxes are compatible with economic growth is that they allow a low tax burden on capital. (He further suggests that low capital taxation could be achieved by differentiating between capital and labor income even in progressive tax systems, but he may underestimate the political difficulties of doing so.) Capital flight does not yet seem to have caused the race to the bottom in taxation or social spending that many feared, but some scholars argue that globalization has prevented the tax burden on capital from rising (Genschel 2002b), and this may be the secret to the stability of the European welfare states.

Another claimed advantage of consumption taxes is their effect on the incentive to save: "If you are subject only to a 15 percent consumption tax now and forever, with no income tax, your incentive to save is not strongly affected. . . . Income taxes, by contrast, take from your saved income twice, both when you initially earned the income you decided to save and again when your savings earns new capital income" (Lindert 2004, 241–242; Hines 2007). This should lead to higher savings in regimes reliant on consumption taxes and consequently higher economic growth. For these reasons, Lindert argues, regressive taxes are more compatible with economic growth, while progressive taxes distort economic growth. In this telling the political and popular support for cutting income and property taxes is not a direct consequence of their visibility but an indirect consequence of their effect on economic growth. Several economic studies support the argument that consumption taxes are associated with higher growth (Summers 1981; Kneller, Bleaneay, and Gemmell 1999 for an overview; Pecorino 1993; Pecorino 1994; Johansson, Heady, Arnold, Brys, and Vartia 2008; Jorgenson and Yun 1986; Widmalm 2001; but see Angelopoulos, Economides, and Kammas 2007). Lucas (1990) famously argued that the efficient rate of tax on capital is zero.

Thus, the existing work on the link between taxation and welfare-state spending emphasizes the negative political and economic consequences of progressive taxation, especially after the economic difficulties of the 1970s. Although the specific mechanisms by which progressive taxation undermines the welfare state remain a matter of debate, these explanations implicate a regime of progressive taxation in the increased difficulty of developing or maintaining welfare states in recent decades. Some scholars and policymakers argue that there is no guarantee that in the American context the greater revenues of regressive taxation would have gone to welfare spending rather than to military expenditures or other such concerns; this has always been one reason the American Left has been wary of regressive taxation. As one of Sven Steinmo's interviewees, a liberal senator, explained in his opposition to a national consumption tax: "[N]o one can guarantee me that the money taxed out of the grocery bills of American workers will ever be used to benefit those same workers. How am I to know whether that tax money will be used for social spending or for more waste at the Pentagon?" (Quoted in Steinmo 1989, 515.) But bargains of regressive taxation for progressive spending have been struck several times in American history, as we have seen above in the Agricultural Adjustment Act and the Social Security Act. Once again the perceived differences between the United States and other countries may be exaggerated.

A third way in which the unusual American tax system affected the development of its welfare state has been emphasized by historians and historically oriented social scientists focusing on an earlier time period. Between 1913 and 1954 a series of tax decisions excluded fringe benefits such as employer-provided pensions and health insurance from taxation. Corporations searching for ways to lower their tax bills found fringe benefits a useful way to increase effective wages, especially during the wage freeze of 1942 when more direct increases in compensation were impossible. The widespread adoption of fringe benefits crowded out the governmental role in pensions and health care, because those covered under private welfare programs feared that government alternatives would be of lower quality than their current employment-based coverage. (Quadagno 1984, 1988; Stevens 1988; Brown 1997–1998; Dobbin 1992; Jacoby 1993; Howard 1997; Hacker 2002; Thomasson 2003; Gordon 2003; Klein 2003; Jacobs and Skocpol 2010).

Jacob Hacker (2002, 218) warns that tax decisions were not the only factor behind the rise of employment-based coverage (see also Jacoby 1998, Klein 2003). Nor was employment-based coverage the only reason for the repeated failure of national health care (see, e.g., Gordon 2003; Quadagno 2004). Nevertheless, all analysts agree that tax decisions are one important factor in the development of employment-based coverage and that employment-based coverage is an important part of the explanation for the underdeveloped public welfare state. What the analysts in this tradition have been unable to answer, however, is where the system of tax preferences for fringe benefits came from, often treating it as exogenous.

The next section of this chapter reviews the history of these tax preferences for fringe benefits and shows that these features of the tax code were rooted in the very progressivity that actors such as Huey Long had demanded. Even before the rise of neoliberalism in the 1970s, progressive taxation was important because it generated a new political world centered on the politics of tax preferences, which channeled the American welfare state down private rather than public lines.

The Rise of Tax Preferences for Private Welfare

One of the most unusual features of the American tax state in comparative perspective is the predominance of tax preferences. A *tax preference* is a provision in the tax code that reduces a taxpayer's total obligation, such as an exemption for certain kinds of income, a deduction for certain activities, or a tax credit. The preference is usually given for behaving in a particular way. For example, the mortgage interest tax deduction rewards taxpayers for making mortgage payments by allowing them to deduct the interest on their mortgage payments from their taxable income. The Earned Income Tax Credit rewards taxpayers for working. Tax preferences are popularly called *loopholes* in the tax code, although that term is imprecise. Some scholars call them *tax expenditures*, but I have argued that this terminology is misleading (Prasad 2011), and I will refer to them as tax preferences here.

The American tax code is riddled with tax preferences (Howard 1997). Tax preferences were enshrined in the American tax state at its very origins, with the income tax act of 1913 including a deduction for home-mortgage interest. Deductions for employers and exclusions for employees on fringe benefits were ratified through decisions on several occasions—in 1926, in 1939, in 1942–1943, and in 1954—that each produced an uptick in demand for private health insurance. In 1926, Congress passed legislation formalizing the Department of the Treasury's practice of deferring corporate taxes for amounts spent on company pensions. Particularly important for the development of private welfare were the following series of decisions: in 1939, the IRS clarified an uncertainty about which fringe benefits were taxable; in 1943, an IRS administrative ruling found employer payments to private group plans subject to the tax exclusion; and in 1954, Congress codified the 1943 ruling in the Internal Revenue Code, ending uncertainty about whether it could survive a court challenge and extending it to all arrangements of health insurance, including firm-based insurance (Jacoby 1993; Dobbin 1992; Howard 1997; Hacker 2002; Thomasson 2003).

Despite the extraordinary importance of tax preferences in the United States, their origins are murky. The Civil War tax code already recognized deductions for "[e]xpenses necessarily incurred and paid in carrying on any trade, business, or vocation, such as rent of store, clerk hire" (United States Internal Revenue Service, 1863), and American law followed British precedent in allowing "ordinary and necessary" deductions. It is in grappling with the definition of this phrase that the tax code eventually grew to a tangled wasteland. The earliest tax preference, the home mortgage interest deduction, is "one of the earliest building blocks of the hidden welfare state" (Howard 1997, 49). It entered history in the 1913 income tax act, which excluded "interest paid on all indebtedness, including but not limited to home mortgages. Thus, from the very beginning, individuals who went into debt to buy a home shared with all indebted consumers a special place in the tax code. This design effectively broadened the potential base of support for the home mortgage interest deduction" (Howard 1997). The original intention had not been to focus on home mortgages in particular. The language of the legislation says only that "all interest paid within the year by a taxable person on indebtedness" is to be deducted (quoted in Ventry 2010, 236).

The absence of explicit debate in Congress has led scholars to suggest that it was a matter of administrative necessity and a wish for simplification, and this is perhaps the orthodox understanding of interest deductions. Howard notes that Congress worried about confusing business debt—which everyone agreed should be deducted from taxation as a necessary business expense—with personal debt. Favoring simplicity, Congress extended the principle of deduction to all debts (Howard 1997, 53–54). Although this was later rationalized with the argument that deductions on interest for borrowers are logically required as lenders are already paying taxes on interest received, the historical record suggests that deductions for interest were "accidental" and not part of a logical design (Ventry 2010). Howard also speculates that the larger social context might have led Congress to specifically allow deductions for all indebtedness, as "this treatment of indebtedness favored . . . agricultural interests in the South and West" (Howard 1997, 53–54). Debt was such a central issue to the turn-of-the-century Populists that deduction of debt of all kinds simply continued a Populist tradition. Given the established practice of allowing deductions for particular kinds of debt from legal proceedings and sheltering homesteads from bankruptcy (McKnight 1983; Goodman 1993; Morantz 2006), it should not be surprising that measures favoring debtors received little comment when introduced into the first federal tax legislation. Thus, although the origins remain speculative, the larger political context suggests that deductions for debt were the intersection of a partisan struggle in which manufacturing interests wanted lower taxes in general (and saw deductions as one way to lower taxes), while Populist agrarians wanted favorable treatment of debtors in general (and accepted deductions on debt as one aspect of that favorable treatment).

Similarly, the first legislation enshrining the principle of exclusion of fringe benefits from taxation was an amendment to the Revenue Act of 1926, introduced by Republican Senator George McLean of Connecticut, but scholarship on the reasons behind the passage of this legislation has been hampered by the absence of discussion of it at the time it was passed. McLean said in introducing the amendment only that pension funds operate "on the same basis as those which provide stock bonuses or profit-sharing plans," which were already excluded from taxation (quoted in Howard 1997, 61). There was no debate on the amendment on the floor or in the Treasury reports, and no discussion of it is to be found in newspaper coverage or in memoirs of the key actors (Howard 1997). Howard therefore interprets it as part of the general partisan struggle over taxation that took place in the aftermath of the First World War when Republicans, recently returned to power, sought to reduce taxes in general and the progressive taxes levied during the war in particular, to intense opposition from Democrats and insurgent Republicans. Republicans sought to lower rates and to add provisions to help businesses, and the taxation of pensions was included as part of this new Republican approach to taxation (63). The amendment regarding company pensions was tacked on by a senator who was "a pro-business northeastern Republican who, like Mellon, believed that tax cuts for wealthy individuals and corporations were the key to economic growth" (61). For these reasons, Howard concludes that the origin of the practice of tax preferences for pensions was in the general partisan struggle over progressive taxation in the 1920s, in which they represented a means of reducing business taxes. They gave firms a means to reduce their tax obligations while providing greater compensation to employees.

The next major decision came in 1939, when Congress ruled that fringe benefits did not constitute taxable income. The Internal Revenue Code of 1939 specified "the following items shall not be included in gross income and shall be exempt from taxation under this chapter. . . . Amounts received, through accident or health insurance or under workmen's compensation acts, as compensation for personal injuries or sickness, plus the amount of any damages received whether by suit or agreement on account of such injuries or sickness" (Internal Revenue Code of 1939, chapter 1, section 22(b)(5), 53 statute 10, cited in White 1968–1969, 1603). However, this applied only to programs that were run through commercial insurance groups, not to internal programs funded directly by the employer. Employers were also allowed to deduct amounts paid for pension plans from taxable income, reaffirming prior policies (Internal Revenue Code of 1939, chapter 1, section 23(p)(1), 53 statute 15), and Congress ruled that payroll taxes did not have to be paid on fringe benefits (Jacoby 1993, 546). Prior to this ruling the Treasury had considered health benefits to be taxable income, but since 1919 it had also recognized some fringe benefits—such as meals or accommodations—to be excluded from the definition of taxable income if they were given "for the convenience of the employer" (Simon 1984, 892; Landman 1955, 177). This created an uncertainty in the tax code that some believed held back the adoption of health plans in private companies. The 1939 language clarified this in favor of declaring health benefits that were provided through commercial firms nontaxable (Jacoby 1993).

The 1939 legislation helps to explain the rise in private plans in the early 1940s. Hacker's argument that taxation was not as central as has been thought draws on Dobbin (1992). Dobbin argues that public policy explanations for the rise in private welfare are not supported, because that rise began before the Second World War. Dobbin equates public policy with wartime excess profits taxes, wage freezes, and the Revenue Act of 1942, arguing that all of these came too late to cause the rise in the early 1940s (1992, 1419, 1437). But Dobbin, perhaps following the secondary sources available at the time, does not consider the 1939 tax legislation. His data show a significant increase after 1939 consistent with an argument for the effect of this legislation: for example, health and accident insurance was found in 25.7% of small firms and 38.3% of large firms in 1939, but in 1946, the numbers were 53.3% of small firms and 67.2% of large firms (Dobbin 1992, 1424). Pension plans also grew in this period, and the greatest rise occurred in 1942–1944, at just around the time the government determined that supplemental pensions to high-wage employees were excluded from taxation and just after the Revenue Act of 1942 (Jacoby 1993, 546–547). Informal pension plans and mutual benefit associations declined at the same time that formal private health and pension programs increased (Dobbin 1992, 1427). Zelenak argues that the tax legislation of 1939 and earlier years cannot explain the rise in private welfare before 1940, because the majority of Americans would not begin to pay income tax until 1942 (2010a, 194). But the important tax preference here is the deduction for *employers,* who were already paying comparatively high taxes and who were allowed to deduct or exclude amounts paid for fringe benefits from corporate income tax and payroll tax whether or not the employees who received these amounts were subject to income tax. Because of this, the 1939 legislation supports the argument that tax decisions were one factor in the sharp rise in private welfare programs of the early 1940s.

A few years later, the Revenue Act of 1942 introduced several new features that combined to make health plans even more attractive. It increased top corporate rates and added a wartime excess profits tax of 90%. Moreover, an IRS administrative ruling in 1943 declared employer payments to private insurers for health coverage for employees excluded from taxation. Michael Brown (1997–1998) writes that the ruling was particularly popular with employers because "[i]n the context of the wartime excess profits tax, 85 percent of the costs of health insurance was sheltered income or profits that would have been taxed" (651). The ruling became particularly effective because of the interaction with other wartime policies, for this was one of the few moments at mid-century when the government was actually attempting to restrain consumption in an effort to fight inflation. Through the National War Labor Board, Roosevelt was preventing workers from acquiring wage increases. Caught between the President's attempt to control inflation by limiting wage increases and union members spurred by that same inflation to demand wage increases, the Board encouraged unions to fight for fringe benefits instead, and fringe benefits became a central element of union strategy (651–657). Many union members were paying income taxes for the first time and paying attention to the consequences of tax exemptions (Stevens 1988, 135). As Brown notes, the union decision cannot be explained as a reaction to the failure of the public welfare state, because in fact these decisions were made at a moment—the Truman administration— when the prospects for the public welfare state looked quite high (1997– 1998, 659). Indeed, the 1940s were a moment when the United States might have followed the path taken in other countries—as recently as a decade earlier in some cases—of turning a system of private welfare provision into a state system, as some union leaders and employers were voicing dissatisfaction with the existing system of private health insurance and supporting alternatives (Brown 1997–1998; Quadagno 1984). In this context, Brown argues that the rise of fringe benefits is to be understood as an element in the power struggle between unions and corporations. Fringe benefits were the central element of unions' strategy in cementing workers' loyalty.

If unions saw private welfare provision as an element in preserving loyalty of workers to unions, firms saw private welfare provision as an element in preserving loyalty of workers to firms: "The postwar businessmen advocating privatization of social welfare were inclined to see private social benefits as a bulwark against state socialism . . . the older, anti-union rationale for corporate social benefits remained a vital feature of managerial ideology and strategic practice" (Brown 1997–1998, 648– 649). In addition to tax status, Jacoby also sees the War Labor Board's exclusion of health and pension benefits from wartime wage controls as consequential as well as employers' general attempt to use fringe benefits to fight unionization. While firms did not want collective *bargaining* over private welfare as unions did, they did want private welfare for the same reasons that employers in all other countries have always wanted systems of private welfare—to solidify worker loyalty to firms.

However, the 1943 administrative decision also contained ambiguities, particularly around the specific arrangements that qualified for exclusion, and there was uncertainty over whether the decision could survive a challenge in court (Thomasson 2003, 1374). Some firms testified to inconsistent treatment by the Internal Revenue Service. For example, the Bell Telephone Company had an industrial paternalist health care program from the turn of the century that had developed into in-house health care. In 1918, the IRS deemed the program excluded from taxation, but in 1938, it reversed that ruling and declared the program taxable, reversed itself again in 1941 and deemed it nontaxable, and reversed itself again in 1943, declaring these payments taxable since they were made in-house and not to a commercial insurance firm (Helm 1953). The Revenue Code of 1954 removed this ambiguity by codifying the exclusion. Thomasson uses state-level data to conclude that this tax decision alone raised the amount of group health insurance purchased by nearly 10% (2003, 1382).

After 1954 the effect of taxes on the demand for private health insurance is unclear, with investigations reaching a wide range of estimates (see Gruber and Poterba 1994). But at this point, as Hacker and others have argued, political considerations began to reinforce the path that had been chosen, as those with private health insurance began to fear that public health insurance would lead to dilution or loss of quality in their private programs.

Scholars continue to debate the exact influence of these decisions of 1939, 1942–1943, and 1954, but together these policies have presented American employers with a way to shield a proportion of employee compensation from taxes, contributing to the growth of the system of private welfare. In the early and mid-twentieth century, these tax policies encouraged the replacement of informal pension plans and mutual benefit associations with formal private programs of health and pension insurance.

Comparative Perspectives: Private Welfare in Other Countries

Before exploring the tax code comparatively, we take a brief detour to show that, in fact, private welfare was common in many countries in the late nineteenth and early twentieth centuries. This is necessary because the contemporary scholarship on the welfare state consistently overstates the degree to which the American system of private welfare was unique. As Kinzley (2006) notes, "In the nineteenth century employers throughout Western Europe relied on paternalist family models of employment relations . . . [private welfare programs] were part of a common, international vocabulary of programs and strategies for dealing with the complexities and challenges of modern industrial development" (190; 205).

Private welfare flourished in Britain. Perhaps the most famous example is the Cadbury company, which implemented many private welfare programs between 1902 and 1918, including sickness and pension benefits and free medical and dental care (Dellheim 1987, 29). Robert Fitzgerald (1988) examines company records from before the First World War and finds private welfare all over British industry: railways, gas, iron and steel, chemicals, breweries, textiles, coal mining, shipbuilding, engineering, electrical goods, and food and tobacco, as well as the motor car industry after the First World War. Many industries had exactly the same gamut of private welfare as in the United States, including private health programs.

In railways, welfare programs had a long history, extending as far back as the 1830s, when the railways established "provident societies" for their workers to cover illness, pension, and other benefits. In iron and steel, voluntary sickness benefit funds, infirmaries, health insurance, workers' sick clubs, sick pay, and company-appointed medical personnel were common (84–87). The two firms that dominated the chemicals industry—Imperial Chemicals Industries (ICI) and Unilever—had extensive health and accident programs. As Britain's largest company measured by capital holdings, Unilever's welfare policies were extremely visible in early twentieth century British political economy. One of its welfare schemes was a model village (Port Sunlight) that would be familiar to students of American industrial paternalism, complete with an illness society and, in 1907, a hospital. These two companies, the dominant firms in one of the most important of British industries, "became recognised exponents of all-embracing industrial welfare schemes" (115). Small British firms and even those characterized by more casual labor also turned to industrial welfare, including breweries, shipbuilding, engineering, electrical goods, and food and tobacco companies (137–183).

Fitzgerald argues that, as a method of raising productivity and lessening worker turnover, industrial welfare in Britain was an alternative to Scientific Management and Taylorist principles. At times, these company schemes raised opposition to national health insurance, for example, when the *Brewer's Journal* worried in 1911 about the effects of national insurance on their company programs (142). But eventually, Fitzgerald argues, the British public welfare state arose out of private welfare, particularly through the innovation of allowing firms with private welfare schemes to "contract out" of the public scheme if they met certain minimum levels (212).

Private welfare flourished in Canada. Around the First World War employers resisted a rising wave of labor unrest by supporting private welfare alternatives including "company pension plans, profit-sharing, medical services, recreational facilities, and improved working conditions" (Yarmie 2003, 598). Yarmie argues, "Employers in both countries [Canada and the United States] also began to use welfarism to contain the labor movement [in the period around the First World War]. The parallel approaches to industrial relations by employers and governments undermine any claim of American uniqueness" (613).

Naylor writes that in Ontario in 1919, "innovative measures in industrial relations were generally the result of private, not state, activity. As the product of the initiatives of individual firms, they were generally modelled on the Rockefeller Plan and provided no space for trade-union participation.... Employers were guided by an image of pre-capitalist paternalism" (1991, 165). He notes that after the First World War, a "wide range of measures was introduced to instil [sic] a loyalty to the firm and a degree of satisfaction with the workplace. These post-war welfare programs were notable not for their novelty but for the sheer number of companies that became involved in providing new and often elaborate services to their employees.... In 1882, McClary's had established an Employee Benefit Society to provide workers with sickness and death benefits. In 1910, the company turned to a more generalized welfare system ... [including] some medical care" (166). Some of these measures were clearly oriented to controlling workers, such as a company nurse employed to make home visits on ill workers. After the war, other employers were "caught up in the movement and had implemented similar and even more extensive programs. All the policies that combined to form a more-or-less coherent strategy of welfare capitalism represented responses to major problems of labour control" (168). Benefit plans, with sickness benefits as the norm, were very popular, with Canadian branches of international companies often leading the trend.

Private welfare flourished in Germany, and German historians have tended to see it as a template for the welfare state rather than as an alternative to it. McCreary (1968) provides the most dramatic example, suggesting a direct link between German social legislation and the private welfare systems of Krupp, one of the larger German firms of the latter part of the nineteenth century: "On the national level, it is no accident that health insurance legislation was the first welfare measure to be enacted, against the express wishes of Bismarck. . . . Nor is it any accident that Germany led other industrial nations in the general field of social legislation. . . . The Reichstag accepted the chancellor's proposals because they were *not* revolutionary. They simply took programs, formerly voluntary and private, with which all the greater industrialists had long been familiar, and, making them compulsory, extended them to the national sphere" (26–27, emphasis in original).

The Krupp plan, he notes, was not the first in the country, not even in Essen (28). The Krupp programs included an extensive health care plan, pension plans, life insurance, housing, schools, and various other smaller welfare benefits. Extensive documentation has been preserved on Alfred Krupp's motivations, which prove to be similar to all welfare capitalists everywhere: a mixture of charitable ideals and hardheaded calculations about worker loyalty (39–41). His efforts at inculcating loyalty to the firm seem to have been very successful: "Natives of Essen still speak of the sense of status enjoyed by Krupp's employees prior to World War I. They were not 'hands' or laborers or even steelworkers. They were 'Kruppians.' " (47). As evidence for the proposition that the Krupp voluntary plan influenced the national compulsory plan, McCreary mentions that the Krupps were personally close to Wilhelm I and Wilhelm II as well as to Bismarck (30) and writes: "While it is impossible to gauge precisely the extent of Krupp's influence on the national program, given the size and importance of the firm, the success of its welfare program, and these personal contacts, it seems fair to conclude that such an influence did exist" (30–31).

Kocka (1971) and Kastl and Moore (2006) examine private welfare provision in Siemens and Halske; Berghoff (1997) examines Hohner; and Sweeney (2009) considers heavy industry in the Saar. Private welfare provision was so important in Germany that in the 1970s scholars began to debate whether such systems were holdovers from a feudal past or whether they were driven by instrumental concerns; consequences for German industrialization were also considered (see Berghoff 1997 for an overview). The details of this debate do not concern us here as much as the fact that these and later scholars found enough private welfare in Germany to generate rival theories of its place in German history.

Private welfare flourished in Japan. Kinzley (2006) discusses a survey in the early 1920s "of 233 companies by the Tokyo city government [which] reported the existence of well-staffed medical clinics in many companies" (189). This range of protections and benefits was similar to that found elsewhere, including health programs, for example, in the textile industry, the largest industry in Japan at the turn of the century: "The 1903 Ministry of Agriculture and Commerce survey of company welfare facilities in 123 textile firms reported 65 having in-house medical facilities of some sort with most claiming some kind of worker protection assistance as well" (195–196). In another important industry, railroads, private health benefits were central, among other welfare benefits (198–201). In Japan private and public welfare benefits were not mutually exclusive. State action helped to further the development of private welfare through models of welfare provision in state-owned firms as well as through legislation (194–195).

Private welfare flourished in France. For example, Paul Dutton (2002) notes, "Employment-dependent programs made up the core of France's family welfare and social insurance programs from the late 1920s until the end of the Second World War" (11). Michael B. Miller, in a thorough history of the French department store Bon Marché, provides the best investigation of private welfare, using the term "industrial paternalism" common among French scholars. He argues that "paternalism did not readily die out as Western economies became more advanced, nor was it simply a prolongation of labor policies determined in an earlier era. . . . In France it could be found most prominently among some of the largest, the most dynamic, and the most innovative firms in the French economy well into the twentieth century, where it served purposes in accordance with its times" (1994, 8). He concludes that paternalism helped to reconcile citizens with corporations (9–10). Donald Reid (1985) finds this industrial paternalism in France as early as the nineteenth century. As in the United States, firms saw these paternalist measures as a way to keep state control over industry at bay (587). In the 1850s calico-printing firms had developed "a savings society, an old-age home, public baths, worker housing, a society for maternity care, and associations to prevent and investigate industrial accidents" (Piore and Sabel 1984, 34).

Peter Stearns (1978) conducts a systematic study of industrial paternalism in France in the nineteenth century, concluding that the majority of large firms had paternalist programs: "At least 461 companies identifiable by name began to develop a paternalistic program before 1848. Given the inadequacy of records, this understates the actual situation. Since fewer than 656 factories employed over fifty workers in the 1840s, we are talking about the majority of firms in this category" (1978, 89). By the 1840s, "at least fifty large companies gradually extended the coverage of their aid groups to include pensions, sometimes just to widows and orphans, always modest in amount . . . but increasingly aiding adult males if they devoted their life to the firm" (95). Moreover, companies were starting to provide on-site medical care, including surgery rooms or even hospitals (96). Stearns writes: "There was no sharp change, but the evolution was clear: policies adopted reluctantly at first or with a self-satisfied sense of generosity, now became standard expenses" (99).

In stark opposition to the recent American historiography that has seen American welfare capitalism as crowding out the state's role in welfare provision, French historians see industrial paternalism as having generated a model upon which the welfare state would be built. Dutton, for example, argues that social insurance and welfare programs "grew out of employer initiatives and private mutual aid societies" and that when state legislation came, private mutual aid societies managed to acquire administrative responsibility for social insurance (2002, 3). Far from seeing private and public welfare provision as mutually exclusive, Dutton views them in a complicated engagement with each other in which private provision often leads to public provision, or in which private schemes are given administrative responsibility for public provision. (This resembles Lloyd George's strategy of overcoming the resistance of the private "friendly societies" to public welfare in Britain by giving the societies responsibility for the administration of the new public program [Sokolovsky 1998]).

Dutton argues that the imprint of the early private provision is visible in the fragmented and decentralized nature of the early French welfare state: "Mutual aid societies served as the model for social insurance while industrialists' family allowance institutions became the archetype for family welfare . . . the choice of the mutual model also proved fateful for France's postwar welfare state. The creation of a 'mutualized' social insurance system immortalized decentralization along occupational lines" (2002, 5). Moreover, the separation of family welfare and social insurance is a legacy of their origins in separate private models (5).

Although quantitative examination of the extent of private welfare provision in each country is rare, and the inadequacy of historical records may never allow for systematic comparisons of the percent of the labor force covered by these policies, these case studies show that private welfare clearly existed in every country.[1] Jacoby (1998) argues that although private welfare existed in other countries it was relatively less important and "was preempted by the early development of the European welfare states; conversely, U.S. welfare capitalism preceded and in important ways constrained the New Deal welfare programs. For example, in 1939—when the foundations had been laid for the Swedish welfare state but Social Security had not yet taken hold in the United States—the percentage of the Swedish elderly population receiving a public pension already was 79 percent, as opposed to only 5 percent in the United States" (164–165). But the example of pensions seems to undermine Jacoby's case rather than support it, because old age pensions are the one area of the welfare state where the United States is not a laggard (see Scruggs and Allan 2006, 62–64 for a discussion of why an earlier generation of scholarship may have underestimated the importance of public pensions in the United States). The early template of private provision did not prevent the elaboration of a comprehensive public pensions program in the United States, just as clearly established systems of private benefits did not preempt the turn to the state in other countries. Analysts have argued for more rupture between private and public systems of welfare than the histories seem to warrant; in Europe, the welfare state developed in tight relation to systems of private welfare, borrowing models from them, or ceding responsibility to them, and even in the United States, a vigorous public pensions program has grown alongside private programs. Thus, we cannot simply argue that private welfare provision in the United States inevitably crowded out public provision, as the currently most popular explanation for the underdeveloped welfare state contends. We need to answer the question of why the United States was unable to overcome the resistance of these private welfare programs in the early and mid-twentieth century when every other advanced industrial country was able to prevail.

It is here that the role of tax preferences becomes clear. At midcentury, while European systems of private welfare were replaced by public welfare states, the United States passed a series of tax laws and policies that reinforced the American commitment to private welfare by encouraging the formation of formal private health and pension programs. Where informal private systems gave rise to welfare states in Europe, informal private systems such as mutual benefit associations gave way to formal private systems of welfare in the United States. Particularly in health care, a domain in which public and private programs may not coexist as easily as in pensions (Hacker 2002, 202), the tax laws encouraged and codified the private alternative. This is the juncture at which the relative underdevelopment of the American welfare state began, suggesting that examination of the reasons for the unusual development of health care in the United States requires a broader understanding of the origins of that mid-century series of tax legislation and a comparative perspective on tax progressivity and the role of tax preferences.

The Consequences of Progressivity

Despite the sparse historical record on the origins of tax preferences in the United States, we can gain some analytical perspective on them by examining why other countries did not develop a series of tax policies similar to the United States in the early twentieth century. One element that has not been emphasized in the literature on the origins of tax preferences is the very different structure of corporate taxation in the United States compared to other countries in the early twentieth century. Because of the American political focus on progressive taxation, in the early twentieth century the United States was unusual in having a separate corporate tax at all, as well as in the way that corporate tax operated. The 1913 income tax had introduced a 1% tax on corporations, raised to 12% in 1918 and 24% in 1940. In the 1930s the exclusion in the individual income tax for corporate dividends was repealed, leading to what has been called "double taxation" of corporate earnings (Brownlee 2004; Bank 2010).[2] No other country had this combination of progressive taxation and a fragmented democratic context early in the twentieth century. Although fully comparative data on taxes in the early twentieth century are not available, the evidence that does exist shows higher and more progressive taxes on corporations and dividends in the United States by mid-century. In 1938, one comparative study of taxation of dividends noted "[t]he most striking variance between the countries is in the very high rates imposed in this country [the United States] on those with very large incomes. . . . On the other hand rates in this country are relatively moderate in the lower and middle brackets" (*Wall Street Journal* 1940). The first year in which systematic comparisons of corporate taxation across countries become available is 1955. In this year the United States was second only to the United Kingdom in corporation tax as a percent of GDP (OECD 1981, calculated from tables 1 and 8). Ten years later, corporation tax as a percentage of GDP had plunged in the United Kingdom to one of the lowest figures among the OECD countries but remained high in the United States (OECD 2010b). This reflects both the instability and incoherence that characterizes British tax policy (Steinmo 1989), as well as American commitment to corporate taxation in this period. Corporate taxes have fallen in America since then, and risen elsewhere, so that today the United States is no longer unusually progressive in corporate taxation; however, if our aim is to understand the origins of the politics of tax preferences, the relevant comparison is corporate tax structure earlier in the twentieth century, when tax preferences arose and became politically central. (While there is a debate on who ultimately pays the corporate tax burden, the concern here is the political, not the economic, consequences of corporate taxes.)

In France, there was no separate tax on corporate income until 1948 (Delalande 2011, 382; Shoup 1955), but since 1917 there had been a tax on the profits of industrial and commercial interests (replacing the older *patente*), and securities were taxed separately. These two taxes together constituted a large part of total revenue, but their yield was lessened by routine underassessment in both cases (Owen 1982, 348–349). The reluctance to implement reliable procedures of assessment was an outgrowth of widespread French fear of the "fiscal inquisition" by the state that direct taxes represented at the time (Morgan and Prasad 2009). Although the Socialists led a long interwar effort to enact a onetime capital levy as a means of retiring war debt, weak governments and the opposition of the right forced a turn toward indirect taxation (Owen 1982; Delalande 2011). The result was that by 1965 corporate tax as a percentage of GDP in France was less than half the level in the United States (OECD 2010b).[3] France did have a long tradition of tax exemptions (see, e.g., Hoffman 1986), but in the context of the country's emerging regressive tax regime tax preferences do not seem to have been a major concern of corporations or their political defenders. Rather than escape taxation through tax preferences, taxpayers escaped taxation through policies that systematically underassessed values subject to direct taxation, ultimately forcing a turn to indirect taxation.

Sweden has been marked by a tax regime unusually hospitable to capital not only during this time but also ever since. In 1938, corporate taxes were reformed in a manner that benefited large and capital-intensive firms, a key factor in reconciling employer groups to the welfare state (Högfeldt 2005, 541). In successive years, "Social Democratic governments have extended a set of deep tax expenditures . . . designed to encourage investment and savings, iron out fluctuations in the business cycle, and concentrate Sweden's economic resources into its largest and most profitable corporations. In Sweden, unlike any other country that this author is aware of, taxes on corporate profits are inversely related to both profitability and size. In other words, the larger and more profitable a corporation, the lower its tax rates" (Steinmo 1988, 407). In 1965, corporate tax as a percent of GDP in Sweden was just over half the level in the United States (OECD 2010b). In Sweden, capital income is also taxed at lower top rates than wages (Ganghof 2008, 73). Tax preferences exist in Sweden, but they are nowhere near as important as in the United States (Steinmo 1989). In general, capital in Sweden has been granted low taxes outright as part of the grand bargain of economic growth for welfare and does not need to fight for lower taxes through the back door of tax preferences.

In Britain, despite an overall progressive tax structure and high taxes paid by corporations in the early postwar period, there was no separate corporate tax rate until 1965 (apart from temporary wartime measures, Daunton 2001, 211; 2002); corporations paid the general income tax, and Britain used "a shareholder imputation system, where shareholders are provided a credit for dividend payments. Depending upon the size of this credit, it reduces or eliminates the second layer of tax" (Bank 2004, 2). Corporate tax yields also varied in accordance with the volatile pattern of British tax policymaking, and by 1965 they were among the lowest of the advanced industrial countries (OECD 2010b). Because corporations paid the general income tax, the practice of carving out special exceptions to corporate tax rates was not feasible. And the pattern of tax policymaking was hostile to the proliferation of tax preferences: where Congress was the site for intensive lobbying in the United States, "[i]n Britain, tax measures emanated from the executive, in circumstances of some secrecy: the budget was written by the chancellor, often with minimal discussion with his colleagues in Cabinet, following the advice of a small group of Treasury officials who had a strong commitment to general measures" (Daunton 2001, 72). As far back as the nineteenth century, comparison of Britain to France shows that "there were no glaring exemptions to taxation in Britain" (7). At the turn of the century, Inland Revenue worried that even granting exemptions for charitable donations would be the thin edge of the wedge that would undoubtedly lead to a chaotic pressure for exemptions of different kinds and end up reducing the government's collective capacity. The British code did come to include some preferences, for example, the exclusion of mortgage interest, but even here the limits of the loan amounts that can be excluded are so low that "mortgage subsidies provide almost no incentive at the margin for most taxpayers" and because of inflation "decline in the value of mortgage interest subsidies has been gradual but gigantic" (Gale 1997, 352–353). Britain's concentrated budget-making procedure ensured that tax preferences would not become politically central.

Germany is closer to the American model, with corporate taxation including the "double taxation" of dividends established since 1920 and eliminated only in 1977 (Genschel 2002a; Mehrotra 2010; King and Fullerton 1984, 157). Although Germany did have a corporation tax that could have become a site for the politics of tax preferences, at mid-century Germany's revenue from corporate taxation was much lower than the United States (OECD 2010b), weakening corporations' incentives to press for preferences. The different nature of agrarian politics in the early part of the century may also have played a role. While both the United States and Germany had about one-third of their labor forces in agriculture in the early twentieth century, a key difference between the two countries was the predominance of what Kane and Mann (1992) call "peasant farmers" in the United States, that is, farmers who owned property but did not hire other laborers to farm it, relying on household production. While these American agrarians were pushing for measures such as favorable policies for debtors that led to the context in which tax preferences arose, large landowners were the only agrarians who were able to wield much influence in Germany, and for the reasons discussed in Chapter 3, their concerns at this time were dominated by protectionism (Kane and Mann 1992; Koning 1994). In Germany, corporations experienced neither the high levels of taxation nor the political context that gave rise to tax preferences.

For these reasons, politicians in other countries were not trying to punch holes in the tax rate for corporations in the first half of the twentieth century: taxes on corporations did not even exist in some cases and were much less onerous in most cases, or tax preferences were not politically viable for other reasons. All of these capitalist countries developed policies to favor capital in the early twentieth century, but the power of a mobilized agrarian contingent forced the United States to place high rates on corporations and then offer them exceptions through the back door of tax preferences. Tax preferences became a key element of the early- to mid-twentieth-century political world, and this is the background against which exclusions for fringe benefits are to be understood.

Comparatively heavy corporate taxation unleashed a political sequence that ended with a proliferation of tax preferences.

This politics of tax preferences became extremely resilient and undermined the prospects for national health care. Scholars have shown that both corporations and unions fought for employer-provided health benefits, rather than national health care, partly because employer-provided benefits were excluded from taxes. But the deeper question that this research has so far failed to answer is why tax preferences were so important in the United States. I argue here that the politics of tax preferences—and therefore the politics of health care—is tied to progressive taxation. Progressive taxation at the turn of the twentieth century placed extremely high tax rates on corporations and the wealthy. Given the established practice of excluding certain kinds of income from taxation, legislators responded by seeking tax preferences of all kinds. The combination of progressive taxation and a fragmented policymaking structure was particularly consequential, because it made broad cuts in rates difficult and led, therefore, to a search for other ways to reduce taxes. This created a specific relational structure between capital and the state that made tax preferences a central part of politics. This politics eventually resulted in tax preferences for private welfare benefits that corporations gave their employees. Because most other countries did not have such high corporate taxes early in the twentieth century, they did not develop this politics of tax preferences. Powerful corporations in other countries did not need to resort to tax preferences because they could count on lower corporate taxes in general. And national health insurance in other countries did not get tangled up in and eventually sidelined by fights over tax preferences because the political structure and the tax structure of these other countries did not produce the odd curiosity of a polity focused on tax preferences to begin with.

This chapter has identified three ways in which the American tax structure interacts with the welfare state. Progressive taxes may lead to more political protest than regressive taxes because of their greater visibility. Taxes on income and capital may be more economically distorting than taxes on labor and consumption. And in a situation of fragmented government, progressive taxation gave rise to a regime of tax preferences that privileged the development of a private system of welfare that was ultimately detrimental to the development of the public welfare state. Certainly progressive taxation is not the only factor relevant to an examination of the development of the American welfare state, but I hope to have shown here that it is one important factor, and that an examination of welfare programs separate from examination of the fiscal capacity of the state is incomplete.

This part of the book has examined the curious process by which overproduction led to a focus on tax progressivity, which in turn constrained the welfare state. Part III takes a broader and more explicitly comparative focus to examine the other main policy attempt that arose out of American abundance: consumer credit.

PART THREE

THE AGRARIAN
REGULATION OF FINANCE

7

AMERICAN ADVERSARIAL REGULATION

One of the most curious issues raised by the financial crisis of 2007–2008 is that while the financial deregulations of the 1990s are cited by many as contributing to the crisis, the U.S. financial system has traditionally been more heavily regulated than the financial systems of Europe in some central areas. Indeed, this tradition of heavier regulations compared to Europe was often given as a reason for the deregulation of the 1990s. And yet, those deregulations in the American context seemed to have significantly worse outcomes than in the European countries, causing a financial and economic crisis second only to the Great Depression in the postwar period: European style deregulation does not work in the United States. This leads to two questions for comparative political economy. First, how can the "liberal" United States, the paradigmatic example of a market economy, have had heavier financial regulation? And second, when the United States attempted to imitate the less regulated systems of Europe, why were the consequences so much worse than in Europe?

Surprisingly, there is not much literature on comparative financial regulation. There is increasing research on the issue of *global* financial regulation (e.g., Herring and Litan 1995; Singer 1997; Posner 2009), but the global financial regulatory regime is a work in progress. At the moment it consists only of a patchwork set of standards on a limited number of issues. For example, the Basel Accords, the centerpiece of global financial regulation, are limited to the issue of minimum capital requirements. They do not address either the issues of credit rating and securitization that were central to the recent financial crisis or the regulation of banking activities in multiple sectors and the conflicts of interest that some argue stem from such activities, the main concern of Glass-Steagall (see Tarullo [2008] for a critique of the reliance on capital requirements as the lynchpin of international financial regulation). To understand contemporary financial dynamics we need to turn our attention to national-level regulation.

The literature comparing national-level financial regulation is most developed on the issue of banking regulation. This literature suggests that the United States had more stringent regulation than other countries at least until the 1990s and on some dimensions even after the 1990s. As Andreas Busch writes, "Contrary to popular conceptions of economic life in the United States, American banks operate in a highly regulated banking environment" (2009, 33); this has been the case since the Great Depression. Busch notes that in the United Kingdom no formal regulatory agency exists at all to regulate banks and that both Germany and Switzerland responded to the Great Depression with lighter regulation than the United States.

Howell Jackson compares the intensity of financial regulation in several countries by comparing regulatory budgets, personnel levels, and enforcement efforts. He finds as a general trend that "the common law countries—the United States, United Kingdom, and countries formerly connected to the British Empire—report markedly higher levels of regulatory intensity on all dimensions I have studied" (Jackson 2007, 256) and that in terms of total regulatory costs as a percent of GDP and total regulatory staff as a percent of the population, the United States has higher costs of financial regulation than Australia, Canada, France, Germany, Ireland, Sweden, and the United Kingdom. In securities enforcement, "the United States had substantially more enforcement actions than the United Kingdom and Germany" (283). Duffie and Hu compare the United States to the United Kingdom and find: "U.K.-style prudential supervision has resulted in levels of enforcement that are orders of magnitude lower than those of the United States"(2008, 29). John Coffee further notes that even in the cases when the United States seems similar to other common law countries on enforcement inputs (budgets and staffing), it is much more stringent in terms of enforcement outputs (enforcement actions, monetary sanctions, class action suits, criminal enforcement) than its closest common law rival, the United Kingdom (Coffee 2007–2008).

One may wonder if American financiers are more likely to take risks or to bend rules, requiring higher regulation and greater efforts of enforcement. But what is considered rule breaking in the United States is considered rule following elsewhere: the United States criminalizes actions that other countries do not. The most painstaking study of comparative financial regulation to date is a study of banking regulation that was undertaken for the World Bank (Barth, Caprio, and Levine 2001). The results, as shown in Figure 7.1, were that the United States had the most stringent banking regulation of any of the advanced industrial countries other than Japan until 1999 (before the repeal of Glass-Steagall) (see Barth, Caprio, and Levine 2005). Financial actions that would have been criminal in the United States before the repeal of Glass Steagall were perfectly legal in other countries. Even countries with greater government ownership of banks saw those state-owned banks operating with fewer restrictions than private banks in the United States, complicating recent attempts to draw conclusions about the effect of government ownership of banks on financial development (e.g., La Porta, Lopez-de-Silanes, and Shleifer 2002).

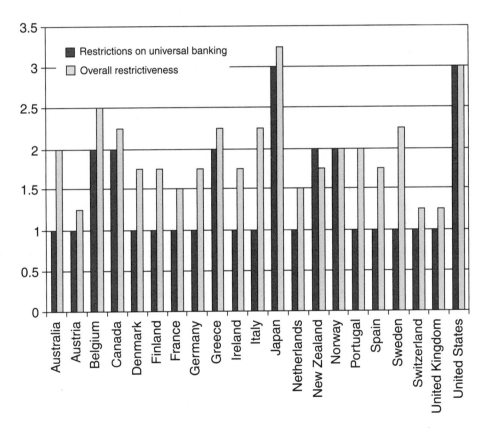

Figure 7.1. Restrictiveness of banking regulation before 1999. (*Source:* Barth, Caprio, and Levine 2001.)

Having seen other areas of greater regulation in previous chapters, this picture of heavier financial regulation in the United States should not surprise us. Not all areas of the financial system show this pattern; most notably, shadow banking has escaped regulation in the United States (Gorton and Metrick 2010). But the heavier regulation of entry barriers was consequential because it was often given as a reason for deregulation. From the late 1980s through the 1990s, observers repeatedly pointed out that European countries have never had legislation separating commercial and investment banking (Canals 1997; and that European banks were much less restricted in setting up branches, as we will discuss in the next chapter). This was taken as evidence that the United States did not need such a separation either. This argument was cited as a reason for enacting Gramm Leach Bliley (GLB), which repealed the separation of commercial and investment banking that the Glass-Steagall Act had implemented. This argument was made by scholars (e.g., Benston 1994; Calomiris 2000) as well as by financiers themselves ("Today banks, insurance companies and securities firms ... must be able to compete with the same flexibility their European and Asian counterparts already enjoy. U.S. financial corporations cannot do that unless Congress sweeps aside our antiquated banking laws" [Komansky, Purcell, and Weill 1997]; "I think that if you look to Europe or you look to Asia, organizations like ours already exist, where banks and insurance companies and investment companies are all part of what they call universal banks" [Weill, quoted in "Financial Powerhouse," 1998]).

It was cited on the floors of Congress by members of both parties, including Daniel Patrick Moynihan ("London does it. Tokyo too. Why not New York ... ?" *Congressional Record* 1999, 28357), Richard Lugar ("This bill will finally break down inefficient barriers between insurance, banking, and securities and allow United States financial services corporations to compete on an even basis with their European and Asian counterparts" *Congressional Record* 1999, 28356), and Pete Domenici ("Currently, European laws are much more flexible, allowing financial services firms across the Atlantic to be better integrated than United States firms. Our laws need to keep pace. This conference report will allow our various banking, insurance, and securities firms to combine through financial holding companies so that they may be even stronger competitors in the increasingly international financial services marketplace" *Congressional Record* 1999, 28356).

This argument was cited in defense of Gramm Leach Bliley after the financial crisis erupted: "It seems clear that if GLB was the problem, the crisis would have been expected to have originated in Europe where they never had Glass-Steagall requirements to begin with" (Gramm 2009).

It was given by President Obama in 2009 as one of the main reasons to resist reimposing the separation of commercial and investment banking ("You know, I've looked at the evidence so far that indicates that other countries that have not seen some of the problems in their financial markets that we have nevertheless don't separate between investment banks and commercial banks, for example." Barack Obama, quoted in Leonhardt 2009). The common wisdom is that if the European countries can function well with lower levels of financial regulation, then the United States can too. This was not the only reason for the passage of Gramm Leach Bliley, but it was one important reason (Barth, Brumbaugh, and Wilcox 2000).

And yet, many think that this series of deregulations was a factor in the unraveling of the American financial system. For example, much work remains to be done to measure the specific effects of the repeal of Glass-Steagall, but it is clear that unqualified optimism on Gramm Leach Bliley is unwarranted. Eleven studies have been conducted on the effect of Gramm Leach Bliley on financial sector risk. Four (Mamun, Hassan, and Lai 2004; Neale and Peterson 2005; Mamun, Hassan, and Maroney 2005; Yildirim, Kwag, and Collins 2006) find that GLB reduced risk in the financial sector, three (Stiroh and Rumble 2005, Allen and Bali 2007; Geyfman and Yeager 2009) find the opposite, and four (Allen, Jagtiani, and Moser 2001; Elyasiani, Mansur, Pagano 2007; Baele, De Jonghe, and Vander Vennet 2007; Cebula 2010) reach mixed conclusions or find no effect. Moreover, the studies finding greater risk may be measuring the independent variable more accurately: all of the studies that find reduced risk of GLB compare the period immediately preceding GLB to the period during and after it. But as many scholars have noted, GLB simply formalized a process of circumventing Glass-Steagall restrictions that had been underway for many years, suggesting that a continuous measure is more appropriate; the studies finding greater risk after GLB are more likely to use a continuous and therefore more accurate measure of the independent variable. More research is necessary, but it is already clear that the optimism that GLB had nothing to do with the crisis rests on extremely shaky analytical foundations.

The mechanisms by which the repeal of Glass-Steagall may have contributed to the crisis are also starting to be understood. First, the repeal of Glass-Steagall increased the sheer size of financial institutions, allowing their health to affect larger and larger parts of the economy, creating what some analysts have called "systemic risk" (Moss 2009). Second, while studies have reached contradictory findings on the ability of the financial system as a whole to diversify risk following GLB, the volatility of earnings and stock market performance of traditional commercial banks seems to have increased after the act (Rajan 2006, Stiroh and Rumble 2006). Akhigbe and Whyte (2004) suggest that while securities firms have been able to reduce risk by diversifying into traditional commercial banks, traditional commercial banks have increased risk by diversifying into the riskier securities business. Finally, even before GLB, banking possessed greater uncertainty than other areas of the financial system, as measured by divergence in ratings produced by different credit rating agencies (Morgan 2002); the exposure of greater areas of the financial system to banking suggests the spread of this opacity throughout the system, leading to the credit rating agencies' now widely acknowledged failure. Gramm Leach Bliley was not the only consequential regulatory reform (the nonregulation of the Commodity Futures Modernization Act had the most direct consequences), but it was one of several changes in regulatory governance that collectively reduced the ability of the state to constrain finance. The mixing of investment and commercial lending made each vulnerable to the other, as new financial instruments for commercial lending were developed that were ultimately derived from consumer lending, and consumer lending became subject to fluctuations in the stock market.

In short, the United States deregulated partly because European countries were much less heavily regulated, but those deregulations seem to have had worse consequences in the United States. This chapter and the next two chapters examine why this was the case.

There are three key differences between the United States and other countries in the regulation of consumer finance. First, for most of the century the United States had more debtor-friendly bankruptcy laws, which made taking on debt a less onerous proposition. Second, and in some tension with this, during and after the Depression the United States implemented the most extensive regulation of banking of any country, including the Glass-Steagall prohibition against the universal banking practised in other countries, as well as a prohibition on interstate branch banking as found in other countries. Third, after the Second World War the United States developed a political economy driven by home-mortgage financing.

These differences coalesced into a regime that was unusually dependent on the flow of credit, making credit easier to get and bankruptcy easier to survive, but the banks that provided this credit were also strictly regulated. This chapter and the next trace the emergence of this complex of regulatory techniques—what I have summarized under the term the *agrarian regulation of finance*—by investigating the origins of the more debtor-friendly bankruptcy laws, the more extensive regulation, and the reliance on home mortgage financing. Chapter 9 pulls these arguments together to answer the questions posed above: why the "liberal" United States had such interventionist banking regulations, and why attempts to move in the direction of less regulated Europe had such negative consequences.

Bankruptcy

Colonial America borrowed English bankruptcy laws on debtors' prisons and implemented draconian punishments such as cropping the ears or branding the thumbs of debtors (Mann 2002, 78ff; Noel 1919, 54, 71). The nineteenth century saw a slow but continuous easing of the condition of debtors. A weak federal bankruptcy law was passed as early as 1800 but repealed just three years later (Balleisen 2001; Sandage 2005). The states began abolishing debtors' prisons in the 1820s and 1830s (Warren 1935). In 1841 the first federal bankruptcy law that applied to all debtors and allowed debtors themselves to declare bankruptcy came on the books, but was repealed just over a year later (Balleisen 2001). Another such law came into effect in 1867, attended by rhetorical flourishes comparing debt bondage to slavery, but in 1878 this too was repealed (Sandage 2005).

Only in 1898 did a federal bankruptcy law pass that stayed on the books. In this year the "fresh start" policy of bankruptcy took effect, and until the bankruptcy reforms of 2005 "most individual consumer debtors in the United States enjoyed broad access to an immediate and unconditional discharge of debts, unhampered even by a corresponding requirement of future income contribution. The only other countries with a hint of a 'liberal' policy for debtors have been England and its Commonwealth countries, most notably Canada. But, even in those jurisdictions, the law historically could hardly be characterized as debtor friendly: Debtors have never been able to get an immediate debt discharge as in the States, facing instead various restrictions imposing limited, conditional, and suspended discharge rules" (Tabb 2005, 763–764).

Debtor-friendly bankruptcy laws would seem to violate the cardinal principle of capitalism, the protection of private property. But some observers have seen in this attitude towards debt and bankruptcy a peculiarly American brand of freewheeling, risk-taking capitalism. Tocqueville wrote: "Commercial business is [in America] like a vast lottery, by which a small number of men continually lose, but the State is always a gainer; such a people ought therefore to encourage and do honor to boldness in commercial speculations. But any bold speculation risks the fortune of the speculator and of all those who put their trust in him. The Americans, who make a virtue of commercial temerity, have no right in any case to brand with disgrace those who practise it. Hence arises the strange indulgence which is shown to bankrupts in the United States; their honor does not suffer by such an accident. In this respect the Americans differ, not only from the nations of Europe, but from all the commercial nations of our time" (1840, 152).

Scott Sandage has recently brought together evidence suggesting that Tocqueville was wrong about the absence of dishonor associated with economic failure. In 1812 proponents of a bankruptcy law were complaining that debtors were "no longer recognized as a citizen of the community . . . doomed to slavery, misery, and bondage for life" (quoted in Sandage 2005, 194). In the years before the passage of the 1867 law an outpouring of letters from debtors testifies to how they perceived their state: "I have passed Ten years in worse bondage than that of the black man at the South, more humiliating and degrading for I was no longer regarded as an equal amongst my old associates" (quoted in Sandage 2005, 202). Others considered themselves "bound down with a bondage worse than slavery" (quoted in Sandage 2005, 190). There was a clear stigma attached to economic failure in America in the nineteenth century at the time when the bankruptcy laws diverged from European precedents, and debtors did not have the luxury of knowing that "their honor does not suffer."[1]

It is worth pausing here to consider these arguments in relation to each other, because they show why cultural arguments are so resilient. Where Tocqueville argued that absence of dishonor associated with economic failure proved the market orientation of the American regime, Sandage (2005) argues that the exact opposite—the dishonor associated with economic failure—proves the market orientation of the American regime. Sandage argues that economic failure was read as moral failure and therefore served to discipline Americans into behaving in accordance with the needs of a market economy. Sandage does not offer comparative evidence showing that nonmarket economies or less fully marketized economies read economic failure as morally neutral, but if Tocqueville is right that this too would show a cultural preference for the market, then it is hard to see any of this evidence as relevant to the question of why the laws were instituted. But the ability to read directly opposed empirical patterns as proving the existence of a market-friendly culture in the United States demonstrates why the cultural argument has remained so prominent, as it is easy for scholars to argue that any pattern they find supports the argument.

A deeper look into the origin of these laws suggests that, rather than a culture unusually favorable to the market, the bankruptcy law of 1898 was the outcome of an uneasy marriage between commercial interests and debtors' rights proponents, particularly farmers. Manufacturers and capitalists did want a systematic bankruptcy law, because it would prevent the reigning practice of debtors paying off favored creditors (particularly family and relatives) first. After the repeal of the 1867 law commercial interests pushed relentlessly for another federal bankruptcy law. However, the feature of the 1898 law that is unusual in comparative perspective—its debtor-friendly characteristic—was a result of the influence of debtors' groups. Skeel writes: "At the heart of this resistance to a creditor-oriented bankruptcy law in the 1880s and 1890s were the agrarian and populist movements that emerged in the last half of the nineteenth century, and which overlapped with the states' rights movement that remained influential in the South. . . . bankruptcy was an extraordinarily prominent issue, and lawmakers from farm states actively promoted the ideological views of their rural constituents. . . . In the populist imagination, bankruptcy law was often linked with the gold standard as the two greatest scourges of the common laborer" (2001, 38–39). One legislator summarized the argument thus: the gold standard was "the seed which was sown to the great crop of ruin, and this bankruptcy bill follows as a harvester and thrasher to enable Shylock to gather in his crop" (quoted in Skeel, 39). The perspectives of the agrarians were amplified by the federalist structure of the American state. Pro-creditor Republicans from the manufacturing Northeast found themselves forced to give concessions to Republicans from the Midwest to have any hopes of a bankruptcy bill passing. Without this pressure from the agrarians, the bankruptcy bill that emerged would have been similar to the more creditor-friendly bankruptcy law that England, for example, passed in the same period. Thus, the peculiarly American concept of bankruptcy as a "fresh start," as the complete forgiveness of debt, was introduced as a direct result of populist agitation, in the same burst of reform that we examined in Chapter 3.

Adversarial Regulation

While bankruptcy is an important difference, another extremely unusual facet of American-style regulation is the reliance on regulatory agencies that are uniquely adversarial to capital. Because this feature is so consequential to the story being tracked in this book, in this section we take a step back to understand the broader development of American regulation.

Over the course of the twentieth century the United States developed a system of regulation of the market that was unique in relying on regulatory agencies. These federal regulatory agencies—the familiar "alphabet soup" from the ICC and the FDA to the SEC, the EEOC, the EPA, OSHA, and many more—accrued autonomous power and applied rules in a legalistic manner unseen in any other country. Some of these agencies are housed within the executive branch, and others are independent from all three branches of government. While the heads of these agencies are politically appointed, the agencies have a measure of state autonomy, so much so that some observers worry that they constitute a "fourth branch" of American government. On their limited policy terrain they sometimes have the power of all three of the other branches—they can set rules, enforce them, and interpret them (Meier 1979; Smith and Licari 2006). They are the American version of the Weberian bureaucratic state.

The formal and legalistic style of regulation applied by these agencies has been called "adversarial legalism" (Kagan 2003). The dominant scholarly view is that this regulation was more interventionist and more harmful to industry than regulation in Europe, at least until the rise of neoliberalism in the 1980s. In some cases, the more costly and state interventionist American regulations did not produce superior regulatory outcomes, and the European countries' more cooperative approaches were more successful. In other cases, such as the Thalidomide affair, American regulations were much more successful at protecting consumers from industry. This chapter first reviews the literature on adversarial legalism and then turns to a case study of the rise and increasing autonomy of the first independent regulatory agency, the Interstate Commerce Commission, to examine the unfolding of adversarial regulation.

Regulatory agencies seem to be exactly what one prominent commentator claims Americans have never wanted their government to be: "cosmopolitan, expert, authoritative, efficient, confidential, articulated in its parts, progressive, elite, mechanical, duties-oriented, secular, regulatory, and delegative" (Wills 1999, 17–18). Unlike the "government out of sight" that characterized the nineteenth century (Balogh 2009), regulatory agencies are centralized, bureaucratic, and extremely visible. This pattern of American regulation is so contrary to our usual stereotypes about the United States that it warrants more careful examination.

Throughout the 1980s and 1990s, individual scholars examining particular aspects of regulation produced the string of findings of greater adversarialism discussed in the introduction—for example, that the United States was more stringent on climate regulation and health and safety regulation (Lundqvist 1980; Braithwaite 1985; Vogel 1986; Benedick 1998; Verweij 2000; Jasanoff 1991; Kelman 1981; Badaracco 1985).

Berkeley law professor Robert A. Kagan[2] connected the dots and argued that American regulation is more "adversarial" than regulation in other countries; this is part of his larger argument about the United States as marked by "adversarial legalism," a style of governing characterized by the dominance of lawyers and an unusual reliance on a formal, transparent, rule-bound, and expensive process of adversarial litigation, as opposed to the negotiated approaches to policy making and implementation found in other countries (Kagan 2003). Even when the laws are similar, Kagan argues, American policies are implemented differently, with "(1) more complex bodies of legal rules; (2) more formal, adversarial procedures for resolving political and scientific disputes; (3) more costly forms of legal contestation; (4) stronger, more punitive legal sanctions; (5) more frequent judicial review of and intervention into administrative decisions and processes; (6) more political controversy about legal rules and institutions; (7) more politically fragmented, less closely coordinated decision; and (8) more legal uncertainty and instability" (7). Kagan sees regulation as one of many spheres in which adversarial legalism can be found, from the criminal justice system to tort law, from the rights of welfare recipients to school finance reform.

While the studies of the 1980s consistently found greater regulation in the United States, starting in the 1990s the picture became more mixed, as the United States saw a backlash to regulation emerge in the deregulatory movement—which included consumers' groups such as the AIDS activists who protested the FDA delays—while the rising power of the European Union (E.U.) brought a more adversarial and legalistic approach to Europe. In the 1990s Kagan led a team examining the treatment of multinational corporations in different countries. By holding constant the stimulus—the same corporation conducting parallel activities in different countries—Kagan and his team attempted to isolate the different natures of the regulatory regimes. Using this methodology the researchers found greater or more costly and interventionist regulation in the United States in waste management, land and groundwater contamination, air pollution, employee termination, debt collection, and patent protection; however, the process of drug approval had become more similar to other countries, and chemical notification laws were less burdensome, while the regulation of landfills was more burdensome in some American states than in others (see contributors to Kagan and Axelrad 2000). Thus, the more recent picture is mixed. Some scholars have even suggested that after the 1980s a "great flip-flop" occurred, in which the United States systematically attempted to deregulate, while the E.U. moved towards the American adversarial mode of regulation (Löfstedt and Vogel 2001).

The most recent attempt to answer the question of who has the more strict regulatory laws is the work of Jonathan Wiener and his colleagues (Wiener, Rogers, and Hammitt 2011; Hammitt, Wiener, Swedlow, Kall, and Zhou 2005; Wiener and Rogers 2002), who find general parity between the United States and Europe from 1970 to today, with some weak support for the theory of a flip-flop. This work, while clearly the best study of its kind to date, restricts itself to examining the laws on the books, and does not examine the implementation or enforcement of the laws. Since many of the case studies cited above reveal differences at the level of implementation, an examination of the laws is only part of the picture; nevertheless their study shows that at that level, the United States does not have significantly less regulation than Europe. As Wiener and Rogers write: "differences in relative precaution depend more on the context of the particular risk than on broad differences in national regulatory regimes" (2002, 317). They note that while Europe takes a more precautionary stance on issues such as genetically modified organisms, hormones in beef, and climate change, the United States is more precautionary in areas from drug approval to nuclear energy to policies to protect the ozone layer to particulates in the air (322).

We can conclude from these studies that there is no evidence that the American state is less interventionist overall in the regulation of business. There is some evidence from case studies that prior to the 1980s the American state was overall more interventionist than European states and that regulation took a more adversarial form in the United States whereas it took a more cooperative form in Europe. A debate continues about the current situation, but there is no support even today for the picture of a less regulatory United States. Whatever the specific extent of the intervention and the recent changes, these studies show that we cannot automatically assume a less interventionist mode of governance in the United States. At the minimum, the United States has been more regulatory than Europe in some areas at some times, and at the maximum, it is more regulatory in most areas. No serious student of comparative regulation claims that regulation in the United States accords with the minimal state interventionist picture found in the theories of comparative political economy examined in Chapter 2.

Where the scholarship has been less successful, however, is in explaining where these American regulations came from, and none of our theories can offer guidance here, as there are simply too many of these instances of greater regulation to be swept aside as occasional exceptions to a liberal state.

In attempting to explain adversarial legalism Kagan cites a national culture that values the freedom to challenge government in court, and fragmented institutions that make other forms of authority more difficult to exercise (1994). As mentioned above, the cultural argument is hard to take seriously as an analytical tool, since it can be stretched to fit any empirical pattern. For example, if we had found the exact opposite empirical pattern, proponents of the cultural argument would surely see that as evidence for their claim: if we found that European countries were entrusting issues of market regulation to independent centralized regulatory bureaucracies, defenders of the cultural argument would surely argue that this shows European statism and deference to expertise and preference for centralized power at work, and absence of independent regulatory agencies would be seen as proof of American anti-statism. If Europe was more formalistic and legalistic and the American system less rules-based, then this would be used as evidence that the American system is more populist. Even the prominent role of lawyers, if it were found in Europe, would be seen as deference to highly educated experts. In fact, all three empirical patterns go in the other direction: it is the United States that is marked by independent centralized regulatory bureaucracies, formalism and legalism, and the prominent position of lawyers. A theory that sees the presence of centralized Weberian bureaucracies as proof of American antistatist culture and also sees absence of centralized Weberian bureaucracies as proof of American antistatist culture is not very helpful in trying to make sense of the world.

Both of these elements might well be compatible with antistatist culture, but if so, then we need to look for other factors to explain why a polity with an antistatist culture might take one rather than the other route.

While fragmentation of power is an important element, it cannot be the whole story, because fragmentation of power is also compatible with no independent regulatory commissions at all. Indeed, if the empirical pattern were reversed—if independent regulatory commissions were a European phenomenon and were absent or only recently arisen in the United States—we would have learned treatises showing how difficult it is to get the various "veto points" in the political system to agree on establishing an independent regulatory commission.

For the actual story of how these commissions came into being, we need to leave behind the legal and public policy scholarship and turn to the debates on the origins of Progressivism that have raged across the disciplines of history, sociology, and political science. These disciplines, and particularly the scholars who study American political development, have given careful attention to independent regulatory commissions as well as to executive branch agencies.

The first independent regulatory agency, the Interstate Commerce Commission (ICC), established rules on railroad rates and eventually acquired extensive authority over the railroads. It was based on models of independent commissions that had been implemented in the states. The ICC in turn was the guide that all other independent regulatory agencies followed, and in developing the pattern of regulation by agencies that were independent from politics and staffed by experts, it established the American mode of regulation.

Because of its centrality, the ICC has been examined exhaustively, and a vigorous debate continues on whether the key agents were agrarian populists, who wanted lower railroad rates; the railroads themselves, who supported it as a means of stabilizing what would otherwise have been destructive competition; northeastern merchants, who supported it for the same reason agrarian populists did; or bureaucrats such as Charles Francis Adams of Massachusetts, who used their energies to create a space of autonomous state power (see, e.g., Benson 1955; Bernstein 1955; Skowronek 1982; McCraw 1984; Fiorina 1986; Gilligan, Marshall, and Weingast 1989; Berk 1997; Sanders 1999; James 2000). Despite the divergences, these accounts agree on a few basics: the pressure to do *something* about railroad rates came from the agrarians; the idea for a commission came from other groups and was initially opposed by agrarians; and the result of the Interstate Commerce Act benefited short-haul shippers at the expense of long-haul shippers.

To understand the rise of the first independent regulatory commission, it is necessary to understand the central conflict between short- and long-haul shipping. The capital-intensive nature of railroads led to a situation in which all but the largest cities had only one railroad line. A farmer or merchant shipping from Chicago to the East Coast—a long-haul shipper—had multiple options, forcing the railroads to compete to attract the shipper's business. However, a farmer or merchant shipping between two cities in the Midwest—a short-haul shipper—had only one railroad option. The capital requirements of the railroads and the large size of the American landmass produced natural monopolies between terminus points. And because railroads were forced to reduce long-haul prices to compete for the long-haul trade, they raised short-haul prices to subsidize the losses incurred from the long-haul side of the business. Moreover, given economies of scale in railroading—where it was only slightly more expensive to send a full freight train than a half-full freight train—railroad operators attempted to attain higher and higher shipping volume, for example, by forming cartels (known as "pools"). And the sheer size of some corporations allowed them to promise railroads significant volume for reduced costs, until the practice of giving "rebates" to large corporations such as Standard Oil took hold. (Benson 1955; Skowronek 1982; Sanders 1999; James 2000).

These practices resulted in price differentials that affected all sectors within a region. Between the railroad terminus points, farmers paid more to get their goods to market, consumers paid more for those goods, and industries were hampered by the higher transportation costs. Meanwhile, farmers, consumers, and industry west of Chicago depended on low long-haul prices. This is why scholars emphasize that the ensuing conflict was a sectional rather than a class conflict (Sanders 1999, 187; Bensel 1984). A long debate in economic history casts doubt on the populist claim that railroad rates were objectively high (see Eichengreen 1984 for an overview), but there is no doubt that long-haul shippers were getting lower rates than short-haul shippers and that high-volume shippers were getting rebates. When the price deflations of the 1880s and 1890s led farmers to cast about for causes of their distress, they identified these visible issues of price discrimination and pooling as the problem, and demanded railroad regulation. Thus, the original demand for railroad regulation came from agrarians. Agrarian influences found an outlet in the House of

Representatives, where Texas congressman John Reagan emerged as the champion of railroad regulation. The House repeatedly introduced bills attempting railroad regulation of various kinds over the course of the 1870s and 1880s (Benson 1955; Sanders 1999; James 2000).

But agrarians were not behind the specific idea of a commission; rather, this emerged from the Senate, which was less favorable to agrarian interests. Throughout the 1870s and 1880s the dozens of railroad regulation bills passed by the House met with either inaction on the side of the Senate, or Senate bills that could not be reconciled with the more populist House bills. The Senate was not opposed to railroad regulation, but it was more favorable to railroad interests and favored regulation that would stabilize the market by legalizing pooling. This was anathema to the House, which interpreted pools as farmers did. By the mid-1880s, a series of House bills prohibiting pooling and price discrimination came up against Senate bills legalizing pooling and not mentioning price discrimination. The logjam finally broke when in 1886 the Supreme Court declared state-level railroad regulation unconstitutional, leaving the entire industry unregulated. Congress acted quickly to reconcile the House and Senate versions of the bill and the Interstate Commerce Act passed in 1887—with the House version triumphing in a ban against pooling and price discrimination but with the addition of the idea of a commission taken from the Senate side of the battle. (Benson 1955; Sanders 1999; James 2000).

The Interstate Commerce Commission had an inauspicious beginning. In a string of rulings in the 1890s, the increasingly conservative Supreme Court successively overturned the Commission's attempts to set rates or determine transportation policy, ruling that the Commission could only pass judgment on the reasonableness of rates—and then when the Commission attempted to act in even this restricted domain, the Court overturned all but one of its rulings (Skowronek 1982, 160). By the turn of the century the Commission was widely seen to be a powerless body. But rising regulatory fervor in the new century brightened its fortunes, particularly with the rise of Theodore Roosevelt's multipronged attack on monopolies. Strong anti-rebating legislation passed in 1903, and legislation allowing the ICC to set maximum rates passed in 1906. Commissions also became popular with agrarians: whereas in the 1870s and 1880s they had been opposed to the idea of a commission, a string of judicial rejections of agrarian legislation in the 1890s had pitted agrarians against the judiciary. In the battle between the judiciary and the Commission, agrarian radicals took the Commission's side (Skowronek 1982, 254).

The Progressives' faith in impartial expertise made commissions popular throughout the Wilson presidency, with the Federal Reserve and the Federal Trade Commission borrowing from the ICC template. But the Progressives held out hope that the state itself would take over responsibility for the public interest; as Herbert Croly put it, "Any legislation which seeks to promote this neglected public interest is consequently to be welcomed; but the welcome accorded to these commissions should not be very enthusiastic. It should not be any more enthusiastic than the welcome accorded by the citizens of a kingdom to the birth of a first child to the reigning monarchs,—a child who turns out to be a girl, incapable under the law of inheriting the crown. A female heir is under such circumstances merely the promise of better things; and so these commissions are merely an evidence of good will and promise of something better. As initial experiments in the attempt to redeem a neglected responsibility, they may be tolerated; but if they are tolerated too long, they may well work more harm than good" (Croly, quoted in Bernstein 1955, 41).

Over the next few decades the female heir inherited the crown. The independent regulatory commissions were eclipsed by the more radical planning that took over during World War I, but as the country entered the Depression, independent regulatory commissions proliferated. New Deal reformers discovered that the commission offered an American form of government regulation of business. The promise of expert management of the economy was irresistible at a time when the economy seemed to be going haywire. Senate investigations of stock market scandals resulted in the Securities and Exchange Commission; the Federal Communications Commission, the National Labor Relations Board, and the Civil Aeronautics Board also date from this time. Many politicians saw the commission as a way to *prevent* the concentration of state power under the President (Bernstein 1955, 53), but this hope turned out to be frustrated as the executive branch developed its own version of regulatory commissions, such as the Food and Drug Administration (FDA) (Carpenter 2010).

At each point in the rise of independent regulatory agencies, we see the mark of the American state's unusual size and economic growth. In placing the story in comparative context, we need to compare three issues: the origins of the commission model, when price discrimination between long- and short-haul shippers inaugurated the pressure to do something about railroad rates; the reasons why delegation to a commission was particularly appealing in the United States; and the reasons why the ICC was strengthened under Theodore Roosevelt and Wilson. At each of these points the unusual American pattern of state formation caused the American path to diverge from the European. Despite differences between the European countries in economic and social structure, all of the European countries saw a pattern in which railroads did not witness the central conflict between long- and short-haul shipping because of the more concentrated nature of the railroad network; delegation was not so attractive because corruption was not so endemic there; and independent regulatory commissions were not the answer to monopoly because Europe had neither the large monopoly concerns, nor agrarian groups to inciting opposition to monopoly.

First, while price differentials between short- and long-haul shipping focused farmers' attention on railroads in the United States, in Europe railroads did not witness the major economies of scale with long-haul shipping that the size of the American landmass produced. The main reason for this difference is that railroads were everywhere national enterprises. Whether they were privately or publicly financed, regulated by the state or by independent commissions, they never crossed national borders. Since long-haul trade in Europe meant trade between countries, long-haul trade continued to use the waterways. This made long-haul trade and short-haul trade incommensurable. While railroads did discriminate between shippers of different distances (Chandler 1990), long-haul shipping in Europe could never mean shipping of the same scale as in the United States and thus never produced the same political cleavages. For example, in the 1880s the United States had over 119,764 miles of railroad lines compared to 18,867 in Germany (the second largest of any country in the world), 18,370 in Great Britain and Ireland, 17,194 in France, and only 2,531 in Sweden; even Russia, with a landmass equivalent to the continental United States, boasted only 15,840 miles of railroad at this point, a victim of slower economic development (McArthur, 1884, 6). Although canals might have been almost as effective economically as railroads in the United States (Fogel 1964), this was not clear at the time, and in the decades after the Civil War, stitching the nation together was a political imperative. This gave rail transport a higher share of the transport market than any other country (only Russia came close [Hannah 2008]) and produced the political divisions examined here.

The problems that the United States faced—pulling together a continent-wide market in the decades after part of that landmass had attempted to secede, in the face of rapid economic growth—were quite different from Europe. The reliance on railroads for long-haul trade and the falling prices of long-haul trade led to the perception of price discrimination that began the chain of events that resulted in the ICC.

Even if the problems were different, however, the European countries did have problems associated with railroads such as with siting or standardization, and one could imagine them coming up with the idea of commissions to solve them. The particular appeal of a commission in the United States was that it got the issue of railroads out of politics. The idea of a commission came from Senator Shelby Cullom of Illinois, the dominant figure in the Senate on the issue of railroad regulation. Like many other states, Illinois had implemented a commission at the state level to oversee railroad rates. The Illinois commission was the first "strong" commission, as opposed to the more well-known but weaker "sunshine" commission of Massachusetts, which restricted itself to publicizing the railroads' misdeeds. It was the strong version of a commission that was implemented in the Interstate Commerce Act. The state commissions in turn emerged from failed experiments with public operation of the railroads. For example, the Western and Atlantic Railroad of Georgia was publicly operated until 1870 but was continually accused of sacrificing economic efficiency for political expedience, resulting in scandal (Wimbish 1912, 323–324). It was fear of corruption that channeled Charles Francis Adams of Massachusetts away from the idea of public ownership: "Imagine the Erie [railroad] and Tammany rings rolled into one and turned loose on the field of politics, and the result of State ownership would be realized" (quoted in McCraw 1984, 11). The fact that the first big business—railroads—were appearing before the development of state infrastructure to control them led to concerns about the political operation of railroads, and states experimented with independent commissions of experts. When the Supreme Court invalidated these state regulatory commissions, the national legislature copied the model they had created. Thus, the independent regulatory commission emerged as an alternative to *politicized* public ownership at a time of heightened patronage concerns. This was less of a concern in most European countries, which had all established meritocratic systems of state recruitment by this point. Although recent scholarship has overturned the idea of a passive or absent national government in the nineteenth century, the American state was not yet composed of bureaucracies staffed by meritocratic recruitment, and this produced an unusual regulatory response. In this case, the American fear of state corruption would eventually flower into agencies that had the effect of strengthening the state.

Finally, the particular context that strengthened the ICC in the early twentieth century was the trust-busting fervor of the first decades of the century. The natural monopolies generated by the large utilities as well as the capital-intensive nature of the new technologies for exploiting natural resources had created the sudden rise of a set of organizations with what seemed to observers to be vast wealth and power. A central line of conflict was between these large businesses and the small businesses (including agrarian concerns) they often replaced or with whom they traded. Conflicts also proliferated with labor. Especially crucial was that a developing public sphere made possible by the increasing wealth of the country was able to chronicle and publicize the abuses of these large corporations and mobilize public opinion. By the end of the century, these developments coalesced into a widespread movement against monopoly power. Although conflicts between small and big business occurred everywhere, no European country experienced anything like this popular fervor against monopolies, as American firms were significantly larger than the firms of other countries, and American farmers could not be bought off with protectionism as other farmers could. These large American firms with their seemingly endless wealth became magnets for publicity and popular agitation; railways and other natural monopolies were assimilated into this general antimonopoly fervor (Goodwyn 1978; Cooper 1990; McGerr 2003; Postel 2007).

Thus, at each stage in the story—the rise of the initial grievance, the solution of delegation, and the strengthening of the ICC—the unique features of American state formation in the context of rapid economic growth channeled politics down the line of independent regulatory agencies. The size of the American landmass combined with rapid economic development triggered the original conflict between long- and short-haul shippers. The corruption of politics in a context in which the meritocratic bureaucracies that would soon dot the landscape had not yet been developed led to the solution of the independent commission. And the fear of monopoly caused by the unusual scale of monopoly power in the United States led to the strengthening of the commission.

Over the years, the pattern developed by the ICC would be employed both inside and outside the state, as executive department agencies such as Frances Kelsey's FDA learned from the practices of the ICC. By midcentury, the flowering of independent regulatory agencies as well as executive department agencies had produced the adversarial legalism that Kagan and his collaborators document. It was this tradition of adver-

194

sarial regulation, particularly the agrarian concern with concentration of wealth, that interacted with the Great Depression to produce the unusual strictures against universal banking and branch banking—and the consequence they led to, of the democratization of credit—that we will examine in more detail in the next chapter.

8

THE DEMOCRATIZATION OF CREDIT

The financial crisis has cast a spotlight on the role that credit plays in American life, and many analysts wonder how to explain the "financialization" of the American economy. One explanation that has become prominent in recent years is that credit provided Americans with a way to overcome the economic crisis of the 1970s. Greta Krippner (2011) makes the most systematic version of this argument (see also Rajan 2010). Krippner argues that by turning to credit, politicians avoided the conflicts that might have erupted because of the economic crisis of the 1970s. She suggests that these attempts to expand credit allowed policymakers to depoliticize what would otherwise have been difficult distributional decisions and that "a series of unresolved distributional questions lurk just below the surface of the credit expansion that has occurred in the U.S. economy in the decades since the 1970s" (165). Krippner sees policymakers as the central actors in this depoliticization because "as conditions supporting broadly based prosperity in the economy eroded, efforts to shift aspects of policy implementation from state institutions to markets allowed policymakers to shield themselves from responsibility for unfavorable events such as inflation or unemployment" (147). Thus, "policymakers transformed an era of capital scarcity and perennial credit shortages into apparent prosperity, obviating the need for an emergent social consensus" on issues of distribution (149). By allowing consumers, businesses, and government to borrow from the future, they papered over the economic problems of the present. Krippner warns that the task now is "to define a public philosophy to guide decisions about distribution. We are less equipped for this task because for more than two decades the problem of distribution has been eclipsed by financialization, eroding collective capacities to engage questions of economic justice" (150).

In focusing on financialization of the last several decades as a response to economic crisis, Krippner is following the lead of scholars such as Giovanni Arrighi (1994) and Robert Boyer (2000). One problem with the view that financialization is a response to the economic crisis of the 1970s, however, is that by 1970 the United States was already more financialized on several dimensions than most other countries. The United States ranked second only to Switzerland in 1970 in credit to the private sector as a share of GDP (Demirgüç-Kunt and Levine 2001, and associated database), while International Monetary Fund (IMF) data show the United States trailing only Switzerland and Norway as far back as 1948 (International Monetary Fund, 2009, ratio of lines 22d + 42d to line 99b following Djankov, McLiesh, and Shleifer 2007). In stock market capitalization and several other measures the United States was already more financialized than France, Germany, and Sweden by 1960 (Rajan and Zingales 2003, 14–15). As Krippner has noted, there is debate about exactly what the relevant measure for "financialization" should be; her preferred measure is rise in profits associated with financial activity, but part of her causal argument focuses on the expansion of consumer credit and the political peace this bought. But credit in the household sector as a percent of GDP had been rising since the 1940s (James and Sylla, 2006a). In comparative perspective, while one-half of Americans used some form of installment credit in 1971, only one-tenth of Germans did so (Logemann 2008, 525). In France in 1965, consumer credit rested at 2% of GDP, compared to 6% in the United States (Effosse 2010, 79). Already in the 1960s, David Caplovitz was writing about the extraordinary reliance of American consumers on credit (1963, 1968). Finance was a characteristic of prosperity, not just a response to crisis.

We also know that the habit of borrowing and the institutional innovations that made it possible had been established before the 1970s in the United States. Louis Hyman argues that what changed after the 1970s is that borrowers continued to borrow but were less able to repay their loans because of macroeconomic difficulties: "A credit system premised on rising wages and stable employment [before the 1970s] was reappropriated to shore up uncertain employment and income inequality [after the 1970s]" (2011, 4).

Krippner and others are not wrong to focus on the 1970s, as there is no intrinsic reason why the credit system should have been "reappropriated" after the crisis in this way. The economic crisis could have led to a conscious choice of a different path, and macroeconomic troubles could have led consumers to change their behavior. Instead, debt levels rose to new heights while savings rates plunged. However, examining the history of credit before the 1970s helps to explain *why* this particular credit-oriented path was chosen in the 1970s—it shows the trade-offs decision makers faced and the infrastructure in place that made some choices easier than others.

This chapter begins with a brief overview of the rise of credit in the United States, drawing particularly on the work of Louis Hyman, Sarah Quinn, and Martha Olney. The focus is on consumer credit, including mortgage credit, rather than credit for business, as it is household debt that was particularly consequential for the recent crisis (as I will argue in Chapter 9). The following section examines the origins of the Federal Housing Administration (FHA) in comparative perspective to identify some of the factors responsible for its emergence. The final section of this chapter uses this history to present a different perspective on what happened in the 1970s. For Krippner, the central actors in the rise of credit in the 1970s were policymakers seeking to avoid blame for the economic crisis, and they stumbled their way to these policies in an ad hoc manner. As we will see in Chapter 9, Krippner is right to draw our attention to the trade-off between credit and redistribution. But this chapter agues that policymakers were following the lead of a widespread campaign at the grassroots for greater credit access. This campaign intersected with calls for removal of biases against African Americans and women in many areas of life, and it helped to feed the movement for financial deregulation that was gaining steam at this time. It was not an accidental or ad hoc strategy at all; rather, it was rooted in developments earlier in the century that had made credit a central facet of American life.

Credit in Early Twentieth Century America

The paucity of long-run comparative data makes it hard to identify with certainty when the United States began to diverge from other countries in its reliance on credit, but we do know that it was not always unusually credit oriented. In 1913, the ratio of private credit to GDP in the United States was lower than in Switzerland, Denmark, France, the United Kingdom, and Germany (Eichengreen and Mitchener 2003, 64), and Rajan and Zingales find the United States trailing most other industrializing countries on four different measures of financialization in 1913 (Rajan and Zingales 2003, 14–17). On the issue of consumer and mortgage credit in particular, historians point to two moments prior to the 1970s when consumer credit rose in America: the credit boom of the 1920s and the New Deal.

Although informal credit arrangements with merchants have always been part of capitalism, the systematic development of consumer credit in the United States begins in the nineteenth century, when Americans moving westward needed to borrow to buy their farms (or to work them even if the land itself was free, Quinn 2010). After the Civil War the development of the crop-lien system in the South as well as the innovation of installment payments produced another rise in the use of consumer credit (Olney 1998, 409). In the late nineteenth century the American agrarian Left made the easier availability of credit a rallying cry, most famously in the arguments of William Jennings Bryan.

These Progressive-era precedents flowered in the 1920s when government, the private sector, and the nonprofit sector all independently developed several key institutions to facilitate the democratization of credit. Although the American states had been involved with banks since the nineteenth century (Callender 1902), the national government had stayed out of credit financing. But repeated boom and bust cycles convinced observers that stabilization at the national level was necessary (Quinn 2010). The first major instance of the national government successfully taking responsibility for the management of credit was the Federal Farm Loan Act (FFLA) of 1916, "an important halfway point between the ad hoc credit programs of the nineteenth century and the government's systematic extensive use of direct loans and guarantees following the New Deal" (Quinn 2010; 99). Quinn argues that the FFLA, driven by farmers who had become organized as a response to the depression of the 1890s, set a precedent for the use of amortized loans in particular (Quinn n.d., 27–31; Quinn 2010, 107), a central element in the ballooning use of credit after the New Deal.

The private sector was also innovating in credit markets. Firms began to formalize such credit arrangements with the development of installment payments, increasingly used in the first decades of the twentieth century to sell big-ticket items like reapers, sewing machines, pianos, phonographs, furniture, and eventually the expensive new appliances of twentieth century life, such as the refrigerator (Olney 1998, 409–413; Calder 1999; Hyman 2011). The implementation of installment payments in the automobile industry in 1915 was particularly consequential (Olney 1991,

Hyman 2011). Installment payments were not subject to usury laws, since the arrangement was not seen as a loan (Carruthers and Ariovich 2010, 94). Consequently, with the implementation of installment selling in the automobile industry in 1915, consumer credit rose dramatically. Installment purchases of major durable goods moved from 3.7% of income in 1898–1916 to nearly double, 7.2% of income in 1922–1929 (Olney 1990). By 1926, 15% of all retail sales were sold on installment, with automobiles making up over half of this amount (Cohen 1989, 8), and by 1930 over two-thirds of furniture and washing machines were sold on installment (Carruthers and Arovich 2010, 95).

At the same time, a movement in the nonprofit sector against loan sharks resulted in the rise of "small loan lending" (Carruthers and Ariovich 2010; Anderson 2008). Where credit had been necessary for settling the agrarian frontier, Arthur Ham of the Russell Sage Foundation argued that credit was also necessary for the rising urban economy, in which workers were unmoored from the land and could no longer be self-sufficient from the market. An illness or a spell of unemployment led to debt, but usury laws made legitimate lenders wary of making small loans, leaving the field to loan sharks who operated outside the law. The Russell Sage Foundation pushed for reform of usury laws, and eventually saw such reform adopted in the majority of states (Anderson 2008; Trumbull 2012).

All of these movements were backed by the Federal Reserve's loose monetary policy in the 1920s, and all of these movements led in the same direction: making consumer credit more easily available, particularly in the boom years of the 1920s. This credit boom can be seen in figures for debt in the early twentieth century. In 1900, debt stood at 4.46% of income, rising and falling moderately over the next two decades. Starting in 1920 a sustained increase is seen, from 4.68% that year to 9.34% in 1930 (Olney 1991, 87–90). However, this credit boom of the 1920s was not unique in the developed world. Several countries saw increases in credit in this period, some quite markedly so (Eichengreen and Mitchener 2003). Even some of the institutional innovations were not unique: for example, the FFLA was actually based on German precedents, and up to this point American credit development seems to have been in line with European (Wiprud 1921, Shulman 2003).

More unusual in comparative perspective are the credit innovations that were implemented during the Depression and the New Deal, the major one of which is the affordable home mortgage. Today, the mortgage is one of the central institutions of American political economy. Despite its familiar role in middle-class life, however, the American home mortgage is unique in the world in the degree to which it facilitates homeownership. All developed countries have mortgages and mortgage-finance markets, but a combination of characteristics makes the American home mortgage stand out. The United States has high loan to value ratios, so homeowners can borrow more of the cost of the home. Mortgages are available at fixed rates for very long terms, including over 20 years; this makes monthly payment costs lower and more certain and brings homeownership into the purview of middle-income and even lower-income socioeconomic strata. Early repayment of a mortgage is easily available, which means that mortgages can be easily refinanced, and second mortgages are also common. Other countries share some of these features, but no other country scores as high across the board. Denmark comes closest, but Danish home buyers are required to put more money down (20%, as opposed to as little as 3% in the American case), which automatically excludes a large segment of citizens from the housing market, and the criteria by which creditworthiness is determined are stricter in Denmark. In making homeownership easier to attain by making debt easier to take on and to manage, the United States is unparalleled (Green and Wachter 2005).

These institutional innovations were implemented in the middle of the twentieth century. At the beginning of the century, mortgage loans in the United States often required down payments as high as 50% of the value of the house, and loan terms were short, usually under 10 years and sometimes as short as 3 to 5 years. Fixed interest rates were rare, and most mortgages were "balloon" mortgages, in which borrowers only paid interest payments for the life of the loan, and were expected to pay off the whole amount of the principal in one lump sum at the end of the loan period. This proved particularly difficult for borrowers to manage and most simply rolled one mortgage into another, never actually completing the purchase of the home. This periodic need for new loans made them vulnerable to banks' unwillingness to lend in uncertain times, a prime cause of foreclosures and exacerbation of economic crises. While the principle of amortization—paying down the principal over the life of the loan—had been adopted by the thrifts in the late nineteenth century, it was not yet widespread, and since it resulted in higher monthly payments when combined with the traditional short-term loans, it was not very popular. Most mortgages were essentially just loans made with the house as collateral (Jackson 1985; Weiss 1989; Green and Wachter 2005; Quinn 2010, n.d.; Hyman 2011).

201

There were important precursors to the contemporary mortgage, such as the nineteenth century thrifts and the development of credit mechanisms in the Federal Farmers' Loan Act of 1916, and there was important legislation that came later, such as the Veterans Administration loan program of 1944 and changes to the financial regulatory structure in the 1960s (Green and Wachter 2005; Quigley 2006; Quinn 2010, n.d.). But the characteristics that make the American mortgage unique in international perspective largely grew out of the economic crisis of the 1930s. Housing construction had collapsed in the early 1930s. Residential building permits fell from a peak of nearly 500,000 a year in 1925 to just over 25,000 in 1933, and housing investment fell from $68 billion to $17.6 billion in just 3 years (Gotham 2000, 296; Hyman 2011, 48). Foreclosures more than tripled (Gotham 2000, 296). Several other elements of the economy depended on housing. For example, significant portions of industry were tied to provisioning or servicing the construction industry, from building materials to freight cars; at one point the families of construction workers constituted one-third of the relief rolls (Hyman 2011, 48). Homeownership may also have what economists call "wealth effects" on consumption, in that owning a home may make consumers feel wealthier and willing to spend more.[1]

For all of these reasons, Roosevelt and many other observers of the economy saw the construction industry as central to economic revival and saw housing as the most important part of the construction industry. Because they believed that the housing collapse rippled out to the rest of the economy, they saw reviving homeownership as a key lever with which to get the economy moving. Mariner Eccles, Chairman of the Federal Reserve, wrote:

> The significance of a new housing program that could revive the economy was not lost on President Roosevelt. He knew that almost a third of the unemployed were to be found in the building trades, and housing was by far the most important part of that trade. A program of new home construction, launched on an adequate scale, not only would gradually help put those men back to work but would act as the wheel within the wheel to move the whole economic engine. It would affect everyone, from the manufacturer of lace curtains to the manufacturer of lumber, bricks, furniture, cement, and electrical appliances. The mere shipment of these supplies would affect the railroads, which in turn would

need the produce of steel mills for rails, freight cars, and so on. (Quoted in Quinn 2010, 149–150; Quinn n.d., 36; Gotham 2000, 299; Radford 1996, 179)

On this point observers from many walks were united, including the American Federation of Labor, which argued that "home reconstruction provides the broadest single base for production and re-employment in major industries. In keeping with other plans for an economy of abundance, we should carry on slum clearance and rehousing of families whose incomes keep them out of reach of the private building markets" (quoted in Logemann 2007, 245).

Congress and the President—first Hoover and then Roosevelt—experimented with several different means of rescuing housing. Under Hoover the Federal Home Loan Banking System set up a supplementary credit system. Housing became a central thrust of Roosevelt's response to the Great Depression. The first New Deal housing policy experiment was the Home Owners' Loan Corporation (HOLC), a temporary measure that allowed borrowers to trade their mortgage obligations for government bonds, aiming to prevent foreclosures while ensuring the flow of capital in the housing industry. Shortly afterwards came the unsuccessful housing division of the Public Works Administration, which aimed to directly fund housing for the urban poor but fell to criticism—from the Right for too much government intervention and from the Left for too little—and eventually to a lack of funds. These experiments finally gave way to the centerpiece of New Deal housing policy, the Federal Housing Administration (FHA) and the Federal National Mortgage Association (FNMA) (Radford 1996; Green and Wachter 2005; Quinn 2010, n.d.; Hyman 2011, 49–70).

The National Housing Act of 1934 inaugurated the FHA, authorized home mortgage associations, and implemented a small but important program of home improvement loans. It was a remarkably creative piece of legislation. It went beyond traditional categories of state and market. Ignoring those who called on the state to directly subsidize the distressed, and ignoring the admonitions from conservatives to let the market fend for itself, the National Housing Act used the state to jump-start the market. Such a strategy was not uncommon among the industrialized countries in the Great Depression, but what made the American case unique was the particular shape that this market making took. The FHA standardized a particular kind of mortgage—long-term (10 to 20 years), low-interest (below 5%), high loan to value (up to 80%), and fully amortized—and created an insurance program for lenders that would repay up to 20% of lenders' total losses. The insurance came not out of tax funds, but out of the interest on the loans itself. The insurance program meant that as long as lenders were not wildly imprudent in making loans, they could be sure to avoid large losses. As the national mortgage associations that the Housing Act of 1934 envisioned and authorized failed to develop spontaneously in the private sector, in 1938 Roosevelt established the FNMA, widely called "Fannie Mae." Fannie Mae created a nationwide secondary market for these insured mortgages so that they could be easily bought and sold. This made the market for mortgages much more liquid, as lenders could quickly resell mortgages, and allowed capital to flow across the country to where it was most needed. As an FHA Commissioner wrote in the early 1950s, "It is now customary to find mortgages secured by properties in one part of the country held in the portfolios of mortgagees whose home offices are hundreds or even thousands of miles away from the location of the security and, to a large degree, an FHA insured mortgage is 'its own courier and carries no luggage' in that it speaks for itself and practically all persons experienced in the mortgage business instantly recognize it. This element of liquidity is a relatively new and very valuable asset in mortgage finance. . . . Very substantial incomes have been and are now being derived through the servicing of FHA insured mortgages"[2] (on FHA and liquidity see also Bartke 1966–1967; Harris 2009; Quinn 2010, n.d.; Hyman 2011).

These New Deal financial institutions did seem to increase the rate of homeownership. The longer term of the loans lowered monthly payments, and the high loan to value ratios, low interest rates, and amortization helped middle class and working class purchasers borrow from their future earnings in a generally safe and stable way. For the first decades of the twentieth century the U.S. homeownership rate hovered just under 45%. After the implementation of these institutional features of American mortgages in the 1940s, the U.S. homeownership rate sprang to around 65% and has never fallen below that level since. Econometric studies suggest that the policy implementation of the fixed-rate mortgage explains at least half of this rise in homeownership rates and find continued effects of the FHA on homeownership decades after its implementation (Monroe 2001; Chambers, Garriga, and Schlagenhauf 2009). Housing starts (a slightly different measure from residential building permits) went from 93,000 in 1933 to 332,000 in 1937 (Jackson 1985, 205). Between

1935 and 1945 FHA-insured housing starts represented 30%–45% of the single-family market and hit 80% of the market for multifamily homes in 1946–1950.[3] Moreover, the demonstrated profitability of the government-backed mortgage industry drew private-sector lenders into the mortgage market until the form of mortgage insurance that the FHA pioneered became standard, and capital markets began to offer even better terms, such as 30-year loans with as little as 3% down (Hyman 2011). And the FHA provided a stimulus to the economy: in 1952 the deputy administrator of the Housing and Home Finance Agency calculated that Federal government aid to housing resulted in more than $50 billion of benefit to the national economy, or nearly 14% of GDP at a cost of one-eighth of 1% of the total budget.[4] The influence of the FHA on household debt was delayed, as during the Depression and the war public debt crowded out private debt and credit controls held down levels of borrowing. As soon as the war was over, however, private borrowing rebounded. Mortgages for single-family homes jumped from a wartime trough of below 8% of GDP in 1944 to 30% in 1965, and consumer credit from less than 2% to over 12% of GDP in the same time period (Sutch 2006; James and Sylla 2006b). What commentators had thought was a credit bubble in the 1920s had by the 1960s become the normal pattern for the household sector.

Thus, the FHA and the panoply of related New Deal legislation are prime candidates for having created the American model of *credit-based* homeownership: these mortgage innovations did not simply subsidize housing or make it easier for aspiring homeowners to save money through higher interest rates on home saving accounts, as was the case in other countries. Rather, they made it easy and widely popular for Americans to take on significant levels of debt—levels that might have been unimaginable a few decades before these policies. What is important in macroeconomic terms is not only the homeownership rates but the rise in debt for the middle and working classes that came with them.

The FHA in Comparative Perspective

Perhaps the dominant interpretation of the FHA is that it represented a way for Roosevelt to reward business even in the depths of the Depression, as it was the most business friendly of several policies being proposed at the time (e.g., Radford 1996). This is true, but all countries at the time were trying to save capitalism and avoid socialism, and as we have seen, helping business was a major aim all across the advanced industrial world. In Europe as in the United States, the Depression did not prove to be the death knell of the capitalist system but the beginning of a long tradition of using the state to preserve capital. But why did the United States move in the direction of restoring credit when other countries that also wanted to save capitalism did not? While the story of the FHA has often been told, given its centrality to political economy, it is surprising that no comparative historical work asks why there were no FHAs in other countries. If the Great Depression was international and if programs to prop up housing seemed such a natural remedy for it in the United States, why did other countries not respond by adopting programs of housing finance?

Figure 8.1, which shows the fate of the construction industry in different countries between 1925 and 1932, gives part of the answer: no other country was as hard hit in this sector as the United States. Even

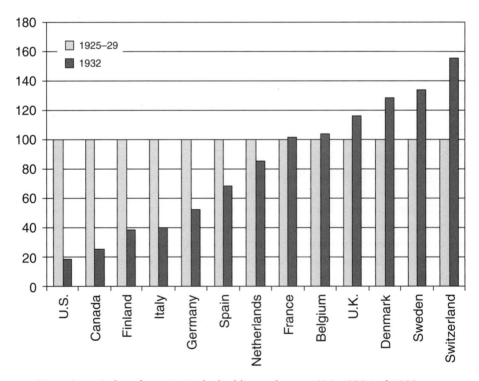

Figure 8.1. Index of activity in the building industry, 1925–1929 and 1932. 1925–1929 = 100. (*Source:* League of Nations, 1933, 136.)

other countries that had seen credit booms in the 1920s, such as the United Kingdom, did not see a similar collapse in construction in the 1930s. Although the measure for each country in Figure 8.1 is slightly different (dwellings completed where available, permits in others), the over-time comparisons of the same measure give comparative indications of the extent of the crisis in different countries. Sweden and Switzerland actually saw growth in construction in 1932, and the United Kingdom held even, but many countries saw declines. Aside from the United States, the worst outcomes were in Canada, Finland, Italy, Germany, and Spain. Exploring the response in two of the worst hit countries—Germany and Canada—helps to put the American response in context.

Germany

Germany's general approach to the Great Depression was Keynesian in that it seemed to have achieved lower unemployment through public spending—"Hitler had already found how to cure unemployment before Keynes had finished explaining why it occurred" (1972, 8), as Joan Robinson wrote. But most of that spending went to feed Hitler's foreign policy preoccupations, with military rearmament the top concern until 1934. Even the heavy expenditures on the highway system, which aided civilians, had an important military aim. And the German response to the Depression focused on public works to a greater extent than did the American, while the Nazis kept tight restrictions on private demand and consumption (Temin 1990). Although there were some exceptions, such as marriage loans (Garraty 1973), in general high tax rates, high interest rates and other means depressed consumption. For this reason scholars (e.g., Overy 1996) hesitate to call the policies Keynesian since they were not oriented to increasing consumer demand; they were rather in the long historical tradition of military policies that have the side effect of stimulating the economy. Jan Logemann suggests that we think of it instead as a different form of Keynesianism, which worked through the increase of "public consumption" as opposed to the increase of "private consumption" (Logemann 2007, 2012; see also Garraty 1973; Overy 1982, 1996; James 1986; Cohn 1992; Ritschl 2002; Weir and Skocpol 1985).

German and American policy differences were starkest in the area of agriculture: while Arthur Koestler watched pigs being slaughtered as the United States struggled to limit output, Germany sought steadfastly to increase agricultural output. "As late as 1930 Germany needed annual imports of food and animal feed . . . which placed a heavy burden on the balance of payments. Through patriotic appeals and a generous policy of easy farm credits the government had, therefore, encouraged the farmers to increase output" (Hardach 1980, 36; see also Garraty 1973, 921). Here as well, rather than increasing consumption, the German focus was on increasing supply.

The main reason for the focus on public rather than private consumption was of course the Nazis' single-minded preoccupation with mobilizing for war (Simpson 1959), but a secondary concern was the German concern with inflation. Where the United States was gently moving towards expansion of credit, Germany at mid-century was doing everything it could to restrict the availability of consumer credit as a means of restraining inflation (Eichengreen and Mitchener 2003). The shocking inflations of the Weimar era had led to a sustained attempt to restrict purchasing power, and in the 1920s the Reichsbank under Hjalmar Schacht implemented a heavy series of credit restrictions, persuading banks to reduce lending (Voth 2003; Eichengreen and Michener 2003). In addition to restraining inflation, German authorities were concerned about the availability of credit for rebuilding infrastructure destroyed by the First World War and developing the export industries on which economic growth would depend. The scale of the destruction was such that from 1919 to 1924 industrial production was only a fraction of what it had been in 1913 (Overy 1996, 5). The need for reconstruction guided German attempts to reduce the availability of consumer credit throughout the first half of the twentieth century and channel these funds to investment (Logemann 2007, 2012). The German growth model "subordinated domestic demand to the needs of industrial capital" (Allen 1989, 263). Over the course of several decades, "[m]oderate wages enabled the buildup of plant and equipment to take place, ensured the stability of the new currency, and permitted Germany's return to the world market through competitive exports" (Hardach 1980, 171). Although Hitler's focus on the military was unusual, the emphasis on public consumption and restraint of private consumption were of a piece with what came before and after.

A comparison of the role that inflationary fears played in Germany and the United States is particularly revealing. As discussed above, the work of Meg Jacobs (2005) has shown that although there have been experiments with voluntary rationing and price control in the United States, starting in the 1920s fears of inflation became linked to an argument that the problem was putting more purchasing power in workers' hands. Rather than seeing the problem of inflation as one of too much money chasing too few goods, in the United States the problem was seen as *too little money* in the hands of wage earners to be able to afford the outpouring of goods that American productivity had brought. Given current understandings of inflation, this consumers' critique of inflation as caused by not enough money is hard to understand. This critique is best conceptualized, as Jacobs argues, as an argument about distributional equity and a form of proto-Keynesianism that relied not on fiscal policy but on a direct shift of profits from capital to labor. Jacobs argues that there was nothing apolitical about this. This was the American version of social democracy, conceiving of a process in which money would be taken from capitalists, put into the hands of consumers, and spent on purchases including agricultural products. Although agricultural producers came into conflict with consumers on occasion, such as when price support programs for farmers raised the price of bread (Jacobs 2005, 116–117), and while the two movements never formed a coalition, what united the two sides was a focus on mending the monetary mechanism, if possible at the expense of capitalist profits: "Linking the politics of inflation with the politics of income distribution, [labor Progressives and liberal thinkers] developed their critique into a theory of underconsumption and argued that workers had to be able to consume for the economy to prosper" (Jacobs 2005, 75). The rise of credit was part of this attempt to encourage consumption.

The picture was starkly different in Germany. Although Germany has a long tradition of mortgage financing, and small credit schemes have proliferated at particular moments (such as in the immediate aftermath of the Second World War as an emergency measure for getting household goods into the hands of a devastated population), consumer credit never became as important in Germany as in the United States. Jan Logemann (2007, 2008, 2012) argues that instead of building its market through the development of consumer purchasing power, Germany developed it by using private savings to jump-start production, much of which was geared toward the export market. Public policy subsidized savings, because politicians feared a return to the post-World War I patterns of inflation. This restrained reliance on credit was aided by the increasing development of the welfare state. The elaboration of the Bismarckian welfare state became particularly pressing as the Federal Republic informally competed with the German Democratic Republic on the issue of citizens' welfare. Although the Social Democratic Party did occasionally push for the democratization of credit, its main focus was on the extension of the welfare state. Credit did increase in the 1950s and the 1960s (see, e.g., Stücker 2007), but by 1971,

Germans were using credit at much lower rates than Americans (Logemann 2007, 2008, 2012). And while the mortgage market was relatively large, it was characterized by features that limited its ability to lead to a greater financialization of the economy (Green and Wachter 2005, 103–104).

This approach to credit was part of the wider effort to increase investment in industry while restraining consumption examined in Chapter 3; as Adenauer put it in 1951, "the federal government must take measures to increase the capacity of heavy industry . . . this can only be achieved by a purposeful utilization of funds that have previously flown into less necessary investments or excessive consumption" (quoted in Van Hook 2004, 221). It was Germany that agreed with Hayek's lessons about the dangers of easy credit, while it was the United States that adopted Keynesian expansion of consumption.

These divergent approaches to consumption were ultimately guided by the different economic problems that the countries were facing: the rapid economic growth that the United States was experiencing in contrast to the political conflict and lower economic growth of Europe. The rapid growth of credit in the United States was a response to the rapid rise in productivity, while the attempt to restrain credit in Germany was an attempt to restrain inflation and increase productivity, necessitated partly by the devastation of the war. Indeed, the Nazis were highly traditional in following the previous administration's insistence on savings. Their preference for channeling the government's fiscal and monetary expansions down public lines—construction and roads as well as rearmament—laid the foundations for the German focus on increasing investment and strengthening the export sector at the expense of private consumption. Germany, in short, had a supply-side response to the Great Depression.

Although France did not experience the collapse in construction that frames our questions in this chapter, a brief glance there shows a history of credit very similar to Germany. While France had a well-developed tradition of consumer credit in auto loans and through pawnshops (*monts-de-piété*) and slightly *greater* popular support for credit than the United States at mid-century, policymakers deliberately restricted the availability of consumer credit after the Second World War in order to have sufficient capital available for investment in the export industries (Trumbull 2010a, 2012). Moreover, Trumbull points out that the reason for the collapse of the monts-de-piété was that: "Under partial German occupation, non-payment rates rose, and the government placed a ban on auctions of unclaimed pawn. This drove the monts-de-piété into insolvency" (2010b,

33). The failure of this credit institution was thus a direct result of the effect of war on credit markets. Moreover, as in Germany, French policymakers feared that credit would fuel inflation (2010b, 34). While the first government of Léon Blum did try to increase purchasing power by increasing wages, in general the short-lived nature of Third Republic governments led to incoherent and half-hearted policy responses to the Depression and no consistent focus on credit or purchasing power (Garraty 1973).

The difference between the French and American regulation of credit was put into sharp relief by events in 1953. The Minister of Economic Affairs Robert Buron proposed a law to facilitate credit in remarkably American terms, arguing that it would make "the development of credit one of the means to revive the French economy" (translated from Effosse 2010, 72). The law was controversial from the start and was eventually abandoned after two years of discussion; although it did have effects on making consumer credit more easily available, in 1965 French consumers used credit much less than American consumers (Effosse 2010, 79). (Note that France, like Germany, was in this period generous with the provision of *industrial* credit (Zysman 1983; Loriaux 1991), but this generosity did not extend to consumers.)

Trumbull argues that these differences in the role of consumer credit between France and the United States are ultimately historical accidents, that "national differences in regulation may trace to historically contingent conditions under which markets are constructed as legitimate" (Trumbull 2010b, 1; Trumbull 2012)—American policymakers contingently developed the idea that credit would be welfare promoting, while French policymakers developed the conviction that it would be worse for the economy. But a look at the context in which these decisions were made suggests that those decisions might have arisen from the different economic situations the countries were facing: as in Germany, France was trying to rebuild a war-torn economy. In this context policymakers worried that consumer credit would divert resources from production. As we have seen, this was not the concern in the United States—there, the concern was that production was overwhelming traditional mechanisms of consumption and distribution, leading to price declines that pulled the whole system into crisis. Preserving credit for production by restraining the development of consumer credit was not necessary in the American case as it was in both Germany and France.

Thus, the comparisons with Germany and France highlight the concerted effort in those countries to husband resources from consumption and channel them into production, in contrast with the emerging and relentless focus on policies to encourage consumption in the United States, of which home mortgage financing was one.

Canada

A comparison with Canada is even more revealing because of the Canadian resemblance to the United States. Canada, too, was a lightly populated country settled by the British and with a federal tradition of government. Like all the settler countries, it experienced rapid economic growth. Canada even had radicalized agrarian movements during the Depression (Lipset 1950; Ascah 1999). But like Australia and New Zealand, Canada's small population, constrained by the size of the country's habitable land, could never match the total productivity of its southern neighbor, and its industrialization depended on American capital and technology (Naylor [1975] 1997).

The Depression in Canada shared many similarities with the Depression in the United States (Amaral and MacGee 2002; Betts, Bordo, and Redish 1996). Canada consciously attempted to copy American-style New Deal programs, but a federal attempt to do so was stymied over questions of states' rights. Canada did adopt something similar to the American National Recovery Administration (NRA), and there was a provincial movement that echoed some American themes: William "Bible Bill" Aberhart of Alberta also argued that capitalism produced so much that people did not have the means to enjoy it. The direction he took was to draw on C.H. Douglas's theories of "social credit," one of the proto-Keynesian theories that Keynes mentions in the *General Theory* ([1935] 1964). The effort petered out when the federal government declared unconstitutional Alberta's attempt to control banks and finances as would have been required for "social credit." (Ascah 1999)

Construction and housing were particularly hard hit during the Depression. As Figure 8.1 shows, the construction industry collapse of 1932 was almost as bad in Canada as in the United States. During the Depression, "[e]xtensive studies of Halifax, Hamilton, Ottawa, Winnipeg, Montreal, and Toronto in the 1930s showed a proliferation of dilapidated housing conditions, lack of affordable housing units and rampant social distress" (Purdy 2003, 460). As Hulchanski summarizes: "Virtually all aspects of the housing system had ceased to function normally. . . . By 1933, for example, residential construction fell to 31 per cent of the 1929 level. . . . The insurance, trust and loan companies were increasingly unwilling to provide mortgage money due to falling real estate and rental values and the growing number of defaults" (1986, 21).

Canada, however, did not respond with the massive range of policies seen in the United States. When the United States set up a temporary program to stop foreclosures in the HOLC, Canada passed no similar policy. As the United States implemented the FHA and set up Fannie Mae, Canada passed the Dominion Housing Act of 1935 and the National Housing Act of 1938, but both of these had only minor effects (Hulchanski 1986). The United States even experimented with public housing during the Depression, but Canada refused to do so until decades later. Well until the late twentieth century, Canada had a housing policy that was much more hesitant to turn to government intervention; because of this Harris calls it "more American than the United States" (2000; see also Bacher 1993; Harris and Ragonetti 1998; and the exchange between Wexler 1996, Harris 1999, and Wexler 1999). In recent years Canadian mortgage debt has represented 44% of GDP, compared to 69% in the United States; Canadians could not rely on long-term fixed rate mortgages or absence of prepayment penalties. On average they borrowed 65% of the cost of a house, compared to 75% in the United States (Green and Wachter 2005).

The reasons for Canadian inaction during the Depression have not been convincingly explored (see Harris 2000). In other areas of policy, Canada has been more likely than the United States to turn to state intervention, to the extent that some have argued that the two countries have entirely different cultural traditions. Seymour Martin Lipset famously argued that the result of the American Revolution was to create two nations with exactly opposing founding myths: popular sovereignty in the United States and fear of it in Canada (1990, 1). These "organizing principles" (2) flowered in the nineteenth and twentieth centuries into a tradition of distrust of the state in the United States and one of governmental intervention in Canada. We have seen in Chapter 1 reasons to be skeptical of this argument in general, but more to the point here, this argument cannot make sense of the inaction in housing policy in Canada during the Depression compared to the extensive state intervention in the United States.

Canadian businesses responded to the contraction just as American businesses did, with direct lobbying of government for state intervention. In 1933, the Canadian Construction Association and the Canadian Manufacturers Association together with representatives of engineers and architects organized the National Construction Council (NCC) to put pressure on the federal government for a housing program (Hulchanski 1986, 22). "For the first time in Canadian history . . . municipal officials, civic organizations and an influential part of the business community shared a common conclusion on housing—that government ought to do something and do it quickly. There was general agreement on what the problem was and how best to address it, and there was general agreement as well that the federal government ought to intervene" (Hulchanski 1986, 22). Just as business favored government intervention in the United States, so business also favored government intervention in Canada. But in Canada, the government "was able to brush aside suggestions from the construction lobby that a public housing program be introduced to reduce unemployment in the building trades" (Harris 2000, 470).

Harris (2000) wonders if the Canadian parliamentary system was simply less open to pressure than the American political system. But comparative scholars usually argue that the parliamentary system makes the Canadian government *more* open to outside pressure than the American government; this is the central factor in Antonia Maioni's (1998) explanation of why Canada has health care while the United States does not, as we saw in previous chapters. Maioni builds on common institutionalist arguments to suggest that while Canadian parliamentary democracy allows the organic emergence of pressure groups and third parties, American winner-takes-all majoritarianism prevents such emergence, and moreover allows multiple points where new ideas can be vetoed.

While it is not fully clear why the Canadian government took no action, one key difference between the countries is that the banking crisis that shaped housing policy in the United States was absent in Canada. As Harris writes: "The financial system in Canada was more centralized and hence stable: during the Depression, virtually none of the Canadian banks, trusts, or loan companies went bankrupt. In general, then, the need for federal intervention was less than in the United States" (2000, 470). We have seen, however, that there was a clearly demonstrated need for housing during the Depression in Canada. I would therefore qualify Harris's statement: the need for federal intervention *that saved the financial industry as much as it saved construction* was absent in Canada. Construction was equally in crisis in the two countries. But banking was not.

Although Canada was hit as hard by the Depression as the United States, not a single bank failed in Canada. Indeed only one Canadian bank failed in the entire period between 1920 and 1980, holding 1% of total bank capital; compare this to the one-fifth of all banks that failed in the United States during the Depression, with failed banks in one peak year alone holding 2.5% of total bank capital (Haubrich 1990; White 1984; Bordo, Rockoff, and Redish 1994). Agricultural debt levels were as high in Canada as in the United States, suggesting that in the absence of bank failures debt does not disturb the real economy (Haubrich 1990). Banking did contract slightly in Canada, with a 10% decline in bank branch offices, but this was much lower than the 35% decline in bank offices in the United States, and "far from leading a decline [as they did in the United States, Canadian] banks did better than other industries during the Depression" (Haubrich 1990, 250; White 1984).

Most scholars who have compared the different course of the Depression in the two countries believe that Canadian banking stability was rooted in branch banking—one bank opening offices in many different areas. American banks, on the other hand, were not permitted to engage in branch banking across state lines, and in many cases they were not even allowed to open branches in the same state or city. This is a system called *unit banking*. Branch banking is generally held to be more stable than unit banking because the many offices of a branch bank can come to the aid of a local office that runs into trouble. Because branches make loans and deposits in many different areas, they provide diversification against purely local or seasonal economic conditions as well as a more diversified base of loans and deposits that can withstand local bank runs (Grossman 1994, 658). In addition, the sheer size and depth of branch banks give them greater funds with which to ride out minor economic winds and prevent them from turning into major storms (White 1984). Aside from the United States, France also had many small banks that failed, and aside from Canada, Sweden and the United Kingdom are also said to have benefited from diversified branches (Bernanke and James 1991, 54–55).

Thus, a key difference between the United States and Canada is that "in the presence of a stable branch banking system, financial shocks were not magnified by their effects on bank risk and, therefore, had more limited effects on economic activity" (Calomiris 2000, 102). This seems to be the general consensus on the course of the Depression in Canada and the United States (Carr, Mathewson, and Quigley 1995; Calomiris, 2000; Haubrich 1990; White 1984, 131–132; Grossman 1994; Bordo, Rockoff and Redish, 1994; see also their update after the financial crisis, Bordo, Redish, Rockoff 2011). There is still some controversy over the specific mechanisms that make branch banking more stable, e.g., Kryzanowski and Roberts (1993) argue that branch banking implied a government guarantee of insolvent banks because the banks became literally too big to fail (but see Calomiris 2000, 19), while Carlson and Mitchener (2006) argue that branch banking leads to heightened competition and therefore to the removal from the system of unstable banks. But all sides agree that branch banking makes banks more likely to withstand at least *local and regional* shocks of the kind that the United States witnessed (even if it cannot prevent banks from national and international shocks [Kryza-nowski and Roberts 1993, 374]) and that Canadian banks survived be-cause of the large size and diversification that branch banking allowed. Although radical agrarian organizations developed in Canada in the early part of the twentieth century and particularly during the Depression, and although these organizations did complain about the monopoly in finance and call for the nationalization of banks, the stability of the financial sys-tem prevented their proposals from gaining much support (Lipset 1950; Bordo and Redish 1987; Ascah 1999).

In the United States most banks that failed were unit banks, and states that allowed branch banking saw fewer failures and faster recovery (Grossman 1994, 658; Calomiris 2000; Wheelock 1992). There are a few exceptions involving failures of banks that had state-wide branches, but there were no banks that had nationwide branches as in other countries (Grossman, 1994, 658; Calomiris and Mason 2003).

The unit bank system had developed after the National Bank Act of 1863, which prohibited branching in national banks. The reason for the prohibition seems to have been the wish to stamp out a corrupt practice by which banks opened nominal branches in obscure locations to hold onto currency notes longer, which benefited the banks (Federal Reserve 1932, 52–61). Branch banking per se was not really the concern of the National Bank Act, and it was not discussed in the Congressional de-bates or bankers' discussions around the issue (Federal Reserve 1932, 65; Southworth 1928, 11). Nevertheless, the prohibition led to a unit bank-ing system. These constraints restricted the amount of capital available to finance Reconstruction. Although in the first decades of the system this does not seem to have been a particular concern, increasing industrializa-tion demanded more capital, and calls for looser banking regulations in-creased. Several states responded with loosened regulations for state banks in the 1880s. A dual banking system emerged, with both national and state banks competing for clients. A large number of very small banks that would soon provide a lobby against change sprang up. Meeting increasing competition from the state banks, the national bank system began to consider branch banking (Federal Reserve 1932; Southworth 1928).

Starting around 1900, intrastate bank branches proliferated, particularly in California and in Massachusetts, Michigan, New York, and Ohio (Federal Reserve 1932, 28, 1197). The turn of the century witnessed a long debate on branching, with supporters arguing that branched banks would be more stable, more efficient, and able to generate larger sums of money for the larger projects that were now being envisioned. The opposition argued that branch banking would allow the development of giant financial monopolies insensitive to local concerns and credit needs. The movement for branching was led by the large banks and bankers' associations, particularly the Bank of America under A. P. Giannini. The debate ended with the McFadden Act of 1927, which reinforced the prohibition against interstate branch banking but allowed intra-city branching for national banks where state regulations permitted it for state banks. The Banking Act of 1933 further allowed intrastate branching where state regulations permitted it, but branching across state lines would not be permitted until the Riegle-Neal Act of 1994 (White 1982; Hendrickson 2010; Southworth 1928; Federal Reserve 1932; Langevoort 1985–1986). Although it is true that American banking had been small and fragile even before the McFadden Act, the Act was the first to codify into law what had until then only been practice.

When we look more closely at the McFadden Act—the first policy that explicitly codified the prohibition against branch banking—we find a familiar cast of characters and events, with Insurgent Republicans and Southern Democrats leading the opposition. There is not much scholarship on the McFadden Act, but to date the handful of historians and economists who have examined it agree on the Southern/Midwestern and agrarian provenance of the opposition. In an early history, Southworth (1928) noted that the organized opposition to branch banking came from the Midwest; in Illinois small rural banks had convinced the "loop banks," the large urban financial centers of Chicago who did not themselves fear branch banking, to organize with them in opposition to the bill. Preston (1927) traced the (unsuccessful) attempt by this group of Chicago bankers to include provisions opposed even to intra-city branching in the bill. Chapman and Westerfield ([1942] 1980) note the importance of the legislative horse trade of support for the McFadden Act in exchange for support for the McNary-Haugen Farm Relief bill, which was necessary because opposition to branch banking was concentrated in agrarian areas. While Roe (1994) traces the uniqueness of American financial regulation to populism more generally, Carney (2010) shows that it was not labor but agrarians driving these reforms. Economides, Hubbard, and Palia (1996) show that opposition to branch banking came from areas where small and poorly capitalized unit banks predominated. The most explicit attempt to trace the socioeconomic status of opposition to branch banking is in a still unpublished paper by Rajan and Ramcharan (2010), who argue that "landed agrarian interests were strongly opposed to any reforms perceived to be fostering more local bank competition" (12). However, although opposition to branch banking came from rural areas, Rajan and Ramcharan as well as Calomiris (2000) argue that it was the relatively well-off rural areas that opposed branch banking.

In Congress, the debate was conducted in terms of fear of monopoly. For example, Alan Goldsborough, Democrat from Maryland, opened the debate in January 1926 with: "A great thinker once said: Give me control of the credit of a country and I care not who makes it laws. He could have said with equal truth 'Give me control of the credit of a country and I will make its laws.' . . . there is no way to control a credit monopoly." (*Congressional Record,* 1926, 2839). Henry Steagall, Democrat of Alabama, whose name would go down in history linked with another instance of unusual American regulation, said: "[Branch banking] is condemned by nearly all leaders of thought in the banking world. . . . It is absentee banking; it is carpet-bag banking. The men in control of the branch banks are not identified with the interests of the community in a commercial way nor in social life. Their business is to get what they can out of the investment, to be distributed elsewhere, and to absorb the deposits of the community, to be withdrawn at will, and in times of distress to be transferred to favored centers selected by the few who control the parent institution" (*Congressional Record,* 1926, 2850).

Midwestern Republicans were equally vociferous. John Nelson of Wisconsin threatened: "This bill means, if it passes, inevitably the end of our independent banking system and in its stead the Canadian, the British, and the continental system of branch banking in this country. . . . No one disputes the monopoly feature of branch banking. Branch banking inevitably tends toward concentration of money and credit in the hands of the few" (*Congressional Record,* 1926, 2840–2844).

The bill that eventually passed was an amalgam of compromises and trades. Some opponents of branch banking supported the bill because they saw it as a matter of leveling the playing field for national banks, given that state banks were allowed to branch (and Congress would have had to meddle in the affairs of the states to prevent state bank branching). Some opponents were won over by compromises that would prevent branch banking from being extended across state lines. And some votes were bought in exchange for support for the McNary-Haugen Farm Relief bill, which directly benefited agrarian areas (Federal Reserve 1932; Chapman and Westerfield [1942] 1980, 107).

Because of the compromises in the bill, it was just plausible for McFadden himself to call his bill an "anti-branch banking measure severely restricting the further spread of branch banking in the United States" (Louis McFadden, quoted in Langevoort 1985–1986, 1267–1268). But most analysts agree that at the end of the twists and turns of the legislative process, the bill "had become again what it was at the time of its introduction . . . a mildly *pro*-branch banking measure" (Federal Reserve 1932, 149).

These compromises and trades make it difficult to track opposition to branch banking with precision based on the votes on the bill, but doing so does give an approximate picture of the regional patterns, especially if we look at the first vote—before the heaviest logrolling and dealing— rather than the final vote. In the vote of February 1926, we can see a regional split in the House, where the strongest opposition to branch banking comes from the South (Table 8.1). The strongest support for the measure comes from the Northeast. The small number of Republican legislators from the West tended to support it, but the even smaller number of western Democrats tended to oppose it. Although midwestern opposition had been central to the early fight against the bill, when it came time to vote many midwestern legislators were satisfied with the compromises. The opponents who remained were the hard core who could not be won over to branch banking through any means, even branch banking only within metropolitan areas. What is important to keep in mind about this table is that a "no" vote on the McFadden Act does not indicate support for branch banking—rather, as we know from the congressional and historical sources, it indicates opposition to even the very weak branching measures contained in the bill. Almost all of the opponents come from the South and the Midwest. While the opponents lost this particular argument, they won the larger battle, as branch banking across state lines was never seriously considered for many decades.

Although the rhetoric against the McFadden Act was couched in terms of fear of monopoly, opposition to branch banking allowed small

Table 8.1. Regional voting on McFadden Act in House of Representatives, February 4, 1926

	Republicans				Democrats			
	Northeast	South	Midwest	West	Northeast	South	Midwest	West
Yes	78	11	88	20	19	54	17	1
No	1	1	11	1	1	56	13	4
Fisher's exact		0.04*				0.000***		

Source: Votes in all tables from *Congressional Record.*
Notes: Definition of regions from U.S. Census Bureau.
Fisher's exact test of independence between region and voting.
* p < .05, ** p < .01, *** p < .001

unit banks in rural areas to preserve their local monopolies against the competitive threat that large branch banks would have posed; many analysts argue that these were the real reasons for the opposition (Rajan and Ramcharan 2010). In this, the dynamics behind the prohibition against branch banking are remarkably similar to those behind antitrust. Some analysts argue that this prohibition on the size of banks led to the rise of the shadow banking system and to the greater importance of the stock market in the United States compared to other countries (Roe 1994). Only years later did the Riegle-Neal Act of 1994 repeal the prohibition against interstate branch banking.

Agrarian influence over financial regulation continued through the Great Depression. For example, Richard Carney (2010) has shown that agrarian interests were also crucial in the Securities Exchange Act of 1934. The story of the Glass-Steagall regulations is similar in the outcome of unusual American regulations on banking; there is still controversy over the details of the history (Burk 1985; Benston 1990; Tabarrok 1998; Eichengreen 1992), but there is little doubt that agrarian attempts to control finance were at least partly responsible for Glass-Steagall (Roe 1994; Carney 2010).

The irony of the McFadden Act is that the sequence of events that ended with the democratization of credit in the United States was triggered off by *stricter* regulation of finance than in other countries. The agrarian opposition to branch banking led to a more fragile financial system in the United States. Hit with similar falls in construction activity, the Canadian financial system survived while the American system needed to be resuscitated by the creation of a large new source of financial flows. Price deflations, combined with the small size of banks—kept small by the McFadden Act—and the absence of deposit insurance, led to a sequence in which farmers defaulting on their loans pushed small banks into bankruptcy. Of course, that sequence might have remained a recession and not become a depression, if not for the actions of the Fed examined in Chapter 3. But the point here is that this sequence led to a particular set of policy actions by the Roosevelt administration to attempt to resuscitate the financial sector. The consequences of this historical sequence were an economy that was more dependent on credit than in Europe but also a greater regulation of credit-granting institutions—a contradiction that belies the claims of scholars who focus on the complementarities between political economic institutions. Access to credit was ultimately the result of antimonopoly fervor, and this antimonopoly fervor was so strong because of the strength of the growing American economy and the role of agrarians in export markets. The resulting political economy was unique in the world. The United States developed a form of "mortgage Keynesianism" in which credit-financed consumption of homes became a central element of the functioning of the economy as well as of the organization of people's lives.

Credit as Justice

After the Second World War, the institutional innovation of the FHA continued to underpin growing access to consumer credit, and to spin off innovations such as Veterans' Administration loans that worked on similar principles. Although credit in the household sector would never again return below the high levels reached in the 1960s, from the mid-1960s to the mid-1970s the numbers did not grow any further—for credit had not grown evenly over the landscape. The innovations of the Depression era had established access to credit as a central feature of American life at the same time that credit access remained constrained for many Americans.

The result was that almost as soon as the institutions of mortgage credit were established, they began to be criticized for their discriminatory lending practices. As is well known, the FHA sanctioned the practice of privately operated racially restrictive covenants in its early years, and other practices of lending institutions severely restricted credit for African Americans (for just the most prominent examples of the enormous literature on this issue see Jackson 1985; Massey and Denton 1993;

Sugrue [1996] 2005; Cohen 2003; Freund 2007). Minority applicants were confronted with either absence of financing altogether or with "higher interest rates, lower appraisals, smaller loan-value ratios, and shorter amortization periods."[5] Real estate brokers would pre-screen black applicants away from certain sources of credit and steer them towards ultimately more expensive forms of credit.[6] Although researchers find that the HOLC did invest impartially (Jackson 1985, 202) and policies in the 1920s and 1930s seemed to affect black and white home-ownership rates equally (Kollman and Fishback 2011), these institutions aimed to invest impartially *in segregated neighborhoods*. As late as 1949, the first draft of the FHA Underwriting Manual—revised only after the explicit intervention of Thurgood Marshall, then lead counsel of the NAACP—included the sentence: "If there is introduced into a neighborhood an interracial mixture of occupants, and analysis shows that the value of the property to be insured has been or will be adversely affected, or if that result is indicated by precedent or experience in comparable areas under similar conditions, such effect upon valuation shall, of course, be recognized in the same manner as though it emanated from any other cause," nodding to the issue of racial discrimination by adding, "It shall not be assumed that such effect has occurred or will occur in the absence of evidence of such effect."[7]

This situation of more difficult credit access for African Americans dampened homeownership and created odd market consequences. In 1962, the Chicago Commission on Human Relations studied one block of Chicago intensively and noted that black families were charged much more for houses than white families had sold them for, while white speculators were making a tidy business of the fact that black families could not get low interest rates: "the speculator is buying the house on a low interest mortgage from a bank or saving loan association [available only to whites] while at the same time he is selling it to the Negro purchaser on a high interest contract [because blacks could not get lower interest loans]. . . . The reason white families do not sell directly to Negro families (which would save them both a lot of money) is that Negro families can rarely get financing for a mortgage. The white family cannot sell on contract to a Negro family because the white family needs all the equity out of the sale in order to buy a house in the suburbs or 'safer' section of the city. The only alternative is the speculator."[8]

Civil rights organizations such as the National Urban League attempted to attack the problem.[9] Reformers such as Illinois Senator Paul

222

Douglas made valiant attempts to ease credit access, but through the 1950s and 1960s, these efforts were largely unsuccessful (Hyman 2011, 182). It was only with the urban riots of the 1960s that efforts to address credit access for the urban poor began to gain traction (Hyman 2011, 181–190). Senator William Proxmire led a series of hearings into the issue of credit access and introduced a number of measures "to increase the flow of private credit for consumer, business and mortgage purposes to urban and rural poverty areas and to expand the opportunities for business ownership by the residents of such areas."[10] Some legislative successes followed, including the Consumer Credit Protection Act of 1968, which made it easier for consumers to compare credit offers (Hyman 2011, 190).

Discriminatory credit practices were finally outlawed in the 1970s, as a result of the work of activists fighting on behalf of women's access to credit. It was common at the time for married women to be denied credit without a husband's co-signature because wives' incomes were presumed to be unstable; moreover, although a wife's unstable income history meant that the husband was required to cosign, in situations where the wife was the stable earner and the husband the unstable earner, the husband was still required to cosign, which would bring the couple's credit rating down. Women's credit ratings were commonly extinguished upon marriage as well as upon divorce so that a divorced woman found herself without a credit history precisely when she most needed it.[11] Widows were sometimes advised to keep the credit accounts in their dead husbands' names and newly married women were on occasion asked to bring in doctors' reports on their childbearing potential or birth control methods to ensure that they would not quit working on account of pregnancy.[12] FNMA tried in 1971 to codify these practices and to make it standard that "only half a wife's income could be counted in determining family credit eligibility," a position the agency dropped only at the insistence of Representative Patsy T. Mink of Hawaii, a leader on the question of women's access to credit.[13]

The reason for these restrictive policies was a perception that women were greater credit risks than men. A credit union official wrote: "In some credit unions, we found that they have had bad experience in making loans to young married wives, who in a short period of time become pregnant and the loan is delinquent. They look to the husband for assistance in making the payments, but in many cases, they are told that they are not legally responsible. This experience is not predominate [sic] in the credit unions here, but it does create a problem."[14] Instead of quantifying the risk of such scenarios, however, credit unions used them as a broad heuristic, categorizing all women as bad risks. For example, one credit union manager complained that women would buy furniture, get married, and then quit payment; but when asked "how many such losses his credit union suffered in the past five years" he could think of only three or four out of several hundred, a remarkably low default rate.[15] In 1973, over a quarter of the mortgage lenders in DC who responded to a survey by the Women's Legal Defense Fund admitted to discriminating against women, and department stores were found to discriminate against women in granting charge accounts.[16] An audit study in Minnesota sent a male and a female investigator to apply for credit separately. Despite identical applications, over half of the banks refused credit to the woman, but treated the man generously, even waiving the requirement for a cosigner (Hyman 2011, 195).

Feminist groups took action on the issue because, as Arline Lotman, executive director of the Pennsylvania Commission on the Status of Women, put it, "Denial of credit is not a one-time action. . . . In our credit-oriented economy, it determines where and how a person lives, what kind of home she lives in, whether she owns a car or can obtain a loan to send her children to college . . . these practices cause a double hardship on minority women. Denying credit because of marital status, sharply limits the ability of the minority woman who is head of a household— and that includes 57 percent of minority women—to provide for her dependents."[17] Rates of separation and divorce were rising, and divorced and abandoned women who suddenly found themselves without a credit history—even if they had been steadily employed for years and had never missed a payment on their family's debts—could experience real penury (Hyman 2011, 198).

Activism on the issue took many forms. Some activists set up local female-friendly credit unions, starting with the "Feminist Federal Credit Union" in Detroit in 1973, with the aim of "making women aware of and securing for them their rights, responsibilities, heritage, etc. . . . [and] to help protect the membership from discrimination in lending at other financial institutions."[18] Three more followed in Pennsylvania and New York.[19]

Others attempted to prove that women were not worse credit risks than men, for example, in a Department of Housing and Urban Development study, which found "the income growth and stability for single women during the longitudinal study period 1966 to 1970, was on a par with the industry standard—the traditional male-headed, one-earner family. Projected 1970 income for two-earner families in which the working wife makes the substantial contribution of 40 percent to family income was, for every income level considered, only 10 percent below the industry standard—and 25 to 125 percent above mortgage bankers' estimates, depending on the underwriting guidelines adopted to discount the wife's earnings. Income growth patterns for women family heads fell within 8 or 9 percentage points of their male counterparts."[20]

Within two and a half years of the first hearings on the issue, the Equal Credit Opportunity Act became law.[21] One of its main accomplishments by many accounts was to allow women who were separated or divorced "who up to now have had very little legal standing" equal access to credit.[22] The next year the bill was amended to outlaw discrimination based on other criteria, including race, religion, and age, finally fulfilling the dream of equal legal access to credit.[23] And soon, the Department of Housing and Urban Development launched an eighteen-month, million-dollar "Women and Mortgage Credit Project" to ensure conformity with the law, to inform women of their legal rights, and to collect research on discrimination as well as on the credit risk women posed.[24]

This history suggests the degree to which the movement for access to credit required action from grassroots activists as well as from organized groups. The reason for the focus of these groups on credit was that credit had become a necessity in American life, determining in Arline Lotman's words quoted above "where and how a person lives, what kind of home she lives in, whether she owns a car or can obtain a loan to send her children to college . . . [her ability] to provide for her dependents." While policymakers may have abetted the financialization of the economy for their own reasons, in aiding the growth of consumer and mortgage credit they were following the lead of social groups who saw equal access to credit as a social goal. In pushing for access to credit, these groups were making reformist and not radical calls for change. Because an extensive infrastructure of credit had already been laid down in the postwar era, they saw access to credit as an issue of justice, as well as a straightforward means of improving the lives of those who had been excluded from credit-financed consumption. The next decades would see an intensification of this trend, as credit rose to new levels and both Republicans and Democrats joined in the push toward making the United States a homeowner society. The story of the rise of credit cards, the increasing predominance of financial activity in nonfinancial firms, and the plunging American savings rate is well known (Hyman 2011; Davis 2009; Krippner 2011). But this chapter has suggested that these developments resulted in part because the democratization of credit at mid-century had created support for credit access from *across* the political spectrum by the 1970s. Keeping this in mind leads to a different perspective on the financial crisis, as we will see in Chapter 9.

9

THE CREDIT/WELFARE STATE TRADE-OFF

Chapter 7 argued that there may be reason to believe that the deregulations of the 1980s and 1990s had a role to play in the financial crisis. Chapter 8 showed that, because the democratization of credit had already become an important part of American political economy at mid-century, grassroots activists pushed for easier credit access for women and African Americans in the 1970s. This chapter puts these arguments together. The first section shows that there is a trade-off between credit and social spending across the advanced industrial countries and that although deregulation was a factor in the rise of credit in countries with less well-developed welfare states, in countries with well-developed welfare states deregulation had no effect on credit. The chapter suggests that in countries such as the United States, deregulation allowed an underlying demand for credit to be met, whereas in countries with well-developed welfare states, there was no such demand. The following sections examine the implications of this for the recent financial crisis.

Credit and Welfare across Countries

Scholars of bankruptcy have long argued that credit serves welfare functions and that in the absence of extensive welfare states a system that couples relatively generous credit with easier rules for debt relief through consumer bankruptcy can provide a measure of welfare for those in need (Sullivan, Warren, and Westbrook 2000; Ramsay 2003; Tabb 2005; Warren and Tyagi 2004; Barba and Pivetti 2009). Krippner and other scholars have argued that policymakers in several cases explicitly saw the development of credit as an alternative to the welfare state (Krippner 2011; Quinn 2010, n.d.). These arguments suggest that there should be an inverse correlation between reliance on credit and the development of the welfare state across countries, yielding higher reliance on credit where the welfare state is less well developed.

On the other hand, there are also several factors that should temper this inverse correlation. A smaller welfare state implies lower taxation, and this should increase purchasing power, lowering consumers' need to turn to credit. A welfare state can itself raise the level of credit in an economy if welfare funds are invested in credit instruments. And according to the most popular theory of consumption in economics, the life cycle hypothesis, people should be more willing to take on high levels of debt if they do not feel it necessary to save for their own future health care and pension needs (see, e.g., Feldstein 1974). Since these factors would produce a direct correlation between welfare state spending and credit, it is not obvious what kind of relationship to expect between credit and the welfare state. The first section of this chapter conducts a multivariate analysis of the advanced industrial countries to identify whether systems with lower levels of welfare provision display systematically different levels of household credit.

This analysis builds on a well-developed research tradition of multivariate analysis on the relationship between home ownership and welfare state development. Jim Kemeny (1980) first identified the trade-off between home ownership and welfare state development across countries and explained it by suggesting that home ownership allows citizens to get by with smaller pensions later in the life course and makes them resistant to taxes which compete with mortgage payments earlier in the life course (see also Esping-Andersen 1985). In recent years home equity credit lines have given home owners a way to tide themselves over in difficult times, and they may have become even less interested in subsidizing provision for others who are not so lucky. Castles (1998) repeated and found strong support for Kemeny's analysis but suggested that the causal sequence could be the other way around, with citizens seeking homes for protection where they do not have a welfare state or the tax demands of a welfare state making it difficult for citizens to acquire savings for homes. Ben Ansell (n.d.) has replicated and updated this work using both data on individuals in the United States and cross-national data, finding in both cases that appreciation of house prices leads to declines in support for welfare spending. Conley and Gifford (2006) show that the relationship holds even when controlling for income inequality. They argue, "[H]ome ownership acts as a major source of income security, particularly for the aged, and confers access to a valuable fungible or collateral asset"

(56). Home ownership also serves as the lynchpin for the long-term distribution of resources, because home ownership enables intergenerational capital accumulation for investment as well as consumption (Conley 1999; Schwartz, 2012). House prices in the United States are entangled with educational quality and channel access to education; as Robert H. Frank notes, the quality of public education rises with the median value of homes in a school district (Frank 2007, 44–45). Finally, with the rise of home equity credit lines, housing has become a way to overcome medical setbacks. While this political economy of home ownership—and the larger regime of private welfare in general—serves as the form of improvement of life chances for a large segment of the populace (Howard 1997; Hacker 2002), it does not fulfill the functions of redistribution and collectivization of risk that are the basic functions of the public welfare state as traditionally understood and therefore does not have the same effects on poverty reduction as the welfare states of Europe (Prasad 2011). While it is a political and historical alternative to the welfare state, it is not equivalent to the welfare state.

This research tradition does give us some reason to suspect a relationship between credit and the welfare state. However, as home ownership rates can be increased by a range of policies other than mortgage finance, such as subsidies for savings accounts destined for housing purchases, the implications of this trade-off for the financial system are not clear, and it is necessary to examine the relationship between credit and welfare more directly.

Herman Schwartz and Leonard Seabrooke (2008, 244) have conducted a more direct examination, noting that a bivariate correlation seems to exist across countries between mortgage debt as a share of GDP and the type of welfare state (liberal-market, corporatist-market, statist-developmental, or familial). But no research has yet examined whether this correlation holds controlling for other factors that may affect both credit and welfare state spending.

To address this gap, I conducted a regression analysis on the relationship of credit and welfare across the advanced industrial countries. The dependent variable, *Debt*, is measured as household debt minus household assets as a percent of GDP. This is a measure of credit that takes into account the value of assets against the value of debts (this is reasonable for our purposes, as debts that are balanced by assets on individual household balance sheets will not have the same macroeconomic consequences as debts that are not balanced by assets). The measure comes from the Organisation for Economic Cooperation and Development's (OECD) measure of net lending and borrowing in the household sector, which was made available for a range of countries in the 2009 *National Accounts*. I have inverted the negative and positive values to turn it into a measure of debt for ease of exposition, with positive values representing greater levels of household debt.

The main predictor of interest is *Socx*, the OECD's measure of gross public social expenditure as a percent of GDP, which is available from 1980 to 2005. I have not included mandatory private welfare spending in this measure, because private systems of welfare provision have very different effects on poverty, inequality, and well-being than the public welfare state (Prasad 2011); there is therefore no reason to expect a trade-off between private welfare and high levels of credit, as these should be able to coexist within the same economic system. Similarly, I did not include expenditures on public education (Garfinkel, Rainwater, and Smeeding 2010) because these do not seem to have similar outcomes on issues of poverty and inequality as the traditional welfare state programs, and therefore they do not represent the heart of the trade-off being measured here.

As control variables I included three measures of economic performance (GDP per capita, unemployment, and the consumer price index), because credit is likely to rise with economic development regardless of what is happening to the welfare state, unemployment may affect demand for credit regardless of welfare state developments, and credit may rise in inflationary periods because inflation makes borrowing less costly; and two demographic measures (female labor force participation and the percent of the population between the ages of 15 and 64), because a higher proportion of female workers and a larger working age population may affect the demand for credit. I also included the annual real interest rate to control for the availability of credit and a measure of central government debt to test the possibility that government debt might absorb all the available credit and thereby crowd out household debt. In the second analysis below I also included a measure of deregulation of the banking sector. If credit and welfare are trade-offs, then we should not expect deregulation to have the same effects in more and less extensive welfare states; instead, deregulation will have more of an effect on credit where welfare states are less developed. In accordance with the discussion in Chapter 7, the measure of deregulation tracks liberalization of entry barriers in the financial sector, such as the repeal of Glass-Steagall. Note that I have consciously chosen a measure of financial deregulation in which the Unites States starts at a point of high regulation at the beginning of the time period examined here in order to measure the effect of the United States moving toward other countries. There are many other aspects of finance in which the United States was already liberalized by 1980, but these would not allow us to measure the effect of deregulation over this time period nor to answer the question of why the United States saw such different outcomes when it liberalized entry barriers to match the norm in Europe.

All data are from the OECD (2010a) except for the measure of real interest rates, which is from the World Bank (2012) and the measure of bank deregulation, which is from the International Monetary Fund (Abiad, Detragiache, and Tressel 2010). For more details on definitions, sources, and means and standard deviations of all variables, as well as all data and calculations, please see the author's website or the University of Michigan data repository.[1]

The time period for the analysis was 1980–2005; while the choice of this date range was driven by availability of data, this range captures the peak period of recent financial sector growth. The countries in the analysis are the advanced industrial countries (see notes to Tables 9.1 and 9.2); because our focus here is on the effect of developed welfare states on credit, the broad conclusions reached by analyses that pool the developed and developing world (e.g., Djankov, McLiesh, and Shleifer 2007) are less relevant.

Unit root tests showed that several variables were not initially stationary. Consequently all variables were first differenced, which also solved problems of autocorrelation. While first differencing is not ideal in substantive terms, as it throws out information about levels, in the presence of unit roots estimations may reach spurious conclusions as a result of historical factors affecting the long-term evolution of the variables. First differencing is the simplest means of overcoming this.

While some of the bivariate correlations are high, variance inflation factor analysis was conducted on all models, and problems of multicollinearity were not detected in any of the models.

Three different models are estimated. The first model is estimated with ordinary least squares with panel corrected standard errors, the second model repeats this estimation with a lagged dependent variable, and the third model uses country fixed effects. In the first two models panel corrected standard errors were used because the number of time points and countries suggests generalized least square methods will understate the size of standard errors and overstate significance (Beck and Katz 1995).

The third model uses fixed effects to control for unobserved heterogeneity between countries. Jackknife post-estimation was conducted on all models, and all results were robust to the exclusion of individual data points as well as to the exclusion of individual countries.

Table 9.1 shows the results of the analysis. Across all models, *Socx* has a significant and robust negative effect. Model 1 shows that a 1 percentage point increase in the growth of social spending as percent of GDP is associated with a .474 percentage point decrease in the growth of debt as percent of GDP. Model 2 repeats the estimation including a lagged dependent variable and shows that a 1 percentage point increase in the growth of social spending as percent of GDP is associated with a .581 percentage point decrease in the growth of debt as percent of GDP. Model 3 repeats the estimation with country fixed effects, and shows that a 1 percentage point increase in the growth of social spending as percent of GDP is associated with a .521 percentage point decrease in the growth of debt as percent of GDP.

Next, I examined whether banking sector deregulation has an effect on household indebtedness. If the discussion above is correct, banking regulation should have an effect where the welfare state is less developed but not where the welfare state is more developed. To conduct this analysis a variable *HighSocx* was generated and assigned a value of zero if a country-year was in the lower half of the distribution on the *Socx* measure, and a value of one if a country-year was in the upper half of the distribution on the *Socx* measure. Table 9.2 shows the results of this analysis. Models 1–3 were estimated on cases where *HighSocx* was equal to zero, and models 4–6 were estimated on cases where *HighSocx* was equal to one. Within each set of estimations, the same three methods were used as in Table 9.1—OLS with panel corrected standard errors, OLS-PCSE with a lagged dependent variable, and country fixed effects.[2]

The table shows that in cases where *HighSocx* is equal to zero—that is, cases with low values on the *Socx* measure—a 1 unit increase in change in entry barrier deregulation is associated with a .824 percentage point increase in growth of debt as percent of GDP. Model 2 repeats the estimation including a lagged dependent variable and shows that a 1 unit increase in change in deregulation is associated with a .820 percentage point increase in growth of debt as percent of GDP. Model 3 repeats the estimation with fixed effects and finds that a 1 unit increase in change in deregulation is associated with a .880 percentage point increase in debt as percent of GDP. In models 4–6, on the other hand, change in deregula-

Table 9.1. The demand for credit, 1980–2005 (first differences)

	Model 1	Model 2	Model 3
Lagged dep var			
Debt.L1	—	−.110	—
		(.106)	
Welfare state			
Socx	−.474***	−.581***	−.521***
	(.132)	(.153)	(.139)
Economic			
Per capita GDP	.001**	.001**	.001***
	(.000)	(.000)	(.000)
Consumer price index	−.268***	−.259**	−.235**
	(.075)	(.078)	(.069)
Central gov't debt	.041	.050†	.062*
	(.028)	(.030)	(.029)
Unemployment	.074	.052	.146
	(.124)	(.136)	(.131)
Demographic			
Population aged 15–64	−.000	−.000	.000
	(.000)	(.000)	(.000)
Female labor force participation	.173†	.221*	.088
	(.097)	(.104)	(.117)
Political			
Real interest rate	−.014	.006	−.013
	(.027)	(.035)	(.030)
R^2	.27	.30	.31

Notes: Standard errors in parentheses. Countries in analysis: Australia, Austria, Belgium, Canada, Denmark, Finland, France, Germany, Greece, Ireland, Italy, Japan, Netherlands, New Zealand, Norway, Portugal, Spain, Sweden, Switzerland, United Kingdom, United States.
    Dependent variable: household debt net of household assets as percent of GDP.
    Model 1: OLS with panel corrected standard errors.
    Model 2: OLS with panel corrected standard errors, lagged dependent variable.
    Model 3: Country fixed-effects.
    $p<.001$***, $p<.01$**, $p<.05$*, $p<.1$†

tion has no statistically significant association with growth in household indebtedness in cases where *HighSocx* is equal to 1, that is, in cases with high levels of welfare spending.

These analyses suggest that there is a relationship between credit and the welfare state, such that where we see greater growth in credit we see less growth in the welfare state since the 1980s. These analyses also show

Table 9.2. The effect of deregulation on credit for different levels of social spending (first differences)

	High Socx = 0 (low social spending)			High socx = 1 (high social spending)		
	Model 1	Model 2	Model 3	Model 4	Model 5	Model 6
Lagged dep var						
Debt.L1	—	−.147	—	—	−.018	—
		(.138)			(.147)	
Deregulation						
Deregulation	.824*	.820*	.880†	−.046	−.021	−.274
	(.376)	(.387)	(.495)	(.528)	(.537)	(.810)
Economic						
Per capita GDP	.001**	.001**	.001*	.001**	.001***	.002***
	(.000)	(.000)	(.000)	(.000)	(.000)	(.000)
Consumer price	−.316***	−.277**	−.275**	−.171	−.168	−.151
index	(.089)	(.101)	(.095)	(.138)	(.139)	(.141)
Central gov't debt	.042	.045	.077	.019	.033	.033
	(.033)	(.034)	(.053)	(.039)	(.041)	(.043)
Unemployment	−.216	−.284	−.255	.104	.080	.357†
	(.179)	(.202)	(.217)	(.176)	(.180)	(.183)
Demographic						
Population aged	−.000	−.000	.000	−.000	−.000	.000
15–64	(.000)	(.000)	(.000)	(.001)	(.001)	(.001)
Female labor force	−.011	−.000	−.078	.245†	.252†	.086
participation	(.181)	(.217)	(.215)	(.145)	(.149)	(.180)
Political						
Real interest rate	−.060†	−.063	−.059	−.045	−.061	−.051
	(.032)	(.052)	(.044)	(.046)	(.049)	(.040)
R^2	.27	.28	.25	.23	.25	.38

Notes: Standard errors in parentheses. Countries in analysis: Australia, Austria, Belgium, Canada, Denmark, Finland, France, Germany, Greece, Ireland, Italy, Japan, Netherlands, New Zealand, Norway, Portugal, Spain, Sweden, Switzerland, United Kingdom, United States.
　Dependent variable: household debt net of household assets as percent of GDP.
　Models 1 and 4: OLS with panel corrected standard errors.
　Models 2 and 5: OLS with panel corrected standard errors, lagged dependent variable.
　Models 3 and 6: Country fixed-effects.
　$p < .001$***, $p < .01$**, $p < .05$*, $p < .1$†

that deregulation is associated with a higher demand for credit in countries where the welfare state is less well developed but not in countries where the welfare state is well developed. If the rise of credit were simply a response to the easier availability of credit rather than to demand for credit (as some suggest, e.g., Rajan 2010, 40), deregulation would lead to a similar rise in credit in developed welfare states. Because it does not, we may conclude that deregulation *allows* the credit-welfare state trade-off to emerge: regulation suppresses credit in less well-developed welfare states, while deregulation allows the credit-financed consumption of goods and services that would be provided by the welfare state elsewhere.

While the use of country fixed effects and the inclusion of the lagged dependent variable give some confidence as to the direction of the causal relationship, I have not included here technical controls for endogeneity, and there is a possibility of reverse causation in both analyses. In the first case, this would suggest not that credit results from a constrained welfare state but that where there is easy access to credit, there is less need for welfare state spending. This possibility cannot be excluded on theoretical or empirical grounds, and for this reason the relationship identified here is best conceptualized as a trade-off between credit and welfare state spending, in which feedback effects are also possible. In the second analysis, rising credit may be the cause, not the result, of deregulation in contexts of lower social spending. For example, it may be that as credit increases, political support for deregulation increases. While this would reverse the causal model, it would be in keeping with the overarching interpretation that rising levels of credit are associated with political support for deregulation in the absence of welfare state spending. The difference of interpretation here is subtle: if deregulation causes an increase in credit, this suggests that deregulation allows a pent-up demand for credit to be met in less well-developed welfare states; whereas if an increase in credit causes deregulation, this suggests that rising credit changes political preferences and increases support for deregulation, whether or not there is a pent-up demand. Both possibilities are compatible with the argument that the politics of credit and regulation work differently in states with different levels of welfare provision, and both may be at work in producing these results.

Credit and Consumption

Is there reason to think that the relationship seen in Table 9.1 is more than spurious and that Americans are in fact using credit to purchase the kinds of goods or services that welfare states provide in other countries? The stereotype is that in recent decades Americans have gotten in the habit of using home equity credit lines or maxing out credit cards to finance the purchase of flat-screen televisions, foreign travel, restaurant meals, and other such sources of instant gratification. If this is the case, then the increase in credit seen above might be a result of Americans using credit to finance luxury consumption rather than the kinds of goods or services that welfare states provide in other countries.

But there is little evidence to back up this stereotype. First, according to the Federal Reserve's *Survey of Consumer Finances* (2007), home equity credit lines and credit cards are insignificant fractions of consumer credit (6.6% and 1.2% respectively in 2007) while home mortgages and other types of loans secured by residential property constitute over half of consumer credit. Americans could still be taking out loans on their homes and spending that money on luxuries, but Bureau of Economic Analysis (2012) data show a clear decline in the percent of consumption expenditure that has gone towards luxuries in recent decades. Home furnishings ("furnishings and durable household equipment") have declined from 4.3% of personal consumption expenditures in 1970, to 2.8% in 2007, the height of the credit bubble. Clothing and footwear represented 7% of consumption in 1970, and 3.4% in 2007. Motor vehicles and parts constituted 5.3% of consumption in 1970, and 4.1% in 2007. Despite perceptions of an explosion in restaurant consumption, "purchased meals and beverages" made up 5.6% of the budget in 1970, and 5.1% in 2007. Foreign travel is the only luxury category to have grown slightly, from 0.8% of total consumption in 1970 to 1.1% in 2007. (All figures from Bureau of Economic Analysis, 2012, *National Income and Product Accounts*, table 2.4.5, "Personal Consumption Expenditures by Type of Product.")

Rather, what Americans are spending on is housing and health care. "Housing and utilities" represent the largest major category of expenditure at 18% in 2007, with the major increase in the role of housing occurring from 1945 to 1960. The next largest category is "health care" at 14.9% in 2007, with a continuous rise throughout the post-war period. (Bureau of Economic Analysis, 2012, *National Income and Product Accounts*, table 2.4.5, "Personal Consumption Expenditures by Type of Product.")

In comparative perspective, it is health care that is the outlier in spending patterns between the United States and other countries. According to the OECD's *Dataset on Final Consumption Expenditures* (2010c), if rental costs are included then Americans do not actually spend much more on housing as a percent of GDP than citizens in other countries, and in all other categories, Americans spend about as much as others. However, in health care, where the average in other countries is slightly over 2% of GDP, Americans have spent over 12% of GDP in recent years. This is an increase from 5.5% in 1970. The picture that arises from these sources of data is of Americans taking out loans backed by their homes to finance health-care spending.

Given the underdeveloped public health system, some of that health-care consumption is providing medicines or services that would be provided out of general taxation in other countries. It can be argued that a large segment of this spending is going towards the uniquely high-cost pattern of American healthcare, with its extensive administrative costs, aggressive high-tech treatments, and weak cost controls. But this, too, can be seen as a consequence of the private nature of the American medical system, as a publicly financed welfare system can be expected to have constrained incentives to this kind of growth, and much of this expenditure is beyond the choice or control of consumers. In short, there is reason to think that private consumer spending on health care—which constitutes the main difference between American and European expenditure patterns—results from an underdeveloped public system of health provision. The American consumer is not maxing out on luxuries but is stretched thin because of health-care costs.

While health care is the clear outlier in terms of consumption, there are other good reasons to take on credit in the United States, including education. Consider the story of James Rouse, who lost both his father and his mother in 1930 as the Depression hit. Struggling to get to law school, he convinced the dean of the University of Maryland Law School to enroll him for five dollars a week, which Rouse was making parking cars, plus a hundred dollars down: "So then I went back to my hometown of Easton, and I went to see the President of the Easton National Bank, a man named James Dixon, who had a son who was a friend of mine, who I'd known, family had known their family well. And I told him my story. And I said, 'I need to borrow a hundred dollars.' Of course I couldn't even sign a legal note, and there was nobody to guarantee my note, which is what he first suggested. I said, 'There isn't anyone.' So he arranged that the bank would lend me a hundred dollars on my signature. Which they did. And that was a very important financial transaction. And with that hundred dollars and five dollars a week, I went to night law school." Appropriately, Rouse ended up an administrator for the FHA.[3] Credit finances American education, mobility, health care, and welfare. In the developed welfare states education and health care are at least partially financed through taxation, and home buying is not caught up in the struggle for quality education.

Credit and the Crisis

The problems with a credit-driven system may seem obvious to us in the wake of an economic crisis caused partly by high levels of consumer debt, but these problems were not necessarily obvious at the time that the credit system was being developed. Although it may seem to be common sense that money borrowed under interest must eventually reduce purchasing power when the loan comes due, the argument for credit is that the *productive* use of credit will lead to economic growth such that the debt will be repaid by a much richer borrower to whom that amount of debt is worth much less. If the credit is used in a way that contributes to the household's upward mobility—access to good schools, overcoming emergencies that would otherwise impoverish the household, investment in business, capital accumulation through house purchases—and if credit is used at the macroeconomic level in productive investments that make the economy grow, it increases purchasing power and pays for itself out of the higher growth. Once interest rates are low enough, and the returns to education or investment are high enough, credit makes sense. The borrower is borrowing from her much richer future self—a future self who is *made* much richer precisely because of the borrowed money. This is the privatized version of the fundamental insight about economic growth that also drives Keynesian thinking. Winfield Riefler, developer of the amortized mortgage and an author of the Federal Housing Act, gave exactly this response to those who questioned the FHA: "If senators questioned Riefler's plan for adding 'another billion and a half to the debts of the Nation,' Riefler's response echoed the new economic thinking of the day: Any measure that increases employment, would add wealth and thereby repay that debt" (Hyman 2011, 55).

Of course, this scenario only works as long as the economy is indeed growing. Robert Collins (2000) traces American dependence on economic growth to the New Deal. Charles Maier (1977) demonstrates how Americans relied on "superseding class conflict with economic growth" (629) throughout the postwar period and traces the origins of this strategy to

238

even before the New Deal. But after all, the welfare state also works only as long as the economy is growing. Under conditions of decline and unemployment, welfare measures quickly become unaffordable, as the number of those drawing on welfare grows and the number of taxpayers shrinks. The logic of the welfare state—that productive public investments will lead to growth and therefore pay for themselves—is not so different from the logic of credit. We should therefore be careful to avoid a teleological interpretation of the credit/welfare state trade-off, because if we did not have the knowledge that we currently have about financial sector volatility, it is not obvious which of these methods—redistribution from the future or redistribution in the present—would make the most sense. In this analysis, credit *is* a resolution of distributional issues, a resolution that comes out of the same insights about economic growth that fed Keynesianism. The welfare state and credit may both be conceptualized as twentieth century versions of reciprocal exchange, marked not only by reciprocity between social actors but also by reciprocity with a more prosperous future.

Understanding credit as an alternative form of redistribution makes sense of an otherwise puzzling feature of the politics of deregulation: why the American Left was so supportive of financial deregulation in the 1970s. We have already seen in Chapter 8 the unceasing efforts of groups that worked to ease access to credit for African Americans and women. It is also the case that the Depository Institutions Deregulation and Monetary Control Act of 1980, which deregulated interest rates, was passed when Democrats were in control of the White House and both houses of Congress. Even consumer advocate Ralph Nader testified to Congress that Depression-era regulations were less relevant now that the United States was (already in 1973) "truly a credit-oriented installment payment economy. Houses are purchased on time payments, so are the appliances and furniture that are in the houses. Indeed, consumers even pay for vacations, clothes, and almost anything on the easy-payment plan. All of these factors indicate that we may have now become a capital deficit country in the sense that there is generated more demand for loanable funds than we have capacity to supply . . . The effect of credit, and most importantly the denial of credit . . . is so great in today's world" (U.S. Congress, House, 1973, 467, 469). Similarly, one of the main reasons for the crisis of the late 2000s was that the development of home-mortgage securitization had enabled the rise of an originate to distribute model of loans, in which lenders were decreasingly concerned with the quality of the loan (Purnanandam

239

2009); but while securitization has been around in some form since the nineteenth century, mortgage-backed securities were originally developed by the government in the Housing Act of 1968 as a means of satisfying a clearly demonstrated demand for credit that had developed in the credit crunch of 1966 (Sellon and VanNahmen 1988; Quinn 2010; Hyman 2011).

These examples suggest that in the United States, deregulation of the financial sector resulted at least partly because groups from across political lines joined together to argue in favor of it. They supported deregulation for the same reason that they supported easier access to credit for underprivileged groups: since the institutional innovations of the Depression and postwar period, credit had become the main mechanism of ensuring welfare. Deregulation was not driven by business interests alone, and it was not an ad hoc result of policymakers' experimentations. It was the logical outcome of a system in which welfare needs were met through credit and the limits that this system hit during the macroeconomic difficulties of the 1970s (for a discussion of the broader politics of deregulation see Prasad 2006).

Of course, we are now aware of some things that the developers of this system may not have understood well. Not only does the credit-based model do a worse job of addressing poverty, but one may also wonder what role the relationship explored here may have played in the recent financial crisis. Specifically, if rising household credit was a factor in the crisis, and if an underdeveloped welfare state was one factor in rising credit, can we conclude that the underdeveloped American welfare state was a partial cause of the financial crisis?

While much remains unclear about the financial crisis that began in 2007, some main lines of causation have been identified. Economic growth throughout the world, and particularly in China, increased the amount of savings worldwide. Financial market deregulation attracted those funds to the United States. One of the new financial innovations was an acceleration of securitization, which intensified in the 1980s and 1990s. Being able to sell forward bad debts increased lenders' willingness to take on riskier loans. Rule changes also allowed firms to take on ever-greater degrees of leverage, and credit-rating agencies that were paid by the very firms they were rating continued to highly rate financial products that were, in fact, quite risky. Separately, a bubble in the home mortgage market began when interest rates were cut to historic lows, but when home prices began to decline speculative investments in homes failed and the bubble burst. This caused mortgage-backed financial products to fail simultaneously in a way that had not been foreseen in models. As firms began to lose money, lack of clarity on the question of how deeply invested any firm was in mortgage-backed financial products led to a slowing of liquidity across the financial sector. This led to reduced spending, disinvestment, and ultimately increased unemployment. (Tomaskovic-Devey and Lin 2011; Mackenzie 2011; Prasad 2009; and see the contributors to Lounsbury and Hirsch 2010).[4]

A debate has ensued in the public sphere with Republicans seeking to blame attempts to increase home ownership for the poor as the central problem, and Democrats seeking to blame financial-sector deregulation (either as a fundamental cause, allowing excessive risk-taking in the financial sector, or as a proximate cause that allows worldwide savings to flow into the United States rather than financing investment and consumption in developing countries. See Prasad 2009). Both of these factors do share the blame, but the Democratic argument ignores the fact that *Democrats themselves* were also in support of financial sector deregulation, as explored in this chapter and Chapter 7; deregulations were not exogenous to the system, and they were not just driven by moneyed interests. They were the outgrowth of a system in which, because of the central role of credit in the political economy, *there was no natural constituency for regulation.* Because credit was a mechanism for addressing poverty, deregulation developed support from all political camps.

The problem with the conservative argument, on the other hand, is that it does not offer alternative means to address poverty. After all, attempting to address poverty by extending credit access can be seen as a market-friendly mechanism. This is why it received support from Democrats such as Jimmy Carter and Bill Clinton as well as Republicans such as George W. Bush. Clinton said, "Expanding homeownership will strengthen our nation's families and communities, strengthen our economy, and expand this country's great middle class. Rekindling the dream of home-ownership for America's working families can prepare our nation to embrace the rich possibilities of the twenty-first century" (quoted in Rajan 2010, 36). George W. Bush remarked, "I believe owning something is part of the American Dream. . . . I believe when somebody owns their own home, they're realizing the American Dream" (quoted in Rajan 2010, 37). Both administrations took steps to extend the dream of home ownership and encountered no significant opposition to doing so.

Because of this, it makes sense to conclude that the underdeveloped welfare state was indeed a factor in the financial crisis, for it led to a political situation in which all actors supported deregulation of the financial sector and increasing access to credit-financed home ownership, the proximate causes of the crisis.

The regulation of finance that emerged in the early twentieth century included three features that were unique in comparative perspective: the ease of bankruptcy, the extensive banking regulations, and the democratization of credit. Easy bankruptcy and easy credit interacted to increase American reliance on credit; however, heavier regulations such as the McFadden Act and the Glass-Steagall Act were in some tension with this, as they kept financial institutions smaller and less stable than in other countries—contrary to what theorists of institutional complementarity might suggest, these two features worked in opposite directions, with the McFadden and Glass-Steagall Acts preventing the further development of credit. The United States developed an economy focused on credit at the same time that it pioneered a set of laws during the New Deal that limited the availability of credit.

The prosperity of the three decades after the Second World War hid those tensions under generally rising income streams, producing a slow and steady increase in both demand for credit and supply of credit, interrupted by frightening—but rare—credit crunches when depositors withdrew their funds to seek higher returns elsewhere in an effort to beat inflation (Wojnilower 1980). But the whole arrangement unraveled in the 1970s when the recession and economic slowdown of that decade meant the demand for credit outpaced available credit, hitting the ceilings imposed by the New Deal regulations. It was certainly the case that the financial services industry argued that the separation of commercial and investment banking was hindering the further development of the industry and preventing the industry from meeting a clearly demonstrated and widespread demand for credit (e.g., Peek and Rosengren 1995). But as we have seen, activists on the Left also supported widening the availability of credit. It was this acknowledged need for credit that came from *across* the political spectrum that stoked the rapidly building deregulatory fervor. Under assault from all quarters, criticized as preventing access to credit without generating any visible benefits, the American tradition of more stringent banking regulation began to give way. The financial sector began a dizzy, decades-long era of innovation (Miller 1986; Coval, Jurek, and Stafford 2009). And the deregulatory movement entered a new phase when the (supposedly) demonstrated success of deregulation led to ever greater deregulation, including the Riegle-Neal Act of 1994, which repealed restrictions against branch banking, the Financial Services Modernization Act of 1999, which repealed Glass-Steagall, and the Commodity Futures Modernization Act of 2000, which prevented the regulation of over-the-counter derivatives.

While some scholars blame those deregulations that allowed innovation in the financial sector, the underlying *reason* for the deregulations was the seemingly endless demand for credit in the United States. The perception of success with these earlier deregulations and a demonstrated ability to sell these new financial instruments led to arguments that the regulations of the New Deal period had been shown to be unnecessary, and even the savings and loan crisis of the 1980s could not stem the popularity of credit access.

In short, the central role of credit and credit-driven home ownership in channeling welfare in the United States meant that large numbers of people were willing to take on debts amounting to large multiples of their incomes and increasingly demanded credit over the postwar period. This resulted in credit crunches and a persistent credit crisis in the 1970s, which led to experiments with increasing deregulation of the financial system that were supported by actors from all parts of the political world.

The answer to the two questions posed in Chapter 7 is that the United States had heavier financial regulation because the United States is not a liberal political economy at all, and theories of comparative political economy ignore this at their peril. Rather, the United States is an adversarial political economy in which heavy state regulation disciplines capitalist firms through antitrust, adversarial regulation, capital taxation, and other measures. In the postwar period this led the United States to develop a heavily regulated economy that was also marked by high demand for credit, while it led to an increasingly strong welfare state in Europe. As the countries entered the economic recession of the 1970s, however, the demand for credit in the United States led to calls for deregulation. But in the absence of heavy regulation, the demand for credit in the United States created financial bubbles and led to the consequences that we have recently witnessed. European-style financial regulations do not work in the United States because the demand for credit is higher in the United States than in Europe. The ultimate lesson of the story is that an economy dependent on credit needs heavy regulation to remain stable but that the demand for credit leads to calls for deregulation; consequently, an economy with a more extensive welfare state is an economy that is more financially stable.

The American credit-driven model also has consequences for economic growth, as Hermann Schwartz (2009) has explained. Schwartz shows that the United States and countries with housing systems similar to the United States sustained higher growth in the 1990s than other countries. Housing spurred growth, Schwartz argues, because in a disinflationary environment home owners could take advantage of lower interest rates by refinancing or taking home equity loans, thus freeing up purchasing power in a manner that was not possible in countries without this kind of reliance on credit.

Ironically, although European regulatory schemes have functioned well for decades within Europe (with the possible exception of the early 1990s in Finland and Switzerland, see Gylfason, Holmström, Korkman, Söderström, and Vihriälä 2010), European countries were drawn into the 2007–2008 crisis to the extent that they were exposed to the American financial system. It is important to clarify a common misconception about the recent economic crisis in Europe. Two separate processes have taken place in Europe in the last several years: first, countries that were exposed to the American financial system—or that imitated it, like Ireland and Iceland—have been punished for that exposure; second, and separately, the process of economic integration produced bubbles in weaker European economies, which have fallen into debt crisis (Hardie and Howarth 2009; Shirai 2009). These processes became interlinked because bailouts for troubled banks worsened budget deficits. But these outcomes were not a result of the regulatory structure. The current crisis in Europe should not obscure the underlying point that a regulatory scheme that had worked well for decades in European countries failed spectacularly when it was imported into the United States.

Finally, while this chapter has shown a trade-off between credit and welfare, it is worth underlining that these two alternatives have very different consequences for poverty. While a political economy based on credit may offer a measure of relief to those who are able to borrow, it leaves unprotected those who are not. In undermining the welfare state, the American path of democratization of credit condemns a segment of the populace to poverty. Moreover, if the links forged in this chapter are correct, then a more developed welfare state in the United States would have constrained the growth of American credit and thus the growth of American consumption. As the world economy has depended for many years on the foundation of strong consumption in the United States, it may not be unwarranted to conclude that the prosperity of the world in recent decades has been built on the consignment of a segment of the American population to poverty.

PART FOUR

CONCLUSION

10

AMERICAN MORTGAGE KEYNESIANISM:
SUMMARY AND POLICY IMPLICATIONS

I have attempted to do four things in this book. First, to draw attention to the many ways in which the United States departs from the ideal type of a liberal or laissez-faire state, to the point that these labels are now harming scholarship. Second, to show how New World wealth created a disequilibrium in the world economy starting in the late nineteenth century that had identifiable consequences for the development of political economy in every country. While the economic might of the United States has been visible to all, its consequences for political economy have remained unexplored, and all of our major traditions of comparative political economy proceed as if this substantial difference between the United States and other countries did not exist. Geography is not destiny, and a particular set of social structures was necessary to translate geographical resources into economic wealth—social structures that were not found in other large, resource-rich countries—but this book comes down in favor of the argument that geography matters. Third, I have attempted to extend Elizabeth Sanders's rubric of "agrarian statism" and show that the political power of American farmers, catalyzed by the rise of New World wealth and made possible by the structure of the American state, lasted into the Great Depression and the early New Deal to produce many aspects of the greater state intervention catalogued here. The interventionism of the American state began as agrarian intervention. Once established, however, this tradition of intervention extended far beyond questions specific to agrarians: for example, consumer protection traces its roots to the technique of intervention through independent regulatory agencies that resulted from agrarian agitation over railroads. But consumer protection today affects all Americans, including the hundreds or perhaps thousands who were directly saved by Frances Kelsey. And fourth, I have sought to show the unexpected results of those agrarian interventions in the postwar period, as progressive taxation closed off the path to a European-style welfare state, and the decentralization of finance resulted in the democratization of credit and an economy based on private consumption. This book thus links the fortunes of the contemporary welfare state to the political economy of trade in the "first" era of globalization in the late nineteenth century (O'Rourke and Williamson 1999, 4) and shows how that first moment of globalization laid a pattern for political economy that came to fruition in the interwar years. The story of greater poverty in the United States is that a set of progressive interventions taken during the early twentieth century produced decidedly non-progressive results.

The theoretical argument of this book is that a state's approach to consumption is the best predictor of whether it will develop an extensive public welfare state that reduces poverty. While I have only examined one case in depth, the logic of the relations examined in that case lead to the theoretical prediction that higher rates of poverty result from a governmental focus on encouraging consumption rather than investment. States that encourage consumption will develop less extensive welfare states, while states that restrain consumption will be forced to develop more extensive welfare states. Of course, a state's approach to consumption does not arise *ex nihilo*. It is the outcome of a complicated set of factors including a country's track record on economic growth and inflation, its role in geopolitics and war, and the structure of finance and the role that finance plays in the economy. A state's approach to consumption is not an exogenous or ultimately determining factor but rather a moment when a causal chain that ends with a particular approach to consumption inaugurates a new causal chain that ends with a particular approach to the welfare state. This is a Durkheimian answer to the problem in historical social science of how far back in history to trace a causal chain. History produces sequences in which phenomena become *sui generis*, that is, no longer reducible to the events that brought them into being. These moments are where our causal sequences should begin. *Whatever* the factors that produce a particular approach to consumption, once established the approach to consumption independently influences the development of the welfare state. Consequences for the welfare state are driven by politicians responding to constituents' needs and constituents making those needs known. Although this book does find an element of path dependence in the stories, in that prior decisions affect future decisions and make some outcomes less likely, it does not find support for the strongest version of path dependence, which posits moments of contingency followed by sequences where processes are "locked" in and cannot change (Mahoney 2000, 2001; Pierson 2000). We do not find contingent events of the kind called for in that vision, as there is nothing contingent about any of the events here: the response of states around the world to the disequilibrium caused by American abundance is well understood through examination of groups' attempts to act in their perceived interests; even the geographical contingency that begins the sequence can be understood in structural terms as human migration ex- tending to ever-newer lands. Nor do we find narrow critical junctures, as the events span several decades from the 1890s to the 1930s. As others have argued, the strong vision of path dependence does not map well onto fluid historical processes (Thelen 2004). But we do find weaker versions of path dependence in the story. For example, the United States has, to date, not embraced national sales tax. In the immediate postwar period there was no reason to leave this path, as the income tax proved to be an effi- cient revenue-raising mechanism. After the economic crisis of the 1970s, when there was reason to turn to a new tax, there was no ability to do so, because in conditions of economic crisis citizens were less tolerant of pro- posals for new taxation. As Kato (2003) notes, this is an instance of path dependence, in that paths chosen before the First World War proved resis- tant to change for decades afterward, even if the stronger arguments about critical junctures and contingency are not supported. Moreover, the appro- aches to consumption established between the First and Second World Wars have remained dominant in each country ever since—explaining German resistance to demand-side policies in the current crisis. Perhaps the main lesson on this score is the importance of unintended and unforeseen consequences in history. Even where groups and actors intend to behave rationally, the systems of social action are too complicated to predict their interactions, at least at current levels of human understanding.

The empirical argument of the book is that experiences with New World wealth drove the advanced industrial countries' different approaches to consumption and consequently the shape of their welfare states, as summarized in Figure 10.1. In the nineteenth and early twentieth centu- ries, European states responded to the collapsing prices caused by Ameri- can growth under the gold standard by raising their tariff barriers—a development that may have intensified conflict between them (Hobson 1997). The conflicts that these protectionist powers engaged in further decimated their economic capacities, such that in each country the political

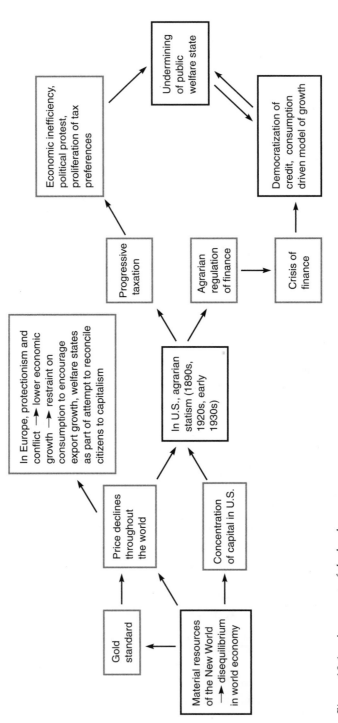

Figure 10.1. Argument of the book.

authorities desperately sought to boost output. Welfare states were one element of postwar reconstruction as a bargain with labor in return for wage restraint and as a means of reconciling citizens to economic growth imposed from above. Agrarians were often powerful in European countries as well, but because of their manner of integration into export markets, price declines for them were caused by foreign grain, and they joined and strengthened protectionist coalitions.

Protection was not enough for American farmers, because it was their own productivity that caused the problem, and consequently in the United States the price volatility of the 1890s and then the 1920s set off a long process of policymaking creativity. Huey Long and others like him could not fathom how it could be that in a land that had so much and could produce so much, people could nevertheless remain hungry and homeless. Something was wrong, they concluded, with the mechanisms of distribution that came between the successful production and the ability to consume. As we have examined, that intense and fertile period of rethinking led to arguments that the money supply needed to grow more quickly to keep pace with the growing economy and that concentrations of wealth needed to be dispersed so that the productivity of the land could flow through the economy. In particular, as Meg Jacobs and other scholars have explored, this period saw the development of a "purchasing power paradigm" that guided mid-century American political economy. Through the twists of the political process, these insights became policy in two particularly important ways. First, American politicians sought to break up concentrations of wealth through a tax structure that was unusually progressive in comparative perspective. Second, the concern to break up concentrated wealth also led to a series of laws designed to keep banks small. These were certainly not the only policies that resulted, but these policies were unusually consequential for the subsequent development of American political economy. This political attempt to protect consumers and suppliers from the power of the great corporations was largely driven by agrarians and their representatives, who were in pivotal positions in the policymaking process at the turn of the century and into the 1930s.

This unique form of state intervention undermined the public welfare state. Progressive taxation seems to be a more politically vulnerable form of revenue generation and may also be less economically efficient, so American resistance to regressive taxation closed off the easy source of revenue that the European states had found. And because the pro-debtor pattern of policy-making had led to a tradition of tax preferences, one way corporations avoided high tax rates was by granting fringe benefits, which received preferential tax treatment. These tax preferences codified and helped to develop the American system of private welfare and conversely to starve the public welfare state of support. This explanation makes it easier to understand why employers began to change their preferences late in the century. In the 1980s and 1990s corporate rates were lowered, lowering the value of tax preferences for fringe benefits and leaving employers with less reason to back the fringe benefits that were becoming increasingly costly. By the 1990s, businesses were moving cautiously towards favoring measures for universal health care, and unions were no longer fighting battles for private welfare provision (for a full examination of the changing politics of health care see Hacker 2002; Jacobs and Skocpol 2010; Daschle 2010).

The American form of state intervention also led to a credit-based political economy. The agrarian regulation of finance caused a financial collapse during the Great Depression. To resuscitate finance—and thereby the economy—the Roosevelt administration began a process of the democratization of credit. At the same time, the financial regulations that emerged from the Great Depression kept a cap on credit by keeping banks small and limiting their activities. While this contradiction was not a major problem during the postwar decades of economic development, as the world entered recession in the 1970s observers from all points of the political spectrum began to agitate for the easier availability of credit, leading to a period of deregulation. Those deregulations developed their own dynamics, ultimately leading to crisis.

In the military-fiscal model that is dominant in studies of state formation, wars are the main junctures of history (Tilly 1985). In the story I have told here, wars are consequential in two key ways: the devastation caused by the world wars was an important impetus for the coordinated project of market-building upon which the European states embarked in the early twentieth century, and the abundance of the American economy that initiated the sequence of events was bound up with the Civil War and the First World War, both of which catalyzed American economic capacity. To that extent this work extends rather than challenges the military-fiscal model. But it is also notable that wars primarily changed the scale, not the shape, of the political economy. For example, the Second World War was the crucial pivot in the history of the American tax state, as it raised revenue levels to new heights, from which they never again returned (Campbell and Allen 1994; Jones 1996; Sparrow 2008). But the war failed to transform the American state's reliance on income tax and rejection of national sales tax, which predated the war and survived the war. Similarly, the main events in the democratization of credit were the result of economic crisis, not geopolitical crisis, and preceded the Second World War. The relative economic decline of Europe compared to the United States predates the world wars, and if the wars intensified the decline, the decline and the protectionism it led to may also have contributed to the atmosphere of conflict that produced the wars. Wars interact with domestic political and economic institutions in ways that do not allow for easy identification of the primacy of any of these factors.

I explored in an earlier book, *The Politics of Free Markets* (Prasad 2006), the consequences of these different models of political economy for the rise of neoliberalism in the United States and Britain in the 1970s and 1980s. In the United States, this political movement was associated with the presidency of Ronald Reagan and in Britain with the administration of Margaret Thatcher. Reagan's neoliberalism took the form of sustained tax cuts and deregulations, many of which persist to this day. Thatcher's took the form of extensive privatizations that have also not been reversed. But although conservative leaders came to power in both France and Germany at similar times and with similar promises to reduce the role of government in the market, in neither of those two countries was neoliberalism very extensive.

Contrary to some prominent explanations, neoliberalism did not result from the influence of business or economists (Prasad 2006; Prasad 2012). Rather, neoliberalism was stronger in the United States and Britain than in France and West Germany because American and British tax structures were more progressive at this time than their French and German counterparts; American regulation was more adversarial to business, specifically in the costly area of environmental regulation, where German firms were allowed to regulate themselves; nationalized firms in Britain were run with the goal of full employment, while nationalized firms in France were run with the goal of efficiency; and while the American and British welfare states gave more to the poor than to the wealthy, France actually had a reverse redistributive welfare state, which gave more to the wealthy than to the poor. These policies laid the foundations for neoliberalism in the United States and Britain because over the postwar period, the majority of Americans and Britons experienced an unprecedented rise in their standards of living. This meant that adversarial policies that had been vote-winners in an earlier period ("soak the rich" progressive taxation in the United States and pro-union policies in the United Kingdom) became less attractive to the electorate, especially after the stagflation of the 1970s. Instead, politicians of the Right discovered that tax cuts (in the United States) and antilabor and pro-homeowner policies (in the United Kingdom) had become vote-winners.

The story does not end with the conservative victories, however, because electoral victory did not translate so easily into policy victory. The Thatcher administration's main promise as it entered government was monetarism. But when the administration actually moved to implement monetary policy, it turned out that no one knew what "money" was. The different ways to define money centrally determined what the policy would mean. Amid this uncertainty, the Treasury was able to assert its power by defining money in such a way that *monetarism* became the equivalent of *balanced budgets*—a process that the proponents of monetarism strongly opposed. This defanged the policy in such a subtle way that even the main actors did not really understand what had happened. A similar episode occurred under Reagan, when the left-wing cause of deregulation was, in an equally startling manner, turned into a right-wing cause. (For details on these episodes see Prasad 2006.)

In short, greater intervention produced a backlash after the economic crisis of the 1970s. This is the reason why the greater state intervention chronicled in Chapter 1 nevertheless gave way to the very different current models of political economy summarized in Table 1.1, in which the United States looks much different from continental Europe (Britain occupies an intermediate position). European state interventions were driven by the overarching focus on encouraging economic growth by investing in business, and therefore survived the economic crises of the 1970s more easily.

I suggested above three criteria for a good explanation of the differences between the United States and Europe: it must explain the heavier state intervention in some domains in the United States *as well as* the country's less developed public welfare state that results in greater poverty and inequality; it must explain why European states were able to combine economic growth with redistribution for several decades; and it must explain the origins of the divergences in the American and European trajectories. I have argued in this book that the role of agrarians in politics in the first part of the twentieth century explains state intervention in areas important to farmers, state interventions that went on to undermine the public welfare state. Because of the agrarian resistance to regressive taxation, the United States never adopted the less economically-distorting taxes that underpin the European welfare states and that allow Europe to combine economic growth with redistribution. The ultimate cause of this divergence was the explosive economic growth of the United States, caused by British institutions imported onto the immense landmass of North America and bearing fruit starting in the nineteenth century.

This book also argues that the differences between the American and European models of capitalism have little to do with culture, the preferences of employers, or the power of labor unions, and everything to do with the unusual productivity of American capitalism and the crises it caused during the interwar period and the Great Depression. Public mobilization or support for welfare policies was not a major factor in the origin of the policies in any of the developed welfare states. Although systematic polling data do not exist for the whole period, historical studies suggest that the greater support that we see now came after the policies were implemented. Likewise, employers usually resisted welfare policies when they were first suggested and only acquiesced to them later. And the pattern of labor strength and mobilization does not fit the unusual trajectory of the American welfare state.

Rather, the explanation I have advanced here is built on the principle that capitalism can be analyzed by examining the demand side of the economy, specifically, whether states encourage or restrain consumption. That lens leads, further, to an appreciation of the importance of the international economic context, in which the United States played a very different role than the European countries because American abundance created a disequilibrium in the world economy starting in the late nineteenth century from which the world only slowly, and only at great cost, recovered.

Although much of the explanation given here is specific to the advanced industrial countries, there are also several elements that can be fashioned into a more general explanation that can be tested on currently developing countries. First, as Karl Polanyi taught us, inflation and especially deflation are the great destabilizers of history. In the absence of a gold standard and in the presence of central banks and completely different institutions for managing international exchange, the monetary questions will not be the same today. But there will still be episodes of price volatility, and examining these is a good entry point into political economy. Economic grievances are rarely sufficient to explain the course of historical events, but we may put it this way: price volatility occurs; when price volatility occurs, governments intervene; but *how* governments intervene is a result of other factors. A second more general conclusion of this work is of the importance of agrarian politics to the welfare state. Welfare states have historically developed as societies began to industrialize, at times when agrarian classes remained politically important. Esping-Andersen (1990) saw this clearly, but did not appreciate the complicated paths that agrarian politics could take. A particularly important feature of agrarian politics is the productivity of farmers and their integration into export markets. In uncompetitive agrarian markets, farmers can be bought off with protectionism. But the uncompetitiveness of agrarian markets may be an index of a general uncompetitiveness of the economy (which protectionism can exacerbate); in this situation welfare states may be part of the attempt to stimulate economic growth by restraining private consumption and channeling savings to investment. On the other hand, where farmers are exporters, protectionism is not enough to defuse their activism during moments of price decline. While the results of this activism are less predictable, a natural target of agrarian energies is the concentration of wealth that industrialization produces.

The politics of the 1920s and 1930s cast a long shadow, consigning the United States to a smaller welfare state and higher poverty and inequality levels for the next eighty years. The shadow of the era chronicled here is so long that it leads to some clear policy implications for the economic crisis that the world is experiencing as I write. This book is a history and not a policy manual, so I leave the full development of these arguments for other venues, but I suggest here some preliminary thoughts.

1. Consider lower taxes on savings. The uniqueness of American rejection of national sales tax has been a topic of discussion among students of "fiscal sociology" for some time now (see Martin, Mehtortra, and Prasad 2009). Many scholars have drawn the lesson that the United States should follow the example of every other industrialized country and adopt a Value Added Tax (VAT) (see Zelenak 2010b for an overview). For example, Andrea Campbell's proposal for a 10% VAT would "raise a significant amount of revenue with relative political and economic ease—while carefully blunting [the VAT's] regressivity" (2010, 55) with several design features such as exempting necessities, allowing refunds for low-income households, and imposing higher rates on luxury goods.

The history discussed in this book accords with the calls for a serious consideration of the VAT, which has been an important element in the

European countries' attempt to restrain consumption and foster investment and capital accumulation, and which finances a state large enough to reduce poverty. The arguments in this work also suggest that, in addition to addressing regressivity, such proposals would need to alleviate the fear of the states that a national VAT would cut into their revenue base. A successful VAT could either add VAT on top of state sales taxes or replace state sales taxes and explicitly dedicate some portion of the proceeds of the VAT to the states.

However, if Harold Wilensky is right, then the VAT's main political benefit is that it makes taxes less visible. Adopting a mechanism precisely because of its lower visibility contradicts the trend to greater transparency that is a feature of American politics in recent decades. Another approach that has become popular in recent years, and that captures some of the benefits of consumption taxation while avoiding its politically questionable aspects, would be to raise taxes overall while lowering taxation on savings. This is the economic equivalent of increasing consumption taxes, which could help to increase the American savings rate and thereby aid growth. Such a policy could be graduated so that lower-income taxpayers reap most of the benefits, and indeed, savings for the lowest-income taxpayers could be rewarded with refundable tax credits, as has been attempted on a temporary basis in the past. The only problem with such a measure would be avoiding undue complication of the tax code.

2. *Simplify the tax code.* Simplification of the tax code seems to be one of those abstract and technical issues of good government that cannot generate much excitement. But the complexity of the tax code explains many important problems in American politics today. One problem is that this complexity offers a back door for corporate interests to carve out exemptions. Many Americans conclude from this that corporations have overweening power in the political system. But the end result of this corporate backroom wheeling and dealing is simply to *bring the corporate tax rate down to levels similar to other countries*. That is to say, the United States today has on paper a very progressive corporate tax rate, 35% as compared to around 25% in other OECD countries. But in practice the effective corporate tax rates—what corporations actually pay—are not so different (Avi-Yonah and Lahav 2011).

This leads to the obvious question: Why not just set the corporate tax rates at the same level as in other countries in the first place? Why all this drama involving armies of lobbyists and complicated exemptions if the rates are just going to end up where other countries start out? One reason for this curious state of affairs may be that this way of doing things benefits politicians. It brings them symbolic benefits by allowing them to claim that tax rates on corporations are high, and it brings them material benefits because corporations must pay politicians in the form of campaign contributions to get the tax rates down to the level of other countries. McCaffery and Cohen (2005–2006) have argued that this constitutes a "shakedown" by politicians. The situation does not really benefit corporations, who have to purchase tax rates that corporations in other countries take for granted, nor does it benefit the economy in general, as much productive effort is wasted in lobbying and lawyering. But it brings politicians campaign funds and saves them from having to visibly lower corporate rates, which may explain the hardiness of this system despite efforts such as the Tax Reform Act of 1986. Perhaps the most pernicious effect of this set of affairs, however, is that it produces alienation among the public, who are turned off by the perception of corruption that arises. The politics of tax preferences also leads to consequences that are not predictable or controllable—indeed, the welfare state itself got caught in the complexities of the tax code, which led to a situation in which corporations and labor both preferred private welfare spending to public welfare spending.

3. Don't just regulate the supply of credit; consider also the demand for credit. In the United States, the main response to the financial crisis has been a call for greater financial regulation (Schwartz 2012; Rajan 2010). Certainly regulation is part of the answer, and regulation of credit-rating agencies in particular seems a necessary lynchpin for any viable financial system. But what regulations do is reduce the *supply* of credit. They make credit harder to get by constraining how much banks and financial institutions can provide. Another approach is to examine the demand for credit: why are people borrowing so much to begin with? Why are they so susceptible to offers from predatory lenders? We saw that in countries that have well-developed welfare states, deregulation of entry barriers did not increase the debt that households carry as it did in the United States, which means that something beyond regulation is going on. We also saw that in the United States, pressure to ease access to credit came from across the political spectrum, from advocates of the marginalized as well as from business interests. These two features suggest there is an underlying demand for credit caused by the absence of sustaining welfare institutions in the United States. In the absence of the welfare institutions common in

Europe, credit is how Americans survive. What this means is that if we simply constrain the supply of credit, we *create hardship* by making it harder for people to meet health care needs or to turn to housing as a means of security and mobility. This guarantees the emergence of calls for increased access to credit from all quarters. This is the dynamic that saw feminists and African American groups and Democrats and consumer advocates supporting easier credit access and financial deregulation in the 1970s. We are sure to see a repeat of these dynamics if we constrain the supply of credit without considering why people turn to credit in the first place. Regulation of the financial sector cannot work in the absence of a focus on the demand for credit.

4. Finance is not the answer. The postwar world has been living under a consumption order that ends with massive credit-financed consumption in the United States. This consumption makes possible export-led growth in other countries, while American consumers benefit from low-priced goods. But this order is showing its weaknesses, as a regime founded on credit-financed private consumption can fall prey to financial bubbles that can devastate the system, and this order does nothing to foster consumption where it is most needed, in currently developing countries.

There has been little enthusiasm in the American government for moving away from reliance on finance. For example, Treasury Secretary Timothy Geithner envisions a future in which American finance is even more developed, and in which America's comparative advantage is its highly developed financial sector. The American financial sector, according to Geithner, will draw in the savings of the rapidly rising middle classes of the world, and this will be a major source of economic growth in the United States. America will become the world's bank. Geithner believes that prudent regulation will prevent the kinds of crises we have seen, but he does not want regulation to damage the financial sector. "I don't have any enthusiasm for . . . trying to shrink the relative importance of the financial system in our economy as a test of reform, because we have to think about the fact that we operate in the broader world. . . . It's the same thing for Microsoft or anything else. We want U.S. firms to benefit from that . . . Now financial firms are different because of the risk, but you can contain that through regulation" (Scheiber 2011, 17).

But there are several reasons to be cautious about this vision. First, putting finance at the center of the economic system means that everyone— from consumer advocates to groups working on behalf of the poor to big business—ends up wanting finance to be unrestrained. In a finance-driven economy, there is no natural social constituency that supports and pushes for regulation because finance seems to meet people's needs while providing profits. Perhaps regulations that channel finance away from the United States, and into the developing world, could lessen American reliance on finance without reducing the size of the financial sector; but it is precisely such regulations that are difficult to implement given the centrality of finance. In this situation regulation of the kind Geithner thinks is necessary may not be possible.

Second, the financial sector is moving into uncharted territory. Economists often argue that the development of finance benefits the economy, based on historical correlations between financial development and economic growth (see, e.g., King and Levine 1993; Rajan and Zingales 1998), but it is unclear whether these historical relationships apply for the levels of financialization that the contemporary United States is reaching. Some studies have found that financialization of the nonfinancial sector actually harmed capital accumulation in recent decades (Stockhammer 2004; Orhangazi 2008). Many observers have noted that finance is drawing away not only resources but also highly educated labor, and the latest crisis suggests that much of that talent may have been wasted in the production of worthless and even harmful financial innovations.

Perhaps Geithner's vision is most dangerous because it pushes off the stage all the alternative visions of economic growth within the Democratic Party. Republicans have for decades been offering a coherent program of lower taxes and less regulation as the means to sustained economic growth. This program was a sincere attempt to respond to the economic slowdowns of the 1970s in a way that would find favor among a democratic majority (Prasad 2006; Prasad 2012). The problems with these policies have been well explored, but the program continues to resonate because Democrats have not offered a clear alternative. Democrats do have an alternative nation-building program of economic growth, consisting of investments in education, transportation, renewable energy, research and development, and controlling health care costs. But no Democratic politician has managed to articulate these into an agenda as politically compelling as lower taxes and less regulation, perhaps because Democrats like the Treasury secretary have been as beguiled by finance as the Republicans.

5. For the United States, poverty reduction is a growth strategy. The welfare state affects the financial system, and vice versa. If the arguments in this book are correct, then one of the unexpected benefits of the welfare state is that it may stabilize the financial system. If credit is an alternative to the public welfare state, developing the public welfare state will lessen the demand for credit, and thereby reduce financial volatility. Rather than attacking the demand for credit by attacking home ownership (such as by getting rid of tax privileges for home ownership or making home mortgages harder to get, which will simply make it harder for Americans to provide for their own welfare), we need to address the underlying security needs that lead Americans to focus on home ownership, such as the cost of health care, the search for good schools, and the search for assets to guard against financial reversals. One of the main benefits of extending the public welfare state, and consequently limiting citizens' reliance on credit to finance their welfare needs, would be the constraints this would put on the financial sector.

A more well developed welfare state will lessen the appetite for mortgages and credit that is built into American political economy. Far from hurting American economic growth, it will pave the way for it, because as demand for finance lessens, rewards to the financial sector will lessen, and other, more productive and less bubble-inclined sectors will attract resources and skilled workers. For the United States, poverty reduction is a growth strategy.

To conclude with the implications of this work for scholarship, this book has aimed to demonstrate that the United States possesses a political tradition in many respects as radical as that of any western European country. While there are many differences between American and European capitalism, at the heart of American history is a critique of unfettered capitalism and a strong belief in state intervention, particularly in using the power of the state against the power of capital.

This investigation suggests that analysts have dismissed prematurely the "logic of industrialism" argument—the argument of Polanyi and others that industrialization brings with it state intervention—with the observation that this thesis could not explain the different form and timing of the welfare state in different countries. This is true and important; but if we broaden our focus from the welfare state to state intervention more generally, it is clear that no country has managed to make capitalism work without heavy state intervention. Indeed, the United States is not a laissez-faire or liberal political economy at all, and it never has been.

Rather than draw our attention to the rich history of American intervention, our theories of comparative political economy have obscured it,
and have consequently been unable to help us understand the American
state's past or its contemporary development. To fully investigate the
trajectory of this unusual political economy, scholars will have to leave
behind the fiction of the weak American state and take the actual history
into account in developing our theories.

NOTES

REFERENCES

ACKNOWLEDGMENTS

INDEX

1. THE FARMERS' TOUR

1. Many years later researchers discovered other uses for the drug, including treatment of leprosy and cancer, and it has been approved and distributed for these purposes. Although there are warnings against prescribing it to pregnant women, it has once again produced birth defects in newborns, particularly in Brazil (Brynner and Stephens 2001; Fraser 2004; Gorman, McCluskey, and Mondi 1994).

2. "Briefing Statement for Secretary," December 11, 1962, Frances Oldham Kelsey Papers, Box 34, Folder 2, Thalidomide Miscellaneous 1962, Manuscript Division, Library of Congress.

3. Things changed suddenly in the 1980s when AIDS activists, frustrated with delays in approval of AIDS treatment drugs, began to dramatize the issue. Larry Kramer called the FDA "the single most incomprehensible bottleneck in American bureaucratic history—one that is actually prolonging the roll call of death" (quoted in Daemmrich and Krücken 2000, 514). In 1988, AIDS activists protested FDA headquarters, lying down before mock tombstones with mock engravings like, "Killed by FDA Inertia," "Baby Doe Died Waiting for Drug Approval," "As a Person of Color I was Exempt from Drug Trials," "I Got the Placebo" (Daemmrich and Krücken 2000, 515; Duggan 1988; Epstein 1996). No such protests arose in Germany because AIDS drug approvals had been expedited there (Daemmrich and Krücken 2000, 517). Faced with a barrage of criticism, the FDA became very sensitive to the drug-lag issue, and worked hard to speed up its approval process. By the 1990s, studies were claiming there was no more drug lag in the United States (Kessler, Hass, Feiden, Lumpkin, Temple 1996).

2. COMPARING CAPITALISMS

1. Hooks and McQueen (2010) argue that American military hegemony had something to do with the welfare state because it reduced the power of the Democrats. Although the welfare state is what they claim to be explaining, their model only tests the effect of military hegemony on Democratic party success; they take the effect of parties on welfare states as given, and therefore, like the other class-based or power-resources arguments, have nothing to say to the issue of heavier

regulation in some domains. Note also that American military hegemony is ultimately a consequence of the rising economic power discussed in this book.

3. A DEMAND-SIDE THEORY OF COMPARATIVE POLITICAL ECONOMY

1. Koestler remembers these events taking place in 1931 and 1932; he may be misremembering the years, or he may be confusing hesitant Hoover administration attempts with the much more extensive slaughtering of pigs and destruction of crops of the Roosevelt years, seeing all of these as part of a searing whole.

2. But see Sweezy 1967 for an overview and critique of Luxemburg's arguments.

3. Will Rogers agreed: his diagnosis of agricultural overproduction was, "the farmers don't use their own heads a whole lot and some of 'em don't use anybody's," *Times-Picayune* 1931a.

4. There is some support for the view that credit expansion was a factor in the Depression (see, e.g., Eichengreen and Mitchener 2003; Wicker 1980), but the choice between a stable economy based on gold and a much richer one not tied to gold but supported by government interventions and threatened by occasional crises is not an obvious one.

5. Gregory Clark puts it in the strongest and most colorful terms: "All the numbers Maddison estimates for the years before 1820 are fictions, as real as the relics peddled around Europe in the Middle Ages. Many of the numbers for the years 1820, 1870, and 1913 are equally fictive." [(Clark 2009, 1156–1157). For the earliest years Clark cites anthropological and physiological evidence that puts Maddison's assumptions into doubt. For the period from 1250 to 1820 Clark cites the work of economic historians whom Maddison has not consulted. It is true that Maddison's numbers are rife with speculation for the period before 1820: for example, he simply assumes that French growth was equivalent to growth in Belgium (245) or that Ireland grew half as fast as England and Wales (246). But Clark does not give any specific instances of data problems after 1820.

6. Belich (2009, 196) has argued that comparisons of per capita GDP understate the explosive growth of the settler countries, because in the face of migration that increased the population several-fold, even stable levels of per capita GDP indicate great economic growth.

7. Henry A. Wallace, "How Permanent is the Farm Program?" December 5, 1939, Center for Legislative Archives, Record Group 46, Records of the U.S. Senate, 76th Congress, Box No. 185, Papers Relating to Specific Bills and Resolutions, Sen 76A-E6, H.R. 10413-H.R. 10683, Folder H.R. 10413, National Archives and Records Administration, Washington, DC.

4. THE NON-HISTORY OF NATIONAL SALES TAX

1. "The payers of direct taxes, Walpole once remarked, were pigs that squealed if they were touched; the payers of indirect taxes were only sheep that let themselves be sheared in silence" (Barker 1944, 57).

2. For this section I used three sources to identify major attempts at implementing a national sales tax. First, I conducted a keyword search of the New York

Times for articles with the keywords *sales tax* or its alternatives (*consumption tax, expenditure tax, v.a.t., value added tax, turnover tax, cascade tax, tax on sales, tax on consumption,* or *tax on expenditures*) AND the keywords *ways and means,* or *finance committee* in the citation or abstract, from 1857 to the present. Articles that were about excise taxes (sales taxes on specific goods rather than a general sales tax), luxury taxes, or sales taxes in other countries were excluded from the results. I also examined the Congressional Record's Index of roll-call votes in the House and Senate, specifically the index heading "yea or nea votes" from 1919 to 1984 (the heading becomes "voting in House/Senate" starting in 1971), and Lexis-Nexis records of roll-call votes after 1984. And finally, I consulted secondary sources on tax history. After identifying the major sales tax attempts, I investigated each using media accounts, the Congressional Record, and archival materials. These methods are biased toward attempts that achieved some traction in the political arena, as minor incidents (such as a congressman's call for sales tax that was not followed up or a group of economists' push toward sales taxes that was not reported in national media) may not show up in either the newspaper or scholarly record and will not be listed in the Congressional Record Index of roll-call votes. Future research on more minor attempts may qualify some of the conclusions this chapter reaches, although it is unlikely to overturn the general findings.

3. Blydenburg (1971) has argued that given general opposition to any tax, the 1932 bill was subject to the paradox of voting, and whichever proposal had been proposed last would have won. However, by his own calculations, the opposition to the sales tax was stronger (236 against) than opposition to income tax (211 against) or excise tax (187 against). Blydenburg's demonstration that whichever proposal had been raised last in the head-to- head competitions would have won is convincing, yet in the end the least unpopular proposal (the excise tax) did win.

4. Count of letters in favor and opposed, and all quotes, from Records of the Committee on Finance 1901–1946, Committee Papers H.R. 7378, 77th Congress, 2d Session, Box 149, "Sales Tax," National Archives, Washington, DC.

5. THE LAND OF TOO MUCH

1. Republican legislators from midwestern states did not completely reject tariffs, but they did oppose the large, politically motivated tariffs of the old guard Republicans, favoring instead "scientific" tariffs on only those industries that truly needed protection (Sanders 1999, 223).

2. Baack and Ray (1985) suggest that reluctant states were persuaded to support the income tax amendment through the use of military pensions; they show that military pensions and military spending are correlated with support of the income tax. But Sanders (1999) has shown that military pensions were distributed by Republicans, with the intent of protecting the tariff. In other words, there may be a correlation between pensions and income tax votes, but if so, it was because the Republicans tried and failed to target states where support for the tax was strong, and did not need to spend on states where opposition to the tax was strong.

3. The practice of naming babies after Huey had become so common that Long's office established a routine procedure of sending to parents who wrote to him silver cups engraved with the baby's name (Huey P. Long Papers, folder "Baby

Cups," Mss. 2005, Louisiana and Lower Mississippi Valley Collections, LSU Libraries, Baton Rouge, LA). At least one baby girl, born on the day of his inauguration
as governor, was named after him (Ken Burns, *Huey Long*, October 15, 1986, Arling-
ton, VA, Public Broadcasting Service).

4. Harvey Peltier interview, Oral History Interviews, March 3, 1960, T. Harry
Williams Papers, Mss. 2489, 2510, Louisiana and Lower Mississippi Valley Collection, LSU Libraries, Baton Rouge, LA.

5. Huey P. Long, (speech), Alexandria, LA, August 3, 1927, Scrapbook #9, Huey
Long Scrapbooks, Mss. 1666, Louisiana and Lower Mississippi Valley Collection,
LSU Libraries, Baton Rouge, LA.

6. "Cooper," Oral History Interviews, July 16, 1963, T. Harry Williams Papers,
Mss. 2489, 2510, Louisiana and Lower Mississippi Valley Collection, LSU Libraries,
Baton Rouge, LA.

7. Hermann Deutsch, "The Incredible Heterocrat" (draft), n.d., 340, Hermann
Bacher Deutsch Papers, collection 130, Box 20, Louisiana Research Collection,
Tulane University, New Orleans, LA.

8. Huey P. Long, "Huey Long speech for re-election of Senator Hattie Caraway,"
n.d., "stenographic report of extemporaneous speech [not prepared] delivered in
Arkansas, for the reelection of Senator Hattie W. Caraway", Hermann Bacher
Deutsch Papers, collection 130, Box 20, folder 130-20-3, Louisiana Research Collection, Tulane University, New Orleans, LA.

9. Hermann Deutsch, "The Incredible Heterocrat" (draft), n.d., 339, Hermann
Bacher Deutsch Papers, collection 130, Box 20, Louisiana Research Collection, Tulane University, New Orleans, LA.

10. Hermann Deutsch, "The Incredible Heterocrat" (draft), n.d., 339–340,
Hermann Bacher Deutsch Papers, collection 130, Box 20, Louisiana Research Collection, Tulane University, New Orleans, LA.

6. PROGRESSIVE TAXATION AND THE WELFARE STATE

1. The literature written in English on private welfare in Sweden is sparse but
see Swenson (1999).

2. Some question whether this term is appropriate, as all taxes are double or
even multiple taxes in some sense—for example, wages can be taxed once when
paid to the employee and again when they are spent. The point here is not the terminology but the comparative practices.

3. This does not seem to be caused by unusually high corporate profits in the
United States, at least to judge from historical measures of the wealth of the top
1%, which show U.S. measures in line with French and British at this time (Piketty
2007, 48).

7. AMERICAN ADVERSARIAL REGULATION

1. Some scholars have argued that the stigma of bankruptcy began to lessen in
the late twentieth century. For example, Efrat (2006) finds newspaper articles
showing more favorable attitudes towards bankrupt debtors starting in the 1960s.

But this may well be part of a general attitude change towards the poor and the oppressed in the United States rather than a specific example of American support for the free market. On the other hand Sullivan, Warren, and Westbrook (2006–2007) argue that the stigma of bankruptcy actually seems to be increasing recently. (See particularly their amusing footnote 16 on the tautological reasoning of scholars who argue that there is less stigma associated with bankruptcy.)

2. Not to be confused with journalist and historian Robert Kagan, author of *Of Paradise and Power,* cited in the introduction.

8. THE DEMOCRATIZATION OF CREDIT

1. For example, in the 1980s, households that experienced gains in the worth of their houses did not change their spending behavior, but households that experienced losses in the worth of their houses dramatically reduced their spending (Engelhardt 1996). If this mechanism were at work in the 1930s, it would be another transmission route from housing to the larger economy.

2. Curt C. Mack, "What FHA Means to a Real Estate Broker Today," September 13–15, National Urban League Papers, Box I: C9, Folder Federal Housing Administration 1951–1955, General, Manuscript Division, Library of Congress.

3. "Future of FHA: Background," n.d., Patricia Robert Harris Papers, Box 37, Folder Briefing Books: Welfare Reform; Subsidized Housing and Welfare Reform 1977, Manuscript Division, Library of Congress.

4. B. T. Fitzpatrick, "Remarks of B. T. Fitzpatrick, Deputy Administrator and General Counsel, Housing and Home Finance Agency, Before the Annual Conference of the National Associate of Housing Officials," October 15, 1952, National Urban League Papers, Box I: C14, Folder Housing and Home Finance Agency Miscellaneous 1952–1959, Manuscript Division, Library of Congress.

5. B. T. McGraw, "The Neglected Tenth in Housing and Home Finance," July 19–24, 1948, NAACP Papers, II: B81, Folder I, Housing and Home Finance Agency 1947–1949, Manuscript Division, Library of Congress.

6. "Equal Credit Opportunity and Arrangers of Consumer Credit," n.d., FTC Staff, Leadership Conference on Civil Rights Papers, Box II: 13, Folder 12, Task Forces–Housing–Equal Credit Opportunity 1977–1978, Manuscript Division, Library of Congress.

7. Philip B. Perlman to B. T. Fitzpatrick, June 3, 1949, and draft letter Roy Wilkins to Harry S. Truman, December 16, 1949, NAACP Papers, Box II: B72, Folder 1, Federal Housing Administration General 1949, April 1955, Manuscript Division, Library of Congress.

8. Bill Moyer, "An Analysis of the System of Housing Negroes in Chicago," American Friends Service Committee, February 18, 1966, Leadership Conference on Civil Rights Papers, Box I: 96, Folder 3, Government Agencies Housing and Home Finance Agency 1964–1969, Manuscript Division, Library of Congress.

9. See, for example, "Mortgage Financing for Properties Available to Negro Occupancy," January 1954, National Urban League 1954, National Urban League Papers, Box I: C21 Folder "Mortgage Financing for Properties Available to Negro Occupancy Miscellaneous," Manuscript Division, Library of Congress.

10. William Proxmire to Marvin Caplan, June 9, 1969, Leadership Conference on Civil Rights Papers, Box I: 115, Folder 8, Community Credit Expansion Act 1969, Manuscript Division, Library of Congress.

11. "For Release Sunday, March 25, 1973," Patsy Mink Papers, Box 56, Folder 7, Banking and Currency Credit Unions Sex Discrimination 1972–1976 (1 of 2), Manuscript Division, Library of Congress.

12. "Special Report: Sex, Credit, and Credit Unions," *Credit Union Magazine*, July 1974, Patsy Mink Papers, Box 58, Folder 5, Banking and Currency Credit Unions Sex Discrimination 1971–1974, Manuscript Division, Library of Congress.

13. "Statement by Representative Patsy T. Mink Before the Hearing on Availability of Credit to Women of the National Commission on Consumer Finance at Washington, DC, May 24, 1972," Patsy Mink Papers, Box 56, Folder 7, Banking and Currency Credit Unions Sex Discrimination 1972–1976 (1 of 2), Manuscript Division, Library of Congress.

14. Frank R. Kahookele to Patsy T. Mink, December 17, 1971, Patsy Mink Papers, Box 58, Folder 5, Banking and Currency Credit Unions Sex Discrimination 1971–1974, Manuscript Division, Library of Congress.

15. "Special Report: Sex, Credit, and Credit Unions," *Credit Union Magazine*, July 1974, Patsy Mink Papers, Box 58, Folder 5, Banking and Currency Credit Unions Sex Discrimination 1971–1974, Manuscript Division, Library of Congress.

16. William H. Jones, "Lenders' Bias Hits Women," *Washington Post*, October 13, 1973, E1, E6, Patsy Mink Papers, Box 56, Folder 7, Banking and Currency Credit Unions Sex Discrimination 1972–1976 (1 of 2), Manuscript Division, Library of Congress.

17. "For Release Sunday, March 25, 1973," Patsy Mink Papers, Box 56, Folder 7, Banking and Currency Credit Unions Sex Discrimination 1972–1976 (1 of 2), Manuscript Division, Library of Congress.

18. "'Feminist Federal Credit Union' Chartered in Detroit," August 31, 1973, Patsy Mink Papers, Box 58, Folder 5, Banking and Currency Credit Unions Sex Discrimination 1971–1974, Manuscript Division, Library of Congress.

19. "Special Report: Sex, Credit, and Credit Unions," *Credit Union Magazine*, July 1974, Patsy Mink Papers, Box 58, Folder 5, Banking and Currency Credit Unions Sex Discrimination 1971–1974, Manuscript Division, Library of Congress.

20. "Women in the Mortgage Market," March 1976, 11, Patricia Robert Harris Papers, Box 29, Folder "Women and Mortgage Credit Project," Manuscript Division, Library of Congress.

21. Morrigene Holcomb, "Credit: Availability to Women," January 9, 1975, Congressional Research Service, Patsy Mink Papers, Box 56, Folder 7, Banking and Currency Credit Unions Sex Discrimination 1972–1976 (1 of 2), Manuscript Division, Library of Congress.

22. Lynn Langway, "Now, Women Will Get Equal Credit," *Chicago Daily News*, October 23, 1974, Patsy Mink Papers, Box 56, Folder 7, Banking and Currency Credit Unions Sex Discrimination 1972–1976 (1 of 2), Manuscript Division, Library of Congress.

23. "Equal Credit Opportunity Act Amendments," May 16, 1975, Patsy Mink Papers, Box 56, Folder 7, Banking and Currency Credit Unions Sex Discrimination 1972–1976 (1 of 2), Manuscript Division, Library of Congress.

24. "Women and Mortgage Credit Project," n.d., Patricia Robert Harris Papers, Box 29, Folder "Women and Mortgage Credit Project," Manuscript Division, Library of Congress.

9. THE CREDIT/WELFARE STATE TRADE-OFF

1. http://www.sociology.northwestern.edu/people/faculty/monica-prasad.html or http://www.icpsr.umich.edu/icpsrweb/ICPSR/

2. In separate analyses I also estimated this model using an interaction term between *Socx* and *deregulation* (dividing *deregulation* by *Socx* to capture the dynamic of rising credit where *deregulation* is rising but *Socx* is declining). This interaction term was significant in the OLS-PCSE models, and was significant in the estimation using country fixed effects if outliers were excluded. These estimations are available in the data and calculations.

3. "Interview with James Rouse by Dr. Morton J. Schussheim, March 14 1995," p.7, Pioneers in Housing, Box 3/2, Rouse, James W. 1991–1995, Manuscript Division, Library of Congress.

4. Some have wondered if the crisis really can be blamed on these policies that privileged home ownership, as there was also a bubble in commercial real estate. But the bubble seems to have been much smaller in commercial real estate (Bureau of Economic Analysis, 2012, *National Income and Product Accounts*, table 1.1 5), and rising prices in nonresidential construction may have been driven by competition from the residential sector for construction goods and labor (Mulligan 2010).

Abbott, Andrew. 2012. "Abundance." Hollingshead Lecture. Yale University, February 28.

Abdelal, Rawi. 2007. *Capital Rules: The Construction of Global Finance.* Cambridge: Harvard University Press.

Abiad, Abdul, Enrica Detragiache, and Thierry Tressel. 2010. "A New Database of Financial Reforms." *International Monetary Fund Staff Papers* 47(2): 281–302. Database available at http://www.imf.org/external/pubs/ft/wp/2008/data/wp08266.zip.

Adams, William James. 1989. *Restructuring the French Economy: Government and the Rise of Market Competition since World War II.* Washington, DC: The Brookings Institution.

Advisory Commission on Intergovernmental Relations (ACIR). 1993. *Changing Public Attitudes on Government and Taxes.* Washington, DC: ACIR.

Aglietta, Michel. 2000. *A Theory of Capitalist Regulation: The US Experience.* New York: Verso.

Akhigbe, Aigbe, and Ann Marie Whyte. 2004. "The Gramm-Leach-Bliley Act of 1999: Risk Implications for the Financial Services Industry." *The Journal of Financial Research* 27(3): 435–446.

Akhurst, Rosemary. 2010. "Taking Thalidomide Out of Rehab." *Nature Medicine* 16(4): 370–372.

Albright, Robert C. 1942a. "Tax Bill Hit By Industry And Labor: Measure Is Unfair To Corporations, Says One; Other Asserts It 'Soaks the Poor.' " *Washington Post,* July 30, 1.

———. 1942b. "Gallery Glimpses." *Washington Post*, September 6, B3.

Alesina, Alberto, and Edward L. Glaeser. 2006. *Fighting Poverty in the U.S. and Europe: A World of Difference.* Oxford: Oxford University Press.

Allen, Christopher S. 1989. "The Underdevelopment of Keynesianism in the Federal Republic of Germany." In *The Political Power of Economic Ideas: Keynesianism across Nations*, edited by Peter A. Hall, 263–289. Princeton: Princeton University Press.

Allen, Linda, and Turan G. Bali. 2007. "Cyclicality in Catastrophic and Operational Risk Measurements." *Journal of Banking and Finance* 31(4): 1191–1235.

Allen, Linda, Julapa Jagtiani, and James T. Moser. 2001. "Further Evidence on the Information Content of Bank Examination Ratings: A Study of BHC-to-FHC Conversion Applications." *Journal of Financial Services Research* 20(2/3): 213–232.

Allen, Robert Loring. 1993. *Irving Fisher.* Cambridge, MA: Wiley-Blackwell.

Alston, Lee J. 1983. "Farm Foreclosures in the Interwar Period." *Journal of Economic History* 43(4): 885–903.

Amaral, Pedro S., and James C. MacGee. 2002. "The Great Depression in Canada and the United States: A Neoclassical Perspective." *Review of Economic Dynamics* 5(1): 45–72.

Amenta, Edwin. 2000. *Bold Relief.* Princeton: Princeton University Press.

Amenta, Edwin, Kathleen Dunleavy, and Mary Bernstein. 1994. "Stolen Thunder? Huey Long's 'Share Our Wealth,' Political Mediation, and the Second New Deal." *American Sociological Review* 59(5): 678–702.

Anderson, Elisabeth. 2008. "Experts, Ideas, and Policy Change: the Russell Sage Foundation and Small Loan Reform, 1909–1941." *Theory and Society* 37(3): 271–310.

Andrews, Edmund L. 2004. "Bush Remark Touches Off New Debate on Income Tax." *New York Times,* August 12, A20.

Angelopoulos, Konstantinos, George Economides, and Pantelis Kammas. 2007. "Tax-Spending Policies and Economic Growth: Theoretical Predictions and Evidence from the OECD." *European Journal of Political Economy* 23(4): 885–902.

Ansell, Ben W. n.d. "The Political Economy of Ownership: Housing Markets and the Welfare State." Working Paper, Department of Political Science, University of Minnesota.

Appadurai, Arjun. 1996. *Modernity at Large: Cultural Dimensions of Globalization.* Minneapolis: University of Minnesota Press.

Arrighi, Giovanni. 1993. *The Long Twentieth Century.* London: Verso.

Ascah, Robert Laurence. 1999. *Politics and Public Debt: The Dominion, The Banks and Alberta's Social Credit.* Edmonton, Canada: University of Alberta Press.

Atlanta Constitution. 1929. "Woman's Hanging Stayed by Judge." January 4, 1.

———. 1931. "Potlikker and Cornpone May Split Solid South If Huey Long Wins Out." February 17, 1.

Avi-Yonah, Reuven S., and Yaron Lahav. 2011. "The Effective Tax Rate of the Largest US and EU Multinationals." University of Michigan Law School Program in Law and Economics, Working Paper 41. http://law.bepress.com/umichlwps/empirical/art41.

Baack, Bennett D., and Edward John Ray. 1985. "Special Interests and the Adoption of the Income Tax in the United States." *Journal of Economic History* 45(3): 607–625.

Bacher, John. 1993. *Keeping to the Marketplace: The Evolution of Canadian Housing Policy.* Montreal and Kingston: McGill-Queen's University Press.

Badaracco, Joseph L., Jr. 1985. *Loading the Dice: A Five-Country Study of Vinyl Chloride Regulation.* Boston: Harvard Business School.

Baele, Lieven, Olivier De Jonghe, and Rudi Vander Vennet. 2007. "Does the Stock Market Value Bank Diversification?" *Journal of Banking and Finance* 31(7): 1999–2023.

Bairoch, Paul. 1982. "International Industrialization Levels from 1750 to 1980." *Journal of European Economic History* 11(2): 269–333.

Baker, Dean. 2007. *The United States Since 1980.* Cambridge: Cambridge University Press.

Baldwin, Peter. 1992. *The Politics of Social Solidarity: Class Bases of the European Welfare State 1875–1975.* Cambridge: Cambridge University Press.

Balleisen, Edward J. 2001. *Navigating Failure: Bankruptcy and Commercial Society in Antebellum America.* Chapel Hill: University of North Carolina Press.

Balogh, Brian. 2009. *A Government Out of Sight: The Mystery of National Authority in Nineteenth-Century America.* Cambridge: Cambridge University Press.

Baltimore Sun. 1932. "50 Democrats Unite in Fight Upon Sales Tax." March 17, 1.

Bank, Steven. 2002–2003. "The Progressive Consumption Tax Revisited." *Michigan Law Review* 101(6): 2238–2260.

———. 2004. "The Dividend Divide in Anglo-American Corporate Taxation." *Journal of Corporation Law* 30(1): 1–50.

———. 2010. *From Sword to Shield: The Transformation of the Corporate Income Tax, 1861 to Present.* New York: Oxford University Press.

Baran, Paul A., and Paul M. Sweezy. 1966. *Monopoly Capital: An Essay on the American Economic and Social Order.* New York: Monthly Review Press.

Barba, Aldo, and Massimo Pivetti. 2009. "Rising Household Debt: Its Causes and Macroeconomic Implications—A Long-Period Analysis." *Cambridge Journal of Economics* 33(1): 113–137.

Barker, Ernest. 1944. *The Development of Public Services in Western Europe 1660–1930.* London: Oxford University Press.

Barkin, Kenneth D. 1970. *The Controversy over German Industrialization, 1890–1902.* Chicago: University of Chicago Press.

Barkley, Frederick R. 1942. "Senators Stand by 'Victory Tax' Plan." *The New York Times*, September 10, 19.

Barth, James R., R. Dan Brumbaugh Jr., and James A. Wilcox. 2000. "Policy Watch: The Repeal of Glass-Steagall and the Advent of Broad Banking." *The Journal of Economic Perspectives* 14(2): 191–204.

Barth, James R., Gerard Caprio Jr., and Ross Levine. 2001. "The Regulation and Supervision of Banks Around the World: A New Database." *The World Bank Development Research Group* Policy Research Working Paper 2588.

Bartke, Richard W. 1966–67. "The Federal Housing Administration: Its History and Operations." *Wayne Law Review* 13(4): 651–677.

Beck, Nathaniel, and Jonathan N. Katz. 1995. "What to Do (and Not to Do) with Time-Series Cross-Section Data." *American Political Science Review* 89(3): 634–647.

Beckert, Jens. 2008. *Inherited Wealth.* Princeton: Princeton University Press.

Belich, James. 2009. *Replenishing the Earth: The Settler Revolution and the Rise of the Anglo-World, 1783–1939.* Oxford: Oxford University Press.

Benedick, Richard. 1998. *Ozone Diplomacy.* Cambridge: Harvard University Press.

Benedict, Murray R. 1966. *Farm Policies of the United States, 1790–1950: A Study of their Origins and Development.* New York: Octagon Books.

Bensel, Richard F. 1984. *Sectionalism and American Political Development, 1880–1980.* Madison: University of Wisconsin Press.

———. 2000. *The Political Economy of American Industrialism, 1877–1900.* New York: Cambridge University Press.

Benson, Lee. 1955. *Merchants, Farmers, and Railroads: Railroad Regulation and New York Politics, 1850–1887.* Cambridge: Harvard University Press.

Benston, George J. 1990. *The Separation of Commercial and Investment Banking: The Glass-Steagall Act Revisited and Reconsidered.* New York: Oxford University Press.

———. 1994. "Universal Banking." *Journal of Economic Perspectives* 8(3): 121–143.

Beramendi, Pablo, and David Rueda. 2007. "Social Democracy Constrained: Indirect Taxation in Industrialized Democracies." *British Journal of Political Science* 37(4): 619–641.

Berg, Maxine. 1994. *The Age of Manufactures, 1700–1820: Industry, Innovation, and Work in Britain.* London: Routledge.

Berghoff, Hartmut. 1997. "Unternehmenskultur und Herrschaftstechnik: Industrieller Paternalismus: Hohner von 1857 bis 1918." *Geschichte und Gesellschaft* 23(2): 167–204.

Berk, Gerald. 1997. *Alternative Tracks: The Constitution of American Industrial Order, 1865–1917.* Baltimore: Johns Hopkins University Press.

———. 2009. *Louis D. Brandeis and the Making of Regulated Competition, 1900–1932.* Cambridge: Cambridge University Press.

Bernanke, Ben S. 1983. "Nonmonetary Effects of the Financial Crisis in the Propagation of the Great Depression." *American Economic Review* 73(3): 257–276.

Bernanke, Ben S., and Harold James. 1991. "The Gold Standard, Deflation, and Financial Crisis in the Great Depression: An International Comparison." In *Financial Markets and Financial Crises,* edited by R. Glenn Hubbard, 33–68. Chicago: University of Chicago Press.

Bernstein, Marver. 1955. *Regulating Business by Independent Commission.* Princeton: Princeton University Press.

Bernstein, Michael A. 1987. *The Great Depression: Delayed Recovery and Economic Change in America, 1929–1939.* Cambridge: Cambridge University Press.

Betts, Caroline M., Michael D. Bordo, and Angela Redish. 1996. "A Small Open Economy in Depression: Lessons from Canada in the 1930s." *Canadian Journal of Economics/Revue canadienne d'Economique* 29(1): 1–36.

Blakey, George T. 1967. "Ham That Never Was: The 1933 Emergency Hog Slaughter." *Historian* 30(1): 41–57.

Blakey, Roy G., and Gladys C. Blakey. 1932. "The Revenue Act of 1932." *American Economic Review* 22(4): 620–640.

———. 1942. "The Federal Revenue Act of 1942." *American Political Science Review* 36(6): 1069–1082.

Block, Fred. 2007. "Understanding the Diverging Trajectories of the United States and Western Europe: A Neo-Polanyian Analysis." *Politics and Society* 35(1): 3–33.

———. 2008. "Swimming Against the Current: The Rise of a Hidden Developmental State in the United States." *Politics and Society* 36(2): 169–206.

Blydenburg, John C. 1971. "The Closed Rule and the Paradox of Voting." *The Journal of Politics* 33(1): 57–71.

Board of Governors of the Federal Reserve System (U.S.). 1932. *Branch Banking in the United States*. Accessed June 21, 2012. http://fraser.stlouisfed.org/publica tion/?pid=686.

———. 2007. *Survey of Consumer Finances*. http://www.federalreserve.gov/econresdata/scf/scindex.htm.

Bodde, Derk. 1946. "Henry A. Wallace and the Ever Normal Granary." *The Far Eastern Quarterly* 5(4): 411–426.

Bordo, Michael David, Claudia Dale Goldin, and Eugene Nelson White. 1998. *The Defining Moment: The Great Depression and the American Economy in the Twentieth Century*. Chicago: University of Chicago Press.

Bordo, Michael David, and Lars Jonung. 1981. "The Long Run Behavior of the Income Velocity of Money in Five Advanced Countries: 1870–1975: An Institutional Approach." *Economic Inquiry* 19(1): 96–116.

Bordo, Michael D., John Landon Lane, and Angela Redish. 2004. "Good Versus Bad Deflation: Lessons from the Gold Standard Era." National Bureau of Economic Research Working Paper No. 10329. http://www.nber.org/papers/w10329.

Bordo, Michael D., and Angela Redish. 1987. "Why Did the Bank of Canada Emerge in 1935?" *Journal of Economic History* 47(2): 405–417.

Bordo, Michael D., Angela Redish, and Hugh Rockoff. 2011. "Why Didn't Canada Have a Banking Crisis in 2008 (Or in 1930, or 1907, or . . .)?" National Bureau of Economic Research Working Paper, Working Paper 17312.

Bordo, Michael D., and Hugh Rockoff. 1996. "The Gold Standard as a 'Good Housekeeping Seal of Approval.'" *Journal of Economic History* 56(2): 389–428.

Bordo, Michael D., Hugh Rockoff, and Angela Redish. 1994. "The U.S. Banking System From a Northern Exposure: Stability versus Efficiency." *Journal of Economic History* 54(2): 325–341.

Boudreaux, Donald J., and Thomas J. DiLorenzo. 1993. "The Protectionist Roots of Antitrust." *Review of Austrian Economics* 6(2): 81–96.

Boyer, Robert. 2000. "Is a Finance-Led Growth Regime a Viable Alternative to Fordism? A Preliminary Analysis." *Economy and Society* 29(1): 111–145.

Brady, David. 2009. *Rich Democracies, Poor People*. New York: Oxford University Press.

Braithwaite, John. 1985. *To Punish or Persuade*. Albany: State University of New York Press.

Bren, Linda. 2001. "Frances Oldham Kelsey." *FDA Consumer* 35(2): 24–29.

Brickman, Ronald, Sheila Jasanoff, Thomas Ilgen. 1985. *Controlling Chemicals: The Politics of Regulation in Europe and the United States*. Ithaca, NY: Cornell University Press.

Brinkley, Alan. 1982. *Voices of Protest.* New York: Alfred A. Knopf.

Brooks, Clem, and Jeff Manza. 2008. *Why Welfare States Persist: The Importance of Public Opinion in Democracies.* Chicago: University of Chicago Press.

Brown, Michael K. 1997–1998. "Bargaining for Social Rights: Unions and the Reemergence of Welfare Capitalism, 1945–1952." *Political Science Quarterly* 112(4): 645–674.

Brownlee, W. Elliot. 1996. *Funding the Modern American State, 1941–1995: The Rise and Fall of the Era of Easy Finance.* Cambridge: Cambridge University Press.

———. 2004. *Federal Taxation in America: A Short History.* Cambridge: Cambridge University Press.

Brynner, Rock, and Trent D. Stephens. 2001. *Dark Remedy: The Impact of Thalidomide and Its Revival as a Vital Medicine.* Cambridge, MA: Basic Books.

Buehler, A. G. 1932. *General Sales Taxation.* New York: The Business Bourse.

Buenker, John D. 1985. *The Income Tax and the Progressive Era.* New York: Garland.

Buhmann, Brigitte, Lee Rainwater, Guenther Schmaus, and Timothy M. Smeeding. 1988. "Equivalence Scales, Well-Being, Inequality and Poverty: Sensitivity Estimates across Ten Countries Using the Luxembourg Income Study (LIS) Database." *Review of Income and Wealth* 34(2): 115–142.

Bureau of Economic Analysis. 2012. *National Income and Product Accounts.* http://www.bea.gov/national/nipaweb/index.asp

Burk, James. 1985. "The Origins of Federal Securities Regulation: A Case Study in the Social Control of Finance." *Social Forces* 63(4): 1010–1029.

Burns, Ken. 1996. *Huey Long.* PBS, October 15.

Busch, Andreas. 2009. *Banking Regulation and Globalization.* Oxford: Oxford University Press.

Calder, Lendol. 1999. *Financing the American Dream: A Cultural History of Consumer Credit.* Princeton: Princeton University Press.

Callender, Guy Stevens. 1902. "The Early Transportation and Banking Enterprises of the States in Relation to the Growth of Corporations." *Quarterly Journal of Economics* 17(1): 111–162.

Calomiris, Charles W. 2000. *U.S. Bank Deregulation in Historical Perspective.* Cambridge: Cambridge University Press.

———. 2010. "Volatile Times and Persistent Conceptual Errors: U.S. Monetary Policy 1914–1951." American Enterprise Institute Papers and Studies http://www.aei.org/papers/economics/monetary-policy/volatile-times-and-persistent-conceptual-errors/.

Calomiris, Charles W. and Joseph R. Mason. 2003. "Fundamentals, Panics, and Bank Distress during the Depression." *American Economic Review* 93(5): 1615–1647.

Cameron, David. 1991. "Continuity and Change in French Social Policy: The Welfare State under Gaullism, Liberalism, and Socialism." In *The French Welfare State,* edited by John Ambler, 58–93. New York: New York University Press.

Campbell, Andrea. 2011. "The 10 Percent Solution: How Progressives Can Stop Worrying and Love a Value-Added Tax." *Democracy: A Journal of Ideas* 19: 54–63.

Campbell, John L., and Michael Patrick Allen. 1994. "State Revenue Extraction from Different Income Groups: Variations in Tax Progressivity in the United States, 1916 to 1986." *American Sociological Review* 59(2): 169–186.

Canals, Jordi. 1997. *Universal Banking: International Comparisons and Theoretical Perspectives.* Oxford: Oxford University Press.

Caplovitz, David. 1963. *The Poor Pay More: Consumer Practices of Low-Income Families.* New York: Free Press of Glencoe.

———. 1968. "Consumer Credit in the Affluent Society." *Law and Contemporary Problems* 33(4): 641–655.

Carey, David, and Josette Rabesona. 2004. "Tax Ratios on Labor and Capital Income and on Consumption." In *Measuring the Tax Burden on Capital and Labor*, Peter Birch Sørensen, ed., 213–262. Cambridge: MIT Press.

Carlson, Mark, and Kris James Mitchener. 2006. "Branch Banking, Bank Competition, and Financial Stability." *Journal of Money, Credit, and Banking* 38(5): 1293–1328.

Carney, Richard. 2010. *Contested Capitalism: The Political Origins of Financial Institutions.* Abingdon: Routledge.

Carpenter, Daniel. 2010. *Reputation and Power: Organizational Image and Pharmaceutical Regulation at the FDA.* Princeton: Princeton University Press.

Carr, Jack, Frank Mathewson, and Neil Quigley. 1995. "Stability in the Absence of Deposit Insurance: The Canadian Banking System, 1890–1966." *Journal of Money, Credit and Banking* 27(4): 1137–1158.

Carruthers, Bruce G., and Laura Ariovich. 2010. *Money and Credit: A Sociological Approach.* Cambridge, UK: Polity Press.

Carruthers, Bruce G., and Sarah Babb. 1996. "The Color of Money and the Nature of Value: Greenbacks and Gold in Postbellum America." *American Journal of Sociology* 101(6): 1556–1591.

Castles, Francis. 1998. "The Really Big Trade-Off: Home Ownership and the Welfare State in the New World and the Old." *Acta Politica* 33(1): 5–19.

Cebula, Richard J. 2010. "Determinants of Bank Failures in the U.S. Revisited." *Applied Economics Letters* 17(13): 1313–1317.

Ceccoli, Stephen. 2002. "Divergent Paths to Drug Regulation in the United States and the United Kingdom." *Journal of Policy History* 14(2): 135–169.

———. 2004. *Pill Politics.* Boulder, CO: Lynne Riener.

Chambers, Matthew, Carlos Garriga, and Don E. Schlagenhauf. 2009. "Accounting for Changes in the Homeownership Rate." *International Economic Review* 50(3): 677–726.

Chandler, Alfred D., Jr. 1990. *Scale and Scope: The Dynamics of Industrial Capitalism.* Cambridge: Harvard University Press.

Chandler, Lester V. 1970. *America's Greatest Depression 1929–1941.* New York: Harper & Row.

Chang, Ha-Joon. 2007. *Bad Samaritans: The Myth of Free Trade and the Secret History of Capitalism.* New York: Bloomsbury Press.

Chapman, John Martin, and Ray Bert Westerfield. [1942] 1980. *Branch Banking: Its Historical and Theoretical Position in America and Abroad.* New York: Arno Press.

Chetty, Raj, Adam Looney, and Kory Kroft. 2009. "Salience and Taxation: Theory and Evidence." *American Economic Review* 99(4): 1145–1177.

Chicago Daily Tribune. 1921a. "Advocates of 1% Sales Tax Open Their Barrage." May 10, 18.

———. 1921b. "Farmers Again Protest Against Turnover Taxes." May 19, 6

———. 1921c. "Sales Tax Foes Arouse Penrose to Hot Retorts." May 20, 7.

———. 1921d. "Labor Hostility to 'Sales Tax' Called Mistake." May 22, A9.

———. 1921e. "Labor Helps to Kill Chance of Sales Tax." May 25, 1.

———. 1921f. "Professor and Attorney Agree on Sales Tax." May 26, 9.

———. 1921g. "Sales Tax Again Condemned by College Expert," May 28, 5.

———. 1921h. "Sales Tax of 1% Seems Doomed by Fights on It." May 30, 10.

———. 1921i. "U.S. May Grant Pension in Lieu of War Bonus." September 4, 3.

———. 1921j. "Forecast Tax Bill Vote This Week in Senate." October 31, 12.

———. 1921k. "Smoot May Put Over His Sales Tax Amendment." November 2, 14.

———. 1921l. "Senate Sales Tax Amendment Gaining Friends." November 3, 5.

———. 1929a. "Long Impeached to Yells, Faints, and Fist Fights," April 7, 3.

———. 1929b. "Hula Hula Girl Sat on Long's Lap, House Hears," April 25, 5.

———. 1931. "3d 'Governor of Louisiana' Takes the Oath," October 15, 1.

———. 1933a. "'New Deal' Pigs Haunt South Suburbs: Towns Protest the Flies and Odors of Dump," September 19, 1–2.

———. 1933b. "Farmers Fight For Equality Under the New Deal." November 26, G4.

———. 1942a. "Retailer Group Advocates Sale Tax of 5 Per Cent." April 1, 33.

———. 1942b. "Expect 10% Sales Tax Bill." April 3, 10.

———. 1942c. "Asks Whether Election Holds Off Sales Levy." August 7, 25.

———. 1942d. "Predicts Doom for Boeing Firm in Revenue Bill." August 14, 9.

———. 1943. "Federal Sales Tax Defeated by House Group." October 29, 16.

Chivvis, Christopher. 2010. *The Monetary Conservative: Jacques Rueff and Twentieth-Century Free Market Thought.* Dekalb: Northern Illinois University Press.

Clark, Geoffrey. 2009. Review of Angus Maddison, *Contours of the World Economy. Journal of Economic History* 69(4): 1156–1161.

Clemens, Elisabeth. 1997. *The People's Lobby: Organizational Innovation and the Rise of the Interest Group.* Chicago: University of Chicago Press.

Coad, George N. 1928. "Louisiana to Have Colorful Governor." *New York Times,* January 29, 52.

Cochrane, Willard W. 2003. *The Curse of American Agricultural Abundance: A Sustainable Solution.* Lincoln: University of Nebraska Press.

Coffee, John C., Jr. 2007–2008. "Law and the Market: The Impact of Enforcement." *University of Pennsylvania Law Review* 156(2): 229–311.

Cohen, Lizabeth. 1989. "Encountering Mass Culture at the Grassroots: The Experience of Chicago Workers in the 1920s." *American Quarterly* 41(1): 6–33.

———. 2003. *A Consumers' Republic: The Politics of Mass Consumption in Postwar America.* New York: Knopf.

Cohn, Raymond L. 1992. "Fiscal Policy in Germany During the Great Depression." *Explorations in Economic History* 29(3): 318–342.

Collins, Robert M. 2000. *More: The Politics of Economic Growth in Postwar America*. Oxford: Oxford University Press.

Conley, Dalton. 1999. *Being Black, Living in the Red: Race, Wealth, and Social Policy in America*. Berkeley and Los Angeles: University of California Press.

Conley, Dalton, and Brian Gifford. 2006. "Home Ownership, Social Insurance, and the Welfare State." *Sociological Forum* 21(1): 55–82.

Cooper, John Milton. 1990. *Pivotal Decades: The United States, 1900–1920*. New York: W. W. Norton.

Corwin, Edward S. 1938. *Court over Constitution*. Princeton, NJ: Princeton University Press.

Coval, Joshua, Jakub Jurek, and Erik Stafford. 2009. "The Economics of Structured Finance." *Journal of Economic Perspectives* 23(1): 3–25.

Craig, Lee A., and Thomas Weiss. 1993. "Agricultural Productivity Growth During the Decade of the Civil War." *Journal of Economic History* 53(3): 527–548.

Crouch, Colin. 2009. "Privatised Keynesianism: an Unacknowledged Policy Regime." *British Journal of Politics and International Studies* 11(3): 382–399.

Curti, Merle. 1950. "America at the World's Fairs, 1851–1893." *American Historical Review* 55(4): 833–856.

Cusack, Thomas R., and Pablo Beramendi. 2006. "Taxing Work." *European Journal of Political Research* 45(1): 43–73.

Daemmrich, Arthur. 2002. "A Tale of Two Experts: Thalidomide and Political Engagement in the United States and West Germany." *Social History of Medicine* 15(1): 137–158.

Daemmrich, Arthur A. 2004. *Pharmacopolitics*. Chapel Hill and London: University of North Carolina Press.

Daemmrich, Arthur, and Georg Krücken. 2000. "Risk Versus Risk: Decision-Making Dilemmas of Drug Regulation in the United States and Germany." *Science as Culture* 9(4): 505–534.

Danbom, David B. 1979. *The Resisted Revolution: Urban America and the Industrialization of Agriculture*. Ames: Iowa State University Press.

Daschle, Tom. 2010. *Getting It Done: How Obama and Congress Finally Broke the Stalemate to Make Way for Health Care Reform*. New York: Thomas Dunne.

Daunton, Martin. 2001. *Trusting Leviathan*. Cambridge: Cambridge University Press.

———. 2002. *Just Taxes*. Cambridge: Cambridge University Press.

David, A. Paul, and Gavin Wright. 1997. "Increasing Returns and the Genesis of American Resource Abundance." *Industrial and Corporate Change* 6(2): 203–245.

Davis, Gerald F. 2009. *Managed by the Markets: How Finance Reshaped America*. Oxford: Oxford University Press.

Davis, Gerald F., and Suzanne K. Stout. 1992. "Organization Theory and the Market for Corporate Control." *Administrative Science Quarterly* 37(4): 605–633.

Dawley, Alan. 1991. *Struggles for Justice*. Cambridge: Harvard University Press.

De Grazia, Victoria. 2005. *Irresistible Empire: America's Advance Through Twentieth-Century Europe*. Cambridge: Harvard University Press.

Delalande, Nicolas. 2011. *Les Batailles de l'Impôt: Consentement et Résistances de 1789 à Nos Jours*. Paris: Editions du Seuil.

Dellheim, Charles. 1987. "The Creation of a Company Culture: Cadburys, 1861–1931." *American Historical Review* 92(1): 13–44.

DeLong, J. Bradford, and Andrei Shleifer. 1991. "The Stock Market Bubble of 1929: Evidence from Closed-end Mutual Funds." *The Journal of Economic History* 51(3): 675–700.

Demirgüç-Kunt, Asli, and Ross Levine, eds. 2001. *Financial Structure and Economic Growth: A Cross-Country Comparison of Banks, Markets, and Development*. Cambridge: MIT Press.

Denoon, Donald. 1983. *Settler Capitalism: The Dynamics of Dependent Development in the Southern Hemisphere*. Oxford: Clarendon Press.

Dessaux, Pierre-Antoine. 2006. "Comment Définir les Produits Alimentaires?" *Histoire, Economie et Societé* 25(1): 83–108.

Deutsch, Herrmann. 1935. "Huey Long—the Last Phase," *Saturday Evening Post*, 208(15): 27–91.

DiLorenzo, Thomas J. 1985. "The Origins of Antitrust: An Interest-Group Perspective." *International Review of Law and Economics* 5(1):73–90.

Dixon, Arthur. 1933. "Voice of the People: A Long Perspective." *Chicago Daily Tribune*, September 20, 12.

Djankov, Simeon, Caralee McLiesh, and Andrei Shleifer. 2007. "Private Credit in 129 Countries." *Journal of Financial Economics* 84(2): 299–329.

Dobbin, Frank R. 1992. "The Origins of Private Social Insurance: Public Policy and Fringe Benefits in America, 1920–1950." *American Journal of Sociology* 97(5): 1416–1450.

———. 1993. "The Social Construction of the Great Depression: Industrial Policy during the 1930s in the United States, Britain, and France." *Theory and Society* 22(1): 1–56.

———. 1994. *Forging Industrial Policy: The United States, Britain, and France in the Railway Age*. New York: Cambridge University Press.

Dobbin, Frank, and Timothy J. Dowd. 2000. "The Market That Antitrust Built: Public Policy, Private Coercion, and Railroad Acquisitions, 1825 to 1922." *American Sociological Review* 65(5): 631–657.

Dornstein, Miriam. 1987. "Taxes: Attitudes and Perceptions and their Social Bases." *Journal of Economic Psychology* 8(1):55–76.

Dorris, Henry N. 1942a. "$3,680,000,000 Yield Seen in Sales Tax: Treasury and Congressional Experts' Estimates Given to House Committee." *The New York Times*, March 17, 15.

———. 1942b. "Chamber Proposes 10-Billion Tax Plan: Sales, Gross-Income Levies and Rises on Individuals and Corporations Suggested." *The New York Times*, April 15, 16.

Due, John. 1955a. "Sales Taxation in Western Europe: A General Survey. Part I: The Single-Stage Tax." *National Tax Journal* 8(2): 171–185.

———. 1955b. "Sales Taxation in Western Europe. Part II: The Multiple-Stage Sales Tax." *National Tax Journal* 8(3): 300–321.

Duffie, Darrell, and Henry T. C. Hu. 2008. "Competing for a Global Share of Derivatives Markets: Trends and Policy Choices for the United States." http://ssrn.com/abstract=1140869

Duggan, Paul. 1988. "1,000 Swarm FDA's Rockville Office to Demand Approval of AIDS Drugs." *The Washington Post*, October 12, B1.

Dunlavy, Colleen A. 1992. "Mirror Images: Political Structure and Early Railroad Policy in the United States and Prussia." *Studies in American Political Development* 5(1): 1–35.

———. 1994. *Politics and Industrialization: Early Railroads in the Unites States and Prussia.* Princeton: Princeton University Press.

Dutton, Paul V. 2002. *Origins of the French Welfare State.* Cambridge: Cambridge University Press.

Eccleston, Richard. 2007. *Taxing Reforms: The Politics of the Consumption Tax in Japan, the United States, Canada, and Australia.* Cheltenham, UK: Edward Elgar Publishing.

Echols, Marsha A. 1998. "Food Safety Regulation in the European Union and the United States: Different Cultures, Different Laws." *Columbia Journal of European Law* 4(3): 525–544.

Economides, Nicholas, R. Glenn Hubbard, and Darius Palia. 1996. "The Political Economy of Branching Restrictions and Deposit Insurance: A Model of Monopolistic Competition Among Small and Large Banks." *Journal of Law and Economics* 39(2): 667–704.

Edwards, Corwin D. 1967. *Control of Cartels and Monopolies: An International Comparison.* Dobbs Ferry, NY: Oceana Publications.

Effosse, Sabine. 2010. "Pour ou Contre le Crédit à la Consommation? Développement et Réglementation du Crédit à la Consommation en France dans les Années 1950 et 1960." *Entreprises et Histoire* 59(2): 68–79.

Efrat, Rafael. 2006. "The Evolution of Bankruptcy Stigma." *Theoretical Inquiries in Law* 7(2): 365–393.

Eichengreen, Barry J. 1984. "Mortgage Interest Rates in the Populist Era." *American Economic Review* 74(5): 995–1015.

———. 1992. *Golden Fetters.* Oxford: Oxford University Press.

———. 1995. "Mainsprings of Economic Recovery in Post-War Europe." In *Europe's Post-War Recovery*, edited by Barry J. Eichengreen, 3–35. Cambridge: Cambridge University Press.

———. 1996. "Institutions and Economic Growth: Europe after World War II." In *Economic Growth in Europe since 1945*, edited by Nicholas Crafts and Gianni Toniolo, 38–72. Cambridge: Cambridge University Press.

———. 2007. *The European Economy Since 1945: Coordinated Capitalism and Beyond.* Princeton and Oxford: Princeton University Press.

———. 2008. *Globalizing Capital: A History of the International Monetary System.* Princeton: Princeton University Press.

Eichengreen, Barry, and Kris Mitchener. 2003. "The Great Depression as a Credit Boom Gone Wrong." Bank for International Settlements, Working Paper No. 137.

Elkins, Caroline, and Susan Pedersen, eds. 2005. *Settler Colonialism in the Twentieth Century.* New York: Routledge.

Ellis, Elmer. 1940. "Public Opinion and the Income Tax, 1860–1900." *Mississippi Valley Historical Review* 27(2): 225–242.

Elyasiani, Elyas, Iqbal Mansur, and Michael S. Pagano. 2007. "Convergence and Risk-Return Linkages Across Financial Service Firms." *Journal of Banking and Finance* 31(4): 1167–1190.

Engelhardt, Gary V. 1996. "House Prices and Home Owner Saving Behavior." *Regional Science and Urban Economics* 26(3–4): 313–336.

Epstein, Steven. 1996. *Impure Science: AIDS, Activism, and the Politics of Knowledge.* Berkeley: University of California Press.

Esping-Andersen, Gøsta 1985. *Politics Against Markets: The Social Democratic Road to Power.* Princeton: Princeton University Press.

———. 1990. *The Three Worlds of Welfare Capitalism.* Princeton: Princeton University Press.

Evans, Peter B., Dietrich Rueschemeyer, and Theda Skocpol. 1985. *Bringing the State Back In.* Cambridge: Cambridge University Press.

Federico, Giovanni. 2005. "Not Guilty? Agriculture in the 1920s and the Great Depression." *Journal of Economic History* 65(4): 949–976.

Feldenkirchen, Wilfried. 1992. "Competition Policy in Germany." *Business and Economic History* 21: 257–269.

Feldstein, Martin. 1974. "Social Security, Induced Retirement and Aggregate Capital Accumulation." *Journal of Political Economy* 82(5): 905–926.

Ferguson, Niall. 2008. *The Ascent of Money: A Financial History of the World.* New York: Penguin.

"Financial Powerhouse." 1998. *Jim Lehrer NewsHour*, PBS, April 7, http://www.pbs.org/newshour/bb/business/jan-june98/merger_4–7.html.

Findlay, Ronald, and Kevin H. O'Rourke. 2003. "Commodity Market Integration, 1500–2000." In *Globalization in Historical Perspective*, edited by Michael D. Bordo, Alan M. Taylor, and Jeffrey G. Williamson, 13–64. Chicago: University of Chicago Press.

Finegold, Kenneth. 1982. "From Agrarianism to Adjustment: The Political Origins of New Deal Agricultural Policy." *Politics and Society* 11(1): 1–27.

———. 1988. "Agriculture and the Politics of U.S. Social Provision: Social Insurance and Food Stamps." In *The Politics of Social Policy in the United States*, edited by Margaret Weir, Ann Shola Orloff, and Theda Skocpol, 199–234. Princeton: Princeton University Press.

Finegold, Kenneth, and Theda Skocpol. 1995. *State and Party in America's New Deal.* Madison: University of Wisconsin Press.

Fink, Gary M. 1973. *Labor's Search for Political Order: The Political Behavior of the Missouri Labor Movement.* Columbia: University of Missouri Press.

Finkelstein, Amy. 2009. "Tax Salience and Tax Rates." *Quarterly Journal of Economics* 124(3): 969–1010.

Fiorina, Morris P. 1986. "Legislator Uncertainty, Legislative Control, and the Delegation of Legislative Power." *Journal of Law, Economics, and Organization* 2(1): 33–51.

Fisher, Irving. 1933. "The Debt-Deflation Theory of Great Depressions." *Econometrica* 1(4): 337–357.

Fisher, John. 1942. "Vote 5% Tax on All Wages Over $12 Week." *Chicago Daily Tribune*, September 9, 1.

Fitzgerald, Deborah. 2003. *Every Farm a Factory: The Industrial Ideal in American Agriculture*. New Haven, CT: Yale University Press.

Fitzgerald, Robert. 1988. *British Labour Management and Industrial Welfare 1846–1939*. London: Croom Helm.

Fleming, Dewey L. 1932a. "Sales Tax Plan Held Aimed at Poor Classes," *Baltimore Sun*, March 12, 1.

———. 1932b. "Tax Hearing Due to End Tomorrow," *Baltimore Sun*, April 20, 2.

Fligstein, Neil. 2001. *The Architecture of Markets: An Economic Sociology of Twenty-First-Century Capitalist Societies*. Princeton: Princeton University Press.

Fogel, Robert W. 1964. *Railroads and American Economic Growth*. Baltimore: Johns Hopkins University Press.

Folliard, Edward. 1930. "Hitler, Who Fought in War Under Kaiser is Without Country." *The Washington Post*, September 28, M13.

Foner, Eric. 1984. "Why Is There No Socialism in the United States?" *History Workshop Journal* 17(1): 57–80.

Fouracde, Marion. 2009. *Economists and Societies: Discipline and Profession in the United States, Britain, and France, 1890s to 1990s*. Princeton: Princeton University Press.

Frank, Robert H. 2007. *Falling Behind: How Rising Inequality Harms the Middle Class*. Berkeley: University of California Press.

Fraser, Mat. 2004. "It's Back . . ." *The Guardian*, March 30, 10.

Freund, David M. P. 2007. *Colored Property: State Policy and White Racial Politics in Suburban America*. Chicago: University of Chicago Press.

Freyer, Tony. 1992. *Regulating Big Business: Antitrust in Great Britain and America, 1880–1990*. Cambridge: Cambridge University Press.

Frieden, Jeffry. 1997. "Monetary Populism in Nineteenth Century America: An Open Economy Interpretation." *Journal of Economic History* 57(2): 367–395.

Friedman, Lawrence. 2005. *A History of American Law*. New York: Simon and Schuster.

Friedman, Milton, and Rose Friedman. 1998. *Two Lucky People: Memoirs*. Chicago: University of Chicago Press.

Friedman, Milton, and Anna J. Schwartz. 1963. *A Monetary History of the United States, 1867–1960*. Princeton: Princeton University Press.

Gale, William. 1997. "What Can America Learn from the British Tax System?" *Fiscal Studies* 18(4): 341–369.

Gallagher, Kelly Sims, and Erich Muehlegger. 2011. "Giving Green to Get Green? Incentives and Consumer Adoption of Hybrid Vehicle Technology." *Journal of Environmental Economics and Management* 61(1): 1–15.

Gallup, George. 1943. "Sales Tax Leads in Gallup's Poll; It Is Preferred to a Rise in Income Levy by 53% of Persons Queried." *The New York Times*, November 3, 23.

Ganghof, Steffen. 2006. "Tax Mixes and the Size of the Welfare State: Causal Mechanisms and Policy Implications." *Journal of European Social Policy* 16(4): 360–373.

———. 2007. "The Political Economy of High Income Taxation: Capital Taxation, Path Dependence, and Political Institutions in Denmark." *Comparative Political Studies* 40(9): 1059–1084.

———. 2008. "The Politics of Tax Structure." In *Divide and Deal: The Politics of Distribution in Democracies,* edited by Ian Shapiro, Peter Swenson, and Daniela Donno, 72–98. New York: New York University Press.

Garber, Peter. 1990. "Famous First Bubbles." *Journal of Economic Perspectives* 4(2): 35–54.

Garfinkel, Irwin, Lee Rainwater, and Timothy Smeeding. 2010. *Wealth and Welfare States: Is America a Laggard or Leader?* Oxford: Oxford University Press.

Garon, Sheldon. 2012. *Beyond Our Means: Why America Spends While the World Saves.* Princeton: Princeton University Press.

Garraty, John A. 1973. "The New Deal, National Socialism, and the Great Depression." *The American Historical Review* 78(4): 907–944.

Genschel, Philipp. 2002a. *Steuerharmonisierung und Steuerwettbewerb in der Europäischen Union.* Frankfurt: Campus Verlag.

Genschel, Philipp. 2002b. "Globalization, Tax Competition, and the Welfare State." *Politics and Society* 30(2): 245–275.

Gerschenkron, Alexander. 1962. *Economic Backwardness in Historical Perspective.* Cambridge: Belknap Press of Harvard University Press.

Gerth, Jeff. 1984. "Treasury's Objections to a Sales Tax." *The New York Times,* December 22, 31, 34.

Geyfman, Victoria and Timothy J. Yeager. 2009. "On the Riskiness of Universal Banking: Evidence from Banks in the Investment Banking Business Pre- and Post-GLBA." *Journal of Money, Credit and Banking* 41(8): 1649–1669.

Gieske, Millard L. 1979. *Minnesota Farmer-Laborism: The Third Party Alternative.* Minneapolis: University of Minnesota Press.

Gilligan, Thomas W., William J. Marshall, and Barry R. Weingast. 1989. "Regulation and the Theory of Legislative Choice: The Interstate Commerce Act of 1887." *Journal of Law and Economics* 32(1): 35–61.

Go, Julian. 2008. *American Empire and the Politics of Meaning: Elite Political Cultures in the Philippines and Puerto Rico during U.S. Colonialism.* Durham, NC: Duke University Press.

Goldsmith, Raymond W. 1985. *Comparative National Balance Sheets.* Chicago and London: University of Chicago Press.

Goodman, Paul. 1993. "The Emergence of Homestead Exemption in the United States: Accommodation and Resistance to the Market Revolution, 1840–1880." *Journal of American History* 80(2): 470–498.

Goodwyn, Lawrence. 1978. *The Populist Moment: A Short History of the Agrarian Revolt in America.* Oxford: Oxford University Press.

Gordon, Colin. 1994. *New Deals: Business, Labor, and Politics in America, 1920–1935.* New York: Cambridge University Press.

————. 2003. *Dead on Arrival: The Politics of Health Care in Twentieth-Century America*. Princeton: Princeton University Press.

Gordon, Robert J. 2004. "Two Centuries of Economic Growth: Europe Chasing the American Frontier." National Bureau of Economic Research Working Paper No. 10662 http://www.nber.org/papers/w10662

Gordon, Robert J., and Robert Krenn. 2010. "The End of the Great Depression 1939–41: Policy Contributions and Fiscal Multipliers." National Bureau of Economic Research Working Paper No. 16380. http://www.nber.org/papers/w16380.

Gordon, Sanford D. 1963. "Attitudes towards Trusts prior to the Sherman Act." *Southern Economic Journal* 30(2): 156–167.

Gorman, Christine, Ian McCluskey, and Lawrence Mondi. 1994. "Thalidomide's Return." *Time*, 143(24): 67.

Gorton, Gary, and Andrew Metrick. 2010. "Regulating the Shadow Banking System." *Brookings Papers on Economic Activity* (Fall) 261–297.

Gotham, Kevin Fox. 2000. "Racialization and the State: The Housing Act of 1934 and the Creation of the Federal Housing Administration." *Sociological Perspectives* 43(2): 291–317.

Gourevitch, Peter. 1986. *Politics in Hard Times: Comparative Responses to International Economic Crisis*. Ithaca, NY: Cornell University Press.

Graetz, Michael J. 2005. "Comments on John B. Shoven and John Walley, 'Irving Fisher's Spendings (Consumption) Tax in Retrospect.'" *American Journal of Economics and Sociology* 64(1): 245–256.

Gramm, Phil. 2009. "Deregulation and the Financial Panic." *Wall Street Journal*, February 20, A17.

Green, Richard K., and Susan M. Wachter. 2005. "The American Mortgage in Historical and International Context." *Journal of Economic Perspectives* 19(4): 93–114.

Grossman, Richard S. 1994. "The Shoe That Didn't Drop: Explaining Banking Stability During the Great Depression." *Journal of Economic History* 54(3): 654–682.

Gruber, Jonathan, and James Poterba. 1994. "Tax Incentives and the Decision to Purchase Health Insurance: Evidence from the Self-Employed." *The Quarterly Journal of Economics* 109(3): 701–733.

Gruning, David. 2003–2004. "Bayou State Bijuralism: Common Law and Civil Law in Louisiana." *University of Detroit Mercy Law Review* 81(4): 437–464.

Gylfason, Thorvaldur, Bengt Holmström, Sixten Korkman, Hans Tson Söderström, and Vesa Vihriälä. 2010. *Nordics in Global Crisis: Vulnerability and Resilience*. Helsinki: The Research Institute of the Finnish Economy (ETLA), Taloustieto Oy.

Hacker, Jacob. 2002. *The Divided Welfare State: The Battle over Public and Private Social Benefits in the United States*. New York: Cambridge University Press.

Hadenius, Axel. 1985. "Citizens Strike a Balance: Discontent with Taxes, Content with Spending." *Journal of Public Policy* 5(3): 349–363.

Haig, Robert Murray, and Carl Shoup. 1934. *The Sales Tax in the American States*. New York: Columbia University Press.

Hall, Peter A., and David W. Soskice. 2001. *Varieties of Capitalism: The Institutional Foundations of Comparative Advantage.* New York: Oxford University Press.

Hamilton, Thomas J. 1942. "10 Billion Increase in Tax Bill Urged." *The New York Times,* August 13, 10.

Hammitt, James K., Jonathan B. Wiener, Brendon Swedlow, Denise Kall, and Zheng Zhou. 2005. "Precautionary Regulation in Europe and the United States: A Quantitative Comparison." *Risk Analysis* 25(5): 1215–1228.

Hamowy, Ronald. 2007. *Government and Public Health in America.* Cheltenham, UK: Edward Elgar.

Hanes, Christopher. 2006. "Wholesale and Producer Price Indexes, by Commodity Group: 1890–1997 [Bureau of Labor Statistics]." Table Cc66-83 in *Historical Statistics of the United States, Earliest Times to the Present: Millennial Edition,* edited by Susan B. Carter, Scott Sigmund Gartner, Michael R. Haines, Alan L. Olmstead, Richard Sutch, and Gavin Wright. New York: Cambridge University Press, 2006. http://dx.doi.org/10.1017/ISBN-9780511132971 .Cc66-20410.1017/ISBN-9780511132971.Cc66-204.

Hannah, Leslie. 2008. "Logistics, Market Size, and Giant Plants in the Early Twentieth Century: A Global View." *Journal of Economic History* 68(1): 46–79.

Hansen, John Mark. 1990. "Taxation and the Political Economy of the Tariff." *International Organization* 44(4): 527–551.

———. 1991. *Gaining Access: Congress and the Farm Lobby, 1919–1981.* Chicago: University of Chicago Press.

Hansen, Susan. 1983. *The Politics of Taxation.* Praeger Publishers.

Hardach, Karl. 1980. *The Political Economy of Germany in the Twentieth Century.* Berkeley: University of California Press.

Hardie, Iain, and David Howarth. 2009. "Die Krise but Not La Crise? The Financial Crisis and the Transformation of German and French Banking Systems." *Journal of Common Market Studies* 47(5): 1017–1039.

Harris, Richard. 1999. "Housing and Social Policy: An Historical Perspective on Canadian-American Differences—A Comment." *Urban Studies* 36(7): 1169–1175.

———. 2000. "More American Than the United States: Housing in Canada in the Twentieth Century." *Journal of Urban History* 26(4): 456–478.

———. 2009. "A New Form of Credit: The State Promotes Home Improvement, 1934–1954." *Journal of Policy History* 21(4): 392–423.

Harris, Richard, and Doris Ragonetti. 1998. "Where Credit is Due: Residential Mortgage Finance in Canada, 1901–1954." *Journal of Real Estate Finance and Economics* 16(2): 223–238.

Hartz, Louis. 1955. *The Liberal Tradition in America: An Interpretation of American Political Thought since the Revolution.* New York: Harcourt, Brace.

Haubrich, Joseph G. 1990. "Nonmonetary Effects of Financial Crises: Lessons from the Great Depression in Canada." *Journal of Monetary Economics* 25(2): 223–252.

Hawley, Ellis. 1966. *The New Deal and the Problem of Monopoly.* Princeton: Princeton University Press.

Hayek, Friedrich A. 1944. *The Road to Serfdom*. Chicago: University of Chicago Press.

———. 1948. *Individualism and Economic Order*. Chicago: University of Chicago Press.

Hazlett, Thomas W. 1992. "The Legislative History of the Sherman Act Re-Examined." *Economic Inquiry* 30(2): 263–276.

Hellerstein, Jerome R. 1950. "Federal Tax Policy During the Roosevelt Era." *Lawyers' Guild Review* 5(3): 160–171.

Helm, William P. 1953. "A Tangle of Rulings on Sick Pay Benefits." *Los Angeles Times*, December 17, A4.

Hendrickson, Jill M. 2010. "The Interstate Banking Debate: A Historical Perspective." *Academy of Banking Studies Journal* 9(2): 95–130.

Hendrickson, Walter B. 1961. "Nineteenth-Century State Geological Surveys: Early Government Support of Science." *Isis* 52(3): 357–371.

Herrigel, Gary. 2000. *Industrial Constructions: The Sources of German Industrial Power*. Cambridge: Cambridge University Press.

Herring, Richard, and Robert E. Litan. 1995. *Financial Regulation in the Global Economy*. Washington: Brookings Institution.

Hicks, Alexander. 1999. *Social Democracy and Welfare Capitalism: A Century of Income Security Politics*. Ithaca, NY: Cornell University Press.

Hicks, John D. [1931] 2009. *The Populist Revolt: A History of the Farmers' Alliance and the People's Party*. Minneapolis: University of Minnesota Press.

Higgens-Evenson, R. Rudy. 2003. *The Price of Progress: Public Services, Taxation, and the American Corporate State, 1877 to 1929*. Baltimore, MD: Johns Hopkins University Press.

Hilzenrath, David S. 1992. "For Clinton's Deficit Fighters, All's Fair Game." *Washington Post*, December 27, H1.

Hindman, Monty. 2010. *The Rise and Fall of Wealth Taxation: An Inquiry into the Fiscal History of the American States*. PhD diss., University of Michigan.

Hines, James R., Jr. 2007. "Taxing Consumption and Other Sins." *Journal of Economic Perspectives* 21(1): 49–68.

Hobson, John M. 1997. *The Wealth of States: A Comparative Sociology of International Economic and Political Change*. Cambridge: Cambridge University Press.

Hoffman, Elizabeth, and Gary D. Libecap. 1991. "Institutional Choice and the Development of U.S. Agricultural Policies in the 1920s." *The Journal of Economic History* 51(2): 397–411.

Hoffman, Philip T. 1986. "Taxes and Agrarian Life in Early Modern France: Land Sales, 1550–1730." *Journal of Economic History* 46(1): 37–55.

Högfeldt, Peter. 2005. "The History and Politics of Corporate Ownership in Sweden." In *A History of Corporate Governance around the World: Family Business Groups to Professional Managers*, edited by Randall K. Morck, 517–579. Chicago: University of Chicago Press.

Hooks, Gregory. 1990. "From an Autonomous to a Captured State Agency: The Decline of the New Deal in Agriculture." *American Sociological Review* 55(1): 29–43.

Hooks, Gregory, and Brian McQueen. 2010. "American Exceptionalism Revisited: The Military-Industrial Complex, Racial Tension, and the Underdeveloped Welfare State." *American Sociological Review* 75(2): 185–204.

Howard, Christopher. 1997. *The Hidden Welfare State: Tax Expenditures and Social Policy in the United States*. Princeton: Princeton University Press.

Huber, Evelyne, and John D. Stephens. 2001. *Development and Crisis of the Welfare State: Parties and Policies in Global Markets*. Chicago: University of Chicago Press.

Huberman, Michael. 2004. "Working Hours of the World Unite? New International Evidence of Worktime, 1870–1913." *The Journal of Economic History* 64(4): 964–1001.

Huey Long Scrapbooks. Mss. 1666, Louisiana and Lower Mississippi Valley Collections, LSU Libraries, Baton Rouge, LA.

Huey Pierce Long Papers. Mss. 2005, Louisiana and Lower Mississippi Valley Collections, LSU Libraries, Baton Rouge, LA.

Hulchanski, David. 1986. "The 1935 Dominion Housing Act: Setting the Stage for a Permanent Federal Presence in Canada's Housing Sector." *Urban History Review* 15(1): 19–40.

Hyman, Louis. 2011. *Debtor Nation: The History of America in Red Ink*. Princeton: Princeton University Press.

Immergut, Ellen. 1990. "Institutions, Veto Points, and Policy Results: A Comparative Analysis of Health Care." *Journal of Public Policy* 10(4): 391–416.

Indiana Farmer's Guide. 1921. "The Sales Tax." April 30, 33(18): 6.

International Monetary Fund. 2009. *International Financial Statistics*. Washington, DC: International Monetary Fund.

Irwin, Douglas. 2010. "Did France Cause the Great Depression?" National Bureau of Economic Research, Working Paper No. 16350. http://www.nber.org/papers/w16350.

Isenberg, Daniel J. 1986. "Group Polarization: A Critical Review and Meta-Analysis." *Journal of Personality and Social Psychology* 50(6): 1141–1151.

Iversen, Torben, and David Soskice. 2009. "Distribution and Redistribution: The Shadow of the Nineteenth Century." *World Politics* 61(3): 438–486.

Jackson, Howell E. 2007. "Variation in the Intensity of Financial Regulation: Preliminary Evidence and Potential Implications." *Yale Journal on Regulation* 24(2): 253–291.

Jackson, Kenneth T. 1985. *Crabgrass Frontier: The Suburbanization of the United States*. New York: Oxford University Press.

Jacobs, Lawrence R. and Theda Skocpol. 2010. *Health Care Reform and American Politics: What Everyone Needs to Know*. New York: Oxford University Press.

Jacobs, Meg. 2005. *Pocketbook Politics: Economic Citizenship in Twentieth-Century America*. Princeton: Princeton University Press.

Jacoby, Sanford M. 1993. "Employers and the Welfare State: The Role of Marion B. Folsom." *The Journal of American History* 80(2): 525–556.

———. 1998. *Modern Manors: Welfare Capitalism Since the New Deal*. Princeton: Princeton University Press.

James, Harold. 1986. *The German Slump: Politics and Economics, 1924–1936.* Oxford: Oxford University Press.

———. 1990. Review of *Lessons from the Great Depression* by Peter Temin. *Business History Review* 64(1): 194–196.

James, John A., and Richard Sylla. 2006a. "Credit Market Debt Outstanding: 1945–1997." Table Cj899-957 in *Historical Statistics of the United States, Earliest Times to the Present: Millennial Edition,* edited by Susan B. Carter, Scott Sigmund Gartner, Michael R. Haines, Alan L. Olmstead, Richard Sutch, and Gavin Wright. New York: Cambridge University Press. http://dx.doi.org/10.1017/ISBN-9780511132971.Cj870-119110.1017/ISBN-9780511132971.Cj870-1191.

———. 2006b. "Net Public and Private Debt, by Major Sector: 1916–1976." Table Cj870-889 in *Historical Statistics of the United States, Earliest Times to the Present: Millennial Edition,* edited by Susan B. Carter, Scott Sigmund Gartner, Michael R. Haines, Alan L. Olmstead, Richard Sutch, and Gavin Wright. New York: Cambridge University Press. http://dx.doi.org/10.1017/ISBN-978051113297 1.Cj870-119110.1017/ISBN-9780511132971.Cj870-1191.

James, Scott C. 2000. *Presidents, Parties, and the State: A Party System Perspective on Democratic Regulatory Choice, 1884–1936.* New York: Cambridge University Press.

Janoski, Thomas. 2010. *The Ironies of Citizenship: Naturalization and Integration in Industrialized Countries.* New York: Cambridge University Press.

Jasanoff, Sheila. 1991. "Acceptable Evidence in a Pluralistic Society." In *Acceptable Evidence: Science and Values in Risk Management,* edited by Deborah J. Mayo and Rachelle D. Hollander, 29–47. New York: Oxford University Press.

Jeansonne, Glen. 1993. *Messiah of the Masses.* New York: Longman.

Jennings, Edward T. 1977. "Some Policy Consequences of the Long Revolution and Bifactional Rivalry in Louisiana." *American Journal of Political Science* 21(2): 225–246.

Johansson, Asa, Christopher Heady, Jens Arnold, Bert Brys, and Laura Vartia. 2008. OECD Economics Department Working Papers. Working Paper No. 620.

Johnson, H. Thomas. 1974. "Postwar Optimism and the Rural Financial Crisis of the 1920's." *Explorations in Economic History* 11(2): 173–192.

Jones, Carolyn. 1996. "Mass-based Income Taxation: Creating a Taxpaying Culture, 1940–1952." In *Funding the Modern American State, 1941–1995: The Rise and Fall of the Era of Easy Finance,* edited by W. Elliot Brownlee, 107–147. Cambridge: Cambridge University Press.

Jones, Harriet. 2000. "'This is Magnificent!': 300,000 Houses a Year and the Tory Revival after 1945." *Contemporary British History* 14(1): 99–121.

Jones, Roland M. 1933. "Corn Belt Puzzled by Farm Policy." *The New York Times,* August 27, E8.

Jones, William. 1973. "Lenders' Bias Hits Women." *Washington Post,* October 13, E1, E6.

Jorgenson, D. W., and K. Y. Yun. 1986. "Tax Policy and Capital Allocation." *The Scandinavian Journal of Economics* 88(2): 355–377.

Kagan, Robert. 2003. *Of Paradise and Power: America and Europe in the New World Order.* New York: Vintage Books.

Kagan, Robert A. 1994. "Do Lawyers Cause Adversarial Legalism? A Preliminary Inquiry." *Law and Social Inquiry* 19(1): 1–62.

———. 2003. *Adversarial Legalism: The American Way of Law*. Cambridge: Harvard University Press.

Kagan, Robert A., and Lee Axelrad. 2000. *Regulatory Encounters: Multinational Corporations and Adversarial Legalism*. Berkeley: University of California Press.

Kane, Anne, and Michael Mann. 1992. "A Theory of Early Twentieth-Century Agrarian Politics." *Social Science History* 16(3): 421–454.

Kastl, Jakub, and Lyndon Moore. 2006. "Wily Welfare Capitalist: Werner von Siemens and the Pension Plan." *Cliometrica* 4(3): 321–348.

Kato, Junko. 2003. *Regressive Taxation and the Welfare State*. Cambridge: Cambridge University Press.

Katznelson, Ira. 2005. *When Affirmative Action Was White*. New York: W. W. Norton.

Kazin, Michael. 1987. *Barons of Labor*. Urbana: University of Illinois Press.

Keller, Morton. 1980. "Regulation of Large Enterprise: The United States Experience in Comparative Perspective." In *Managerial Hierarchies: Comparative Perspectives on the Rise of Modern Industrial Enterprise*, edited by Alfred D. Chandler Jr. and Herman Daems, 161–181. Cambridge: Harvard University Press.

Kelman, Steven. 1981. *Regulating America, Regulating Sweden: A Comparative Study of Occupational Safety and Health*. Cambridge: MIT Press.

Kelsey, Frances. 1965. "Problems Raised for the FDA by the Occurrence of Thalidomide Embryopathy in Germany, 1960–1961." *American Journal of Public Health* 55(5): 703–707.

Kemeny, Jim. 1980. "Home Ownership and Privatisation." *International Journal of Urban and Regional Research* 4(3): 372–388.

Kennedy, David M. 1999. *Freedom from Fear: The American People in Depression and War, 1929–1945*. New York, Oxford: Oxford University Press.

Kenworthy, Lane. 2004. *Egalitarian Capitalism: Jobs, Incomes, and Growth in Affluent Countries*. New York: Russell Sage Foundation.

Kessler David A., Arthur E. Hass, Karyn L. Feiden, Murray Lumpkin, Robert Temple. 1996. "Approval of New Drugs in the U.S.: Comparison with the UK, Germany and Japan." *Journal of the American Medical Association* 276(22): 1826–1831.

Keynes, John Maynard. [1935] 1964. *The General Theory of Unemployment, Interest, and Money*. San Diego: Harcourt.

Kindleberger, Charles. 1951. "Group Behavior and International Trade." *Journal of Political Economy* 59(1): 30–46.

———. 1978. *Manias, Panics, and Crashes: A History of Financial Crises*. New York: Wiley.

King, Mervyn A., and Don Fullerton. 1984. *The Taxation of Income from Capital: A Comparative Study of the United States, the United Kingdom, Sweden, and West Germany*. Chicago: University of Chicago Press.

King, Robert G., and Ross Levine. 1993. "Finance and Growth: Schumpeter Might Be Right." *The Quarterly Journal of Economics* 108(3): 717–737.

Kinghorn, Janice Rye, and John Vincent Nye. 1996. "The Scale of Production in Western Economic Development: A Comparison of Official Industry Statistics in the United States, Britain, France, and Germany, 1905–1913." *Journal of Economic History* 56(1): 90–112.

Kinzley, W. Dean. 2006. "Japan in the World of Welfare Capitalism: Imperial Railroad Experiments with Welfare Work." *Labor History* 47(2): 189–212.

Klein, Jennifer. 2003. *For All These Rights: Business, Labor, and the Shaping of America's Public-Private Welfare State.* Princeton: Princeton University Press.

Klinghard, Daniel P. 2005. "Grover Cleveland, William McKinley, and the Emergence of the President as Party Leader." *Presidential Studies Quarterly* 35(4): 736–760.

Kneller, Richard, Michael F. Bleaney, and Norman Gemmell. 1999. "Fiscal Policy and Growth: Evidence from OECD Countries." *Journal of Public Economics* 74(2): 171–190.

Kocka, Jürgen. 1971. "Family and Bureaucracy in German Industrial Management, 1850–1914: Siemens in Comparative Perspective." *Business History Review* 45(2): 133–156.

Koestler, Arthur. 1961. *Arrow in the Blue: An Autobiography, Vol. 1.* New York: Macmillan.

Kollmann, Trevor M., and Price V. Fishback. 2011. "The New Deal, Race, and Home Ownership in the 1920s and 1930s." *American Economic Review* 101(3): 366–70.

Komansky, David H., Philip J. Purcell, and Sanford I. Weill. 1997. "1930s Rules Ensnare 1990s Finance." *Wall Street Journal,* October 30, A22.

Koning, Niek. 1994. *The Failure of Agrarian Capitalism: Agrarian Politics in the United Kingdom, Germany, the Netherlands and the USA 1846–1919.* London: Routledge.

Korpi, Walter. 1983. *The Democratic Class Struggle.* London: Routledge and Kegan Paul.

———. 2006. "Power Resources and Employer-Centered Approaches in Explanations of Welfare States and Varieties of Capitalism: Protagonists, Consenters, and Antagonists." *World Politics* 58(2): 167–206.

Korpi, Walter, and Joakim Palme. 1998. "The Paradox of Redistribution and Strategies of Equality: Welfare State Institutions, Inequality, and Poverty in the Western Countries." *American Sociological Review* 63(5): 661–687.

Krippner, Greta. 2011. *Capitalizing on Crisis: The Political Origins of the Rise of Finance.* Cambridge: Harvard University Press.

Kryzanowski, Lawrence, and Gordon S. Roberts. 1993. "Canadian Banking Solvency, 1922–1940." *Journal of Money, Credit, and Banking* 25(3): 361–376.

Kuisel, Richard F. 1981. *Capitalism and the State in Modern France.* Cambridge: Cambridge University Press.

———. 1993. *Seducing the French: The Dilemma of Americanization.* Berkeley: University of California Press.

Lake, David A. 1989. "Export, Die, or Subsidize: The International Political Economy of American Agriculture, 1875–1940." *Comparative Studies in Society and History* 31(1): 81–105.

Lamoreaux, Naomi R. 1985. *The Great Merger Movement in American Business, 1895–1904*. Cambridge: Cambridge University Press.

Landman, Henry J. 1955. "The Taxability of Fringe Benefits." *Taxes—The Tax Magazine* 33(3): 173–190.

Lange, Matthew, James Mahoney, and Matthias vom Hau. 2006. "Colonialism and Development: A Comparative Analysis of Spanish and British Colonies." *American Journal of Sociology* 111(5): 1412–1462.

Langevoort, Donald C. 1985–1986. "Interpreting the McFadden Act: The Politics and Economics of Shared ATMs and Discount Brokerage Houses." *The Business Lawyer* 41(4): 1265–1280.

La Porta, Rafael, Florencio Lopez-de-Silanes and Andrei Shleifer. 2002. "Government Ownership of Banks." *Journal of Finance* 57(1): 265–301.

League of Nations. 1933. *World Production and Prices, 1925–1932*. Geneva: League of Nations.

Lebergott, Stanley. 1993. *Pursuing Happiness: American Consumers in the Twentieth Century*. Princeton: Princeton University Press.

Leff, Mark. 1983. "Taxing the Forgotten Man: The Politics of Social Security Finance in the New Deal." *Journal of American History* 70(2): 359–381.

———. 1984. *The Limits of Symbolic Reform: The New Deal and Taxation, 1933–1939*. Cambridge: Cambridge University Press.

Le Grand, Julian, and David Winter. 1986. "The Middle Classes and the Welfare State under Conservative and Labour Governments." *Journal of Public Policy* 6(4): 399–430.

Leonhardt, David. 2009. "After the Great Recession." *The New York Times,* May 3, MM36.

Lester, Connie L. 2006. *Up from the Mudsills of Hell: The Farmers' Alliance, Populism, And Progressive Agriculture in Tennessee, 1870–1915*. Athens, GA: University of Georgia Press.

Letwin, William L. 1956. "Congress and the Sherman Antitrust Law: 1887–1890." *University of Chicago Law Review* 23(2): 221–258.

Libecap, Gary D. 1992. "The Rise of the Chicago Packers and the Origins of Meat Inspection and Antitrust." *Economic Inquiry* 30(2): 242–262.

———. 1998. "The Great Depression and the Regulating State: Federal Government Regulation of Agriculture, 1884–1970." In *The Defining Moment: The Great Depression and the American Economy in the Twentieth Century,* edited by Michael D. Bordo, Claudia Goldin, and Eugene N. White, 181–224. Chicago: University of Chicago Press.

Lieberman, Evan S. 2003. *Race and Regionalism in the Politics of Taxation in Brazil and South Africa*. Cambridge: Cambridge University Press.

Lindert, Peter H. 2004. *Growing Public: Social Spending and Economic Growth since the Eighteenth Century*. New York: Cambridge University Press.

Lindert, Peter H., and Richard Sutch. 2006. "Consumer Price Indexes, For All Items: 1774–2003." Table Cc1-2 in *Historical Statistics of the United States, Earliest Times to the Present: Millennial Edition,* edited by Susan B. Carter, Scott Sigmund Gartner, Michael R. Haines, Alan L. Olmstead, Richard Sutch, and Gavin Wright. New York: Cambridge University Press, 2006. http://dx

.doi.org/10.1017/ISBN-9780511132971.Cc1-6510.1017/ISBN-97805111 32971.Cc1-65.

Link, Arthur S. 1959. "What Happened to the Progressive Movement in the 1920's?" *American Historical Review* 64(4): 833–851.

Lipset, Seymour Martin. 1950. *Agrarian Socialism*. Berkeley: University of California Press.

———. 1990. *Continental Divide: The Values and Institutions of the United States and Canada*. New York and London: Routledge.

Lipset, Seymour Martin, and Gary Marks. 2000. *It Didn't Happen Here*. New York: W. W. Norton.

Löfstedt, Ragnar E., and David Vogel. 2001. "The Changing Character of Regulation: A Comparison of Europe and the United States." *Risk Analysis* 21(3): 399–416.

Logemann, Jan. 2007. "Shaping Affluent Societies: Divergent Paths to Mass Consumer Society in West Germany and the United States during the Postwar Boom Era." PhD diss., Pennsylvania State University.

———. 2008. "Different Paths to Mass Consumption: Consumer Credit in the United States and West Germany during the 1950s and '60s." *Journal of Social History* 41(3): 525–559.

———. 2010. "Cultures of Credit: Consumer Lending and Borrowing in Modern Economies." *Bulletin of the German Historical Institute* 47 (Fall): 102–106.

———. 2012. *Trams or Tailfins? Public and Private Prosperity in Postwar West Germany and the United States*. Chicago: University of Chicago Press.

Long, Huey Pierce. 1930. "Will the God of Greed Pull the Temple Down on Himself?" *Louisiana Progress*, December, 2(1): 1.

———. 1931a. "Could It Ever Have Been or Could It Ever Be?" *Louisiana Progress*, January, 2(2): 1.

———. 1931b. "On the Menace of Concentrated Wealth and Impoverishment of the Masses." *Louisiana Progress*, May, 2(6): 1.

———. 1931c. "The Laws of God: The Concentration of Wealth." *Louisiana Progress*, June, 2(7): 1.

———. 1931d. "Our National Plight." *Louisiana Progress*, August 18, 3(2): 1.

———. 1933a. "Behind the President and In Front of Him." *American Progress*, August 24, 1(1): 1.

———. 1933b. "The First Thing We Must Do." *American Progress*, August 31, 1(2): 1.

———. 1933c. "Poison for the Sick, Stones for the Hungry." *American Progress*, September 7, 1(3): 1.

———. 1933d. "Transfusion With One's Own Blood." *American Progress*, September 21, 1(5): 1.

———. 1933e. "The Long Plan." *American Progress*, October 12 , 1(8): 1.

———. 1933f. "Back to the Mark! The President Can Yet Save His Program." *American Progress*, October 19, 1(9): 1.

———. 1933g. "The Dislocated Pause." *American Progress*, November 9, 1(12): 1.

———. 1933h. "Quo Vadis?" *American Progress*, November 23, 1(14): 1.

———. 1933i. "Why the Wolves Howl!" *American Progress*, December 7, 1(16): 1.

———. 1934a. "A History Making Congress." *American Progress*, January 4, 1(20): 1.

———. 1934b. "The Money Fight." *American Progress*, February 1, 1(24): 1.

———. 1934c. "The Truth Will Set You Free!" *American Progress*, February 15, 1(26): 1.

———. 1934d. "People! People!! PEOPLE!!!" *American Progress*, February 22, 1(27): 1.

———. 1934e. "Vigilance!" *American Progress*, March 1, 1(28): 1.

———. 1934f. "Why Change Tyrants?" American Progress, March 15, 1(30): 1.

———. 1934g. "Why Stand Ye Here Idle?" American Progress, March 29, 1(32): 1.

———. 1934h. "The Way Out." *American Progress*, April 5, 1(33): 1.

———. 1934i. "Moratoriums Necessary." *American Progress*, August 7, 1(35): 1.

———. 1935a. "The Educational Program Of The Share Our Wealth Society." *American Progress*, March, 2(4): 3.

———. 1935b. "Share Our Wealth is Coming." *American Progress*, April, 2(5): 1.

———. 1935c. "Forcing the Truth To Light." *American Progress*, May, 2(6): 1.

———. 1935d. "What Is It They Want to Undo?" *American Progress*, December 7, 2(13): 7.

Loriaux, Michael. 1991. *France After Hegemony: International Change and Financial Reform*. Ithaca, NY: Cornell University Press.

Los Angeles Times. 1921a. "Divergent Views on Sales Tax Law." May 11, I5.

———. 1921b. "Sales Tax Plan." May 21, II4.

———. 1921c. "Auto Industry for Sales Tax." May 24, I4.

———. 1921d. "Pending Tax Bill O.K.'d." October 6, I1.

———. 1921e. "Not Satisfied With Tax Bill." November 25, I6.

———. 1929. "Torrid Charges Name Gov. Long." March 27, 2.

———. 1931. "Hooey, Huey! Cry Gourmets." February 18, 5.

———. 1933. "'Kingfish' Tells New Tax Plan." October 6, 4.

———. 1942. "Pension Tax Plan Opposed." April 11, 6.

Louisiana Weekly. 1935. "Huey Long is Dead." September 14, 8.

Lounsbury, Michael, and Paul M. Hirsch, eds. 2010. *Markets on Trial: The Economic Sociology of the U.S. Financial Crisis*. New York: Emerald Press.

Lowrey, Annie. 2012. "French Duo See (Well) Past Tax Rise for Richest." *The New York Times*, April 17, A1.

Lucas, Robert E., Jr. 1990. "Supply-Side Economics: An Analytical Review." *Oxford Economic Papers* 42(2): 293–316.

Lundqvist, Lennart J. 1980. *The Hare and the Tortoise: Clean Air Policies in the United States and Sweden*. Ann Arbor: University of Michigan Press.

Luxemburg, Rosa. [1913] 2003. *The Accumulation of Capital*. New York: Routledge.

MacCormac, John. 1942. "Senators Consider 3 Sales-Tax Plans." *The New York Times*, September 5, 1.

Mackay, Charles. [1841] 2003. *Extraordinary Popular Delusions and the Madness of Crowds*. Hampshire, UK: Harriman House.

Mackenzie, Donald. 2011. "The Credit Crisis as a Problem in the Sociology of Knowledge." *American Journal of Sociology* 116(6): 1778–1841.

Maddison, Angus. 1995. *Monitoring the World Economy*. Paris: Organisation for Economic Coopeation and Development (OECD) Development Centre.

——— 2006. *The World Economy Volume 1: A Millennial Perspective. Volume 2: Historical Statistics*. Paris: Organisation for Economic Cooperation and Development (OECD) Development Centre. http://www.ggdc.net/MADDISON/oriindex.htm.

Mahoney, James. 2000. "Path Dependence in Historical Sociology." *Theory and Society* 29(4): 507–548.

———. 2001. *The Legacies of Liberalism*. Baltimore, MD: Johns Hopkins University Press.

Maier, Charles S. 1977. "The Politics of Productivity: Foundations of American International Economic Policy after World War II." *International Organization* 31(4): 607–633.

Maioni, Antonia. 1997. "Parting at the Crossroads: The Development of Health Insurance in Canada and the United States, 1940–1965." *Comparative Politics* 29(4): 411–431.

———. 1998. *Parting at the Crossroads*. Princeton: Princeton University Press.

Mamun, Abdullah, M. Kabir Hassan, and Neal Maroney. 2005. "The Wealth and Risk Effects of the Gramm-Leach-Bliley Act (GLBA) on the U.S. Banking Industry." *Journal of Business Finance & Accounting* 32(1–2): 351–388.

Mamun, Abdullah, M. Kabir Hassan, and Van Son Lai. 2004. "The Impact of the Gramm-Leach Bliley Act on the Financial Services Industry." *Journal of Economics and Finance* 28(3): 333–347.

Mann, Bruce H. 2002. *Republic of Debtors: Bankruptcy in the Age of American Independence*. Cambridge: Harvard University Press.

Mares, Isabela. 2003. *The Politics of Social Risk: Business and Welfare State Development*. Cambridge: Cambridge University Press.

Martin, Isaac. 2008. *The Permanent Tax Revolt*. Berkeley: University of California Press.

Martin, Isaac, Ajay Mehrotra, and Monica Prasad. 2009. *The New Fiscal Sociology*. Cambridge: Cambridge University Press.

Massey, Douglas S., and Nancy A. Denton. 1993. *American Apartheid: Segregation and the Making of the Underclass*. Cambridge: Harvard University Press.

Mayer, George H. 1951. *The Political Career of Floyd B. Olson*. St. Paul: Minnesota Historical Society Press.

McArthur, D. 1884. *Foreign Railways of the World, Vol. 1*. St. Louis, MO: The Railway Register.

McCaffery, Edward J., and Linda R. Cohen. 2005–2006. "Shakedown at Gucci Gulch: The New Logic of Collective Action." *North Carolina Law Review* 84(4): 1089–1158.

McCraw, Thomas K. 1984. *Prophets of Regulation*. Cambridge: Harvard University Press.

McCreary, Eugene. 1968. "Social Welfare and Business: The Krupp Welfare Program, 1860–1914." *Business History Review* 42(1): 24–49.

McElvaine, Robert S. 1984. *The Great Depression: America, 1929–1941.* New York: Times Books.

McGerr, Michael. 2003. *A Fierce Discontent.* Oxford: Oxford University Press.

McGrattan, Ellen R., and Edward C. Prescott. 2004. "The 1929 Stock Market: Irving Fisher Was Right." *International Economic Review* 45(4): 991–1009.

McGuire, Robert A. 1981. "Economic Causes of Late-Nineteenth Century Agrarian Unrest: New Evidence." *Journal of Economic History* 41(4): 835–852.

McKnight, Joseph W. 1983. "Protection of the Family Home from Seizure by Creditors: The Sources and Evolution of a Legal Principle." *Southwestern Historical Quarterly* 86(3): 369–399.

McMath, Robert C., Jr. 1975. *Populist Vanguard: A History of the Southern Farmers' Alliance.* Chapel Hill: University of North Carolina Press.

———. 1992. *American Populism: A Social History, 1877–1898.* New York: Hill and Wang.

Mehrotra, Ajay. 2004. "'More Mighty Than the Waves of the Sea': Toilers, Tariffs, and the Income Tax Movement, 1880–1913." *Labor History* 45(2): 165–198.

———. 2010. "The Public Control of Corporate Power: Revisiting the 1909 U.S. Corporate Tax from a Comparative Perspective." *Theoretical Inquiries in Law* 11(2): 497–538.

Meier, Kenneth. 1979. *Politics and the Bureaucracy: Policymaking in the Fourth Branch of Government.* North Scituate, MA: Duxbury Press.

Meltzer, Allan H. 2003. *A History of the Federal Reserve, Vol. 1: 1913–1951.* Chicago: University of Chicago Press.

Mendoza, Enrique G., Assaf Razin, and Linda L. Tesar. 1994. "Effective Tax Rates in Macroeconomics: Cross-country Estimates of Tax Rates on Factor Incomes and Consumption." *Journal of Monetary Economics* 34(3): 297–323.

Mettler, Suzanne. 2011. *The Submerged State: How Invisible Government Policies Undermine American Democracy.* Chicago: University of Chicago Press.

Micheletti, Michele. 1990. *The Swedish Farmers' Movement and Government Agricultural Policy.* New York: Praeger.

Miller, Merton H. 1986. "Financial Innovation: The Last Twenty Years and the Next." *Journal of Financial and Quantitative Analysis* 21(4): 459–471.

Miller, Michael B. 1994. *The Bon Marché: Bourgeois Culture and the Department Store, 1869–1920.* Princeton: Princeton University Press.

Milward, Alan S. 1984. *The Reconstruction of Western Europe 1945–51.* Berkeley: University of California Press.

Mintz, Morton. 1962. "'Heroine' of FDA Keeps Bad Drug Off of Market." *Washington Post,* July 15, A1, A8.

Mishkin, Frederic S. 1978. "The Household Balance Sheet and the Great Depression." *The Journal of Economic History* 38(4): 918–937.

Mishra, Ramesh. 1990. *The Welfare State in Capitalist Society: Policies of Retrenchment and Maintenance in Europe, North America and Australia.* Toronto: University of Toronto Press.

Mitchell, Brian R. 1993. *International Historical Statistics, The Americas 1750–1988, 2nd ed.* New York: Stockton Press.

———. 1998. *International Historical Statistics, Europe 1750–1993, 4th ed.* London: Macmillan.

Monroe, Albert. 2001. "How the Federal Housing Administration Affects Home-ownership." Harvard University Joint Center for Housing Studies Working Paper. http://www.jchs.harvard.edu/.

Morantz, Alison D. 2006. "There's No Place Like Home: Homestead Exemption and Judicial Constructions of Family in Nineteenth-Century America." *Law and History Review* 24(2): 245–295.

Morgan, Donald P. 2002. "Rating Banks: Risk and Uncertainty in an Opaque Industry." *The American Economic Review* 92(4): 874–888.

Morgan, Kimberly J., and Monica Prasad. 2009. "The Origins of Tax Systems." *American Journal of Sociology* 114(5): 1350–1394.

Morning Tribune. 1931. "The Plan Came From Him." August 22, 9.

Moss, B. H. 1977. "Radicalism and Social Reform in France: Progressive Employers and the Comité Mascuraud, 1899–1914." *French History* 11(2): 170–189.

Moss, David. 2004. *When All Else Fails: Government as the Ultimate Risk Manager.* Cambridge: Harvard University Press.

———. 2009. "An Ounce of Prevention: The Power of Public Risk Management in Stabilizing the Financial System." Working Paper 09–087. Harvard Business School, Boston, MA.

Mulligan, Casey. 2010. "Was There a Commercial Real Estate Bubble?" http://economix.blogs.nytimes.com/2010/01/13/was-there-a-commercial-real-estate-bubble/.

Murnane, M. Susan. 2004. "Selling Scientific Taxation: The Treasury Department's Campaign for Tax Reform in the 1920s." *Law and Social Inquiry* 29(4): 819–856.

Musson, A.E. 1978. *The Growth of British Industry.* New York: Holmes & Meier.

National Archives. Records of the Committee on Finance, 1901–1946. Washington, DC.

Naylor, James. 1991. *The New Democracy: Challenging the Social Order in Industrial Ontario, 1914–1925.* Toronto: University of Toronto Press.

Naylor, R. Thomas. [1975] 1997. *The History of Canadian Business: 1897–1914.* Montreal: Black Rose Books.

Neal, Steve. 1980. "House Power Ullman Faces Uphill Race." *Chicago Tribune,* Aug. 27, 1, 4.

Neale, Faith R., and Pamela P. Peterson. 2005. "The Effect of the Gramm-Leach-Bliley Act on the Insurance Industry." *Journal of Economics and Business* 57(4): 317–338.

Nelson, Richard R. and Gavin Wright. 1992. "The Rise and Fall of American Technological Leadership: The Postwar Era in Historical Perspective." *Journal of Economic Literature* 30(4): 1931–1964.

Newman, Katherine S., and Rourke L. O'Brien. 2011. *Taxing the Poor: Doing Damage to the Truly Disadvantaged.* Berkeley and Los Angeles: University of California Press.

New York Times, The. 1921a. "Prepare to Press for Tax on Sales." April 11, 1.

———. 1921b. "The Sales Tax in Congress." April 12, 15.

———. 1921c. "Urges Corporation Tax." April 13, 3.

———. 1921d. "Credit Men Oppose General Sales Tax." May 11, 35.

———. 1921e. "Labor Will Fight Against Sales Tax." May 12, 9.

———. 1921f. "Clash Over Sales Tax." May 14, 8.

———. 1921g. "Harding Signs Emergency Tariff." May 28, 2.

———. 1921h. "Snarls in Congress Threaten to Block Harding Policies." June 20, 1.

———. 1921i. "Smoot Will Offer New Revenue Bill." August 31, 11.

———. 1921j. "Why We Are Badly Taxed." October 22, 12.

———. 1921k. "Bar Sales Tax Now, Want It For Bonus." November 3, 1.

———. 1921l. "Reject Sales Tax By 43 to 25 Vote." November 4, 1.

———. 1921m. "Senate Again Votes Sales Tax Down." November 5, 15.

———. 1921n. "Tax Bill Passed by Vote of 38 to 24 in Early Morning." November 8, 1.

———. 1922. "Sales Tax Rejected by Subcommittee as Raiser of Bonus." February 5, 1.

———. 1927. "Politicians Fight in New Orleans Hotel Lobby When Ex-Governor Calls a Candidate a Liar." November 16, 2.

———. 1929. "Fisher Sees Stocks Permanently High." October 16, 8.

———. 1930. "Accuses Gov. Long of Kidnapping Plot," September 7, 15.

———. 1931a. "Watson Condemns Tax Revision Ideas." September 12, 35.

———. 1931b. "Shun Louisiana Bonds. New York Houses Doubt Legality While Governorship Disputed." October 30, 36.

———. 1932a. "Democrats in House Face Split on Taxes; Raskob Takes Hand." March 12, 1.

———. 1932b. "Woll Denounces Sales Tax Plan." March 13, 26.

———. 1932c. "Urge Substitutes for the Sales Tax." March 15, 5.

———. 1932d. "Tax Rebels March on a State Capitol." March 17, 3.

———. 1942a. "Sales Tax is Urged by State Chamber." March 11, 15.

———. 1942b. "Urges 5% Sales Tax." August 18, 33.

———. 1951. "Mr. Doughton on Taxes." March 9, 24.

———. 1953. "Governors Oppose Federal Sales Tax. June 14, 61.

Nicholas, Tom. 2008. "Does Innovation Cause Stock Market Runups? Evidence from the Great Crash." *American Economic Review* 98(4): 1370–1396.

Niemi, William L. and David J. Plante. 2008. "Antecedents of Resistance: Populism and the Possibilities for Democratic Globalizations." *New Political Science* 30(4): 427–447.

Niemi-Kiesiläinen, Johanna. 1997. "Changing Directions in Consumer Bankruptcy Law and Practice in Europe and U.S.A." *Journal of Consumer Policy* 20(2): 133–142.

Noel, Francis Regis. 1919. *A History of the Bankruptcy Law*. Washington, DC: Chas. A. Potter.

Norr, Martin. 1966. "Taxation in France." *Tax Law Review* 21(3): 387–398.

Norris, Pippa, and Ronald Inglehart. 2006. "God, Guns and Gays: Supply and Demand of Religion in the US and Western Europe." *Public Policy Research* 12(4): 224–233.

North, Douglass. 1966. *Growth and Welfare in the American Past: A New Economic History*. Englewood Cliffs, New Jersey: Prentice-Hall.

Nourse, Edwin G. 1940. *Government in Relation to Agriculture*. Washington, DC: Brookings Institution.

Novak, William. 1994. *The People's Welfare*. Chicago: University of Chicago Press.

———. 2008. "The Myth of the 'Weak' American State." *American Historical Review* 113(3): 752–772.

O'Brien, Patrick. 1973. "A Reexamination of the Senate Farm Bloc 1921–1933." *Agricultural History* 47(3): 248–263.

Olmstead, Alan L., and Paul W. Rhode. 2006. "Beef, veal, pork, and lamb—slaughtering, production, and price: 1899–1999." Table Da995-1019 in *Historical Statistics of the United States, Earliest Times to the Present: Millennial Edition*, edited by Susan B. Carter, Scott Sigmund Gartner, Michael R. Haines, Alan L. Olmstead, Richard Sutch, and Gavin Wright. New York: Cambridge University Press.

———. 2008. *Creating Abundance: Biological Innovation and American Agricultural Development*. Cambridge: Cambridge University Press.

Olney, Martha L. 1990. "Demand for Consumer Durable Goods in 20th Century America." *Explorations in Economic History* 27(3): 322–349.

———. 1991. *Buy Now, Pay Later: Advertising, Credit, and Consumer Durables in the 1920s*. Chapel Hill: University of North Carolina Press.

———. 1998. "When Your Word Is Not Enough: Race, Collateral, and Household Credit." *Journal of Economic History* 58(2): 408–431.

Organisation for Economic Cooperation and Development (OECD). 1981. *Long-Term Trends in Tax Revenues of OECD Member Countries 1955–1980*. Paris: OECD.

———. 2008. *Growing Unequal? Income Distribution and Poverty in OECD Countries*. Paris: OECD.

———. 2010a. *OECD National Accounts Statistics* (database). doi: 10.1787 /data-00369-en.

———. 2010b. "Revenue Statistics: Comparative Tables." *OECD Tax Statistics* (database). doi:10.1787/data-00262-en.

———. 2010c. *Dataset on Final Consumption Expenditures*. doi: 10.1787/ data-00005-en.

Orhangazi, Özgür. 2008. "Financialisation and Capital Accumulation in the Non-Financial Corporate Sector: A Theoretical and Empirical Investigation on the U.S. Economy: 1973–2003." *Cambridge Journal of Economics* 32(6): 863–886.

Orloff, Ann Shola, and Theda Skocpol. 1984. "Why Not Equal Protection? Explaining the Politics of Public Social Spending in Britain, 1900–1911, and the United States, 1880s–1920." *American Sociological Review* 49(6): 726–750.

O'Rourke, Kevin H. 1997. "The European Grain Invasion, 1870–1913." *The Journal of Economic History* 57(4): 775–801.

O'Rourke, Kevin H., and Jeffrey G. Williamson. 1999. *Globalization and History: The Evolution of a Nineteenth-Century Atlantic Economy*. Cambridge: MIT Press.

Orren, Karen. 1991. *Belated Feudalism: Labor, the Law, and Liberal Development in the United States*. Cambridge: Cambridge University Press.

Overy, R. J. 1996. *The Nazi Economic Recovery, 1932–1938. 2nd ed.* London: Macmillan.

Owen, Geoffrey. 1999. *From Empire to Europe: The Decline and Revival of British Industry Since the Second World War.* London: HarperCollins.

Owen, Stephen Walker, Jr. 1982. *The Politics of Tax Reform in France, 1906–1926.* PhD diss., Department of History, University of California, Berkeley.

Park, Gene. 2011. *Spending Without Taxation: FILP and the Politics of Public Finance in Japan.* Stanford: Stanford University Press.

Parker, Randall E. 2007. *The Economics of the Great Depression: A Twenty-First Century Look Back at the Economics of the Interwar Era.* Cheltenham, UK: Edward Elgar Publishing.

Passell, Peter. 1988. "Economic Scene." *New York Times,* February 3, D2.

———. 1995. "The Tax Code Heads into the Operating Room." *The New York Times,* September 3, F1.

Pavanelli , Giovanni. 2004. "The Great Depression in Irving Fisher's Thought." In *Political Events and Economic Ideas,* edited by Ingo Barens, Volker Caspari, and Bertram Schefold, 289–305. Cheltenham, UK: Edward Elgar Publishing.

Pecorino, Paul. 1993. "Tax Structure and Growth in a Model with Human Capital." *Journal of Public Economics* 52 (2): 251–271.

———. 1994. "The Growth Rate Effects of Tax Reform." *Oxford Economic Papers* 46 (3): 492–501.

Peek, Joe, and Eric Rosengren. 1995. "Bank Regulation and the Credit Crunch." *Journal of Banking and Finance* 19(3–4): 679–692.

Pekkarinen, Jukka. 1989. "Keynesianism and the Scandinavian Models of Economic Policy." In *The Political Power of Economic Ideas: Keynesianism across Nations,* edited by Peter A. Hall, 311–345. Princeton: Princeton University Press.

Phillips, Jim, and Michael French. 1998. "Adulteration and Food Law, 1899–1939." *Twentieth Century British History* 9(3): 350–369.

Pierson, Paul. 1995. *Dismantling the Welfare State? Reagan, Thatcher, and the Politics of Retrenchment.* Cambridge: Cambridge University Press.

———. 2000. "Path Dependence, Increasing Returns, and the Study of Politics." *American Political Science Review* 94 (2): 251–267.

Piketty, Thomas. 2007. "Top Incomes Over the Twentieth Century: A Summary of Main Findings." In *Top Incomes Over the Twentieth Century,* edited by A.B. Atkinson and Thomas Piketty, 34–56. Oxford: Oxford University Press.

Piketty, Thomas, and Emanuel Saez. 2003. "Income Inequality in the United States, 1913–1998." *Quarterly Journal of Economics* 143(1): 1–39.

———. 2007. "How Progressive is the U.S. Federal Tax System? A Historical and International Perspective." *Journal of Economic Perspectives* 21(1): 3–24.

Pine, Art. 1980a. "Ullman to Rework Value Added Tax to Satisfy Objections." *Washington Post,* January 21, D12.

———. 1980b. "Opponent Seeks to Cook Ullman in His Own VAT." *Washington Post,* February 10, G1, G4.

Piore, Michael, and Charles Sabel. 1984. *The Second Industrial Divide.* New York: Basic Books.

Polanyi, Karl. [1944] 2001. *The Great Transformation.* Boston: Beacon Press.

Pollack, Norman. 1962. *The Populist Response to Industrial America: Midwestern Populist Thought.* Cambridge: Harvard University Press.

Pomeranz, Kenneth. 2000. *The Great Divergence: China, Europe, and the Making of the Modern World Economy.* Princeton: Princeton University Press.

Pontusson, Jonas. 2006. "The American Welfare State in Comparative Perspective: Reflections on Alberto Alesina and Edward L. Glaeser, 'Fighting Poverty in the US and Europe.'" *Perspectives on Politics* 4(2): 315–326.

Poppendieck, Janet. 1995. "Hunger in America: Typification and Response." In *Eating Agendas,* edited by Donna Maurer and Jeffrey Sobal, 11–34. New York: Transaction Publishers.

Portney, Kent E. 1980. "State Tax Preference Orderings and Partisan Control of Government." *Policy Studies Journal* 9(1): 87–95.

Posner, Elliot. 2009. "Making Rules for Global Finance: Transatlantic Regulatory Cooperation at the Turn of the Millennium." *International Organization* 63(4): 665–699.

Postel, Charles. 2007. *The Populist Vision.* Oxford: Oxford University Press.

Prasad, Monica. 2005. "Why is France So French?" *American Journal of Sociology* 111(2): 357–407.

———. 2006. *The Politics of Free Markets.* Chicago: University of Chicago Press.

———. 2009. "Three Theories of the Crisis." *Accounts: ASA Economic Sociology Newsletter* 8(2): 1–4.

———. 2011. "Tax 'Expenditures' and Welfare States." *Journal of Policy History* 23(2): 251–266.

———. 2012. "The Origins of Neoliberalism in the Reagan Tax Cut of 1981." *Journal of Policy History* 24(3):351–383.

Prasad, Monica, and Yingying Deng. 2009. "Taxation and the Worlds of Welfare." *Socio-Economic Review* 7(3): 431–457.

Preston, H. H. 1927. "The McFadden Banking Act." *American Economic Review* 17(2): 201–218.

Purdy, Sean. 2003. "'It Was Tough on Everybody': Low-Income Families and Housing Hardship in Post-World War II Toronto." *Journal of Social History* 37(2): 457–482.

Purnanandam, Amiyatosh K. 2009. "Originate-to-Distribute Model and the Sub-Prime Mortgage Crisis." American Finance Association 2010 Atlanta Meetings Paper. SSRN: http://ssrn.com/abstract=1167786.

Quadagno, Jill. 1984. "Welfare Capitalism and the Social Security Act of 1935." *American Sociological Review* 49(5): 632–647.

———. 1988. *The Transformation of Old Age Security: Class and Politics in the American Welfare State.* Chicago: University of Chicago Press.

———. 1994. *The Color of Welfare: How Racism Undermined the War on Poverty.* Oxford: Oxford University Press.

———. 2004. "Why the United States Has No National Health Insurance: Stakeholder Mobilization Against the Welfare State, 1945–1996." *Journal of Health and Social Behavior* 45 (Extra Issue): 25–44.

Quigley, John M. 2006. "Federal Credit and Insurance Programs: Housing." *Federal Reserve Bank of St. Louis Review* 88(4): 281–309.

Quinn, Sarah. 2010. *American Securitization: Finance, Technology, and the Politics of Debt,* PhD diss., Department of Sociology, University of California, Berkeley.

———. n.d. "The Credit State." University of Michigan and University of Washington, manuscript in progress.

Radford, Gail. 1996. *Modern Housing for America: Policy Struggles in the New Deal.* Chicago: University of Chicago Press.

Rainwater, Lee, and Timothy Smeeding. 2004. *Poor Kids in a Rich Country.* New York: Russell Sage.

Rajan, Raghuram G. 2006. "Has Finance Made the World Riskier?" *European Financial Management* 12(4): 499–533.

———. 2010. *Fault Lines: How Hidden Fractures Still Threaten the World Economy.* Princeton: Princeton University Press.

Rajan, Raghuram G., and Rodney Ramcharan. 2010. "Constituencies and Legislation: The Fight over the McFadden Act of 1927." http://faculty.chicagobooth.edu/raghuram.rajan/research/papers/Mcfadden%20Aug%202010.pdf.

Rajan, Raghuram G., and Luigi Zingales. 1998. "Financial Dependence and Growth." *American Economic Review* 88(3): 559–586.

———. 2003. "The Great Reversals: the Politics of Financial Development in the Twentieth Century." *Journal of Financial Economics* 69(1): 5–50.

Rampell, Catherine. 2009. "A Tax at Every Turn." *The New York Times,* December 11, B1.

Ramsay, Iain. 2003. "Consumer Credit Society and Consumer Bankruptcy: Reflections on Credit Cards in the Informational Economy." In *Consumer Bankruptcy in a Global Perspective,* edited by Johanna Niemi-Kiesiläinen, Iain Ramsay, and William Whitford, 17–39. Oxford: Hart Publishing.

Randolph, A. Philip. 1933. "Randolph Analyzes World Economic Situation as it Affects Race." *Chicago Defender,* January 21, 10.

Rasmussen, Wayne D. 1965. "The Civil War: A Catalyst of Agricultural Revolution." *Agricultural History* 39(4): 187–195.

Ratner, Sidney. 1942. *American Taxation: Its History as a Social Force in Democracy.* New York: W. W. Norton.

Rattner, Steven. 1980. "Ullman Scrambling After a 13th Term." *The New York Times,* August 17, 31.

Reid, Donald. 1985. "Industrial Paternalism: Discourse and Practice in Nineteenth-Century French Mining and Metallurgy." *Comparative Studies in Society and History* 27(4): 579–607.

Reinert, Erik S. 2007. *How Rich Countries Got Rich . . . and Why Poor Countries Stay Poor.* London: Constable.

Rich, Spencer. 1992. "House Democrats Push Health Care Proposals." *Washington Post,* July 1, A19.

Ritschl, Albrecht. 2002. "Deficit Spending in the Nazi Recovery, 1933–1938: A Critical Reassessment." *Journal of the Japanese and International Economies* 16(4) 559–582.

Ritter, Gretchen. 1997. *Goldbugs and Greenbacks: The Antimonopoly Tradition and the Politics of Finance in America, 1865–1896.* Cambridge: Cambridge University Press.

Robinson, Joan. 1972. "The Second Crisis of Economic Theory." *American Economic Review* 62(1/2): 1–10.

Rockoff, Hugh. 1984. "Some Evidence on the Real Price of Gold, Its Costs of Production, and Commodity Prices." In *A Retrospective on the Classical Gold Standard, 1821–1931,* edited by Michael D. Bordo and Anna J. Schwartz, 613–649. Chicago: University of Chicago Press.

Rodgers, Daniel. 1998. *Atlantic Crossings: Social Politics in a Progressive Age.* Cambridge: Harvard University Press.

Roe, Mark. 1994. *Strong Managers, Weak Owners: The Political Roots of American Corporate Finance.* Princeton: Princeton University Press.

Rogowski, Ronald. 1989. *Commerce and Coalitions: How Trade Affects Domestic Political Alignments.* Princeton: Princeton University Press.

Romer, Christina. 1992. "What Ended the Great Depression?" *Journal of Economic History* 52(4): 757–784.

———. 1993. "The Nation in Depression." *Journal of Economic Perspectives* 7(2): 19–39.

Rosanvallon, Pierre. 1989. "The Development of Keynesianism in France." In *The Political Power of Economic Ideas: Keynesianism across Nations,* edited by Peter A. Hall, 171–193. Princeton: Princeton University Press.

Rosen, Jan M. 1988. "Tax Watch: The Likely Forms of New Taxes." *The New York Times,* December 19, D2.

Rosenberg, Nathan. 1994. *Exploring the Black Box: Technology, Economics, and History.* Cambridge: Cambridge University Press.

Rothbard, Murray N. [1963] 2008. *America's Great Depression.* Auburn, AL: Ludwig von Mises Institute.

Rothstein, Bo. 1998. *Just Institutions Matter: The Moral and Political Logic of the Universal Welfare State.* Cambridge: Cambridge University Press.

Rousseau, Peter L., and Richard Sylla. 2005. "Emerging Financial Markets and Early U.S. Growth." *Explorations in Economic History* 42(1): 1–26.

Sandage, Scott. 2005. *Born Losers: A History of Failure in America.* Cambridge: Harvard University Press.

Sanders, Elizabeth. 1999. *Roots of Reform.* Chicago: University of Chicago Press.

Scheiber, Noam. 2011. "The Escape Artist." *The New Republic,* 242(3): 13–17.

Schlesinger, Arthur M., Jr. [1958] 2003. *The Coming of the New Deal.* New York: Houghton Mifflin.

———. [1960] 2003. *The Politics of Upheaval.* New York: Houghton Mifflin.

Schneiberg, Marc, and Tim Bartley. 2001. "Regulating American Industries: Markets, Politics, and the Institutional Determinants of Fire Insurance Regulation." *American Journal of Sociology* 107(1): 101–146.

Schneiberg, Marc, Marissa King, and Thomas Smith. 2008. "Social Movements and Organizational Form: Cooperative Alternatives to Corporations in the American Insurance, Dairy, and Grain Industries." *American Sociological Review* 73(4): 635–667.

Schwartz, Herman. 2009. *Subprime Nation: American Power, Global Capital, and the Housing Bubble.* Ithaca, NY: Cornell University Press.

———. 2012. "Housing, the Welfare State, and the Global Financial Crisis: What Is the Connection?" *Politics and Society* 40(1): 35–58.

Schwartz, Herman, and Leonard Seabrooke. 2008. "Varieties of Residential Capitalism in the International Political Economy: Old Welfare States and the New Politics of Housing." *Comparative European Politics* 6(3): 237–261.

Schwarz, Jordan A. 1964. "John Nance Garner and the Sales Tax Rebellion of 1932." *Journal of Southern History* 30(2): 162–180.

Scranton, Philip. 1997. *Endless Novelty: Specialty Production and American Industrialization, 1865–1925.* Princeton: Princeton University Press.

Scruggs, Lyle, and James Allan. 2006. "Welfare-State Decommodification in 18 OECD Countries: A Replication and Revision." *Journal of European Social Policy* 16(1): 55–72.

Seaberry, Jane. 1984. "Treasury Dept. Releases VAT Study." *Washington Post,* December 22, B1, B2.

Seligman, Edwin R.A. 1890. "The General Property Tax." *Political Science Quarterly* 5(1): 24–64.

———. 1916. "The Economic Influence of the War on the United States." *The Economic Journal* 26(102): 145–160.

Sellon, Gordon H., Jr., and Deana VanNahmen. 1988. "The Securitization of Housing Finance," *Economic Review,* 73(7), 3–20.

Shafer, Byron E. 1999. "American Exceptionalism." *Annual Review of Political Science* 2: 445–463.

Sheingate, Adam. 2001. *The Rise of the Agricultural Welfare State: Institutions and Interest Group Power in the United States, France, and Japan.* Princeton: Princeton University Press.

———. 2009. "Why Can't Americans See the State?" *The Forum* 7(4): 1–14. http://www.bepress.com/forum/vol7/iss4/art1, DOI: 10.2202/1540-8884.1336.

Sherman, Max, and Steven Strauss. 1986. "Thalidomide: A Twenty-Five Year Perspective." *Food Drug Cosmetic Law Journal* 41(4): 458–466.

Shirai, Sayuri. 2009. "The Impact of the U.S. Mortgage Crisis on the World and East Asia," MPRA Paper No. 14722. http://mpra.ub.uni-muenchen.de/14722/.

Shoup, Carl S. 1955. "Taxation in France." *National Tax Journal,* 8(4): 325–44.

Shover, John L. 1965. *Cornbelt Rebellion—The Farmers' Holiday Association.* Urbana: University of Illinois Press.

Shulman, Stuart W. 2003. "The Origin of the Federal Farm Loan Act: Issue Emergence and Agenda-Setting in the Progressive Era Print Press." In *Fighting for the Farm: Rural America Transformed,* edited by Jane Adams, 113–128. Philadelphia: University of Pennsylvania Press.

Siklos, Pierre L. 2002. *The Changing Face of Central Banking: Evolutionary Trends Since World War II.* Cambridge: Cambridge University Press.

Simon, Karla W. 1984. "Fringe Benefits and Tax Reform Historical Blunders and a Proposal for Structural Change." *University of Florida Law Review* 36(5): 871–956.

Simpson, Amos E. 1959. "The Struggle for Control of the German Economy, 1936–37." *The Journal of Modern History* 31(1): 37–45.

Singer, David Andrew. 1997. *Regulating Capital: Setting Standards for the International Financial System.* Ithaca, NY: Cornell University Press.

Skeel, David A., Jr. 2001. *Debt's Dominion: A History of Bankruptcy Law in America.* Princeton: Princeton University Press.

Skocpol, Theda. 1985. "Bringing the State Back In: Strategies of Analysis in Current Research." In *Bringing the State Back In,* edited by Peter B. Evans, Dietrich Rueschemeyer, and Theda Skocpol, 3–38. Cambridge: Cambridge University Press.

———. 1995. *Protecting Soldiers and Mothers: The Political Origins of Social Policy in the United States.* Cambridge: Harvard University Press.

Skocpol, Theda and Kenneth Finegold. 1982. "State Capacity and Economic Intervention in the Early New Deal." *Political Science Quarterly* 97 (2): 255–278.

Skowronek, Stephen. 1982. *Building a New American State: The Expansion of National Administrative Capacities, 1877–1920.* Cambridge: Cambridge University Press.

Slater, Don. 1997. *Consumer Culture and Modernity.* Cambridge, UK: Polity Press.

Smeeding, Timothy. 2005. "Public Policy, Economic Inequality, and Poverty: The United States in Comparative Perspective." *Social Science Quarterly* 86(s1): 955–983.

———. 2006. "Poor People in Rich Nations: The United States in Comparative Perspective." *Journal of Economic Perspectives* 20(1): 69–90.

Smith, Kevin B., and Michael J. Licari. 2006. *Public Administrations: Power and Politics in the Fourth Branch of Government.* Oxford: Oxford University Press.

Smith, Timothy B. 1997. "The Ideology of Charity, the Image of the English Poor Law, and Debates over the Right to Assistance in France, 1830–1905." *The Historical Journal* 40(4): 997–1032.

Snyder, Robert E. 1984. *Cotton Crisis.* Chapel Hill and London: University of North Carolina Press.

Sokolovsky, Joan. 1998. "The Making of National Health Insurance in Britain and Canada: Institutional Analysis and its Limits." *Journal of Historical Sociology* 11(2): 247–280.

Solvick, Stanley D. 1963. "William Howard Taft and the Payne-Aldrich Tariff." *Mississippi Valley Historical Review* 50(3): 424–442.

Sombart, Werner. [1906] 1976. *Why Is There no Socialism in the United States?* Translated by Patricia M. Hockings and C.T. Husbands. White Plains, NY: M.E. Sharpe.

Sørensen, Peter Birch. 2004. *Measuring the Tax Burden on Capital and Labor.* Cambridge: MIT Press.

Southworth, Shirley D. 1928. *Branch Banking in the United States.* New York: McGraw-Hill.

Sparrow, James. 2008. "Buying Our Boys Back: The Mass Foundations of Fiscal Citizenship in World War II." *Journal of Policy History* 20(2): 263–286.

Stearns, Peter N. 1978. *Paths to Authority: The Middle Class and the Industrial Labor Force in France, 1820–1848.* Urbana, IL: University of Illinois Press.

Steinmetz, George. 2005. "Return to Empire: The New U.S. Imperialism in Comparative Historical Perspective." *Sociological Theory* 23(4): 339–367.

Steinmo, Sven. 1988. "Social Democracy vs. Socialism: Goal Adaptation in Social Democratic Sweden." *Politics and Society* 16(4): 403–446.

———. 1989. "Political Institutions and Tax Policy in the United States, Sweden, and Britain." *World Politics* 41(4): 500–535.

———. 1993. *Taxation and Democracy.* New Haven, CT: Yale University Press.

———. 1994. "The End of Redistribution? International Pressures and Domestic Tax Policy Choices." *Challenge* 37(6): 9–17.

Steinmo, Sven, Kathleen Thelen, and Frank Longstreth. 1992. *Structuring Politics: Historical Institutionalism in Comparative Analysis.* Cambridge: Cambridge University Press.

Stephens, John. 1979. *The Transition from Capitalism to Socialism.* London: Macmillan.

Stevens, Beth. 1988. "Blurring the Boundaries: How the Federal Government Has Influenced Welfare Benefits in the Private Sector." In *The Politics of Social Policy in the United States,* edited by Margaret Weir, Ann Shola Orloff, and Theda Skocpol, 123–148. Princeton: Princeton University Press.

Stigler, George J. 1982. "The Economists and the Problem of Monopoly." *American Economic Review* 72(2): 1–11.

———. 1985. "The Origin of the Sherman Act." *The Journal of Legal Studies* 14(1): 1–12.

Stinchcombe, Arthur. 1985. "The Functional Theory of Social Insurance." *Politics and Society* 14(4): 411–430.

Stiroh, Kevin J., and Adrienne Rumble. 2006. "The Dark Side of Diversification: The Case of U.S. Financial Holding Companies." *Journal of Banking and Finance* 30(8): 2131–2161.

Stockhammer, Engelbert. 2004. "Financialisation and the Slowdown of Accumulation." *Cambridge Journal of Economics* 28(5): 719–741.

Stücker, Britta. 2007. "Konsum auf Kredit in der Bundesrepublik." In *Die bundesdeutsche Massenkonsumgesellschaft, 1950–2000,* edited by Alfred Reckendrees and Toni Pierenkemper, 63–88. Berlin: Akademie Verlag.

Sugrue, Thomas J. [1996] 2005. *The Origins of the Urban Crisis: Race and Inequality in Postwar Detroit.* Princeton: Princeton University Press.

Sullivan, Teresa A., Elizabeth Warren, and Jay Lawrence Westbrook. 2000. *The Fragile Middle Class: Americans in Debt.* New Haven, CT: Yale University Press.

———. 2006–2007. "Less Stigma or More Financial Distress: An Empirical Analysis of the Extraordinary Increase in Bankruptcy Filings." *Stanford Law Review* 59(2): 213–256.

Summers, Lawrence H. 1981. "Capital Taxation and Accumulation in a Life Cycle Growth Model." *American Economic Review* 71(4): 533–544.

Sutch, Richard. 2006. "Gross Domestic Product: 1790–2002 [Continuous Annual Series]." Table Ca9-19 in *Historical Statistics of the United States, Earliest*

Times to the Present: Millennial Edition, edited by Susan B. Carter, Scott Sigmund Gartner, Michael R. Haines, Alan L. Olmstead, Richard Sutch, and Gavin Wright. New York: Cambridge University Press. http://dx.doi.org/10.1017/ISBN-9780511132971.Ca1-2610.1017/ISBN-9780511132971.Ca1-26.

Svennilson, Ingvar. 1954. *Growth and Stagnation in the European Economy.* Geneva: United Nations Economic Commission for Europe.

Swain, Martha H. 1978. *Pat Harrison: The New Deal Years.* Jackson, MS: University Press of Mississippi.

Swann, Jonathan P. 2004. "The FDA and the Practice of Pharmacy: Prescription Drug Regulation Before 1968." In *Federal Drug Control*, edited by Jonathon Erlen and Joseph F. Spillane, 145–174. Binghamton, NY: Haworth Press.

Sweeney, Dennis. 2009. *Work, Race, and the Emergence of Radical Right Corporatism in Imperial Germany.* Ann Arbor: University of Michigan Press.

Sweezy, Paul M. 1967. "Rosa Luxemburg's 'The Accumulation of Capital.'" *Science & Society* 31(4): 474–485.

Swenson, Peter. 1999. "Bad Manors and the Good Welfare State: A Nordic Perspective on Jacoby's Modern Manors and American Welfare Capitalism." *Industrial Relations* 38(2): 145–153.

———. 2002. *Capitalists Against Markets: The Making of Labor Markets and Welfare States in the United States and Sweden.* New York: Oxford University Press.

Swinnen, Johan F. M. 2009. "The Growth of Agricultural Protection in Europe in the 19th and 20th Centuries." *The World Economy* 32(11): 1499–1537.

Tabarrok, Alexander. 1998. "The Separation of Commercial and Investment Banking: The Morgans vs. the Rockefellers." *Quarterly Journal of Austrian Economics* 1(1): 1–18.

Tabb, Charles J. 2005. "Lessons from the Globalization of Consumer Bankruptcy." *Law and Social Inquiry* 30(4): 763–782.

Tanzi, Vito, and Ludger Schuknecht. 2000. *Public Spending in the 20th Century: A Global Perspective.* Cambridge: Cambridge University Press.

Tarullo, Daniel K. 2008. *Banking on Basel: The Future of International Financial Regulation.* Washington, DC: Peterson Institute for International Economics.

Taussig, Helen B. 1962. "A Study of the German Outbreak of Phocomelia." *Journal of the American Medical Association* 180(1106): 840–844.

Temin, Peter. 1976. *Did Monetary Forces Cause the Great Depression?* New York: W. W. Norton.

———. 1989. *Lessons from the Great Depression.* Cambridge: MIT Press.

———. 1990. "Socialism and Wages in the Recovery from the Great Depression in the United States and Germany." *Journal of Economic History* 50(2): 297–307.

Thane, Pat. 1984. "The Working Class and State 'Welfare' in Britain, 1880–1914." *The Historical Journal* 27(4): 877–900.

Thelen, Kathleen. 2004. *How Institutions Evolve: The Political Economy of Skills in Germany, Britain, the United States, and Japan.* Cambridge: Cambridge University Press.

311

Therborn, Göran. 1984. "The Prospects of Labour and the Transformation of Advanced Capitalism." *New Left Review* 145(May–June): 5–38.

Therborn, Göran, and Joop Roebroek. 1986. "The Irreversible Welfare State: Its Recent Maturation, its Encounter With the Economic Crisis, and Its Future Prospects." *International Journal of Health Services* 16(3): 319–338.

Thomasson, Melissa A. 2003. "The Importance of Group Coverage: How Tax Policy Shaped U.S. Health Insurance." *The American Economic Review* 93(4): 1373–1384.

Thompson, Edward Palmer. 1963. *The Making of the English Working Class.* New York: Pantheon.

Thorndike, Joseph. 2009. "The Unfair Advantage of the Few." In *The New Fiscal Sociology,* edited by Isaac Martin, Ajay Mehrotra, and Monica Prasad, 29–47. Cambridge: Cambridge University Press.

Tilly, Charles. 1985. "War Making and State Making as Organized Crime." In *Bringing the State Back In,* edited by Peter Evans, Dietrich Rueschemeyer, and Theda Skocpol, 169–191. Cambridge: Cambridge University Press.

Times-Picayune. 1931a. "Conflict of Farm Counsels." August 10, 8.

———. 1931b. "Long Advocates Limiting World Cotton Output." August 19, 1.

Tocqueville, Alexis de. 1840. *Democracy in America, Vol. 4,* translated by Henry Reeve. New York: The Colonial Press.

Tomaskovic-Devey, Donald, and Ken-Hou Lin. 2011. "Income Dynamics, Economic Rents, and the Financialization of the U.S. Economy." *American Sociological Review* 76(4): 538–559.

Tracy, Michael. [1964] 1989. *Government and Agriculture in Western Europe 1880–1988. 3rd ed.* New York: New York University Press.

Troesken, Werner. 2002. "The Letters of John Sherman and the Origins of Antitrust." *The Review of Austrian Economics* 15(4): 275–295.

Trumbull, Gunnar. 2010a. "The Political Construction of Economic Interest: Consumer Credit in Postwar France and America." Unpublished manuscript.

———. 2010b. "Regulating for Legitimacy: Consumer Credit Access in France and America." Harvard Business School, Working Paper 11–047.

———. 2012. "Credit Access and Social Welfare: The Rise of Consumer Lending in the United States and France. "*Politics and Society* 40(1): 9–34.

Trussell, C. P. 1942. "Plan Rejected." *The New York Times,* September 9, 1.

Turner, Frederick Jackson. [1920] 1996. *The Frontier in American History.* Mineola, NY: Dover Publications.

Turner, Henry Ashby. 1985. *German Big Business and the Rise of Hitler.* New York: Oxford University Press.

United States Congress. 1921. *Congressional Record.* 67 Cong., first sess. vol. 61, pt. 7. Washington, DC.

———. 1926. *Congressional Record.* 69 Cong., first sess. vol. 67, pt. 3. Washington, DC.

———. 1932a. *Congressional Record.* 72 Cong., first sess. vol. 75, pt. 7. Washington, DC.

———. 1932b. *Congressional Record.* 72 Cong., first sess. vol. 75, pt. 10. Washington, DC.

———. 1985. *Congressional Record.* 99 Cong., first sess. vol. 131, pt. 25. Washington, DC.

———. 1999. *Congressional Record.* 106 Cong., first sess. vol. 145, pt. 20. Washington, DC.

———. 1973. House. Committee on Banking and Currency. *Credit Crunch and Reform of Financial Institutions, Part 1.* 93 Cong., first sess. Washington, DC.

United States Internal Revenue Service. 1863. *The Excise Tax Law Approved July 1, 1862.* New York: Fitch, Estee.

Vail, Mark. 2010. *Recasting Welfare Capitalism: Economic Adjustment in Contemporary France and Germany.* Philadelphia: Temple University Press.

Valelly, Richard M. 1989. *Radicalism in the States: The Minnesota Farmer-Labor Party and American Political Economy.* Chicago: University of Chicago Press.

Van Hook, James C. 2004. *Rebuilding Germany: The Creation of the Social Market Economy, 1945–1957.* Cambridge: Cambridge University Press.

Ventry, Dennis J., Jr. 2010. "The Accidental Deduction: A History and Critique of the Tax Subsidy for Mortgage Interest." *Law and Contemporary Problems* 73(1): 233–284.

Veracini, Lorenzo. 2010. *Settler Colonialism: A Theoretical Overview.* Houndmills, Basingstoke, UK: Palgrave MacMillan.

Verdier, Daniel. 1994. *Democracy and International Trade.* Princeton: Princeton University Press.

———. 2002. *Moving Money: Banking and Finance in the Industrialized World.* Cambridge: Cambridge University Press.

Vernon, J. R. 1991. "The 1920–21 Deflation: The Role of Aggregate Supply." *Economic Inquiry* 29(3): 572–580.

Verweij, Marco. 2000. "Why Is the River Rhine Cleaner than the Great Lakes (Despite Looser Regulation?)" *Law and Society Review* (24): 1007–1054.

Vogel, David. 1986. *National Styles of Regulation.* Ithaca, NY: Cornell University Press.

Voth, Hans-Joachim. 2003. "With a Bang, Not a Whimper: Pricking Germany's 'Stock Market Bubble' in 1927 and the Slide into Depression." *Journal of Economic History* 63(1): 65–99.

Wadhwani, R. Daniel. 2011. "The Institutional Foundations of Personal Finance: Innovation in U.S. Savings Banks, 1880s–1920s." *Business History Review* 85(3): 499–528.

Walker, Norman. 1958. "Labor Hits Nixon for 'Brazen' Speech." *Washington Post and Times Herald,* September 27, A2.

Wall Street Journal. 1921. "Crisis in Taxation Confronts the Country." May 10, 13.

———. 1932a. "To Speed Committee Action on Tax Bill." April 13, 5.

———. 1932b. "Mills Recalled to Tax Hearing." April 14, 13.

———. 1933. "Newspaper Specials." September 16, 3.

———. 1940. "U.S. Taxes in 1938 on Stockholder's Share Of Corporate Earnings Higher in Upper Brackets Than in Britain, France, Germany and Canada." February 26, 3.

———. 1942a. "Sales Tax Urged As Substitute in Revenue Program: New York C. of C. Submits Graduated Proposal to House Committee Method Is Opposed by Treasury." March 11, 3.

———. 1942b. "Senate Committee Favors Retaining Present Tax Allowance for Losses on Investments." August 6, 4.

———. 1952. "'Muley Bob' Doughton is Quitting Congress After His 21st Term." February 16, 1.

Wardell, Willam M. 1973. "Introduction of New Therapeutic Drugs in the United States and Great Britain: An International Comparison." *Clinical Pharmacology and Therapeutics* 14(5): 773–90.

Wardell, William M., and Louis Lasagna. 1975. *Regulation and Drug Development.* Washington, DC: American Enterprise Institute for Public Policy Research.

Warren, Charles. 1935. *Bankruptcy in United States History.* Cambridge: Harvard University Press.

Warren, Elizabeth, and Amelia Tyagi. 2004. *The Two Income Trap.* New York: Basic.

Washington Post. 1928. "Militia Raids New Orleans Gaming Clubs." August 13, 1.

———. 1930. "German Officer Forgives Host, Pajamaed Governor," March 5, 4.

———. 1931. "Sales Tax Opposed by More Leaders." September 13, M3.

———. 1932. "Alternate Tax Plans Given Senate by Mills." April 19, 1.

———. 1942. "AFL Asks U.S., State, Local Tax Parley." March 20, 14.

———. 1985. "Voting Down a VAT." December 16, A14.

Watson, Matthew. 2010. "House Price Keynesianism and the Contradictions of the Modern Investor Subject." *Housing Studies* 25(3): 413–426.

Webb, Walter Prescott. [1952] 1980. *The Great Frontier.* Reno: University of Nevada Press.

Weir, Margaret, Ann Shola Orloff, and Theda Skocpol. 1988. "Understanding American Social Politics." In *The Politics of Social Policy in the United States* edited by Margaret Weir, Ann Shola Orloff, and Theda Skocpol, 3–36. Princeton: Princeton University Press.

Weir, Margaret, and Theda Skocpol. 1985. "State Structure and the Possibilities for 'Keynesian' Responses to the Great Depression in Sweden, Britain, and the United States." In *Bringing the State Back In,* edited by Peter B. Evans, Dietrich Rueschemeyer, and Theda Skocpol, 107–163. Cambridge: Cambridge University Press.

Weisman, Steven R. 2002. *The Great Tax Wars: Lincoln to Wilson—The Fierce Battles over Money and Power That Transformed the Nation.* New York: Simon and Schuster.

Weiss, Marc A. 1989. "Marketing and Financing Home Ownership: Mortgage Lending and Public Policy in the United States, 1918–1989." *Business and Economic History* 18: 109–18.

Westin, Alan Furman. 1953. "The Populist Movement and the Campaign of 1896." *Journal of Politics* 15(1): 3–41.

Wexler, Martin E. 1996. "A Comparison of Canadian and American Housing Policies." *Urban Studies* 33(10): 1909–1921.

———. 1999. "Housing and Social Policy—An Historical Perspective on Canadian-American Differences—A Reply." *Urban Studies* 36(7): 1177–1180.

Wheelock, David C. 1992. "Regulation and Bank Failures: New Evidence from the Agricultural Collapse of the 1920s." *Journal of Economic History* 52(4): 806–825.

White, Eugene Nelson. 1982. "The Political Economy of Banking Regulation." *Journal of Economic History* 42(1): 33–40.

———. 1984. "A Reinterpretation of the Banking Crisis of 1930." *The Journal of Economic History* 44(1): 119–138.

White, Jimm F. 1968–1969. "Medical Reimbursement Plans for Close Corporation Stockholders-Employees." *Wayne Law Review* 15(14): 1601–1616.

White, Richard D., Jr. 2006. *Kingfish: The Reign of Huey P. Long.* New York: Random House.

Wicker, Elmus. 1980. "A Reconsideration of the Causes of the Banking Panic of 1930." *Journal of Economic History* 40(3): 571–583.

Widmalm, Frida. 2001. "Tax Structure and Growth: Are Some Taxes Better than Others?" *Public Choice* 107(3–4): 199–219.

Wiener, Jonathan B., and Michael D. Rogers. 2002. "Comparing Precaution in the United States and Europe." *Journal of Risk Research* 5(4): 317–349.

Wiener, Jonathan B., Michael D. Rogers, and James K. Hammitt. 2011. *The Reality of Precaution: Comparing Risk Regulation in the United States and Europe.* Washington, DC: RFF Press.

Wilensky, Harold L. 1975. *The Welfare State and Equality: Structural and Ideological Roots of Public Expenditures.* Berkeley and Los Angeles: University of California Press.

———. 2002. *Rich Democracies: Political Economy, Public Policy, and Performance.* Berkeley and Los Angeles: University of California Press.

Williams, T. Harry. 1981. *Huey Long.* New York: Vintage.

Williams, T. Harry, Papers, Mss. 2489, 2510, Louisiana and Lower Mississippi Valley Collections, LSU Libraries, Baton Rouge, LA.

Williamson, K. M. 1921. "The Literature on the Sales Tax." *The Quarterly Journal of Economics* 35(4): 618–633.

Wills, Garry. 1999. *A Necessary Evil: A History of American Distrust of Government.* New York: Simon and Schuster.

Wilson, Graham K. 1985. *The Politics of Safety and Health.* Oxford: Clarendon Press.

Wimbish, William A. 1912. "Should the Government Own the Railroads?" *The Sewanee Review* 20(3): 318–332.

Wiprud, Arne Clarence. 1921. *The Federal Farm Loan System in Operation.* New York: Harper.

Wojnilower, Albert M. 1980. "The Central Role of Credit Crunches in Recent Financial History." *Brookings Papers on Economic Activity* 1980(2): 277–326.

Wood, John H. 2005. *A History of Central Banking in Great Britain and the United States.* Cambridge: Cambridge University Press.

Woofter, T. J. Jr. 1935–1936. "Rural Relief and the Back-to-the-Farm Movement." *Social Forces* 14(3): 382–388.

World Bank. 2012. *World Development Indicators Online (WDI)* database. http://data.worldbank.org.

Wright, Gavin. 1990. "The Origins of American Industrial Success, 1879–1940." *American Economic Review* 80(4): 651–668.

Yarmie, Andrew. 2003. "Employers and Exceptionalism: A Cross-Border Comparison of Washington State and British Columbia, 1890–1935." *Pacific Historical Review* 72(4): 561–615.

Yates, P. Lamartine. 1959. *Forty Years of Foreign Trade.* London: George Allen & Unwin Ltd.

Yearley, Clifton K. 1970. *Money Machines: The Breakdown and Reform of Governmental and Party Finance in the North, 1860–1920.* New York: SUNY Press.

Yildirim, H. Semih, Seung-Woog (Austin) Kwag and M. Cary Collins. 2006. "An Examination of the Equity Market Response to the Gramm-Leach-Bliley Act Across Commercial Banking, Investment Banking, and Insurance Firms." *Journal of Business Finance & Accounting* 33(9–10): 1629–1649.

Zelenak, Lawrence A. 2010a. "The Federal Retail Sales Tax that Wasn't: An Actual History and an Alternate History." *Law and Contemporary Problems* 73(1): 149–205.

———. 2010b. "Foreword: The Fabulous Invalid Nears 100." *Law and Contemporary Problems* 73 (1): i–vii.

Zysman, John. 1983. *Governments, Markets, and Growth: Financial Systems and the Politics of Industrial Change.* Ithaca, NY: Cornell University Press.

This project has been supported by the National Science Foundation (NSF) under Grant No. 0847725. A Burkhardt Fellowship from the American Council of Learned Societies (ACLS) and support from Northwestern University allowed me to take a research leave at a crucial moment. All conclusions and interpretations in this work are my own and are not necessarily shared by the NSF or the ACLS.

I am grateful to the University of Chicago Press and my co-author Kimberly Morgan for allowing me to reprint portions of "The Origins of Tax Systems: A French-American Comparison" which were originally published in the *American Journal of Sociology*, and constitute pages 125–129 of this book.

I have presented parts of this argument at the Policy History conference, the American Sociological Association conference, the "Past and Present" mini-conference of the American Sociological Association's Comparative Historical section, the University of California, Los Angeles, the University of British Columbia, Brown University, the University of Chicago, the University of Virginia, the Newberry Library, and at multiple annual meetings of the Social Science History Association. I am grateful to suggestions from audience members at these venues and particularly to Herman Schwartz at the University of Virginia and Marion Fourcade at the "Past and Present" conference, who gave especially helpful comments. Michael Aronson, Michael Bernstein, Bruce Carruthers, Greta Krippner, Michael Lansing, Jan Logemann, and Sarah Quinn gave thoughtful critiques of sections of the manuscript, as did Jason Beckfield, David Brady, Cheol-Sung Lee, and Andrés Villarreal, who also helped with the statistics (and who are of course not resposible for any remaining errors).

I am extremely grateful to several people who read drafts of the whole manuscript: Steve Rosenberg, Hamza Yilmaz, and Gary Herrigel waded through a disorganized first draft and provided me with the encouragement and criticism that I needed to improve it; Jim Mahoney, Art Stinchcombe, Louis Cain, and Ajay Mehrotra brought expertise from four social science disciplines, directing me to relevant references and doing their best to save me from errors; and Isaac Martin produced almost a whole chapter of his own in response to the manuscript, which has guided my revisions. The anonymous reviewers at Harvard University Press (who turned out to be Elizabeth Sanders and Richard Lachmann) gave uncompromising comments that have improved the book substantially—it is a completely different book because of their input—and Bruce Raeburn and Judy Bolton gave much appreciated help at the Tulane and Louisiana State University Special Collections, respectively. At Northwestern, the Department of Sociology, the Institute for Policy Research, and the Comparative Historical Social Science workshop have been ideal intellectual homes, providing lively debate in an atmosphere of community.

My parents and siblings continue to inspire me every day. In her seventies, while still on cancer medication, my mother rode a horse to the top of a hill in the Himalayas to see the Vaishnav Devi. For the courage she has always displayed in her life, she is my hero. The older I get, the more I appreciate my father's cheerful willingness to take on the world, the confidence that took him from a tiny village in India to the other end of the earth. He will always be my role model.

This book is dedicated to Stefan Henning, who edited the entire manuscript and who has put up with more tax history in his life than should be required of any anthropologist of religion. He didn't know that's what he was in for that April evening in Ann Arbor when an unexpected conversation changed both of our lives. The nine years since then have been my own private economy of abundance.

Lotman, Arline, 224, 225
Louisiana, legal tradition of, 136
Lugar, Richard, 178
Luxury consumption, 236

Maddison, Angus, 56–58, 268n5
Maioni, Antonia, 214
Manufacturing: American economic
    growth and, 63; severe deflation and, 70;
    progressive taxation and, 125
Market efficiency, antitrust policy and,
    36–39
Marks, Gary, 35–36
Marxism, 26, 35
Mayhew, Anne, 71
McCreary, Eugene, 161–162
McFadden Act (1927), 217–221, 242
McLean, George, 155
McQueen, Brian, 267–268n1
Meltzer, Allan, 53
Military hegemony, 267–268n1
Military pensions and spending, 269n2
Miller, Michael B., 163
Mink, Patsy T., 223
Mississippi Company, 55–56, 60–61
Mitchell, Brian, 58
Mogul Steamship Company, 11–12
Monetarism, 256
Monetary reform, 13–16, 141
Money supply: economic growth and, 87,
    253; Great Depression and, 145–146
Monnet, Jean, 78
Monopoly power: studies on, 11–13;
    antitrust policy and, 36–39; severe
    deflation and, 75–76; consumer society
    and, 90–91; ICC and, 194
Monts-de-piété, 210–211
Morgenthau, Henry, 114–119
Mortgage Keynesianism, xiv, 93, 95, 221
Mortgages: severe deflation and, 72–74;
    home mortgage interest deduction, 154;
    implementation of, 200–202; New Deal
    policies for, 203–205; Canadian, 213;
    discriminatory practices in, 221–224; and
    financial crisis of 2007–2008, 239–240
Moynihan, Daniel Patrick, 178

Nader, Ralph, 239
Nathan, Robert, 88
National Bank Act (1863), 216
National Construction Council (NCC),
    213–214
National culture: poverty and, 35–39;
    national sales tax and, 101
National Housing Act (1934), 203
National Industrial Recovery Act (NIRA)
    (1933), 50
National Labor Relations Board (NLRB), 89
National-level financial regulation: overview
    of, 175–181; bankruptcy and, 181–184;
    adversarial, 184–195
National Recovery Administration (NRA),
    89, 141–142
National sales tax: overview of, 99–100;
    resistance to U.S., 100–103, 122–124,
    251, 258; failed attempts at American,
    103–104; 1921 vote on, 104–109; 1932
    vote on, 109–113; 1942 vote on,
    114–119; postwar attempts at establish-
    ing, 120–122
National War Labor Board, 158
Natural resources, 64
Naylor, James, 161
Nelson, John, 218
Neoliberalism, 92, 255–256
New Deal, 87, 117, 119, 200–204
NIRA (National Industrial Recovery Act)
    (1933), 50
Nixon, Richard, 120
NLRB (National Labor Relations Board), 89
North, Douglas, 71
Novak, William, xi, 7, 23
NRA (National Recovery Administration),
    89, 141–142

Obama, Barack, 179
Office of Price Administration (OPA), 89
OPA (Office of Price Administration), 89
O'Rourke, Kevin, 56, 70
Overproduction crisis: Huey Long and,
    xii–xiii, 138–140, 144–145; overview of,
    46–53; solutions to, 86–88; responses to,
    91–92; consequences of, 108